The Žižek Reader

Edited by
Elizabeth Wright and
Edmond Wright

BLACKWELL
Publishers

Copyright © Blackwell Publishers Ltd, 1999-07-06
Introduction, selection, arrangement and apparatus copyright © Elizabeth Wright and
Edmond Wright 1999

First published 1999
Reprinted 1999

Blackwell Publishers Ltd
108 Cowley Road
Oxford OX4 1JF
UK

Blackwell Publishers Inc.
350 Main Street
Malden, Massachusetts 02148
USA

British Library Cataloguing in Publication Data

A CIP catalogue record for this book is available from the British Library.

Library of Congress Cataloging-in-Publication Data
Žižek, Slavoj.
[Selections. English. 1999]
The Žižek reader / Slavoj Žižek; edited by Elizabeth Wright and Edmond Wright.
p. cm.
Includes bibliographical references and index.
ISBN 0– 631– 21200– 0 (alk. paper) — ISBN 0– 631– 21201– 9 (pbk. : alk. paper)
1.Psychoanalysis. 2. Lacan, Jacques, 1901–. I. Wright, Elizabeth (Eva Elizabeth)
II. Wright, Edmond Leo, 1927–.
III. Title.
BF 173.Z52413 1999
150.19 ' 5—dc 21
CIP

Typeset in Bembo on 10.5 pt/12.5 pt
By Pure Tech India Ltd, Pondicherry
http://www.Puretech.com

Printed in Great Britain by MPG Books, Bodmin, Cornwall
This book is printed on acid-free paper

Contents

Contents

Preface: Burning the Bridges

One of the surprisingly refined moments in James Cameron's *Titanic* occurs when Jack, the film's hero, passes away in the freezing water, with Rose, his great love, safe on a floating piece of wood, desperately clutching his hands. Upon noticing that she is holding a corpse, Rose exclaims, 'Nothing can take us apart! I'll never let you go!'. However, the act that accompanies these pathetic words is the opposite gesture of *letting him go*, of gently pushing him away, so that he gets sucked into the dark water – a perfect exemplification of Lacan's thesis that the elevation to the status of symbolic authority has to be paid for by the death, murder even, of its empirical bearer. T. S. Eliot praised the canonic tradition of Virgil, Dante and Goethe precisely because he was aware that it is no longer possible to write like them, in the same way that the *Cahiers du Cinema* critics of the 1950s elevated Hitchcock and *film noir* into classics at the very moment when it was no longer possible to 'do films like that' (the films of Truffaut and Godard are decidedly not Hitchcockian: even when they refer to Hitchcock, we are dealing with an ironic quote which presupposes that the substantial unity with the quoted author is already lost). So I have to confess that when my dear friends and colleagues Elizabeth and Edmond Wright approached me with the proposal to put together a Žižek Reader, my first reaction to it was: isn't the price for this elevation to the status of an author who deserves a Reader that one is treated as a kind of living dead, no longer acknowledged as a living and developing entity? Isn't it that, at some level, at least, an important aspect of me has to disappear into the dark abyss of the past?

However, after getting acquainted with the details of their proposal, I was immediately converted to the idea, since their cogent choice of texts forced me to confront the unpleasant, but unavoidable, question: where do I stand with regard to the present theoretical imbroglio in which deconstruction and the cognitive sciences, the tradition of the Frankfurt school and that of Heideggerian phenomenology, New Age obscurantism and new historicism, fight for hegemony? In what direction does the decade of my work represented in this volume point? What is its true focus? I am well aware that for many a reader the main attraction of my work resides in the way the theoretical line of argumentation is sustained by numerous examples from cinema and popular culture, by jokes and political anecdotes often dangerously approaching the very limits of good taste – this is the main reason why reviewers repeatedly characterize my style as 'postmodern'. Far from being simply misleading, this aspect of my work is a proper symbolic lure: yes, my jokes often do violate the threshold of 'good taste', and enter the uncanny domain in which amusement turns into disgust in order to signal . . . what? In contrast to the cliché of the academic writer beneath whose impassive style the reader can catch an occasional glimpse of a so-called lively personality, I always perceived myself as the author of books whose excessively and compulsively 'witty' texture serves as the envelope of a fundamental *coldness*, of a 'machinic' deployment of the line of thought which follows its path with utter *indifference* towards the pathology of so-called human considerations. In this respect, I always felt a deep sympathy for Monty Python, whose excessive humour also signals an underlying stance of profound disgust with life.

In his '"The Neglected Technique of the Witticism": A Philosophical Inquiry',[1] Edmond Wright focuses on how, for Lacan, the very fundamental structure of a predicative judgement is that of a joke in which the element first posited as the (logical) subject is retroactively subverted, given an unexpected spin, through the predicate, as in any joke: 'Who's there?' 'Amos'. 'Amos who?' 'A mosquito'. Subject and predicate are never harmonized; there is for ever a gap between the two, a gap on account of which the predicate displaces the subject. (Undoubtedly, 'Amos Quito' would be a nice pseudonym for some of my essays.) The jokes and popular culture examples, as well as the main themes of my work, also undergo a similar displacement; however, the displacement works here in the opposite direction, from the initial gap to the assertion of an unexpected continuity.

One of the commonplaces of today's theory is that transcendental subjectivity is *passé*: if one is to assert again the notion of the subject, one has to displace it with regard to the standard Cartesian *cogito*; that is, the new subject has to be a divided, finite subject, a subject 'thrown' into a non-transparent, contingent life-world. At a different level, the same goes for Marxism: if one is to save its legacy, one has to renounce its crude 'economic essentialism' (the notions of class struggle, the role of the proletariat, socialist revolution, etc.), and maintain just the empty messianic emancipatory promise – the new social order should not be 'ontologized', but should remain an elusive democracy *à venir*. The same goes for revolutionary politics: the horrible experience with the Stalinist terror should teach us how idealism and cruelty are two sides of the same coin – that is, how the social reality of any attempt to realize the ideal of a better society is that of extreme violence. And, last but not least, the same goes for religion: if some form of religion is to survive, it has to abandon its direct ontological claims, and turn into the respect and veneration of a kind of vacuous Otherness *à la* Levinas.

In all these points, my gesture is the exact opposite. My work relies on the full acceptance of the notion of modern subjectivity elaborated by the great German Idealists from Kant to Hegel: for me, this tradition forms the unsurpassable horizon of our philosophical experience, and the core of my entire work is the endeavour to use Lacan as a privileged intellectual tool to reactualize German Idealism. From my perspective, the celebrated postmodern 'displacement' of subjectivity rather exhibits the unreadiness to come to terms with the truly traumatic core of the modern subject. *Mutatis mutandis*, a return to the centrality of the Marxist critique of political economy is crucial for my project: the proliferation of the new forms of postmodern political agents is for me the obverse of the tacit acceptance of global capitalism as 'the only game in town'. Furthermore, the horrible experience of the Stalinist terror should in no way inhibit us in our search for a 'good terror' as the key ingredient of any truly radical politics: there is no effective freedom without 'terror' – that is, without some form of the unconditional pressure that threatens the very core of our being. And, finally, what I find theoretically and politically engaging in the religious legacy is not the abstract messianic promise of some redemptive Otherness, but, on the contrary, religion in its properly dogmatic and institutional aspect. If I were asked to provide a one-line description of where I stand, I would probably choose the paradoxical self-designation of a *Paulinian materialist*.

So here I am today: I contend that one can learn more from a Catholic conservative like Paul Claudel than from Levinas. I contend that the tragic fate of Otto Weininger, that passionate anti-feminist and anti-Semite, holds more lessons for a truly radical feminism than the vast majority of contemporary cultural criticism. In contrast to the proponents of contingency and finitude, and also to the anti-realist misreading of Lacan's thesis that truth has the structure of a fiction, I continue to adhere to the emancipatory pathos of universal Truth. In contrast to the advocates of liberal tolerance, I continue to claim that liberal democracy is not the ultimate horizon of our political imagination. While remaining unabashedly Marxist in my insistence on the necessity to repoliticize the sphere of economy, I also remain unabashedly philosophical in my opposition to any reduction of the proper philosophical stance to a form of social or cultural criticism. The historicism of cultural studies and the evolutionism of the cognitive sciences are for me the two complementary forms of the betrayal of this philosophical stance.

So if the present Reader succeeds in burning the last bridges that may appear to connect me to the hegemonic trends of today's academia and force its readers to perceive my work the way it stands alone, I am well ready to pay the price of assuming the status of a living dead.

Slavoj Žižek
Berlin, 1 April 1998

Note

1 *Proceedings of the 10th International Conference on Literature and Psychology*, ed. Frederico Pereira (Lisbon: Instituto Superior de Pscicologia Aplicada, 1994), pp. 69–79.

Acknowledgements

We should like to thank our editor Andrew McNeillie for his attention and commitment to this project throughout, even in the face of adversity, and his editorial assistant, Jenny Lambert, who was a reassuring presence all along, immediately and effectively dealing with any day-to-day problems. Our thanks also go to the copy-editor, Jean van Altena for her meticulous work. Our warmest thanks go to Slavoj Žižek for unfailing enthusiasm and support for this venture through all its vicissitudes.

The editors and publishers wish to thank the following for permission to use copyright material:

Duke University Press for excerpts from Slavoj Žižek, 'There is No Sexual Relationship' in *Gaze and Voice as Love Objects*, eds S. Žižek and R. Salecl (1996), pp. 208–18, 219–36, 237–46. Copyright © 1996 Duke University Press; and Slavoj Žižek, *Tarrying with the Negative* (1993), pp. 140–61. Copyright © 1993 Duke University Press.

New York University Press for Slavoj Žižek, 'A Hair of a Dog that Bit You' from *Lacanian Theory of Discourse*, eds Mark Bracher et al. (1994), pp. 46–73.

The University of Michigan Press for excerpts from Slavoj Žižek, *The Abyss of Freedom/Ages of the World* (1997), pp. 8–12, 14–18, 37–44.

Verso for material from Slavoj Žižek, 'The Spectre of Ideology' from *Mapping Ideology*, ed. Slavoj Žižek (1994), pp. 1–33; Slavoj Žižek, *The Metastases of Enjoyment* (1994), pp. 137–64; and with MIT Press for Slavoj Žižek,

Looking Awry: An Introduction to Jacques Lacan through Popular Culture (1991), pp. 141–53.

Every effort has been made to trace the copyright holders, but if any have been inadvertently overlooked the publishers will be pleased to make the necessary arrangement at the first opportunity.

Introduction

Slavoj Žižek was born in 1949 in Ljubljana, Slovenia, which was, and is, the matrix of his intellectual and political work. He obtained degrees in sociology and philosophy, a doctorate in philosophy, and later a doctorate in psychoanalysis in Paris. In his student days he turned away from both the official Frankfurt school orientation and the 'dissident' Heideggerian one towards theory coming from France. By the early 1970s he and like-minded others attracted to a variety of French thinkers, such as Lacan, Derrida, Althusser and Foucault, began to publish and translate in one of the Slovene monthly cultural journals, *Problemi*, and by the end of the 1970s had established the book series *Analecta*, where they continue to publish Lacanian-inspired works as well as translations. At the same time, the Society for Theoretical Psychoanalysis was founded, within which a pure Lacanian orientation came to predominate, though not without the price of conflict with less 'orthodox' Lacanians. The orthodox Lacanian stance has become the hallmark of the so-called Ljubljana or Slovene Lacanian school, with a characteristic philosophical bent but no connections with the psychoanalytic clinic. The Slovene Lacanian school, which includes Miram Božovič, Ždravko Kobe, Mladen Dolar, Renata Salecl and Alenka Zupančič, works in three principal areas: (1) Lacanian readings of classical and modern philosophy (particularly the German Idealists); (2) endeavours to elaborate Lacanian theories of ideology and power; (3) Lacanian analyses of culture and art (especially the cinema). Initially, in the late 1970s and early 1980s, the school's international connections were predominantly with France (Jacques-Alain Miller's *École de la cause freudienne*), but over the last ten years their links have shifted to the Anglophone world. Although the group has gained an international reputation, the Slovene establishment remains resistant to their work, to the extent that they have not been able to regularize their activities on a common departmental basis, and are consequently scattered over a number of institutions. Even with all this activity, in Slovenia the group is known not so much for its intellectual work as for its political commitments.

The opposition in Slovenia to the Communist regime was split into a number of main orientations, such as nationalist writers with Heideggerian connections, New Left civil rights groups and Catholic intellectuals, a distribu-tion which turned out to be an advantage when a democratic system was set up after the end of Communism. It enabled Slovenia to escape the fate of Croatia and Serbia, where single nationalist parties gained hegemonic control. In Slovenia the Lacanian group has attached itself politically to the left-of-centre Liberal-Democratic Party, which developed out of the civil rights movement, and takes a clear anti-nationalist stance. In the first election for the five-member presidential body in 1989, Slavoj Žižek stood as a candidate. The group's support of the Liberal-Democratic Party had the strictly tactical aim of preventing seizure of power by the rightist nationalists, thus eschewing the pseudo-leftist lack of concrete commitment. The group's basic position is definitely that of a Marxist Left.[1]

II

The Žižek Reader aims in general to present something of the range of the author's work, and in particular to distinguish in it the centrality of Lacan's concept of the Real. It is with this concept above all that Žižek has brought psychoanalysis to bear on fields traditionally kept apart, performing an extra-ordinary elucidation of Lacanian psychoanalysis in the process. A Žižek Reader should display the recurrence of this concept across the diversity of fields that he covers, yet at the same time show its versatility. We have conceived of these fields as best organized under a broad tripartite division, Culture, Woman and Philosophy, within which specific texts have been selected to foreground the key topics which return throughout his books. It is typical of Žižek's style and method to produce continual elaborations of his basic tenets, with the same theoretical instrument acutely applied in each instance. The organization of the Reader tries to do justice to this feature of his work.

The outlines of Žižek's project can be clearly discerned in his first book *The Sublime Object of Ideology* (1989). Here he considers ideology from the perspect-ive of Lacanian psychoanalysis, revealing the antagonism constitutive of social reality as a counter to political fantasies of unity and authority. In his chapter 5, 'Which Subject of the Real?', he focuses on the failure of language to produce a secure object-world: the Symbolic, which orders our perception of reality, has to select from what is fundamentally continuous and unbounded. Hence there is no safe position from which to say that there is no metalanguage, as the poststructuralists would have it: it is rather the Lacanian case that ordinary language is its own metalanguage. Žižek illustrates this failure of language with the title of a painting, *Lenin in Warsaw* (picturing Lenin's wife in bed with a young Komsomol member) which fits and does not fit the picture (ibid., p. 159). It is a signifier which, through an absence of reference, appears to legitimate the satisfaction of an illicit desire, that of Lenin's wife. But although the Symbolic is constructed to establish agreements to satisfy desire, the joke works between signifier and signified in the impossible gap between desire and law where (real) laughter will appear. Žižek links the title of the picture with the Freudian *Vorstellungsrepräsentanz* ('ideational representative'), a mark left in the psyche by the drive, evidence of a hidden pressure: the title of the picture is a mark of an absence (that of Lenin), just as all signifiers fill out the void of some originally missing representation. By the same token, if in the Symbolic we look on the side of what is referred to, the object, this is also at the mercy of the signifying process, in that it is the Symbolic that is responsible for what is to emerge as an object, a point illustrated with another joke. A reluctant conscript, about to be called up for military service, is pretending to be mad, endlessly picking up bits of paper and saying 'That's not it!' He repeats this procedure in the psychiatrist's office until he is finally issued with an exemption paper, whereupon he cries 'That *is* it!' (ibid., p. 160). Here a search itself produces the desired object, the paradox being that the object is 'found' only through the operations of language, where desire both produces its object and is produced by it.

Žižek looks to the Lacanian Real to account for the failure of language in its attempts at reference. The Real is that which is both inside and outside the subject, resisting the Symbolic's endeavours to contain it. In the imaginary mirror-play of illusion a consistency obtains which leaves no gaps for the Real to manifest itself. The Real shows only in the structural effects it produces in mundane reality, and has no existence from the perspective of the symbolic system, the big Other. The fantasy of the Lacanian *objet a* conceals the gap, itself a proof of the Real that lies outside the illusion of consistency. This is the 'sublime object of ideology'. At its simplest, it is that which we most ardently desire, imagining it to be in the possession of the Other. This object, beyond all else, is what is unconsciously believed will fill the void at the core of being. The void is the effect of the constitution of the subject in language out of the Real of the body with all its undirected drives, which language vainly tries to bring entirely within its laws.

An antagonism thus emerges in ethical and political decisions, in which we constantly discover ourselves to be already defined, with our freedom already circumscribed. However, even where external circumstances seem to have forced upon us an evil choice, we are still responsible, since freedom involves the impossible Real, a hard kernel resisting symbolization. For the Real is both the source of symbolization, yet that which is left out of it. It can be looked upon as positive in so far as it is the being outside our knowing, but it is still felt as negative because its effects are most palpable when it is disregarded. As a 'sublime object' we must not get too close to it, or it will provide the shock which foils our expectations. It is both the 'That', the ontological ground on which signifiers work, and the 'What', the unpredictable signifieds that are produced. Yet although the Real cannot be written, there is one place where it does establish itself as writing, where its traumatic effects are inscribed – namely, in the unconscious.

So where is the subject with respect to the Real? The subject is alienated in the signifier. The Real in the subject is excluded from the Symbolic, para-doxically leaving a void as a positive condition of its existence. Yet it is this very void that distinguishes the subject from the results of the historical determina-tions that have made it what it appears to be. As a result, a series of inner contradictions inevitably arises that can only be resolved in dialectical moves. Yet although there is a Hegelian 'negation of the negation', in that this process will involve a rejection of an earlier identity, this double negation is not a smooth synthesis of thesis and antithesis, but a painful antagonistic transforma-tion, a sharp troping of identity. And because the Other too is alienated in the signifier, the subject will encounter an inexorable antagonism in the external as well, the source of which is again the Real.

Along with this sombre presentation of the subject's predicament, the rhetorically distinctive wittiness of Žižek's work, already illustrated by the jokes above, has the effect not only of providing comic relief, but also of slyly transforming the apparently uncompromising bleakness of his politico-philosophical (psycho) analyses into a buoyantly ironic political programme. As another example there is his citing of a well-known Soviet joke which, over time, through the gloom of historical events, he is able to metamorphose hilariously into its reverse. The joke is about a Jew called Rabinovitch who is being interrogated by an emigration official about his reasons for leaving the Soviet Union. He says he has two reasons, the first being that he is afraid Communism will be overthrown and that the Jews will get the blame for what the Communists have done. The official immediately protests that the power of the Communists will last for ever. 'Well,' responds Rabinovitch calmly, 'that's my second reason' (*For They Know Not What They Do*, p. 1). When this joke first appeared in *The Sublime Object of Ideology* in 1989, the Berlin Wall was still in place, and the joke rested on the notion of Communism as eternal. In 1991 Žižek was able to add a counter-version of the joke, with exactly the same structure, in which Rabinovitch again gives two reasons for his wished-for departure, the first being that Communism is there to stay and he cannot bear the thought. The official immediately protests that Communism is collapsing and that retribution will fall upon those responsible for its crimes. 'That's my second reason!' responds Rabinovitch (ibid.). In both jokes the switch of meanings operates over the same part of the joke – the reason against becomes the reason for – but the difference between them is that the statements of the two speakers have chiasmically changed places. In the first form of the joke, both finally believe that the Symbolic (here Communism) will last for ever, whereas in the second both finally believe that it is on the way out. These two modes of misappropriating the Symbolic, either as whole or as hole, are positions taken up respectively by the naïve and the cynic.

Although the content is bleak, the double joke testifies to a resilient hope for those oppressed by a totalitarian regime, in that the failure of the subject to represent itself – the Jew's two reasons being in absolute contradiction – is actually the subject's only mode of being. Rabinovitch is here the resilient subject who has learned that survival resides in 'tarrying with the negative': he is able to perform a dialectical advance, even if it is at the expense of tacitly acknowledging that he is surplus to requirements. In one sense he knows that the Symbolic can go on very well without him (that is why he is leaving); he recognizes his subject status as that of a remainder (Jewish jokes are invariably about the Jew's 'subjective destitution'). In another sense, the joke is a witness to his survival, his ability to move the Symbolic to another place (the Jew is an expert *émigré*). This makes him representative of any subject who can insert himself into the Symbolic without forgetting that there is lack in it, the lack that arises from the ultimate incompatibility of Symbolic and Real. If this argument seems to contradict Žižek's claim in the Foreword that his wit is an envelope concealing a heartlessly inexorable rhetoric within (p. viii), the apocryphal narrative above demonstrates that the wit and the rhetoric are more like the two sides of Saussure's single piece of paper, bonded together for a more positive programme than would seem to be the case.

III

The choice of extracts constitutes an attempt to trace the Žižekian text's elaborations of a set of ethico-political analyses within a Lacanian ontology. A radical definition of the Lacanian Real in relation to the subject can be found in the Culture section, in 'The Undergrowth of Enjoyment' (chapter 1). Here

Žižek traces out the dialectic of Lacan's theory as evidenced in the move from the fifties to the seventies in an 'introduction' which does not stay with the now familiar received version of his thought, but explicates its later complexities through examples from film and fiction. The emphasis here is on the ubiquity of the Real and the challenge to accommodate it, whereas in 'The Obscene Object of Postmodernity' (chapter 2) the undergrowth turns into a disgusting presence, proliferating into the Law as the 'obscene superego'; postmodernism is distinguished by its preoccupation with an excess of the Real, while in modernism the Real is an absence round which the text/object circulates. Inasmuch as the antagonism between Real and Symbolic continually threatens both individual self and communal solidarity, ideology emerges, constantly endeavouring to bridge the gulf. In 'The Spectre of Ideology' (chapter 3), the metaphor of 'spectre', indicating the apparitional nature of fantasy, none the less makes plain the projective feature of ideology as a necessary constituent of social interaction, albeit with the attendant dangers of cynicism for both those manipulating ideology and those manipulated by it. The theme of ideology is pursued again in 'Fantasy as a Political Category' (chapter 4), through an exploration of the part played by fantasy in the constructing and maintaining of both subject and nation, for the subject requires fantasmatic support in its symbolic identifications. The same problem of identification is explored through the structures of fantasy operating within the minds of cyberspace enthusiasts, posing the question 'Is it Possible to Traverse the Fantasy in Cyberspace?' (chapter 5), the final extract in Part I. A fantasy of a peculiar kind is provoked by the Japanese electronic toy, the *tamagochi*, which allows its keeper to indulge in frenetic activity to make sure it stays passive, so as to hide the fact that there is an Other that has real desires and can make real demands. By contrast, cyberspace can provoke a different response, because in encouraging surfers to experiment with identifications, it can make them participate in the work of imaginatively constructing new identities.

For Lacan, woman is a touchstone of the failure of the Symbolic, and has hence become a significant factor in Žižek's project: in Part II he picks up the polemics that have come to surround the Lacanian dicta on this subject. In 'Otto Weininger, or "Woman doesn't exist"' (chapter 6), Žižek co-opts a notorious work of Weininger's of 1903, strongly anti-feminist, for his argument that woman's whole existence depends on man's sexual pursuit of her. Through a Žižekian move into the Lacanian camp, this unpromisingly conservative view is turned upside down to become a radical one, whereby woman becomes representative of the ontological predicament of all subjects, in that she has to avail herself of masquerade to hide the void within. The insidious survival of the courtly love structure in the twin forms of idealization and denigration of the woman bears witness to the man's attempt to reduce her to a vehicle for his fantasy. The inaccessibility of the Beloved Lady as a device of the courtly lover to keep his fantasy intact is part of the evidence discussed in 'Courtly Love, or Woman as Thing' (chapter 7). In Lacan's view of courtly love, the beloved's being raised to the status of an abstract ideal is a narcissistic manoeuvre to evade her uncanny Otherness. The dire consequence of all this is explored in 'There is No Sexual Relationship' (chapter 8), where Žižek turns to Wagner's operas for their repeated attempts, through staging acts of sacrifice, to compensate for the failure of fantasy to reach the Real in the other – a series of redemptive solutions which did not enable Wagner to resolve the hysterical deadlock between the ethical universe of social obligation, on the one hand, and overwhelming sexual passion, on the other. In 'Death and the Maiden' (chapter 9) Žižek engages with three filmic narratives of sacrifice, corresponding to three diagnostic categories, perversion, hysteria and psychosis, in order to show how a woman's apparent pursuit of goodness towards a man founders on the pathological interlocking of their fantasies.

In Part III Žižek brings the Lacanian Real into a discussion of philosophy. In 'Hegel's "Logic of Essence" as a Theory of Ideology' (chapter 10), Žižek addresses the perennial problem of where to locate freedom in a world of necessity without taking refuge in a tacit acceptance of necessity. This is precisely what ideology seduces us into doing, presenting mundane reality as a set piece, whereas what the act of naming involves is an active responsibility for the selection of what is to constitute the logical essence of a thing. In such an act of responsibility, the Real in the subject confronts the Real in the external, whereby the virtual reality of the Symbolic is transformed into new versions of itself by the free will of subjects. In 'Schelling-in-Itself': 'The Orgasm of Forces' (chapter 11), the source of this transformation is traced in a myth of creation in which an originary chaos (the Real) submits to an act of differentiation by God, with the proviso that whatever limit is imposed allows for a leakage to take place, an 'indivisible remainder'. This is the leftover from the Lacanian moment of symbolic castration, emerging in ethics as the gap between act and will – the impossibility of law to specify in advance its own performance. The gap between act and will is the topic of the next two chapters, both of which examine the conflict between duty and drive. In 'A Hair of the Dog that Bit You' (chapter 12) the limit that duty places upon the drive, the 'wound' that the Symbolic inflicts on the subject, can only be tended by an application of what caused it: namely, by an investment in the Symbolic through a commitment to its empty form, for it is this that allows substantial subjective content to enter into speech. This is a Kantian issue which is taken up in chapter 13, 'Kant with (or against) Sade', where Žižek discusses the connection that Lacan has made between Kant and Sade: namely, that both propose subjects who are autonomous legislators of their own morality, which goes against the claim of others that Kant's unconditional injunction ('Do your duty!') hides an obscene superego. The final chapter, 'Of Cells and Selves', proposes that the subject is not merely an autonomous legislator, but owes its origin to an act of autonomous demarcation. In its attack upon cloning, Deep Ecology fails to see that both the living cell and the human subject come into existence and are maintained through an act of self-limitation, and, consequently, that the self cannot be reduced to a set of material causes.

Note

1   Our thanks go to Slavoj Žižek for kindly supplying the material on which the first section of this chapter is based.

Part I

Culture

1

The Undergrowth of Enjoyment: How Popular Culture can Serve as an Introduction to Lacan

This article was first published in *New Formations* (vol. 9 (1989), pp. 7–29). Here Žižek pursues the difference between the earlier, 'structuralist' Lacan of the 1950s and the later Lacan of the Real of the 1960s onwards, in order to bring out the radicality of this concept within his triad of Imaginary/ Symbolic/Real. The fundamental recalcitrance of the Real, the 'irreducible kernel of *jouissance* that resists all symbolization', is paradoxically the driving force of every discursive formation (see p. 14 of the article).

Žižek turns in particular to the theory of the cinema, here noting the shift from the semiotic approach of the 1970s, its preoccupation with the spectator as subject to visual seduction, to an emphasis on the gaze and the voice as that which cannot be integrated in either Imaginary or Symbolic. Something apparently meaningless invades our familiar 'reality', a disturbance on the side of the object, which seems to have an awareness of me from which I am excluded, so that I become strange to myself, and instead of gazing, I am gazed at. Similarly, the voice as object, as detached from the speaker, becomes alien to the 'diegetic "reality"', the story-line, and has the same effect as the visual intrusion. As one of his examples, Žižek goes to Hitchcock's *Psycho*, which can serve to illustrate how both gaze and voice function as cinematic objects. With respect to the gaze, Norman Bates's house is rendered uncanny because the camera's viewpoint switches from the house coming closer (as seen by the approaching woman) to the woman coming closer (as seen from the house), giving the anxious impression that the house is gazing at her; with respect to the voice, the 'mother's' (Norman's) voice is heard without a body, like a free-floating superego in search of something to attach itself to.

But the apparent meaninglessness which irrupts within ideological formations can also serve to resist the superego demand, constituting what Lacan calls *le sinthome*, that singular element of the Real to be found adrift within each subject. While the *symptom* is a compromise with the Symbolic, a message to the Other, an unconscious act of bad faith, the *sinthome* is the invisible kernel, that meaningless fragment of the Real which nevertheless, as part of being – in its 'pathological' singularity – is the basis of the consistency of the subject. At the same time, this meaninglessness, which inevitably becomes subversive, since it cannot be accommodated, preserves the subject from being swallowed up by a totalizing system (see Žižek's film examples, *Brazil* and *Lili Marleen*). Nevertheless, the subject cannot survive without a certain symbolic support. Although the later Lacan shifted his focus from the boundary between Imaginary and Symbolic to that between Symbolic and Real, moving from desire to drive, he realized that the subject cannot escape the Symbolic injunction, the superego's 'So be it!' The status of this voice is also real, since, indirectly, it stands in for the particularities of all others, and reminds us that the Real of desire cannot all be absorbed into an ideal form of the Law.

Žižek moves from the benign superego to the less benign in examining the catastrophic intrusion of the Real in a science-fiction novel and a Fritz Lang film. He discusses various paranoid constructions which reveal the superego as persecutory in a world where an 'Other of the Other' controls events; the paranoid construction allows us to forget that '"the Other does not exist" as a consistent, closed order', and thus enables us to avoid 'confronting the blind, contingent automatism which is constitutive of the symbolic order'. In the case where there is a collapse of the boundary between Real and Symbolic, the Real either floods reality as in psychotic breakdown (e.g. the painter Mark Rothko) or is absorbed into reality as in the paranoid construction (Jim in *Empire of the Sun*), both producing the effect of an 'answer of the Real'. Since the Real cannot be avoided, the paranoid construction is a way of escaping from madness.

This ubiquity of the Real is what the later Lacan takes account of, in contrast to his earlier concentration on the signifier. He thus moves from the notion that *jouissance* is prohibited in language to that of the letter as permeated with enjoyment, the Real as active in every utterance. In the cinema such pervasion of the sign has been designated as *rendu* (Maurice

Chion), a way of representing reality distinct from the Imaginary and the Symbolic modes, typically through the sound-track, which now takes over as dominant indicator of the narrative reality, while the visual images become a secondary montage (as frequently both in *film noir* and in the contemporary cinema). Žižek shows how in three films an arbitrary stylistic prohibition has the effect of *rendu*, each producing the form of a different psychosis and each reproducing, through being an unnecessary prohibition, the Symbolic Law that forbids 'something *that is already in itself inaccessible*', thus making uncannily palpable the tension between Real and Symbolic.

The psychotic effect is constituted by the refusal of symbolic castration, resulting in the lack of a lack, and hence of the ability to attach words to the world. Whereas the earlier, 'classical' Lacan sees the unconscious as determined by the effects of the signifier (as 'the discourse of the Other'), the later Lacan turns to the ways in which signification is disrupted (in the four discourses). In *Seminar XX* he shifts from the Other to the 'One of jouissance', the singularity in the subject that resists its inclusion in the signifying chain, *le sinthome*. Žižek cites two stories by Patricia Highsmith to illustrate this 'undergrowth of enjoyment', in which strange uncanny excrescences thrust up from the ground, 'ex-sistence', the ontological, breaking through existence, the mundane. There is a dilemma here for the subject, who is caught in this either/or, 'the Thing embodying impossible enjoyment' or the Symbolic that excludes it. In an analysis, this is precisely what requires resolution at the end. For the late Lacan, this resolution comes about through an identification with the *sinthome*, through a recognition of the singularity of this element, the particular form of one's own enjoyment. A Ruth Rendell story allows Žižek to demonstrate what happens when there is an 'acting out' of a symptom instead of a Lacanian 'passage to the act': the spinster who steals the clock and identifies with its ticking is shifting her guilt to the Other, whereas in the 'passage to the act' the subject identifies with its *sinthome*, 'the pathological "tic" structuring the real kernel of our enjoyment'. 'Acting out' remains bound to the Symbolic, and in particular to its apparatus of truth; 'passage to the act' allows a break with symbolic 'truth' in order to establish an internal consistency.

The English reception of Jacques Lacan, predominantly at least, has still not integrated all the consequences of the break marked by the seminar on *Ethics of Psychoanalysis* (1959–60), a break which radically shifted the accent of his teaching: from the dialectics of desire to the inertia of enjoyment (*jouissance*), from the symptom as coded message to the *sinthome* as letter permeated with enjoyment, from the 'unconscious structured like a language' to the Thing in its heart, the irreducible kernel of *jouissance* that resists all symbolization.[1] The aim of the present essay is to exemplify some of the key motifs of this last stage of Lacanian theory via a reading of certain narratives borrowed from popular cinema and literature. What is proposed here is not some kind of 'applied psychoanalysis', a psychoanalytic reading of the products of culture, but on the contrary the articulation of some of the fundamental concepts of Lacanian psychoanalytic theory (gaze and voice as objects, the frontier separating reality from the Real, the role of the 'answer of the Real' in the production of the meaning effect, *rendu* and *sinthome*) by the use of examples taken from popular culture, and first from the cinema.

Why cinema? The use of the Lacanian theoretical apparatus in film theory is well known, and has been especially influential in Britain, from the *suture* theories of *Screen* in the 1970s to the feminist explorations indebted especially to the concepts of fantasy and identification. The Lacan who served as a point of reference for these theories, however, was the Lacan before the break; and it is only in French film theory over the last decade that a shift has occurred which corresponds (and has perhaps been directly indebted) to the late turn in Lacanian teaching, a turn that could be summarized concisely by the formula: 'from the signifier to the object'. If the 1970s were dominated by the semiotic approach best rendered by the title of Christian Metz's *The Imaginary Signifier* (an approach whose aim was to dispel the imaginary fascination, to break through it to the hidden symbolic structure regulating its functioning), in the last decade we can observe a shift of accent to the paradoxical status of those remnants and leftovers of the Real that elude the structuring of the signifier: gaze and voice. The renewal of film theory over the last decade is thus centred around gaze and voice as cinematic objects: the status of the first has been elaborated by Pascal Bonitzer,[2] of the second by Michel Chion.[3] It is of course no accident that Lacan defined the object of psychoanalysis, the celebrated *objet petit a*, precisely as gaze and voice.

The first association that comes to mind in connection with 'gaze' and 'voice', for the reader well versed in 'deconstructivist' texts, is that they are the main target of the Derridean enterprise of deconstruction; for what is the gaze if not *theoria* grasping the 'thing itself' in the presence of its form and the form of its presence, and what is the voice if not the medium of pure 'auto-affection' embodying the presence-to-itself of the speaking subject? The aim of deconstruction is precisely to demonstrate how the gaze is always already determined by the 'infrastructural' network which delimits what can be seen from the unseen, and which thus necessarily eludes capture by the gaze; and how, similarly, the self-presence of the voice is always-already split/deferred by the trace of writing.

Yet there is a radical incommensurability between Lacan and poststructuralist deconstruction; for, in Lacan, the function of gaze and voice is almost
exactly the reverse. First of all, they are not on the side of the subject but on the
side of the object. The gaze marks the point in the object (the picture) from
which the viewing subject is *already gazed at*: it is the object which is gazing at
me. Thus, far from guaranteeing the self-presence of the subject and her/his
vision, the gaze functions as a spot or stain in/on the picture, disturbing its
transparent visibility and introducing an irreducible split in my relation to it.
I can never see the picture at the point from which it is gazing at me: the view
and the gaze are constitutively dissymmetrical. The gaze as object is a blemish
that prevents me from looking at the picture from a safe, 'objective' distance,
framing it as something which is at the disposal of my grasping view. It is, we
might say, the point at which the very frame (of my view) is already inscribed
in the 'content' of the picture. And the same goes, of course, for the voice as
object. That voice, the voice, for example, of the superego, addressing me
without being attached to any particular bearer, floating freely in some horrifying interspace, functions again as a stain or blemish, whose inert presence
interferes like a foreign body and prevents me from achieving self-identity.

To clarify this, let us take as our first example a classic Hitchcockian
procedure. How does Hitchcock shoot a scene in which a character is
approaching some mysterious and 'uncanny' object? He does it by juxtaposing
the subjective view of the approaching object with an objective shot of the
subject in motion. Among many instances, let me mention just two, both of
which figure a house as the uncanny object: Lilah (Vera Miles) approaching
'Mrs Bates's' house towards the end of *Psycho* and Melanie (Tippi Hedren)
approaching Mitch's mother's house in the famous scene from *Birds* analysed in
detail by Raymond Bellour.[4] In both cases, the view of the house as seen by the
approaching woman alternatives with the shot of the woman walking towards
the house. Why does this formal procedure in itself generate such anxiety?
Why does the object being approached become 'uncanny'? What we have here
is precisely the dialectic of view and gaze, mentioned earlier: the subject sees
the house, but what provokes anxiety is the uneasy feeling that the house itself
is somehow already gazing at her, from a point which escapes her view and so
renders her utterly helpless.[5]

The corresponding status of voice as object has been elaborated by Michel
Chion around the notion of the *voix acousmatique*, the voice without bearer
which cannot be attributed to a subject and hovers in some indefinable interspace, implacable precisely because it cannot be properly located, being part
neither of the diegetic 'reality' of the story nor of the sound-accompaniment
(commentary, musical score), but belonging to that mysterious domain
designed by Lacan the 'between-two-deaths' (*l'entre-deux morts*). The first

instance that comes to mind here is once again from *Psycho*. As Chion has
demonstrated in a brilliant analysis,[6] the central problem of *Psycho* is to be
located on a formal level: it consists in the relation of a certain voice (the
'mother's' voice) to the body; a voice, as it were, in search of a body to utter it.
When the voice finally finds a body, it is not the mother's body at all, but the
body of Norman, to which it is artificially appended.

The tension created by the errant voice in search of its body may also explain
the effect of relief, even of poetic beauty, at the moment of 'desacousmatisa-
tion' – the point when the voice finally locates its bearer. Thus at the beginning
of George Miller's *Mad Max II: The Road Warrior*, we have an old man's voice
introducing the story and an unspecified view of Mad Max alone on the road.
Only at the very end does it become clear that the voice and the gaze belong to
the little wild kid with the boomerang who later became chief of his tribe and
is recounting the story to his descendants. The beauty of the final inversion lies
in its unexpectedness: both elements, the gaze-voice and the person who is its
bearer, are given from the outset; but it is only at the very end that the
connection between them is established, and the gaze-voice 'pinned' to one
of the characters of the diegetic reality.

The example of *voix acousmatique* with the most far-reaching implications for
the practice of ideological critique is Terry Gilliam's *Brazil*. We all know
'Brazil' as a stupid song from the 1950s that resounds compulsively throughout
the picture. This song, whose status is never quite clear (when is it part of the
story, when just part of the accompanying score?), embodies in its noisy
repetitions the superego imperative of mindless enjoyment. 'Brazil', to put it
briefly, is the content of the fantasy of the film's hero, the support and point of
reference that structure his enjoyment; and it is precisely for that reason that we
can use it to demonstrate the fundamental ambiguity of fantasy and enjoyment.
Throughout the film, it seems that the mindlessly obtrusive rhythm of the song
serves as a support for totalitarian enjoyment, condensing the fantasy-frame of
the 'insane' totalitarian order that the film depicts; but at the very end, just
when the hero's resistance has apparently been broken by the savage torture to
which he has been subjected, he escapes his torturers by whistling... 'Brazil'!
Thus, whilst functioning as a support of the totalitarian order, fantasy is at the
same time that overspill or residue of the Real that enables us to 'pull ourselves
out', to preserve a kind of distance from the socio-symbolic order. When we
go crazy in our obsession with mindless *jouissance*, even totalitarian manipulation cannot reach us.

Finally, a similarly equivocal instance of the *voix acousmatique* can be found in
Fassbinder's *Lili Marleen*. During the film the popular love-song 'Lili Marlene'
is played and replayed *ad nauseam*, until the endless repetition transforms
a lovely melody into a disgusting parasite that will not release us, even for

a moment. Totalitarian power, personified by Goebbels, tries to manipulate the song to capture the imagination of the exhausted soldiers, but it eludes his grasp; like a genie from a bottle, the song takes on a life of its own. The crucial feature of Fassbinder's film is this insistence on the central ambiguity of 'Lili Marlene', a Nazi love-song which is at the same time on the very edge of transforming itself into a subversive element capable of bursting free from the very ideological apparatus by which it is propagated, and thus always in danger of being prohibited.

Such a fragment of the signifier, inescapably permeated with mindless enjoyment, is what Lacan, in the last phase of his teaching, called *le sinthome*: no longer the 'symptom' (the homophonic *symptome*), the coded message to be deciphered by a process of interpretation, but the fragment of a meaningless letter, the reading of which procures an immediate *jouis-sense* or 'meaning-in-enjoyment'.

It should be unnecessary to stress how radically, once we take into account the dimension of the *sinthome* in an ideological structure, we are compelled to modify the procedures of ideological analysis itself. Ideology is usually conceived as a discourse, an enchainment of elements whose meaning is over-determined by their specific articulation, by the way some 'nodal point' or master-signifier totalizes them into a coherent and homogeneous field. We might point, for example, to Laclau's now classic analysis of the ways in which particular ideological elements function as 'floating signifiers', their meanings fixed retrospectively by the operation of hegemonic nodal instances.[7] But what is at stake once we take into account the concept of the *sinthome* is a crucial shift away from deconstruction in this form. It is no longer sufficient to denounce ideological experience as artificial; to seek to demonstrate how the object proffered by ideology as natural and given is the product of a discursive construction, the result of a network of symbolic overdetermination; to locate the ideological text in its context, to render visible its necessarily overloaded margins. What we must do – what is done by Fassbinder and Gilliam – is, on the contrary, to isolate the *sinthome* from the context by virtue of which it exerts its power of fascination, to force us to see it in its utter stupidity, as a meaningless fragment of the Real. In other words, we must (as Lacan puts it in *Seminar XI*) 'change the precious gift into a piece of shit'; we must make it possible to experience the mesmerizing voice as a disgusting piece of sticky excrement.

This form of 'estrangement' is perhaps more radical even than Brechtian *Verfremdung*; for it produces distanciation, not by locating the phenomenon in its historical totality, but by making us experience the utter nullity of its immediate reality; the stupidity of a material presence which escapes historical mediation. Dialectical mediation – the context that bestows meaning on the object – is not added, but rather subtracted.

How Real is Reality?

It is no accident that both films, *Brazil* and *Lili Marleen*, depict a totalitarian universe in which the subjects can survive only by clinging to a superego voice (the title song) that enables them to escape a complete 'loss of reality'. As has been pointed out by Lacan, our 'sense of reality' is never supported solely by the 'reality test' (*Realitatsprüfung*); it always requires a certain superego command: a 'So be it!'. The status of the voice uttering this command is neither imaginary nor symbolic; it is real. We have thus reached the second motif that differentiates Lacan's last stage from the preceding ones. In the earlier stages, the accent fell on the boundary separating the Imaginary from the Symbolic; the aim here was to penetrate through the imaginary fascination to its symbolic cause – to the symbolic overdetermination regulating imaginary effects. In the last stage, the emphasis shifts to the barrier separating the Real from symbolically structured reality: to those leftovers or remnants of the Real that escape symbolic 'mediation'.

To exemplify this, let us refer once again to a popular narrative: Robert Heinlein's sci-fi novel *The Unpleasant Profession of Jonathan Hoag*. The action takes place in contemporary New York; the eponymous hero, Hoag, can remember nothing that happens while he is at work, so he hires the private investigator Teddy Randall to find out what happens to him after he enters his work-place on the thirteenth floor of the Acme Company building. Randall follows Hoag to work; but between the twelfth and fourteenth floors Hoag disappears, and Randall is unable to find the thirteenth floor. That same evening, Randall's double appears in his bedroom mirror and tells the detective to follow him through the mirror, explaining that he has been summoned by 'the committee'. Randall is led to a great meeting-hall, where the president of the committee of twelve informs him that he is now on the thirteenth floor of the Acme building, to which he will be summoned from time to time for nocturnal interrogations.

At the denouement of the story, Hoag invites Randall and his wife to a picnic in the country. He tells them that he has at last become aware of his true identity: he is actually an art critic, though of a peculiar kind. Our universe, he says, is only one of several, and the masters of all the universes are mysterious beings who create different worlds, including our own, as experimental works of art. To maintain the artistic perfection of their efforts, these cosmic artificers from time to time send into their creations one of their own kind disguised as a native, to act as a kind of universal art critic. The mysterious committee members who summoned Randall are representatives of an evil and inferior divinity attempting to corrupt the work of the cosmic artists.

Hoag informs Randall and his wife that, in the course of his visit to this universe, he has discovered one or two minor blemishes which he intends to have put right during the next few hours. Randall and his wife will notice nothing; but on the drive home to New York, they must under no circumstances open the windows of their car. They set off, and the journey is uneventful until they witness a road accident. At first they ignore it and continue on their way; but when they see a patrolman, their sense of duty prevails and they stop to report the accident. Randall asks his wife to lower her window a little:

She complied, then gave a sharp intake of breath and swallowed a scream. He did not scream, but he wanted to. Outside the open windows was no sunlight, no cops, no kids – nothing. Nothing but a grey and formless mist, pulsing slowly as if with inchoate life. They could see nothing of the city through it, not because it was too dense but because it was – empty. No sound came out of it; no movement showed in it. It merged with the frame of the window and began to drift inside. Randall shouted, 'Roll up the window!' She tried to obey, but her hands were nerveless; he reached across her and cranked it up himself, jamming it hard into its seat. The sunny scene was restored; through the glass they saw the patrolman, the boisterous game, the sidewalk, and the city beyond. Cynthia put a hand on his arm. 'Drive on, Teddy!' 'Wait a minute,' he said tensely, and turned to the window beside him. Very cautiously he rolled it down – just a crack, less than an inch. It was enough. The formless grey flux was out there, too; through the glass city traffic and sunny street were plain, through the opening – nothing.

What is this 'grey and formless mist' if not the Lacanian Real – the pulsing of the pre-symbolic substance in all its abhorrent vitality? But what is crucial for us here is the form, or more precisely the place, in which this Real interferes: it irrupts on the very boundary separating the 'outside' from the 'inside', materialized in this case by the car window. Anyone who has ever been inside a car has experienced precisely this phenomenological sense of discord or disproportion between interior and exterior. Though from the outside the car looks small, from the inside it looks all of a sudden far larger; we feel quite comfortable. The price paid for that adjustment is the decisive loss of any continuity between inside and outside. To those sitting inside a car, the outside world appears at a certain distance, separated from them by a barrier or screen symbolized by the windows. They perceive everything outside the car as a mode of reality which is discontinuous with the reality inside. While they remain safely behind the closed windows, however, external objects are as if fundamentally unreal, their reality suspended in parentheses: a kind of cinematic reality, in effect, projected on to the screen of the window. It is precisely this phenomenological experience – the sense of a barrier separating inner and outer, the perception of the outside as a kind of fictional representation of spectacle – that is invoked by the alarming final scene of Heinlein's story. It is as if, for a moment, the 'projection' of the outside world has stopped working; as if we have been confronted momentarily with the formless grey emptiness of the screen itself, with the Mallarmean 'place where nothing takes place but the place'. (The same dissonance and disproportion between inside and outside are reproduced in Kafka's stories, whose sinister architecture – the block of flats where the Court meets in *The Trial*, the uncle's palace in *Amerika* – is characterized by the fact that what appears from outside a modest structure metamorphoses miraculously on entry into an endless maze of halls and stairways reminiscent of Piranesi's drawings of the subterranean labyrinths of prisons.)

It seems that, as soon as we wall in a given space, there is more of it 'inside' than appears possible to an outside view. Continuity and proportion are not possible, because this disproportion, the surplus of inside in relation to outside, is a necessary structural effect of the very separation of the two; it can only be abolished by demolishing the barrier and letting the outside swallow the inside. What I want to suggest, then, is that this excess of 'inside' consists, precisely, in the fantasy-space – the mysterious thirteenth floor, the surplus space which is a persistent motif in science fiction and mystery stories. This, equally, is what underlies the classic cinematic device for evading the unhappy ending, in which, just as the action is approaching its catastrophic climax, we undergo a radical change of perspective, and discover that the whole near-tragic chain of events has been nothing but the protagonist's nightmare – at which point we are returned, awakened and relieved, to the 'real world'.

A notable example is Fritz Lang's *The Woman in the Window*, which begins with a lonely professor of psychology who dozes off one evening in the club. At eleven the attendant wakes him from his nap; and as he is leaving, he glances at the portrait of a beautiful brunette in the window of a store next to the club. The portrait has always been a source of fascination to him, but this time it seems to come alive: the picture in the shop window merges with the reflection of a young woman in the street, who asks him for a match. The professor starts an affair with her and skills her lover in a fight. He is kept informed of the progress of the murder investigation by a friend in the police force; and when he knows his arrest is imminent, he sits in a chair, drinks poison, and dozes off...to be woken by the club attendant because it is eleven o'clock. He returns home, with a renewed appreciation, we presume, of the danger of succumbing to the charms of alluring brunettes.

Contrary to superficial impressions, the final reversal is not a compromise designed to accommodate the narrative to the ideological conventions of Hollywood. The 'message' of the film is not 'Thank God, it was only a dream; I am not really a murderer, just a normal man like everybody else!' Rather, it is that *in our unconscious, in the Real of our desire, we are all murderers.* Paraphrasing the Lacanian reading of Freud's account of the father whose dead son appears in a dream, reproaching him with the cry 'Father, can't you see I'm burning?', we might say that the professor wakes *in order to be able to continue his dream* (of being a normal man like everyone else), to escape the psychic reality of his desire. Awakened into everyday reality, he can say with relief, 'It was only a dream,' overlooking the crucial fact that it is precisely when he is awake that he is 'nothing but the consciousness of his dream' (Lacan). As in the parable of Zhuang-zhi and the butterfly (another Lacanian point of reference), what we have is not a quiet, kind, decent, bourgeois professor dreaming that he is a murderer, but a murderer dreaming, in his everyday life, that he is a quiet, kind, decent, bourgeois professor.

This kind of retroactive displacement of 'real' events into fiction (dreaming) appears as a compromise, an act of ideological conformism, only so long as we hold to the naïve ideological opposition between 'hard reality' and the 'world of dreams'. As soon as we recognize that it is precisely and only in dreams that we encounter the real of our desire, the whole accent shifts radically. Our commonest everyday reality, the reality of the social universe in which we play our usual roles as decent ordinary people, turns out to be an illusion resting on a specific 'repression': on ignorance of the real of our desire. This social reality then becomes nothing more than a fragile symbolic tissue which can be torn at any moment by the intrusion of the real; the most routine everyday conversation, the most familiar event, can suddenly take a dangerous turn, damage can be caused that cannot be undone, things can be said after which the tissue can never be repaired. *The Woman in the Window* exemplifies this in the loop-like line of its narrative progress. Events proceed in a linear fashion until, all of a sudden, at the very instant of catastrophic breakdown, we find ourselves once again back at an earlier point: the route into the catastrophe turns out to be nothing but a fictional detour, returning us to our starting point. To effect this retroactive fictionalization, *The Woman in the Window* employs a repetition of the same scene (in which the professor falls asleep, to be woken at eleven by the attendant); but the repetition retroactively transforms everything that has happened in between into a fiction.

The earlier reference to Kafka in connection with the disproportion between 'outside' and 'inside' was more than merely casual. Kafka's Court, that absurd, obscene agency of guilt, can be located precisely in this surplus of inside over outside, this fantasy-space on the thirteenth floor. Indeed, it is not difficult to recognize in the mysterious 'committee' that interrogates Heinlein's hero a new version of Kafka's tribunal, a classic figure of the evil Law of the superego. Heinlein ultimately eludes the Kafkaesque vision of a world ruled by the agents of a mad God; but he does so only at the cost of resorting to the paranoid notion that the universe is a work of art created by an unknown demiurge. The common feature of paranoid stories of this kind (a further example is Isaac Asimov's 'The Jokester') is that they imply the existence of the 'Other of the Other', a hidden subject who pulls the strings of the great Other, the symbolic order, precisely at those points where the Other starts to speak 'autonomously', where it produces an effect of meaning by means of a senseless contingency, beyond the conscious intention of the speaking subject, as in dreams or jokes. This 'Other of the Other' is exactly the Other of paranoia, the one who speaks through us without our knowledge, controlling our thoughts, manipulating us through the apparent spontaneity of jokes, the hidden Artist whose fantasy-creation is our reality. This paranoid construction enables us to evade the fact that (to cite Lacan again) 'the Other does not exist' as a consistent, closed order: to avoid confronting the blind, contingent auto-matism which is constitutive of the symbolic order.

The Answer of the Real

Faced with a paranoid construction of this kind, we must not forget Freud's warning and mistake it for the 'illness' itself. The paranoid construction, on the contrary, is already an attempt to heal ourselves, to pull ourselves out of the real 'illness', the psychotic breakdown – the 'end of the world', the falling apart of the symbolic universe – with the help of a substitute-formation.

The process of psychotic breakdown corresponds precisely to the break-down of the boundary separating reality from the Real; and, for an example of that breakdown in its pure and, as it were, distilled form, without any admix-ture of 'content', I want first to turn to a sequence of paintings produced in the 1960s, during the last decade of his life, by Mark Rothko, the most tragic exponent of American 'abstract expressionism'. The 'theme' of the paintings is constant: they represent a series of colour variations on the motif of the relation between reality and the Real, rendered in pure geometrical abstraction by the famous painting of Kasimir Malevich, *The Naked Unframed Icon of my Time*: a simple black square on a white ground. In this formulation, 'reality' (the white background surface, the 'liberated nothingness', the open space in which objects can appear) derives its consistency and meaning entirely from the 'black hole' in its centre (the Lacanian *das Ding*, the Thing that gives body to the substance of enjoyment), from, that is, the exclusion of the Real, the transformation of the status of the Real into a central lack. Like all Rothko's late pictures, this is a manifestation of a fight to maintain the frontier separating reality from the Real, to prevent the Real (the central black square) from overflowing the entire field, to preserve the distinction between the square and what must at all costs remain its background; for if the square comes to occupy the whole field, and the difference between figure and ground is lost, we are precipitated into psychotic autism.

Rothko depicts this struggle as a colour tension between a grey background and the central black spot which spreads menacingly from one picture to another. In the late 1960s, the vivacity of red and yellow in his earlier canvases begins to give way to the minimal opposition of black and grey. If we look at these paintings 'cinematically' – putting the reproductions one above the other and turning them over quickly to give an impression of continuous movement – we can trace a line that travels ineluctably to a seemingly inevitable end. In the canvases produced immediately before Rothko's death, the minimal tension between black and grey changes for the last time into a burning conflict of voracious reds and yellows: witness perhaps to a last desperate attempt at redemption, yet at the same time an unmistakable confirmation that the end is imminent. A few weeks later, he was found dead in his New York atelier, in a pool of blood, with his wrists cut.

Far from being a sign of 'madness', the barrier separating the Real from reality is therefore the very condition of a minimum of 'normality'; madness – psychosis – sets in when this barrier falls down and the Real either overflows into reality (as in autistic breakdown) or is itself included in reality (as in paranoia, where it assumes the form of the 'Other of the Other'). Two instances of this can be drawn from popular narratives: the first, Spielberg's *Empire of the Sun*. From the moment at which the protagonist, Jim, is imprisoned in a Japanese camp near Shanghai, his basic problem becomes one of survival, not only in the physical sense but above all psychically: how to avoid a catastrophic 'loss of reality' once his world, his symbolic universe, has literally fallen apart. Early on in the film, Jim's reality is the isolated and artificial world of his expatriate parents; and he perceives the misery of Chinese everyday life only through the safe distance of a screen – which, as in *The Unpleasant Profession of Jonathan Hoag*, is a car window. Through the windows of his parents' Rolls Royce, Jim observes the misery and chaos of the Chinese crowd as a kind of cinematic 'projection', dreamlike and discontinuous with his own reality. His problem, then, is how to survive once this barrier is removed; once he is thrown into the hostile, violent world towards which he has until then sustained a distance based on a suspension of its reality.

His first, automatic reaction to this loss of reality, this encounter with the Real, is to repeat the elementary 'phallic' gesture of symbolization, to invert his utter impotence into omnipotence, to conceive himself as *radically responsible* for the intrusion of the Real. The moment of this intrusion of the Real has been marked by the shell from the Japanese warship which hits the hotel where

Jim and his family have taken refuge. In order to hang on to a sense of reality, Jim immediately assumes responsibility for this disaster. From his room, he has watched the Japanese ship sending out light signals, and has answered them with his pocket torch; and when, a moment later, the shell strikes the hotel and his father rushes into the room, Jim, convinced that the attack was the result of his inadvertent signalling, cries desperately, 'I didn't mean it! It was only a joke!' The same omnipotence surfaces later in the prison camp, when an Englishwoman dies, and Jim, furiously massaging her corpse, is convinced by an involuntary movement of the eyelids that he has succeeded in reviving the dead. We see here how a 'phallic' inversion of impotence into omnipotence is invariably associated with an *answer of the real*: there must always be some 'little piece of the real', wholly contingent but perceived none the less by the subject as a confirmation of his supposed omnipotence.[8]

Far from being limited to so-called pathological cases, the 'answer of the real' is a fundamental prerequisite for intersubjective communication; for there can be no symbolic exchange without some 'bit of the real' to serve as a kind of pawn guaranteeing its consistency. What, then, does this mean for the structure of so-called normal communication? Under what condition can we speak of 'successful' communication?

In a recent novel by Ruth Rendell, *Talking to Strange Men* – which could be read as a kind of 'thesis novel' on this theme (in the sense in which Sartre spoke of his plays as 'thesis plays' exemplifying his philosophical propositions) – an intersubjective constellation is staged which renders perfectly the Lacanian thesis on communication as a 'successful misunderstanding'. As is often the case with Ruth Rendell (cf. also her *Lake of Darkness, The Killing Doll, The Tree of Hands*), the plot is based on the contingent encounter of two intersubjective networks. The hero of the novel is a young man, desperate because his wife has recently left him for another man. Quite by chance, he stumbles upon what he believes to be a spy ring, which communicates through coded messages secreted in the hand of a statue in the park. The hero breaks the code, and places in the hand of the statue a coded message ordering one of the 'agents' to liquidate the man for whom his wife left him.

What the hero does not know is that the 'spy ring' is actually a group of pre-pubescent adolescents playing spy games. When his wife's lover finally dies, it is in fact as a result of pure accident; yet the hero reads his rival's death as a result of his own successful infiltration into the spy ring.

The charm of the novel derives from the parallel description of the inter-subjective networks of the two groups, on the one side the hero, desperately searching for his wife, on the other the spy games of the adolescents. There is a sort of interaction between them, but it is wrongly construed on both sides: the hero believes that he is in contact with a real spy ring which is carrying out his orders, while the adolescents have no idea that an outsider has interfered in the circulation of their messages and attribute the hero's interventions to one of their own members. 'Communication' is achieved, but in such a way that one participant knows nothing at all about it while the other totally misunderstands the nature of the game. The two poles of communication are thus asymmetrical. The adolescent network, we might say, embodies the great Other, the symbolic universe of codes and cyphers, with its senseless automatism; and when as a result of its blind functioning this mechanism produces a body, the subject (the hero) reads this purely arbitrary outcome as an 'answer of the real', a confirmation of successful communication.[9]

Rendering the Real

We have now arrived at the last motif separating the later from the earlier Lacan. The 'standard' Lacanian theory of the signifier aims to produce a suspension of the sign-effect described above: to make us see the pure contingency on which the process of symbolization hangs; to 'denaturalize' the effect of meaning by demonstrating how it is always overdetermined by a series of contingent encounters. In *Seminar XX* (*Encore*), however, Lacan surprisingly rehabilitates the notion of the sign – conceived precisely in its opposition to the signifier – as preserving continuity with the Real. Assuming that we can discount the possibility of a simple theoretical regression, what is meant here?

In the earlier Lacan, the order of the signifier is defined by a vicious circle of differentiality. It is an order of discourse in which the identity of each element is overdetermined by its articulation, in which every element 'is' nothing more than its difference from all the others, without any grounding in the Real. In rehabilitating the notion of 'sign', Lacan attempts, by contrast, at this later stage in his work to indicate the status of a letter which cannot be reduced to the dimension of the signifier, which is prediscursive, still permeated with the substance of enjoyment. Against the classical 'standard' proposition of 1962, 'enjoyment is forbidden to the one who speaks as such', we have now a paradoxical letter which is nothing other than materialized enjoyment.

In film theory, the status of this letter-enjoyment – of a letter continuous with the Real of *jouissance* – has been defined by Michel Chion using the concept of *rendu*, which is opposed both to the (imaginary) simulacrum and the (symbolic) code. *Rendu* is a third means of representing reality in the cinema – not by imaginary imitation or by symbolic codification, but by means of its immediate 'rendition'.[10] Chion has in mind here specifically those contemporary techniques of sound recording and reproduction that enable us not only exactly to reproduce 'original' sound, but to reinforce it and so render audible details which we should not be able to hear if we found ourselves in the 'reality' recorded by the picture. This kind of sound penetrates us, seizes us on an immediate-real level; witness, for example, the obscenely disgusting mucous-slimy sounds, suggestive of some indeterminate activity somewhere between sexual intercourse and the act of childbirth, that accompany the transformation of human beings into their alien clones in the Philip Kaufman version of *The Invasion of the Body Snatchers*. According to Chion, this shift in the status of the sound-track points to a slow but far-reaching silent revolution that is taking place in contemporary cinema. For it is no longer appropriate in such cases to say that the sound 'accompanies' the flow of pictures; rather, the sound-track functions as the primary frame of reference that orientates us in the depicted diegetic reality. Bombarding us with details from every side, the sound-track has in a sense taken over the function once exercised by the establishing shot. It gives us the general perspective, the 'map' of the situation, and guarantees its continuity, while the images on screen are reduced to isolated fragments, visual fishes swimming freely in the encompassing medium of the sound-aquarium.

It would be difficult to invent a better metaphor for psychosis: in contrast to the 'normal' state of affairs, in which the Real is a lack, a hole in the middle of the symbolic order (the central black spot in Rothko's paintings), we have here an 'aquarium' of the Real encircling isolated islands of the Symbolic. In other words, it is no longer enjoyment which drives the proliferation of signifiers by its lack, functioning as a central 'black hole' around which the signifying network is interlaced; it is, on the contrary, the symbolic order itself which is reduced to the status of floating islands of signifiers, albuminous *îles flottantes* basking in a sea of yolky enjoyment.[11]

This effect of *rendu* is not of course limited to the 'silent revolution' currently taking place in the cinema.[12] Close analysis reveals its presence already in classical Hollywood cinema – in *film noir* of the late 1940s and early 1950s, for example. A number of those films are founded in the prohibition of a formal element which is conventionally central to the narrative of sound film: the objective shot, montage, the voice, etc. Robert Montgomery's *Lady in the Lake* is constructed, for example, on a prohibition of the objective shot: except for the introduction and the ending, where Marlowe gazes directly into camera, introducing and commenting on the narrative, the entire story is told in flashback through subjective shots – we see only what the detective himself sees (including himself, seen only when he looks in a mirror). Alfred Hitchcock's *Rope*, contrastingly, is built on a prohibition of montage: the whole picture has the effect of a single unedited and uninterrupted take. Even when a cut is necessary for technical reasons (and in 1948 the longest possible camera-take was ten minutes), it is disguised so as to be undetectable.

Finally, Russell Rouse's *The Thief*, the story of a Communist agent who finally breaks down under moral pressure and gives himself up to the FBI, is built on a prohibition of the voice: it is a 'talking film', certainly, since we hear the usual background noises, but apart from a few distant murmurings we never hear a voice, a spoken word (the film avoids all situations in which dialogue would be necessary); the idea being to convey the spy's painful solitude and isolation from the community.

Each of these three films leaves us with an undeniable sense of dissatisfaction, an impression of failure; they produce a feeling of claustrophobic closure, as if we found ourselves imprisoned in a psychotic universe without symbolic openness. In *The Lady in the Lake*, we long continually for release from the 'glasshouse' of the detective's gaze, so that we can take a 'free' and objective view of the action. In *Rope* we wait desperately for a cut to deliver us from the nightmarish continuity. In *The Thief*, we look forward all the time to some voice to pull us out of the closed autistic universe in which the meaningless noises render all the more palpable the basic silence, the absence of a spoken word.

Each of these three prohibitions thus produces its own kind of psychosis; indeed, taking the three films as a point of reference, it would be possible to elaborate a classification of the three fundamental types of psychosis. By prohibiting the objective shot, *Lady in the Lake* produces an effect of paranoia. Since the point of view of the camera is never 'objective', the field of what is seen is continually menaced by the unseen, and the very proximity of objects to the field of view becomes threatening. All objects assume a potentially minatory character, and there is danger everywhere. (When a woman approaches the camera, for instance, we experience her presence as an aggressive intervention into the sphere of our intimacy.) Through a prohibition of montage, *Rope* enacts the psychotic *passage à l'acte*. The rope of the title is ultimately the rope that connects 'words' and 'deeds'. Like the hangman's rope, it signifies the moment when the symbolic falls into the Real. *The Thief*, by prohibiting the voice, renders a psychotic autism, a terminal isolation from the discursive network of intersubjectivity. We can now see, therefore, wherein lies the dimension of *rendu*: not in the psychotic contents of these movies, but in the way the content, so far from being simply 'depicted', is directly 'rendered' in the very form of the narrative. Here, surely, the 'message' of the film is immediately its form.

The ultimate reason for the 'failure' of these films is that the formal prohibitions they impose are both arbitrary and capricious. It is as if the director had decided to renounce one of the key constituents of the normal talking picture (objective shot, montage, voice) purely for the sake of formal experiment. Thus all three films involve the prohibition of something that could as easily not have been prohibited, not (as in the fundamental paradox that, according to Lacan, defines symbolic castration and the incest taboo, the prohibition of that *jouissance* which is axiomatically impossible) the prohibition of something *that is already in itself inaccessible*. Hence the sense of claustrophobia that they evoke; for the fundamental prohibition that constitutes the symbolic order – the incest prohibition, the 'cutting of the rope' through which we achieve symbolic distance from 'reality' – is absent, and the arbitrary prohibition that takes its place only embodies and bears witness to a second lack, the lack of a lack itself.

Love Thy Sinthome As Thyself

The lack of a lack – the lack, that is, of distance, of the empty space which 'triggers' the process of symbolization – is what, according to Lacan, characterizes psychoses. Thus *rendu* could be defined as the elementary cell or zero point of psychosis. Here we touch on the most radical dimension of the break that separates the later Lacan from the 'standard' version of his theory. The limit of the 'classical' Lacan is the limit of discourse. The field of psychoanalysis is conceived as the field of discourse, and the unconscious is defined as the 'discourse of the Other'. Towards the end of the 1960s, Lacan gave precise form to his theory of discourse by stipulating a matrix of four discourses – the discourses of the Master, the University, Hysteria, and the Analyst – which he saw as representing the four possible types of social bond, four articulations of the network regulating intersubjective relations. The first of these, and the point of departure for all the others, was the discourse of the Master, in which a certain signifier (S_1) represents the subject ($\$$) for another signifier, or more precisely for all other signifiers (S_2). The problem, of course, is that the tidy operation of signification never comes off without producing some annoying, messy, disturbing surplus, a piece of leftover or 'excrement', which Lacan designates as smell *a*. The other three discourses are nothing but three different attempts to 'come to terms' with this tiresome and disruptive residue, the famous *objet petit a*.

The discourse of the University takes the residue for its immediate object, its 'other', and attempts to transform it into a 'subject' by applying to it the network of 'knowledge' (S_2). This is the elementary logic of the pedagogic process: out of an untamed object, the 'unsocialized' child, we produce a subject by the implantation of knowledge. The repressed truth of this discourse is that behind the semblance of neutral knowledge, there is always a gesture of the Master.

The discourse of the Hysteric starts, so to speak, from the opposite side. Its basic constituent is the hysteric's question to the Master, 'Why am I what you say I am?' This question arises as a reaction to what Lacan, in the early 1950s, called the 'founding word', the act of conferring a symbolic mandate which, by naming me, defines and fixes my place in the symbolic network. The hysterical question thus articulates the experience of a fissure, an irreducible gap between the signifier which represents me and the non-symbolized surplus of my being-there. The hysteric embodies this ontological question: her/his basic problem is how to justify and account for her/his existence in the eyes of the Other.[13]

Finally, the discourse of the Analyst is the direct inverse of that of the Master. The analyst occupies the place of the surplus object and identifies directly with the residue of the discursive network. This is why the discourse of the Analyst is far more paradoxical than it might appear at first sight, for it attempts to knit together a discourse starting from the very element that escapes discursive articulation, its fall-out or excrement.

What must not be forgotten here is that Lacan's matrix of the four discourses is a matrix of the four possible positions in the intersubjective network of communication: we remain, here, within the field of communication as mean-ing, in spite or rather because of all the paradoxes implied by the Lacanian conceptualization of these terms. Communication is seen to be structured as a paradoxical circle in which the sender receives from the receiver his/her own message in its reverse (that is, true) form. In this formulation, the decentred Other decides *post facto* the true meaning of what I have said (in this sense, it is the S_2 which is the true master-signifier, conferring retroactive meaning on S_1). What circulates between subjects in symbolic communication is ultimately lack – the constitutive absence itself – for it is this absence which opens up the space in which positive meaning can constitute itself. All these are paradoxes intrinsic to the field of communication *qua* meaning; the very nonsense of the signifier, the signifier-without-signified, the condition of possibility of all other signifiers, is a non-sense strictly internal to the field of meaning, and delimits it *from within*.[14]

All the effort of Lacan's last years, however, is directed at breaking through the field of communication-as-meaning. Having established the definitive, logically purified structure of communication and the social bond through the matrix of the four discourses, he set out to delineate the outlines of a certain space in which signifiers find themselves in a state of 'free floating', logically prior to their discursive binding and articulation; the space of a particular 'prehistory' preceding the 'historicity' of the social bond, a psychotic kernel evading the discursive network. Thus the rather unexpected shift in *Seminar XX (Encore)* – a shift homologous to that from signifier to sign – from the Other to the One. Previously, all Lacan's efforts had been directed towards defining the otherness that precedes the formation of the One. First, in the theory of the signifier as differential, every One is defined by the bundle of its discursive relations to its Other. Every One is conceived in advance as 'one-among-others'. Then, in the very domain of the great Other itself, the symbolic order, Lacan sought to isolate and separate out its extemporal, impossible-real kernel. Thus the *objet petit a* is 'the other in the midst of the Other itself', a foreign body in its very heart. But suddenly, in *Seminar XX*, we stumble upon a One (in *'There is One', Y a de l'Un*) which is not one-among-others, which does not yet partake of the articulation proper to the order of the Other. This One is of course precisely the One of *jouis-sense*, of the signifier not yet enchained but still floating freely, permeated with enjoyment: the enjoyment that prevents it from being articulated into a chain.

To indicate the specificity of this One, Lacan coined the neologism *le sinthome*: the point which functions as the ultimate support of the subject's consistency, the point of 'thou art that', the point marking the dimensions of 'what is in the subject more than itself' and what it therefore 'loves more than itself', that point which is none the less neither symptom (the coded message in which the subject receives from the Other its own message in reverse form, the truth of its desire) nor fantasy (the imaginary scenario which, with its fascinating presence, screens off the lack in the Other, the radical inconsistency of the symbolic order).

Two examples from the work of the novelist Patricia Highsmith may serve to elucidate Lacan's concept of the *sinthome*. Highsmith's short stories often explore the motif of nature's pathological tics, its monstrous deformations that materialize the subject's deepest enjoyment by serving as its objective counter-part and support. In her story 'The Pond', a recently divorced woman with a small son moves into a country house with a deep pond in the garden, from which strange plants sprout. The pond exerts a strange fascination on the boy, and one morning his mother finds him drowned, entangled in the roots. Distraught, she calls the garden service, who spread weedkiller around the pond. But it is no use: the roots grow more vigorously than before. Eventually she tackles them herself, hacking and sawing with obsessive determination. As she struggles with them, the roots seem to respond: the more she attacks them, the more she becomes entangled. Finally she stops resisting and yields to their embrace, recognizing in their power of attraction the call of her dead child. Here we have an image of the *sinthome*: the pond as the 'open wound of nature', the nucleus of an enjoyment that simultaneously attracts and repels us.

An inverted variation on the same motif appears in another Highsmith story, 'The Mysterious Cemetery'. In a small Austrian town, doctors at the local hospital perform radioactive experiments upon their dying patients. In the graveyard behind the hospital where the patients are buried, bizarre protuber-ances appear, red spongy plant-like excrescences whose growth cannot be stopped. After a while, the local people get used to them; they even become a tourist attraction; and poems are written about the uncanny and irrepressible 'undergrowth of enjoyment'.

The ontological status of these excrescences of the Real springing up from the soil of common reality is entirely ambiguous; they both do and do not exist. This ambiguity overlaps perfectly with the two opposed meanings of the word 'existence' in Lacan. First, existence means symbolization, integration into the discursive order: only what is symbolized can be said to exist. This is the sense in which Lacan maintains that 'Woman does not exist', or that 'there is no sexual relationship'. Woman, or the sexual relationship, do not possess signifiers of their own; they resist symbolization, and cannot be inscribed into the signifying network. What is at stake here is what Lacan, alluding to Freud and to Heidegger, calls 'the primordial *Bejahung*', an affirmation prior to denial, an act which 'allows the thing to be', which releases the Real in the 'clarity of its being'. According to Lacan, the well-known 'sense of unreality' we experience in the presence of certain phenomena can be located precisely at this level: it indicates that the object in question has lost its place in the symbolic universe.

Against this, existence is also defined in the opposite sense, as 'ex-sistence', the impossible-real nucleus resisting symbolization. The first traces of such a notion of existence can already be found in *Seminar II*, in the notion that 'there is something so incredible about every existence that we must in fact incessantly question ourselves about its reality'. It is of course this ex-sistence of the Real, of the Thing embodying impossible enjoyment, that is excluded by the very advent of the symbolic order. We could say that we are always caught in a certain *vel*, an either/or; that we are forced to choose between meaning and ex-sistence, and that the price we pay for access to meaning is the exclusion of ex-sistence. In these terms, we might say that it is precisely woman that 'exists', that persists as a residue of enjoyment beyond meaning, resisting symbolization; which is why, as Lacan puts it, woman is 'the *sinthome* of man'.

This notion of the ex-sisting *sinthome* – the proliferating 'undergrowth' in Highsmith's stories – is thus more radical than either symptom or fantasy; for the *sinthome* is the psychotic kernel that can neither be interpreted (like a symptom) nor 'traversed' (like a fantasy). What, then, do we do with it? Lacan's answer, and at the same time the Lacanian definition of the ultimate moment of psychoanalysis, is *identification with the sinthome*. The *sinthome* represents the outermost limit of the psychoanalytic process – the reef on which psychoanalysis sticks. At the same time, is the experience of the radical impossibility of the *sinthome* final proof that the psychoanalytic process has been brought to a conclusion?[15] We reach the end of the psychoanalytic process when we isolate the kernel of enjoyment which is as it were immune to the operative mode of the discourse. This is the ultimate Lacanian reading of Freud's motto 'Wo es war, soll ich werden': in the real of your symptom you must acknowledge the ultimate ground of your being. There, where the symptom already was, is the place with which you must identify, recognizing in its 'pathological' singularity the element that guarantees your consistency.

We can now see how great a distance from the 'standard' version of his theory Lacan covered in the last decade of his teaching. In the 1960s he still conceived the symptom as 'a means, for the subject, of giving way on his desire', a compromise-formation bearing witness to the fact that the subject did not persist in his desire – which is why access to the truth of the desire was possible only through the interpretative dissolution of the symptom. In the later Lacan, by contrast, the analysis is over when we achieve a certain distance in relation to the fantasy and identify precisely with the pathological singularity on which hangs the consistency of our enjoyment.

It now also becomes clear how we may understand Lacan's proposition on the very last page of *Seminar XI*, that 'the desire of the analyst is not a pure desire'. All Lacan's previous determinations of the final moment of the analytic process, the 'passage' (*passe*) of analysand into analyst, implied a kind of purification of the desire, a breakthrough to 'desire in its pure state'. The analytical formula was, first, to get rid of symptoms as compromise-formations; then to traverse the fantasy – the frame which defines the co-ordinates of enjoyment. The 'desire of the analyst' was thus a desire purified of enjoyment, and the analysand's access to pure desire was always paid for by the loss of enjoyment.

In the last stage, however, the whole perspective is reversed: we are asked to identify precisely with the particular form of our enjoyment. How, then, does this identification with the symptom differ from what we usually understand by the term: a hysterical reversion into 'madness'?

In Ruth Rendell's brilliant short story 'Convolvulus Clock', Trixie, an elderly spinster, steals a fine old clock from an antique shop. But once she has it, the clock continually incites uneasiness and guilt. She reads allusions to her little crime in every passing remark of her acquaintances; and when a friend mentions that a similar clock has recently been stolen from the antique shop, the panic-stricken Trixie pushes her under an approaching tube train. When in the end she can stand the ticking of the clock no longer, she throws it into a stream; but the stream is shallow and it seems to Trixie that anyone looking down from the bridge will immediately see it. So she wades into the stream, retrieves the clock, and starts to break it up with stones and to scatter the pieces around. The more she scatters the pieces the more it seems that the whole stream is overflowing with clock; and when some time later a neighbouring farmer pulls her, wet, bruised and shaking, from the water, Trixie is waving her arms like the hands of a clock and repeating 'Tick-tock. Tick-tock. Tick-tock. Convolvulus clock.'

This kind of identification can be distinguished from that marking the final moment of the psychoanalytic procedure via a distinction between acting out and what Lacan calls the 'passage à l'acte'. Broadly speaking, acting out is still a symbolic act, an act addressed to the great Other. The 'passage to the act', by contrast, suspends the dimension of the Other: the act is here transposed into the domain of the Real. In other words, acting out is an attempt to break through a symbolic deadlock (an impossibility of symbolization or putting into words) by means of an act, which none the less still functions as the bearer of a ciphered message. By her final identification with the clock, the unfortunate Trixie tries to attest her innocence to the Other, and thus to shed the intolerable burden of her guilt; her 'acting out' embodies a certain reproach to the Other.

The 'passage to the act', in contrast, entails an exist from the symbolic network, a dissolution of the social bond. We could say that by acting out we identify ourselves with the symptom as Lacan conceived it in the 1950s, as a ciphered message delivered to the Other; whereas by the *passage à l'acte* we identify with the *sinthome*, the pathological 'tic' structuring the real kernel of our enjoyment. In Sergio Leone's *Once Upon a Time in the West*, the protagonist, the 'harmonica man', preserves a minimum of coherence in the face of a childhood trauma (his involuntary part as an accomplice to his brother's murder) through a form of personal 'nuttiness'. His specific 'madness' takes the form of identification with his symptom-harmonica. 'He plays the mouthorgan when he should talk and he talks when he should play the mouthorgan,' as his friend Cheyenne puts it. In Lacanian terms, the man everyone knows as 'Harmonica' has undergone 'subjective destitution'; he has no name, no signifier to represent him (it is perhaps no accident that the last of Leone's westerns is called *My Name Is Nobody*); he can retain his coherence only through identification with his symptom.

With such 'subjective destitution', the very relation to truth undergoes a radical change. In hysteria and its 'dialect', obsessional neurosis, we always partake in the dialectical movement of truth, which is why the acting out at the climax of the hysterical crisis remains throughout determined by the co-ordinates of truth; whereas the *passage à l'acte* so to speak suspends the dimension of truth.[16] In so far as truth has the structure of a (symbolic) fiction, truth and the Real of *jouissance* are incompatible. The spectacle of *Brazil* or *Lili Marlene* does not therefore expose some kind of repressed truth in totalitarianism. It does not confront totalitarian logic with its own inner truth. It simply dissolves it as an effective social bond by isolating the outrageous kernel of its mindless enjoyment.

NOTES

1   References in this article to Lacan's work are based on Jacques Lacan, *Le Séminaire: livre XI* (Paris, Éditions du Seuil, 1973); *livre XX* (Paris, Éditions du Seuil, 1975); *livre II* (Paris, Éditions du Seuil, 1978).

2   Pascal Bonitzer, *Le Champ aveugle* (Paris, Gallimard, 1982).

3   Michel Chion, *La Voix au Cinéma* (Paris, Éditions de L'Étoile, 1982).

4   Raymond Bellour, *L'Analyse du film* (Paris, Éditions Albatros, 1979).

5   Since this gaze is on the side of the object, it cannot be subjectified. As soon as we try to add a subjective shot from the house itself (the camera peeping out tremulously from behind the curtains of the approaching Lilah, perhaps), we descend to the level of the ordinary thriller, since such a shot would represent not the gaze as object but only the point of view of another subject.

6   Chion, *La voix*.

7   Ernesto Laclau and Chantal Mouffe, *Hegemony and Socialist Strategy* (London, Verso, 1985).

8   The ironic and perverse achievement of *Empire of the Sun* consists in offering us, who live in an epoch of postmodern nostalgia, a nostalgic object in the shape of the concentration camp, that intolerable and inescapable instance of the impossible-real of our history. Think how the film depicts everyday life in the camp: children clattering happily down the slope in their handcarts, elderly gentlemen improvising a round of golf, women gossiping cheerfully as they iron the weekly wash, while all the time Jim himself runs errands between them, delivering the linen, bartering vegetables for a pair of shoes, resourceful as a fish in its element; and all to the accompaniment of music which evokes in the traditional Hollywood idiom a vivacious idyll of everyday small-town life. Such is the film's depiction of the concentration camp, the traumatic Real of the twentieth century, that which 'returns as the same' in all social systems. Invented at the turn of the century by the British in the Boer War, it was used not only by the two major totalitarian powers, Nazi Germany and Stalin's USSR, but also by such a pillar of democracy as the United States (for the isolation of the Japanese during the Second World War). Thus every attempt to represent the concentration camp as 'relative', to reduce it to one of its forms, to conceive it as a result of some specific set of social conditions (to prefer the term 'Gulag' or 'holocaust', for example) already betrays an evasion of the unbearable weight of the Real.

9   We encounter the same mechanism in horoscopes and fortune-telling. There too a totally contingent coincidence of a prediction with some detail of our real life is sufficient for an effect of transference to take place. One trivial 'bit of the real' is sufficient to trigger the endless work of interpretation through which we struggle to connect the symbolic – here, the symbolic network of prediction – with the events of the day. Suddenly, everything has meaning; and if the meaning is not clear, that is only because it is still hidden, waiting to be deciphered. The Real does not function here as something which resists symbolization, as a meaningless residue which

cannot be integrated into the symbolic structure, but, on the contrary, as its last support.

10 Michel Chion, 'Révolution douce', in *La Toile Trouée* (Paris, Éditions de L'Étoile, 1988), pp. 25–31.

11 The fact that the Real thus rendered is what Freud called 'psychic reality' is demonstrated by the mysterious beauty of scenes in David Lynch's *Elephant Man* which present the Elephant Man's subjective experience 'from the inside'. The matrix of external sounds, the noise of 'the real world', is suspended or moved to the background; all we hear is a rhythmic beat of uncertain origin and status, something between a heartbeat and the regular ictus of a machine. Here we have *rendu* at its purest, a pulse which does not imitate or symbolize anything but which seizes us directly, 'renders' the thing without mediation. In painting, it is abstract expressionist 'action painting' that most closely corresponds to 'rendu'. The spectator is supposed to view the painting from close up, so as to lose objective distance and be drawn directly into it; and the painting itself neither imitates reality nor represents it through symbolic codes, but rather 'renders' the real by 'seizing' the spectator.

12 The clearest case of *rendu* in Hitchcock's work is the famous backwards tracking shot in *Frenzy*, where the camera movement (serpentine, then straight backwards, reproducing the shape of a necktie) tells us what is happening behind the doors of the apartment from which the movement started. In his study of Hitchcock, François Regnault even ventured the hypothesis that such a relation between form and content offers a clue to the entire Hitchcock *oeuvre*, where the content is always rendered by a particular formal feature (the spirals in *Vertigo*, intersecting lines in *Psycho*, etc.): François Regnault, 'Système formel d'Hitchcock', in *Cahiers du Cinéma*, hors-série 8:[b] *Alfred Hitchcock* (1980), pp. 21–30.

13 In contrast to perversion, which is defined precisely by the lack of a question: the pervert possesses an immediate certainty that his activity serves the enjoyment of the other. Hysteria and its 'dialect' obsessional neurosis differ in terms of the way the subject attempts to justify her/his existence: the hysteric by offering her/himself to the Other as the object of its love, the obsessive by striving to comply with the demand of the Other through frenetic activity. Thus the hysteric's answer is love, the obsessive's work.

14 'Communication *qua* meaning' because the two ultimately overlap; not only because the circulating 'object' is always meaning (albeit in the negative form of nonsense), but because meaning itself is always intersubjective, constituted through the circle of communication: it is the other, the addressee, who retro-actively determines the meaning of what I have said.

15 This is the proper emphasis on Lacan's thesis of the 'Joyce-symptom'. As Jacques-Alain Miller points out, 'The mention of psychosis apropos of Joyce in no way meant a kind of applied psychoanalysis: at stake was, on the contrary, the effort to call into question the very discourse of the analyst *by means of* the Joyce symptom, in so far as the subject, identified with his symptom, is closed to its artifice. And perhaps there is no better end of an analysis': Jacques-Alain Miller, 'Preface', in

Jacques Aubert (ed.), Navanin, *Joyce avec Lacan* (Paris, Navarin, 1988), pp. 9–12, at p. 12.

16   The original hysterical position is characterized by the paradox of 'telling the truth in the form of a lie'. In terms of literal 'truth' (the correspondence of words and things), the hysteric undoubtedly 'lies'; but it is through this lie that the truth of his or her desire erupts and articulates itself. To the extent that obsessional neurosis is a 'dialect of hysteria' (Freud), it implies a kind of inversion of this relation: the obsessive 'lies in the form of a truth'. The obsessive always 'sticks to the facts', striving to efface the traces of his subjective position. He is 'hysterized' – that is, his desire erupts – only when, finally, by some inadvertent slip, he 'succeeds in lying'.

2

The Obscene Object of Postmodernity

This is a chapter from *Looking Awry: An Introduction to Jacques Lacan through Popular Culture* (1991, pp. 141–53), the most accessible of Žižek's surveys of culture. The book analyses a diversity of material from film, opera, drama and fiction, engaging Lacan's thought in the process and intervening in politics, philosophy and aesthetics.

The argument is framed by a distinction Žižek wishes to make between modernism and postmodernism. He detects a false opposition between Habermas's definition of modernism – the claim that reason rather than reliance on traditional authority is the basis of a healthy society – and his definition of postmodernism – as an exposure of the ideology of this claim through revealing the hidden power agenda of 'reason'. In Žižek's analysis, this latter, postmodernist claim is still modernist, since modernism is itself characterized by 'a logic of unmasking', exemplified by the Big Three of a century ago: Marx, Nietzsche and Freud. It was the achievement of another Big Three – Adorno, Horkheimer and Marcuse, the first generation of the Frankfurt school – to have already suspected reason in this way. For Žižek, this places Habermas in the embarrassing position of finding himself suddenly in the postmodernist camp, since Habermas locates the source of freedom in the rejection of a modernist utopia and in the division between different life-worlds – precisely what modernism saw as alienating. By the same token, Habermas takes deconstruction to be a postmodern phenomenon, in that for him it constitutes an attack on reason. But in Žižek's reading, deconstruction is in fact modernist, as it is an unmasking procedure *par excellence*, with meaning produced solely by the movement of signifiers. In this reliance upon language, the deconstructionists are still 'structuralists': it is the 'poststructuralist' Lacan who marks the postmodernist break by focusing upon that which lies outside the signifier and which is detectable only retrospectively, after language has failed in its reference.

Žižek illustrates the contrast between modernism and postmodernism by noting a difference in structure between a scene in the modernist film *Blow Up* and a 'postmodernist' scene in Hitchcock's *Lifeboat*. The theme of *Blow Up* is the disappearance of a body photographed by chance, the film's action centring upon the search for what is to fill this absence. A final sequence shows the photographer watching a 'tennis-match' in which the non-existent 'ball' rolls to his feet; whereupon he throws 'it' back, joining in a game which 'works without an object'. In this fantasy, 'nothing' is taken to be 'something' – a fantasy concealing a gap.

In the postmodernist scene, however, the reverse happens: there is 'something' where there was 'nothing'. In Hitchcock's film, a German U-boat sailor, while being picked up in a lifeboat, reveals himself as a cause of horror by showing in his face his response to the response of the British sailors. The object of fear itself thus becomes the focus for the camera: postmodernism shows the 'obscene object', whereas modernism conceals it.

The 'obscene object of postmodernity' is the Lacanian 'Thing', the incestuous maternal object, brought into horrible proximity. This same menacing proximity of the Thing appears in Kafka's *The Trial*. Žižek picks out two modernist misreadings of the emptiness at the core of Kafka's bureaucracy: (1) as the mark of an 'absent god', (2) as the projection of an inner void into an 'apparition' outside. Both these readings make the same error in believing that there is an absence where there is a disgusting presence that is too present, too near. In *The Trial* the closeness of this presence irrupts in the court in the occurrence of a lewd coupling of a man and a woman at the back of the room, the Law allowing transgression while seeming to forbid it: Kafka is introducing the punitive superego that is driven by an obscene and anarchic *jouissance*, the inconsistency of which bewilders K., the victim unable to escape the Law. Here there is a lack of consistency between the (symbolic) Law and the (real) act of copulation, a 'trespassing of the frontier that separates the vital domain from the judicial domain', investing the Law with a boundless enjoyment. Instead of the Law possessing an empty place as the ideal of justice (as in the parable 'Before the Law'), it is engulfed by uncontrolled drives: the Freudian superego has closer links with the id than the ego does. Paradoxically, at the same time the superego presents itself as all-knowing, as if its prohibitions were consistent throughout, thereby producing a subject haunted by an infinite guilt, ever unable to match its acts to an endless chain of demands. So Kafka's text proclaims that the Law is 'necessary' but not 'true': as K. discovers and pays for with his life, if you cannot invest the Law as necessary, you get flooded with *jouissance*. Kafka's 'postmodern' text articulates the threat that the superego poses to the Law through colonizing it with enjoyment. But since the act of speaking presumes the existence of the big Other as the warrant for signification, a necessary supposition of – rather than a fanatical belief in – the Other's consistency is basic to language; only the psychotic, who cannot handle supposition, is persecuted by the symbolic network.

The Postmodernist Break

Modernism versus Postmodernism

When the topic of 'postmodernism' is discussed in 'deconstructivist' circles, it is obligatory – a sign of good manners, so to speak – to begin with a negative reference to Habermas, with a kind of distancing from him. In complying with this custom, we would like to add a new twist: to propose that Habermas is himself postmodernist, although in a peculiar way, without knowing it. To sustain this thesis, we will question the very way Habermas constructs the opposition between modernism (defined by its claim to a universality of reason, its refusal of the authority of tradition, its acceptance of rational argument as the only way to defend conviction, its ideal of a communal life guided by mutual understanding and recognition and by the absence of constraint) and postmodernism (defined as the 'deconstruction' of this claim to universality, from Nietzsche to 'poststructuralism'; the endeavour to prove that this claim to universality is necessarily, constitutively 'false', that it masks a particular network of power relations; that universal reason is as such, in its very form, 'repressive' and 'totalitarian'; that its truth-claim is nothing but an effect of a series of rhetorical figures.[1] This opposition is simply false: for what Habermas describes as 'postmodernism' is the immanent obverse of the modernist project itself; what he describes as the tension between modernism and postmodernism is the immanent tension that has defined modernism from its very beginning. Was not the aestheticist, anti-universalist ethics of the individual's shaping his life as a work of art always part of the modernist project? Is the genealogic unmasking of universal categories and values, the calling into question of the universality of reason not a modernist procedure *par excellence*? Is not the very essence of theoretical modernism, the revelation of the 'effective contents' behind the 'false consciousness' (of ideology, of morality, of the ego), exemplified by the great triad of Marx–Nietzsche–Freud? Is not the ironic, self-destructive gesture by means of which reason recognizes in itself the force of repression and domination against which it fights – the gesture at work from Nietzsche to Adorno and Horkheimer's *Dialectic of Enlightenment* – is not this gesture the supreme act of modernism? As soon as fissures appear in the unquestionable authority of tradition, the tension between universal reason and the particular contents escaping its grasp is inevitable and irreducible.

The line of demarcation between modernism and postmodernism must, then, lie elsewhere. Ironically, it is Habermas himself who, on account of certain crucial features of his theory, belongs to postmodernism: the break between the first and the second generation of the Frankfurt school – that is, between Adorno, Horkheimer and Marcuse on the one side and Habermas on the other – corresponds precisely to the break between modernism and post-modernism. In Adorno and Horkheimer's *Dialectic of Enlightenment*,[2] in Marcuse's *One-Dimensional Man*,[3] in their unmasking of the repressive potential of 'instrumental reason', aiming at a radical revolution in the historical totality of the contemporary world and at the utopian abolition of the difference between 'alienated' life spheres, between art and 'reality', the modernist project reaches its zenith of self-critical fulfilment. Habermas is, on the other hand, postmodern precisely because he recognizes a positive condition of freedom and emancipation in what appeared to modernism as the very form of alienation: the autonomy of the aesthetic sphere, the functional division of different social domains, etc. This renunciation of the modernist utopia, this acceptance of the fact that freedom is possible only on the basis of a certain fundamental 'alienation', attests to the fact that we are in a postmodernist universe.

This confusion concerning the break between modernism and postmodern-ism comes to a critical point in Habermas's diagnosis of poststructuralist deconstructionism as the dominant form of contemporary philosophical post-modernism. The use of the prefix 'post-' in both cases should not lead us astray (especially if we take into account the crucial, but usually overlooked, fact that the very term 'poststructuralism', although designating a strain of French theory, is an Anglo-Saxon and German invention. The term refers to the way the Anglo-Saxon world perceived and located the theories of Derrida, Foucault, Deleuze, etc. – in France itself, nobody uses the term 'poststructur-alism'). Deconstructionism is a modernist procedure *par excellence*; it presents perhaps the most radical version of the logic of 'unmasking', whereby the very unity of the experience of meaning is conceived as the effect of signifying mechanisms, an effect that can take place only in so far as it ignores the textual movement that produced it. It is only with Lacan that the 'postmodernist' break occurs, in so far as he thematizes a certain real, traumatic kernel whose status remains deeply ambiguous: the Real resists symbolization, but it is at the same time its own retroactive product. In this sense we could even say that deconstructionists are basically still 'structuralists' and that the only 'poststructuralist' is Lacan, who affirms enjoyment as 'the real Thing', the central impossibility around which every signifying network is structured.

Hitchcock as Postmodernist

In what, then, does the postmodernist break consist? Let's begin with Antonioni's *Blow Up*, perhaps the last great modernist film. As the hero develops photographs shot in a park, his attention is attracted to a stain that appears on the edge of one of the photographs. When he enlarges the detail, he discovers the contours of a body there. Though it is the middle of the night, he rushes to the park, and indeed finds the body. But on returning to the scene of the crime the next day, he finds that the body has disappeared without leaving a trace. The first thing to note here is that the body is, according to the code of the detective novel, the object of desire *par excellence*, the cause that starts the interpretative desire of the detective (and the reader): how did it happen? who did it? The key to the film is only given to us, however, in the final scene. The hero, resigned to the cul-de-sac in which his investigation has ended, takes a walk near a tennis court where a group of people – without a tennis ball – mime a game of tennis. In the frame of this supposed game, the imagined ball is hit out of bounds, and lands near the hero. He hesitates a moment, and then accepts the game: bending over, he makes a gesture of picking up the ball and throwing it back into the court. This scene has, of course, a metaphorical function in relation to the rest of the film. It indicates the hero's consenting to the fact that 'the game works without an object': even as the mimed tennis game can be played without a ball, so his own adventure proceeds without a body.

'Postmodernism' is the exact reverse of this process. It consists not in demonstrating that the game works without an object, that the play is set in motion by a central absence, but rather in displaying the object directly, allowing it to make visible its own indifferent and arbitrary character. The same object can function successively as a disgusting reject and as a sublime, charismatic apparition: the difference, strictly structural, does not pertain to the 'effective properties' of the object, but only to its place in the symbolic order.

One can grasp this difference between modernism and postmodernism by analysing the effect of horror in Hitchcock's films. At first, it seems that

Hitchcock simply respects the classical rule (already known by Aeschylus in *The Oresteia*) according to which one must place the terrifying object or event outside the scene and show only its reflections and its effects on the stage. If one does not see the object directly, one fills out its absence with fantasy projections (one sees it as more horrible than it actually is). The elementary procedure for evoking horror would be, then, to limit oneself to reflections of the terrifying object in its witnesses or victims.

As is well known, this is the crucial axis of the revolution in horror movies accomplished in the 1940s by the legendary producer Val Lewton (*Cat People, The Seventh Victim,* etc.). Instead of directly showing the terrifying monster (vampire, murderous beast), its presence is indicated only by means of off-screen sounds, by shadows, and so on, and thus rendered all the more horrible. The properly Hitchcockian approach, however, is to *reverse* this process. Let's take a small detail from *Lifeboat,* from the scene where the group of Allied castaways welcome on board their boat a German sailor from the destroyed submarine: their surprise when they find out that the person saved is an enemy. The traditional way of filming this scene would be to let us hear the screams for help, to show the hands of an unknown person gripping the side of the boat, and then *not* to show the German sailor, but to move the camera to the shipwrecked survivors: it would then be the perplexed expression on their faces that would indicate to us that they had pulled something unexpected out of the water. What? When the suspense was finally built up, the camera would finally reveal the German sailor. But Hitchcock's procedure is *the exact contrary* of this: what he does not show, precisely, is the shipwrecked survivors. He shows the German sailor climbing on board and saying, with a friendly smile, 'Danke schön!' Then he *does not* show the surprised faces of the survivors; the camera remains on the German. If his apparition provoked a terrifying effect, one can only detect it by *his* reaction to the survivors' reaction: his smile dies out, his look becomes perplexed. This demonstrates what Pascal Bonitzer[4] calls the Proustian side of Hitchcock, for this procedure corresponds perfectly to that of Proust in *Un Amour de Swann* when Odette confesses to Swann her lesbian adventures. Proust only describes Odette – that her story has a terrifying effect on Swann is evident only in the change in the tone of her story when she notices its disastrous effect. One shows an ordinary object or an activity, but suddenly, through the reactions of the milieu to this object, *reflecting themselves in the object itself,* one realizes that one is confronting the source of an inexplicable terror. The terror is intensified by the fact that this object is, in its appearance, completely ordinary: what one took only a moment ago for a totally common thing is revealed as Evil incarnate.

Such a postmodernist procedure seems to us much more subversive than the usual modernist one, because the latter, by not showing the Thing, leaves open the possibility of grasping the central emptiness under the perspective of an 'absent God'. The lesson of modernism is that the structure, the intersubjective machine, works as well if the Thing is lacking, if the machine revolves around an emptiness; the postmodernist reversal shows *the Thing itself as the incarnated, materialized emptiness.* This is accomplished by showing the terrifying object directly, and then by revealing its frightening effect to be simply the effect of its place in the structure. The terrifying object is an everyday object that has started to function, by chance, as that which fills in the hole in the Other (the symbolic order). The prototype of a modernist text would be Samuel Beckett's *Waiting for Godot.* The whole futile and senseless action of the play takes place while waiting for Godot's arrival when, finally, 'something might happen'; but one knows very well that 'Godot' can never arrive, because he is just a name for nothingness, for a central absence. What would the 'postmodernist' rewriting of this same story look like? One would have to put Godot himself on-stage: he would be someone exactly like us, someone who lives the same futile, boring life that we do, who enjoys the same stupid pleasures. The only difference would be that, not knowing it himself, he has found himself by chance at the place of the Thing; he would be the incarnation of the Thing whose arrival was awaited.

A lesser-known film by Fritz Lang, *Secret Beyond the Door,* stages in pure (one is almost tempted to say *distilled*) form this logic of an everyday object found in the place of *das Ding.* Celia Barrett, a young businesswoman, travels to Mexico after her older brother's death. She meets Mark Lamphere there, marries him, and moves in with him. A little later, the couple receives his intimate friends, and Mark shows them his gallery of historical rooms, reconstituted in the vault of his mansion. But he forbids their entrance into room number seven, which is locked. Fascinated by the taboo placed on it, Celia gets a key made and enters the room, which turns out to be an exact replica of her room. The most familiar things take on a dimension of the uncanny when one finds them in another place, a place that 'is not right'. And the thrill effect results precisely from the familiar, domestic character of what one finds in this Thing's forbidden place – here we have the perfect illustration of the fundamental ambiguity of the Freudian notion of *das Unheimliche.*

The opposition between modernism and postmodernism is thus far from being reducible to a simple diachrony; we are even tempted to say that postmodernism in a way *precedes* modernism. Like Kafka – who logically, not only temporally, precedes Joyce – the postmodernist *inconsistency* of the Other is retroactively perceived by the modernist gaze as its *incompleteness.* If Joyce is the modernist *par excellence,* the writer of the symptom ('the symptom Joyce', as Lacan puts it), of the interpretative delirium taken to the infinite, of the *time* (to interpret) where each stable moment reveals itself to be nothing but a 'condensation' of a plural signifying process, Kafka is in a certain way already postmodernist, the antipode of Joyce, the writer of fantasy, of the *space* of a nauseous inert presence. If Joyce's text provokes interpretation, Kafka's blocks it.

It is precisely this dimension of a non-dialecticizable, inert presence that is misrecognized by a modernist reading of Kafka, with its accent on the inaccessible, absent, transcendent agency (the Castle, the Court), holding the place of the lack, of the absence as such. From this modernist perspective, the secret of Kafka would be that in the heart of the bureaucratic machinery, there is only an emptiness, nothing: bureaucracy would be a mad machine that 'works by itself', as in *Blow Up* where the game is played without a body-object. One can read this conjunction in two opposed ways, which nevertheless share the same theoretical frame: theological and immanentist. One reading takes the elusive, inaccessible, transcendent character of the centre (of the Castle, of the Court) as a mark of an 'absent God' (the universe of Kafka as an anguished universe, abandoned by God); the other reading takes the emptiness of this transcendence as an 'illusion of perspective', as a reverse form of the apparition of the immanence of desire (the inaccessible transcendence, the central lack, is then only the negative form of the apparition of the surplus of desire, of its productive movement, over the world of objects *qua* representations).[5]

These two readings, although opposed, miss the same point: the way this absence, this empty place, is always already filled out by an inert, obscene, revolting *presence*. The Court in *The Trial* is not simply absent, it is indeed present under the figures of the obscene judges who, during night interrogations, glance through pornographic books; the Castle is indeed present under the figure of subservient, lascivious and corrupt civil servants. Which is why the formula of the 'absent God' in Kafka does not work at all: for Kafka's problem is, on the contrary, that in this universe God is *too present*, in the guise of various obscene, nauseous phenomena. Kafka's universe is a world in which God – who up to now had held himself at an assured distance – has got too close to us. Kafka's universe is a 'universe of anxiety', why not – on condition, however, that one takes into account the Lacanian definition of anxiety (what provokes anxiety is not the loss of the incestuous object but, on the contrary, its very *proximity*). We are too close to *das Ding*; that is the theological lesson of postmodernism: Kafka's mad, obscene God, this 'Supreme Being of Evil', is exactly the same as God *qua* Supreme Good – the difference lies only in the fact that we have got too close to him.

Bureaucracy and Enjoyment

Two doors of the Law

To specify further the status of the Kafkaesque obscene enjoyment, let's take as a starting point the famous apologue concerning the door of the Law in *The Trial*, the anecdote told to K. by the priest in order to explain to him his situation *vis-à-vis* the Law. The patent failure of all the major interpretations of this apologue seems only to confirm the priest's thesis that 'the comments often enough merely express the commentator's bewilderment'. There is, however, another way to penetrate the anecdote's mystery: instead of seeking its meaning directly, it would be preferable to treat it in the way Claude Lévi-Strauss treats a myth: by establishing its relations to a series of other myths and elaborating the rules of their transformation. Where can we find, then, in *The Trial*, another 'myth' that functions as a variation, as an inversion, of the apologue concerning the door of the Law?

We do not have far to look: at the beginning of the second chapter ('First Interrogation'), Josef K. finds himself in front of another door of the Law (the entrance to the interrogation chamber); here also, the door-keeper lets him know that this door is intended only for him. The washerwoman says to him, 'I must shut this door after you, nobody else must come in,' which is clearly a variation of the last words of the door-keeper to the man from the country in the priest's apologue: 'No one but you could gain admittance through this door, since this door was intended only for you. I am now going to shut it.' At the same time, the apologue concerning the door of the Law (let's call it, in the style of Lévi-Strauss, m^1) and the first interrogation (m^2) can be opposed through a whole series of distinctive features. In m^1 we are in front of the entrance to a magnificent Court of Justice, in m^2 we are in a block of workers' flats, full of filth and crawling obscenities; in m^1 the door-keeper is an employee of the court, in m^2 it is an ordinary woman washing children's clothes; in m^1 it's a man, in m^2 a woman; in m^1 the door-keeper prevents the man from the country from passing through the door and entering the Court, in m^2 the washerwoman pushes him into the interrogation chamber half against his will. In short, the frontier separating everyday life from the sacred place of the Law cannot be transgressed in m^1, but in m^2 it is easily transgressed.

The crucial feature of m^2 is already indicated by its location: the Court is located in the middle of the vital promiscuity of worker's lodgings. Reiner Stach is quite justified in recognizing in this detail a distinctive trait of Kafka's universe, 'the trespassing of the frontier that separates the vital domain from the judicial domain'.[6] The structure here, of course, is that of the Moebius strip: if we progress far enough in our descent to the social underground, we find ourselves suddenly on the other side, in the middle of the sublime and noble Law. The place of transition from one domain to the other is a door guarded by an ordinary washerwoman of a provocative sensuality. In m[1], the door-keeper doesn't know anything, whereas here the woman possesses a kind of advance knowledge. Ignoring the naïve cunning of K., the excuse that he is looking for a joiner called Lanz, she makes him understand that his arrival has been awaited for a long time, even though K. himself only chose to enter her room quite by chance, as a last desperate attempt after a long and useless ramble:

The first thing he saw in the little room was a great pendulum clock which already pointed to ten. 'Does a joiner called Lanz live here?' he asked. 'Please go through,' said a young woman with sparkling black eyes, who was washing children's clothes in a tub, and she pointed her damp hand to the open door of the next room.... 'I asked for a joiner, a man called Lanz.' 'I know,' said the woman, 'just go right in.' K. might not have obeyed if she had not come up to him, grasped the handle of the door, and said: 'I must shut this door after you, nobody else must come in.'[7]

The situation here is exactly the same as in the well-known incident from *The Arabian Nights*: one enters a place quite by chance, and learns that one's arrival has been long expected. The paradoxical foreknowledge of the washer-woman has nothing whatsoever to do with so-called feminine intuition — it is based on the simple fact that she is connected with the Law. Her position regarding the Law is far more crucial than that of a minor functionary; K. discovers this for himself soon afterward when his passionate argumentation before the tribunal is interrupted by an obscene intrusion.

Here K. was interrupted by a shriek from the end of the hall; he peered from beneath his hand to see what was happening, for the reek of the room and the dim light together made a whitish dazzle of fog. It was the washerwoman, whom K. had recognized as a potential cause of disturbance from the moment of her entrance. Whether she was at fault now or not, one could not tell. All K. could see was that a man had drawn her into a corner by the door and was clasping her in his arms. Yet it was not she who had uttered the shriek but the man; his mouth was wide open and he was gazing up at the ceiling.[8]

What is the relation, then, between this woman and the Court of the Law? In Kafka's work, the woman as a 'psychological type' is wholly consistent with the anti-feminist ideology of an Otto Weininger: the woman is a being with-out a proper self; she is incapable of assuming an ethical attitude (even when she appears to act on ethical grounds, she is calculating the enjoyment she will derive from her actions); she is a being without any access to the dimension of Truth (even when what she is saying is literally true, she lies as a consequence of her subjective position). It is insufficient to say of such a being that she feigns her affections to seduce a man, for the problem is that there is nothing behind this mask of simulation . . . nothing but a certain glutinous, filthy enjoyment that is her very substance. Confronted with such an image of woman, Kafka does not succumb to the usual critical-feminist temptation (of demonstrating that this figure is the ideological product of specific social conditions, of contrasting it with the outlines of another type of femininity). In a much more subversive gesture, Kafka wholly accepts this Weiningerian portrait of woman as a 'psychological type', while making it occupy an unheard-of, unprecedented place, the place of the Law. This is, perhaps, as has already been pointed out by Stach, the elementary operation of Kafka: this *short circuit between the feminine 'substance' ('psychological type') and the place of the Law.* Smeared by an obscene vitality, the Law itself – traditionally, a pure, neutral universality – assumes the features of a heterogeneous, inconsistent *bricolage* penetrated with enjoyment.

The Obscene Law

In Kafka's universe, the Court is – above all – lawless, in a formal sense: it is as if the chain of 'normal' connections between causes and effects were suspended, put in parenthesis. Every attempt to establish the Court's mode of functioning by logical reasoning is doomed in advance to fail. All the oppositions noted by K. (between the anger of the judges and the laughter of the public on the benches, between the merry right side and the severe left side of the public) prove false as soon as he tries to base his tactics on them; after an ordinary answer by K. the public bursts into laughter:

'Well, then,' said the Examining Magistrate, turning over the leaves and addressing K. with an air of authority, 'you are a house-painter?' 'No,' said K., 'I'm the junior manager of a large Bank.' This answer evoked such a hearty outburst of laughter from the Right party that K. had to laugh too. People doubled up with their hands on their knees and shook as if in spasms of coughing.[9]

The other, positive side of this inconsistency is, of course, enjoyment: it erupts openly when the argument of K. is disturbed by a public act of sexual intercourse. This act, difficult to perceive because of its over-exposure (K. has to 'peer beneath his hands to see what was happening'), marks the moment of the eruption of the traumatic Real, and the error of K. consists in

overlooking the *solidarity* between this obscene disturbance and the
Court. He thinks that everybody will be anxious to have order restored
and the offending couple ejected from the meeting. But when he tries to
rush across the room, the crowd obstructs him. Someone seizes him from
behind, by the collar – at this point, the game is over: puzzled and confused,
K. loses the thread of his argument; filled with important rage, he leaves the
room.

The fatal error of K. was to address the Court, the Other of the Law, as a
homogeneous entity, attainable by means of consistent argument, whereas the
Court can only return him an obscene smile, mixed with signs of perplexity. In
short, K. expects *action* from the Court (legal deeds, decisions), but what he gets
instead is an *act* (a public copulation). Kafka's sensitivity to this 'trespassing of
the frontier that separates the vital domain from the judicial domain' depends
upon his Judaism: the Jewish religion marks the moment of the most radical
separation of these domains. In all previous religions, we encounter a place, a
domain of sacred enjoyment (in the form of ritual orgies, for example), whereas
in Judaism the sacred domain is evacuated of all traces of vitality and the living
substance is subordinated to the dead letter of the Father's Law. Kafka trespasses
the divisions of his inherited religion, flooding the judicial domain, once again,
with enjoyment.

Which is why Kafka's universe is eminently that of the *superego*. The Other
as the Other of the symbolic Law is not only dead, it doesn't even know that
it is dead (like the terrible figure in Freud's dream): it couldn't know it, in so
far as it is totally insensible to the living substance of enjoyment. The super
ego presents, on the contrary, the paradox of a law that, according to Jacques-
Alain Miller,[10] 'proceeds from the time when the Other was not yet dead,
evidenced by the superego, a surviving remainder of that time'. The superego imperative 'Enjoy!', the inversion of the dead Law into the obscene
figure of the superego, implies a disquieting experience: suddenly we become
aware that what a minute ago appeared to us a dead letter is really alive,
breathing, pulsating. Let us recall a short scene from the film *Aliens*.
The group of heroes is advancing through a long tunnel the stone walls
of which are twisted like interlaced plaits of hair. All at once the plaits start
to move and to secrete a glutinous mucus; the petrified corpse comes alive
again.

We must, then, reverse the usual metaphor of 'alienation' whereby the dead,
formal letter, a kind of parasite or vampire, sucks out the living, present force.
Living subjects can no longer be considered prisoners of a dead cobweb. The
dead, formal character of the Law becomes now the *sine qua non* of our
freedom, and the real totalitarian danger arises only when the Law no longer
wants to stay dead.

The result of m^1 is, then, that there is no truth about Truth. Every warrant of the Law has the status of a semblance; the Law is *necessary* without being *true*. To quote the words of the priest in m^1, 'it is not necessary to accept everything as true; one must only accept it as necessary'. The meeting of K with the washerwoman adds to this the obverse, usually passed over in silence: in so far as the Law is not grounded in Truth, it is impregnated with enjoyment. Thus, m^1 and m^2 are complementary, representing the two modes of lack: the lack of incompleteness and the lack of inconsistency. In m^1, the Other of the Law appears as *incomplete*. In its very heart, there is a certain gap; we can never reach the last door of the Law. It is the reference to m^1 that supports the interpretation of Kafka as a 'writer of absence', that is, the negative theological reading of his universe as a crazy bureaucratic machine turning blindly around the central void of an absent God. In m^2, the Other of the Law appears on the contrary, as *inconsistent*: nothing is wanting in it, nothing is lacking, but for all that it still is not 'whole/all'; it remains an inconsistent *bricolage*, a collection following a kind of aleatory logic of enjoyment. This provides the image of Kafka as a 'writer of presence' – the presence of what? Of a blind machinery to which nothing is lacking in so far as it is the very surfeit of enjoyment.

If modern literature can be characterized as 'unreadable', then Kafka exemplifies this characteristic in a way that is different from James Joyce. *Finnegan's Wake* is, of course, an 'unreadable' book: we cannot read it the way we read an ordinary 'realist' novel. To follow the thread of the text we need a kind of 'reader's guide', a commentary that enables us to see our way through the inexhaustible network of ciphered allusions. Yet this 'illegibility' functions precisely as an invitation to an unending process of reading of interpretation (recall Joyce's joke that with *Finnegan's Wake*, he hopes to keep literary scientists occupied for at least the next four hundred years). Compared to this, *The Trial* is quite 'readable'. The main outlines of the story are clear enough Kafka's style is concise and of proverbial purity. But it is this very 'legibility' that, because of its over-exposed character, produces a radical opacity and blocks every essay of interpretation. It is as if Kafka's text were a coagulated, stigmatized, signifying chain repelling signification with an excess of sticky enjoyment.

The superego knows too much

The *bureaucracy* depicted in Kafka's novels – the immense machinery of totally useless, superfluous knowledge, running blindly and provoking an unbearable feeling of 'irrational' guilt – functions as a superegoic knowledge (S_2 in Lacan's mathemes). This fact runs counter to our spontaneous understanding.

Nothing seems more obvious than the connection between the superego and the Lacanian S_1, the master-signifier. Is the superego not the very model of an 'irrational' injunction founded solely in its own process of enunciation, demanding obedience without further justification? Lacanian theory, however, runs counter to this spontaneous intuition: the opposition between S_1 and S_2 that is, between the master-signifier and the chain of knowledge – overlaps the opposition of ego-ideal (the 'unitary trait', the point of symbolic identification) and the superego. The superego is on the side of S_2, it is a fragment of the chain of knowledge whose purest form of apparition is what we call the 'irrational feeling of guilt'. We feel guilty without knowing why, as a result of acts we are certain we did not commit. The Freudian solution to this paradox is, of course, that this feeling is well-founded: we feel guilty because of our repressed unconscious desires. Our conscious ego does not (want to) know anything about them, but the superego 'sees all and knows all', and thus holds the subject responsible for its unacknowledged desires: 'the superego knew more than the ego about the unconscious id'.[11]

We should, then, renounce the usual notion of the unconscious as a kind of 'reservoir' of wild, illicit drives: the unconscious is also (one is even tempted to say: above all) fragments of a traumatic, cruel, capricious, 'unintelligible' and 'irrational' law text, a set of prohibitions and injunctions. In other words, we must 'put forward the paradoxical proposition that the normal man is not only far more immoral than he believes but also far more moral than he knows'.[12] What is the precise meaning of this distinction between belief and knowledge, produced as if by a kind of slip and lost already in the note accompanying the quoted phrase from *The Ego and the Id*? In this note Freud rephrases his proposition by saying that it 'simply states that human nature has a far greater extent, both for good and for evil, than it thinks [*glaubt*: believes] it has, i.e., than ego is aware of through conscious perceptions'.[13] Lacan taught us to be extremely attentive to such distinctions that emerge momentarily and are forgotten immediately afterward, for it is through them that we can detect Freud's crucial insights, the whole dimension of which he himself failed to notice (let us recall only what Lacan has been able to derive from a similar 'slippery' distinction between ego-ideal and ideal ego). What, then, is the import of that ephemeral distinction between belief and knowledge? Ultimately, only one answer is possible: if man is more immoral than he (consciously) believes and more moral than he (consciously) knows – in other words, if his relation toward the id (the illicit drives) is that of (dis)belief, and his relation toward the super-ego (its traumatic prohibitions and injunctions) that of (non-)knowledge, i.e., of ignorance – must we not conclude that *the id in itself already consists of unconscious, repressed beliefs*, and that *the superego consists of an unconscious knowledge*, of a paradoxical knowledge unbeknown to the subject? As we have seen, Freud himself treats the superego as a kind of knowledge ('the superego *knew* more than the ego about the unconscious id'). But where can we grasp this knowledge in a palpable way, where does it acquire – so to speak – a material, external existence? In *paranoia*, in which this agency that 'sees all and knows all' is embodied in the real, in the person of the all-knowing persecutor, able to 'read our thoughts'. Concerning the id, we only have to remember the famous challenge made by Lacan to his audience that they show him one single person who did not unconsciously believe in his own immortality, in God. According to Lacan, the true formula of atheism is 'God is unconscious'. There is a certain fundamental belief – a belief in the Other's basic consistency – that belongs to language as such. By the mere act of speaking, we *suppose* the existence of the big Other as guarantor of our meaning. Even in the most ascetic analytical philosophy, this fundamental belief is maintained in the form of what Donald Davidson called 'the principle of charity', conceiving it as the condition for successful communication.[14] The only subject who can effectively renounce the 'charity principle' – that is, whose relation to the big Other of the symbolic order is characterized by a fundamental disbelief – is the *psychotic* – a paranoiac, for example, who sees in the symbolic network of meaning around him a plot staged by some evil persecutor.

Notes

1   Cf. Jürgen Habermas, *The Philosophical Discourse of Modernity* (Cambridge, Mass., MIT Press, 1987).

2   Theodor Adorno and Max Horkheimer, *Dialectic of Enlightenment* (London, Allen Lane, 1973).

3   Herbert Marcuse, *One-Dimensional Man* (Boston, Beacon Press, 1964).

4   Pascal Bonitzer, 'Longs feux', *L'Ane* 16 (1984).

5   Cf. Gilles Deleuze and Félix Guattari, *Kafka: Toward a Minor Literature* (Minneapolis, University of Minnesota Press, 1986).

6   Reiner Stach, *Kafkas erotischer Mythos* (Frankfurt, Fischer Verlag, 1987), p. 38.

7   Franz Kafka, *The Trial* (New York, Schocken, 1984), p. 37.

8   Ibid., p. 46.

9   Ibid., p. 50.

10 Jacques-Alain Miller, 'Duty and the Drives', *Newsletter of the Freudian Field* 6 (1/2) (1992), pp. 5–15, at p. 13.

11 Sigmund Freud, 'The Ego and the Id', in *The Standard Edition of the Complete Psychological Works*, (London: Hogarth Press and the Institute of Psycho-Analysis, 1953), vol. 19, p. 51. The nicest irony of the title of Freud's 'The Ego and the Id'

is that it leaves out the third crucial notion that contains the real theoretical innovation of this essay: its title should be 'The Superego in its Relations to the Ego and the Id'.

12   Ibid., p. 52.
13   Ibid.
14   Cf. Donald Davidson, 'Mental Events', in *Essays on Actions and Events* (New York, Oxford University Press, 1980).

3

The Spectre of Ideology

This is the introduction to a collection entitled *Mapping Ideology*, edited by Žižek (1994), pp. 1–33, which reassesses the concept of ideology through readings from philosophy, sociology and psychoanalysis. Here Žižek provides a survey of the century's theories of ideology, showing how there is a basic fault-line that shows through in oppositional structures of truth and falsity, which ideology itself serves to conceal.

Three aspects in the current approaches to ideology can be distinguished: (1) the beliefs, arguments, basic assumptions and modes of rhetoric that constitute its conceptual apparatus; (2) the institutions, ritual practices and social organizations that maintain its dominance; (3) the ideology emerging at the core of the social in response to its current formations, such as liberal subjects experiencing themselves as individuals with uncontrolled 'free choice'. First, Žižek questions whether 'true' communication can be distinguished from 'false', as if discourse did not depend on an ideological structure to function at all. Second, it is not correct to regard the 'Ideological State Apparatus' as determining beliefs of subjects, since the Fascist experience shows that the so-called manipulators were indifferent as to whether they were believed or not, as long as the rituals produced a sufficient semblance of solidarity. Third, it is no simple matter to separate supposedly extra-ideological elements from 'spontaneous' ideological ones when the ideological is hidden in self-evident 'facts', such as laws, economic structures and sexual relations.

Whatever the opposition, there is an assumption on which it depends that is never questioned; for example, where an opposition between an early and a late form of capitalism is assumed in order to dismiss Marx's radical insights. This goes with the conviction that such a judgement is made from an unassailable position – the false notion of a 'privileged place'. In every case the very denial that we are free from ideology is the proof of our subjugation, since its successful operation depends precisely upon its own concealment. Where this concealment fails, the official values (of 'the people' under Stalinism, of 'the individual' under capitalism) are cynically observed. These splits are the consequence of the basic opposition between ideology as lived and ideology as imposed. There is no ideology that does not come into being without asserting itself in the guise of one 'truth' against another, as witness the case of the new East European democracies in their belief that they have now reached a 'natural state of things', the 'truth'.

Although at first sight it would appear that Marx made a similar error in opposing ideology to 'actual life', his notion of commodity fetishism – the worship of hidden values in the form of material goods – suggests that, standing in place of a missing real value, there is a ghostly counterpart, a fetish, which functions as a supplement to the official religion. Žižek here returns to his Lacanian conceptual key. Just as commodity fetishism operates as a 'spectral apparition' between the system of production and its spiritualized superstructure, so ideology is a spectre covering the gap between the 'pre-ideological kernel', the locus of failed symbolization (the Real), and mundane reality (the Symbolic). The earlier explanations of ideology which polarized reality and illusion failed to take this triangular structure (spectre, Real, Symbolic) into account.

In order for 'reality' to be taken as 'always-already symbolized', the spectre of ideology rises up to conceal the failed symbolization, the 'pre-ideological kernel', that which is primordially repressed and on which 'reality' is founded. What has not been found a place in the Symbolic produces a fundamental antagonism that interferes with the endeavours of social reality to establish itself as unified. The 'class struggle' that early Marxism saw as the engine of social change in history has to be regarded, not as part of this social reality, but as an effect that hides the antagonism as its cause: it is not simply a case of one class in opposition to another, a dynamic working between classes as given, but of an antagonism that pre-exists any actual clash, and is still there in a time of apparent 'peace'. The result, however, is not that society rends itself apart, but rather that the very antagonism prevents its fixation into a 'rational totalization'. The pseudo-antagonism of class struggle as an effect of the fundamental antagonism provokes new symbolizations, and thus, paradoxically, the 'real' antagonism works to preserve the social bond in an endless attempt to abolish it.

Under Stalinism the spectral utopian promise was treated as if it could actually be realized, which had the effect of preventing any new symbolizations. This misses the Lacanian moment in which detachment from the spectre allows freedom to emerge, a frightening possibility, since it marks a time for change, for redefinition of the Symbolic within the Real. The moment is missed if we 'ontologize' the spectre by taking refuge either in divine intervention or in a quasi-divine occult spirit-world. It is psycho-analysis that has grasped where this freedom comes from: it recognizes the Real of antagonism, whereas Marxism used the notion of ideology to disguise it. Something unfathomable, 'more real than reality itself', reveals ideology to be more than 'mere ideology', as opaque to analysis as the kernel of a dream.

Critique of Ideology, Today?

By way of a simple reflection on how the horizon of historical imagination is subjected to change, we find ourselves *in medias res*, compelled to accept the unrelenting pertinence of the notion of ideology. Up to a decade or two ago, the system production-nature (man's productive-exploitative relationship with nature and its resources) was perceived as a constant, whereas everybody was busy imagining different forms of the social organization of production and commerce (Fascism or Communism as alternatives to liberal capitalism); today, as Fredric Jameson perspicaciously remarked, nobody seriously considers possible alternatives to capitalism any longer, whereas popular imagination is persecuted by the visions of the forthcoming 'breakdown of nature', of the stoppage of all life on Earth – it seems easier to imagine the 'end of the world' than a far more modest change in the mode of production, as if liberal capitalism is the 'real' that will somehow survive even under conditions of a global ecological catastrophe.... One can thus categorically assert the existence of ideology *qua* generative matrix that regulates the relationship between visible and non-visible, between imaginable and non-imaginable, as well as the changes in this relationship.

This matrix can be easily discerned in the dialectics of 'old' and 'new', when an event that announces a wholly new dimension or epoch is (mis)perceived as the continuation of, or return to, the past, or – the opposite case – when an event that is entirely inscribed in the logic of the existing order is (mis)perceived as a radical rupture. The supreme example of the latter, of course, is provided by those critics of Marxism who (mis)perceive our late-capitalist society as a new social formation no longer dominated by the dynamics of capitalism as it was described by Marx. In order to avoid this worn-out example, however, let us turn to the domain of sexuality. One of today's commonplaces is that so-called virtual, or cyber, sex presents a radical break with the past, since in it, actual sexual contact with a 'real other' is losing ground against masturbatory enjoyment, whose sole support is a virtual other – phone sex, pornography, up to computerized 'virtual sex'.... The Lacanian answer to this is that first we have to expose the myth of 'real sex', allegedly possible 'before' the arrival of virtual sex: Lacan's thesis that 'there is no sexual relationship' means precisely that the structure of the 'real' sexual act (of the act with a flesh-and-blood partner) is already inherently phantasmic – the 'real' body of the other serves only as a support for our phantasmic projections. In other words, 'virtual sex', in which a glove simulates the stimuli of what we see on the screen, and so on, is not a monstrous distortion of real sex; it simply renders manifest its underlying phantasmic structure.

An exemplary case of the opposite misperception is provided by the reaction of Western liberal intellectuals to the emergence of new states in the process of the disintegration of real Socialism in Eastern Europe: they (mis)perceived this emergence as a return to the nineteenth-century tradition of the nation-state, whereas what we are actually dealing with is the exact opposite: the 'withering-away' of the traditional nation-state based upon the notion of the abstract citizen identified with the constitutional legal order. In order to characterize this new state of things, Étienne Balibar recently referred to the old Marxian phrase *Es gibt keinen Staat in Europa* – there no longer exists a proper state in Europe'. The old spectre of Leviathan parasitizing on the *Lebenswelt* of society, totalizing it from above, is more and more eroded from both sides. On the one hand, there are the new emerging ethnic communities – although some of them are formally constituted as sovereign states, they are no longer states in the proper modern-age European sense, since they did not cut the umbilical cord between state and ethnic community. (Paradigmatic here is the case of Russia, in which local mafias already function as a kind of parallel power structure.) On the other hand, there are the multiple transnational links, from multinational capital to mafia cartels and inter-state political communities (European Union).

There are two reasons for this limitation of state sovereignty, each of which is in itself compelling enough to justify it: the transnational character of ecological crisis and of nuclear threat. This eroding of state authority from both sides is mirrored in the fact that today the basic political antagonism is that between the universalist 'cosmopolitical' liberal democracy (standing for the force corroding the state from above) and the new 'organic' populism-communitarianism (standing for the force corroding the state from below). And – as Balibar pointed out yet again – this antagonism is to be conceived neither as an external opposition nor as the complementary relationship of the two poles in which one pole balances the excess of its opposite (in the sense that, when we have too much universalism, a little bit of ethnic roots gives people the feeling of belonging, and thus stabilizes the situation), but in a genuinely Hegelian sense – each pole of the antagonism is inherent in its opposite, so that we stumble upon it at the very moment when we endeavour to grasp the opposite pole for itself, to posit it 'as such'.

Because of this inherent character of the two poles, one should avoid the liberal-democratic trap of concentrating exclusively on the horrifying facts and even more horrifying potentials of what is going on today in Russia and some other ex-Communist countries: the new hegemonic ideology of 'Eurasism' preaching the organic link between community and the state as an antidote to the corrosive influence of the 'Jewish' principle of market and social atomism, orthodox national imperialism as an antidote to Western individualism, and so on. In order to combat these new forms of organicist populism effectively, one must, as it were, turn the critical gaze back upon oneself and submit to critical scrutiny liberal-democratic universalism itself – what opens up the space for the organicist populism is the weak point, the 'falsity', of this very universalism.

These same examples of the actuality of the notion of ideology, however, also render clear the reasons why today one hastens to renounce the notion of ideology: does not the critique of ideology involve a privileged place, some-how exempted from the turmoils of social life, which enables some subject-agent to perceive the very hidden mechanism that regulates social visibility and non-visibility? Is not the claim that we can accede to this place the most obvious case of ideology? Consequently, with reference to today's state of epistemological reflection, is not the notion of ideology self-defeating? So why should we cling to a notion with such obviously outdated epistemological implications (the relationship of 'representation' between thought and reality, etc.)? Is not its utterly ambiguous and elusive character in itself a sufficient reason to abandon it? 'Ideology' can designate anything from a contemplative attitude that misrecognizes its dependence on social reality to an action-orientated set of beliefs, from the indispensable medium in which individuals live out their relations to a social structure to false ideas which legitimate a dominant political power. It seems to pop up precisely when we attempt to avoid it, while it fails to appear where one would clearly expect it to dwell.

When some procedure is denounced as 'ideological *par excellence*', one can be sure that its inversion is no less ideological. For example, among the procedures generally acknowledged as 'ideological' is definitely the eternalization of some historically limited condition, the act of discerning some higher Necessity in a contingent occurrence (from the grounding of male domination in the 'nature of things' to interpreting AIDS as a punishment for the sinful life of modern man; or, at a more intimate level, when we encounter our 'true love', it seems as if this is what we have been waiting for all our life, as if, in some mysterious way, all our previous life has led to this encounter . . .): the senseless contingency of the Real is thus 'internalized', symbolized, provided with meaning. Is not ideology, however, also the opposite procedure of failing to notice the necessity, of misperceiving it as an insignificant contingency (from the psychoanalytic cure, in which one of the main forms of the analysand's resistance is his insistence that his symptomatic slip of tongue was a mere lapse without any signification, up to the domain of economics, in which the ideological procedure *par excellence* is to reduce the crisis to an external, ultimately contingent occurrence, thus failing to take note of the inherent logic of the system that begets the crisis)? In this precise sense, ideology is the exact opposite of internalization of the external contingency: it resides in externalization of the result of an inner necessity, and the task of the critique of ideology here is precisely to discern the hidden necessity in what appears as a mere contingency.

The most recent case of a similar inversion was provided by the way Western media reported on the Bosnian war. The first thing that strikes the eye is the contrast to the reporting on the 1991 Gulf War, where we had the standard ideological personification:

Instead of providing information on social, political or religious trends and antagonisms in Iraq, the media ultimately reduced the conflict to a quarrel with Saddam Hussein, Evil Personified, the outlaw who excluded himself from the civilized international community. Even more than the destruction of Iraq's military forces, the true aim was presented as psychological, as the humiliation of Saddam who was to 'lose face'. In the case of the Bosnian war, however, notwithstanding isolated cases of the demonization of the Serbian president Milosevič, the predominant attitude reflects that of a quasi-anthropological observer. The media outdo one another in giving us lessons on the ethnic and religious background of the conflict; traumas hundreds of years old are being replayed and acted out, so that, in order to understand the roots of the conflict, one has to know not only the history of Yugoslavia, but the entire history of the Balkans from medieval times.... In the Bosnian conflict, it is therefore not possible simply to take sides, one can only patiently try to grasp the background of this savage spectacle, alien to our civilized system of values.... Yet this opposite procedure involves an ideological mystification even more cunning than the demonization of Saddam Hussein.[2]

In what, precisely, consists this ideological mystification? To put it somewhat crudely, the evocation of the 'complexity of circumstances' serves to deliver us from the responsibility to act. The comfortable attitude of a distant observer, the evocation of the allegedly intricate context of religious and ethnic struggles in Balkan countries, is here to enable the West to shed its responsibility towards the Balkans – that is, to avoid the bitter truth that, far from presenting the case of an eccentric ethnic conflict, the Bosnian war is a direct result of the West's failure to grasp the political dynamic of the disintegration of Yugoslavia, of the West's silent support of 'ethnic cleansing'.

In the domain of theory, we encounter a homologous reversal apropos of the 'deconstructionist' problematization of the notion of the subject's guilt and personal responsibility. The notion of a subject morally and criminally fully 'responsible' for his acts clearly serves the ideological need to conceal the intricate, always-already operative texture of historico-discursive presuppositions that not only provide the context for the subject's act, but also define in advance the co-ordinates of its meaning: the system can function only if the cause of its malfunction can be located in the responsible subject's 'guilt'. One of the commonplaces of the leftist criticism of Law is that the attribution of personal responsibility and guilt relieves us of the task of probing into the concrete circumstances of the act in question. Suffice it to recall the moral-majority practice of attributing a moral qualification to the higher crime rate among African-Americans ('criminal dispositions', 'moral insensitivity', etc.): this attribution precludes any analysis of the concrete ideological, political and economic conditions of African-Americans.

Is not this logic of 'putting the blame on the circumstances', however, taken to its extremes, self-defeating in so far as it necessarily leads to the unforgettable – and no less ideological – cynicism of Brecht's famous lines from his *Three-penny Opera*: 'Wir wären gut anstatt so roh, doch die Verhältnisse, sie sind nicht so!' (We would be good instead of being so rude, if only the circumstances were not of this kind)? In other words, are we, the speaking subjects, not always-already *engaged* in recounting the circumstances that predetermine the space of our activity?

A more concrete example of the same undecidable ambiguity is provided by the standard 'progressive' criticism of psychoanalysis. The reproach here is that the psychoanalytic explanation of misery and psychic suffering through unconscious libidinal complexes, or even via a direct reference to the 'death drive', renders the true causes of destructiveness invisible. This critique of psychoanalysis found its ultimate theoretical expression in the rehabilitation of the idea that the ultimate cause of psychic trauma is real childhood sexual abuse: by introducing the notion of the phantasmic origin of trauma, Freud allegedly betrayed the truth of his own discovery.[3] Instead of the concrete analysis of external, actual social conditions – the patriarchal family, its role in the totality of the reproduction of the capitalist system, and so on – we are thus given the story of unresolved libidinal deadlocks; instead of the analysis of social conditions that lead to war, we are given the 'death drive'; instead of the change of social relations, a solution is sought in the inner psychic change, in the 'maturation' that should qualify us to accept social reality as it is. In this perspective, the very striving for social change is denounced as an expression of the unresolved Oedipus complex. . . . Is not this notion of a rebel who, by way of his 'irrational' resistance to social authority, acts out his unresolved psychic tensions ideology at its purest? However, as Jacqueline Rose demon-strated,[4] such an externalization of the cause into 'social conditions' is no less false, in so far as it enables the subject to avoid confronting the Real of his or her desire. By means of this externalization of the cause, the subject is no longer *engaged* in what is happening to him; he entertains towards the trauma a simple external relationship: far from stirring up the unacknowledged kernel of his desire, the traumatic event disturbs his balance from outside.[5]

The paradox in all these cases is that *the stepping out of (what we experience as) ideology is the very form of our enslavement to it.* The opposite example of non-ideology which possesses all the standard features of ideology is provided by the role of *Neues Forum* in ex-East Germany. An inherently *tragic* ethical dimension pertains to its fate: it presents a point at which an ideology 'takes itself literally', and ceases to function as an 'objectively cynical' (Marx) legitimization of existing power relations. *Neues Forum* consisted of groups of passionate intel-lectuals who 'took socialism seriously' and were prepared to risk everything in order to destroy the compromised system and replace it with the utopian 'third way' beyond capitalism and 'really existing' socialism. Their sincere belief and insistence that they were not working for the restoration of Western capitalism, of course, proved to be nothing but an insubstantial illusion; we could say, however, that precisely as such (as a thorough illusion without substance) it was *stricto sensu non-ideological*: it did not 'reflect', in an inverted ideological form, any actual relations of power.

The theoretical lesson to be drawn from this is that the concept of ideology must be disengaged from the 'representationalist' problematic: *ideology has nothing to do with 'illusion'*, with a mistaken, distorted representation of its social content. To put it succinctly: a political standpoint can be quite accurate ('true') as to its objective content, yet thoroughly ideological; and, vice versa, the idea that a political standpoint gives of its social content can prove totally wrong, yet there is absolutely nothing 'ideological' about it. With regard to the 'factual truth', the position of *Neues Forum* – taking the disintegration of the Communist regime as the opening-up of a way to invent some new form of social space that would reach beyond the confines of capitalism – was doubtless illusory. Opposing *Neues Forum* were forces who put all their bets on the quickest possible annexation to West Germany – that is to say, on their country's inclusion in the world capitalist system; for them, the people around *Neues Forum* were nothing but a bunch of heroic day-dreamers. This position proved accurate – *yet it was none the less thoroughly ideological.* Why? The conformist adoption of the West German model implied an ideological belief in the unproblematic, non-antagonistic functioning of the late-capitalist 'social state', whereas the first stance, although illusory as to its factual content (its 'enunciated'), attested, by means of its 'scandalous' and exorbitant position of enunciation, to an awareness of the antagonism that pertains to late capitalism. This is one way to conceive of the Lacanian thesis according to which truth has the structure of a fiction: in those confused months of the passage of 'really existing socialism' into capitalism, *the fiction of a 'third way' was the only point at which social antagonism was not obliterated*. Herein lies one of the tasks of the 'postmodern' critique of ideology: to designate the elements within an existing social order which – in the guise of 'fiction', that is, of 'utopian' narratives of possible but failed alternative histories – point towards the system's antagonistic character, and thus 'estrange' us to the self-evidence of its established identity.

Ideology: The Spectral Analysis of a Concept

In all these *ad hoc* analyses, however, we have already *practicized* the critique of ideology, while our initial question concerned the *concept* of ideology presupposed in this practice. Up till now, we have been guided by a 'spontaneous' pre-comprehension which, although it led us to contradictory results, is not to be underestimated, but rather explicated. For example, we somehow implicitly seem to know what is 'no longer' ideology: as long as the Frankfurt school accepted the critique of political economy as its base, it remained within the co-ordinates of the critique of ideology, whereas the notion of 'instrumental reason' no longer appertains to the horizon of the critique of ideology – instrumental reason' designates an attitude that is not simply functional with regard to social domination but, rather, serves as the very foundation of the relationship of domination.[6] An ideology is thus not necessarily 'false': as to its positive content, it can be 'true', quite accurate, since what really matters is not the asserted content as such, but *the way this content is related to the subjective position implied by its own process of enunciation*. We are within ideological space proper the moment this content – 'true' or 'false' (if true, so much the better for the ideological effect) – is functional with regard to some relation of social domination ('power', 'exploitation') in an inherently non-transparent way: *the very logic of legitimizing the relation of domination must remain concealed if it is to be effective*. In other words, the starting point of the critique of ideology has to be full acknowledgement of the fact that it is easily possible to *lie in the guise of truth*. When, for example, some Western power intervenes in a Third World country on account of violations of human rights, it may well be 'true' that in this country the most elementary human rights were not respected, and that the Western intervention will effectively improve the human rights record; yet such a legitimization none the less remains 'ideological' in so far as it fails to mention the true motives of the intervention (economic interests, etc.). The outstanding mode of this 'lying in the guise of truth' today is cynicism: with a disarming frankness one 'admits everything', yet this full acknowledgement of our power interests does not in any way prevent us from pursuing these interests – the formula of cynicism is no longer the classic Marxian 'They do not know it, but they are doing it'; it is 'They know very well what they are doing, yet they are doing it'.

How, then, are we to explicate this implicit pre-comprehension of ours? How are we to pass from *doxa* to truth? The first approach that offers itself is, of course, the Hegelian historical-dialectical transposition of the problem into its own solution: instead of directly evaluating the adequacy or 'truth' of different notions of ideology, one should *read this very multitude of the determinations of ideology as the index of different concrete historical situations* – that is, one should consider what Althusser, in his self-critical phase, referred to as the 'topicality of the thought', the way a thought is inscribed into its object; or, as Derrida would have put it, the way the frame itself is part of the framed content.

When, for example, Leninism – Stalinism suddenly adopted the term 'pro-letarian ideology' in the late 1920s, in order to designate not the 'distortion' of proletarian consciousness under the pressure of bourgeois ideology but the very 'subjective' driving force of proletarian revolutionary activity, this shift in the notion of ideology was strictly correlative to the reinterpretation of Marxism itself as an impartial 'objective science', as a science that does not in itself involve the proletarian subjective position: Marxism first, from a neutral distance of metalanguage, ascertains the objective tendency of history towards Communism; then it elaborates the 'proletarian ideology' in order to induce the working class to fulfil its historical mission. A further example of such a shift is the already mentioned passage of Western Marxism from critique of political economy to critique of instrumental reason: from Lukács's *History and Class Consciousness* and the early Frankfurt school, where ideological distortion is derived from the 'commodity form', to the notion of Instrumental Reason, which is no longer grounded in a concrete social reality but is, rather, con-ceived as a kind of anthropological, even quasi-transcendental, primordial constant that enables us to explain the social reality of domination and exploi-tation. This passage is embedded in the transition from the post-World War I universe, in which hope in the revolutionary outcome of the crisis of capitalism was still alive, into the double trauma of the late 1930s and 1940s: the 'regression' of capitalist societies into Fascism and the 'totalitarian' turn of the Communist movement.[7]

However, such an approach, although it is adequate at its own level, can easily ensnare us in historicist relativism that suspends the inherent cognitive value of the term 'ideology' and makes it into a mere expression of social circumstances. For that reason, it seems preferable to begin with a different, synchronous approach. Apropos of religion (which, for Marx, was ideology *par excellence*), Hegel distinguished three moments: *doctrine, belief* and *ritual*; one is thus tempted to dispose the multitude of notions associated with the term 'ideology' around these three axes: ideology as a complex of ideas (theories, convictions, beliefs, argumentative procedures); ideology in its externality, that is, the materiality of ideology, Ideological State Apparatuses; and finally, the most elusive domain, the 'spontaneous' ideology at work at the heart of social 'reality' itself (it is highly questionable if the term 'ideology' is at all appropriate to designate this domain – here it is exemplary that, apropos of commodity fetishism, Marx never used the term 'ideology'[8]). Let us recall the case of liberalism: liberalism is a doctrine (developed from Locke to Hayek) materialized in rituals and apparatuses (free press, elections, market, etc.) and active in the 'spontaneous' (self-)experience of subjects as 'free individuals'. The order of contributions in this book [*Mapping Ideology*] follows this line that, *grosso modo*, fits the Hegelian triad of In-itself – For-itself – In-and-For-itself.[9] This logico-narrative reconstruction of the notion of ideology will be centred on the repeated occurrence of the already mentioned reversal of non-ideology into ideology – that is, of the sudden awareness of how the very gesture of stepping out of ideology pulls us back into it.

1. So, to begin with, we have ideology 'in-itself': the immanent notion of ideology as a doctrine, a composite of ideas, beliefs, concepts and so on, destined to convince us of its 'truth', yet actually serving some unavowed particular power interest. The mode of the critique of ideology that corresponds to this notion is that of *symptomal reading*: the aim of the critique is to discern the unavowed bias of the official text via its ruptures, blanks and slips – to discern in 'equality and freedom' the equality and freedom of the partners in the market exchange, which, of course, privileges the owner of the means of production, and so on. Habermas, perhaps the last great representative of this tradition, measures the distortion and/or falsity of an ideological edifice with the standard of non-coercive rational argumentation, a kind of 'regulative ideal' that, according to him, inheres in the symbolic order as such. Ideology is a systematically distorted communication: a text in which, under the influence of unavowed social interests (of domination, etc.), a gap separates its 'official', public meaning from its actual intention – that is to say, in which we are dealing with an unreflected tension between the explicit enunciated content of the text and its pragmatic presuppositions.[10]

Today, however, probably the most prestigious tendency in the critique of ideology, one that grew out of discourse analysis, inverts this relationship: what the tradition of Enlightenment dismisses as a mere disturbance of 'normal' communication turns out to be its positive condition. The concrete intersubjective space of symbolic communication is always structured by various (unconscious) textual devices that cannot be reduced to secondary rhetoric. What we are dealing with here is not a complementary move to the traditional Enlightenment or Habermasian approach, but its inherent reversal: what Habermas perceives as the step out of ideology is denounced here as ideology *par excellence*. In the Enlightenment tradition, 'ideology' stands for the blurred ('false') notion of reality caused by various 'pathological' interests (fear of death and of natural forces, power interests, etc.); for discourse analysis, the very notion of an access to reality unbiased by any discursive devices or conjunctions with power is ideological. The 'zero level' of ideology consists in (mis)-perceiving a discursive formation as an extra-discursive fact.

Already in the 1950s, in *Mythologies*, Roland Barthes proposed the notion of ideology as the 'naturalization' of the symbolic order – that is, as the perception that reifies the results of discursive procedures into properties of the 'thing itself'. Paul de Man's notion of the 'resistance to (deconstructionist) theory' runs along the same lines: 'deconstruction' met with such resistance because it 'denaturalizes' the enunciated content by bringing to the light of day the discursive procedures that engender evidence of sense. Arguably the most elaborate version of this approach is Oswald Ducrot's theory of argumentation;[11] although it does not employ the term 'ideology', its ideologico-critical potential is tremendous. Ducrot's basic notion is that one cannot draw a clear line of separation between descriptive and argumentative levels of language: there is no neutral descriptive content; every description (designation) is already a moment of some argumentative scheme; descriptive predicates themselves are ultimately reified-naturalized argumentative gestures. This argumentative thrust relies on *topoi*, on the 'commonplaces' that operate only as naturalized, only in so far as we apply them in an automatic, 'unconscious' way – a successful argumentation presupposes the invisibility of the mechanisms that regulate its efficiency.

One should also mention here Michel Pêcheux, who gave a strict linguistic turn to Althusser's theory of interpellation. His work is centred on the discursive mechanisms that generate the 'evidence' of sense. That is to say, one of the fundamental stratagems of ideology is the reference to some self-evidence – 'Look, you can see for yourself how things are!' 'Let the facts speak for themselves' is perhaps the arch-statement of ideology – the point being, precisely, that facts *never* 'speak for themselves', but are always *made to speak* by a network of discursive devices. Suffice it to recall the notorious anti-abortion film *The Silent Scream* – we 'see' a foetus which 'defends itself', which 'cries' and so on; yet what we 'don't see' in this very act of seeing is that we 'see' all this against the background of a discursively pre-constructed space. Discourse analysis is perhaps at its strongest in answering this precise question: when a racist Englishman says 'There are too many Pakistanis on our streets!', *how – from what place – does he 'see' this* – that is, how is his symbolic space structured so that he can perceive the fact of a Pakistani strolling along a London street as a disturbing surplus? That is to say, here one must bear in mind Lacan's motto that *nothing is lacking in the real*: every perception of a lack or a surplus ('not enough of this', 'too much of that') always involves a *symbolic* universe.[12]

Last but not least, mention should be made here of Ernesto Laclau and his path-breaking approach to Fascism and populism,[13] whose main theoretical result is that meaning does not inhere in elements of an ideology as such – these elements, rather, function as 'free-floating signifiers' whose meaning is fixed by the mode of their hegemonic articulation. Ecology, for example, is never 'ecology as such'; it is always enchained in a specific series of equivalences: it can be conservative (advocating the return to balanced rural communities and traditional ways of life), statist (only a strong state regulation can save us from the impending catastrophe), socialist (the ultimate cause of ecological problems resides in the capitalist profit-orientated exploitation of natural resources), liberal-capitalist (one should include the damage to the environment in the price of the product, and thus leave the market to regulate the ecological balance), feminist (the exploitation of nature follows from the male attitude of domination), anarchic self-managerial (humanity can survive only if it reorganizes itself into small self-reliant communities that live in balance with nature), and so on. The point, of course, is that none of these enchainments is in itself 'true', inscribed in the very nature of the ecological problematic: which discourse will succeed in 'appropriating' ecology depends on the fight for discursive hegemony, whose outcome is not guaranteed by any underlying necessity or 'natural alliance'. The other inevitable consequence of such a notion of hegemonic articulation is that statist, conservative, socialist, and so on, inscription of ecology does not designate a secondary connotation that supplements its primary 'literal' meaning: as Derrida would have put it, this supplement retroactively (re)defines the very nature of 'literal' identity – a conservative enchainment, for example, throws a specific light on the ecological problematic itself ('owing to his false arrogance, man forsook his roots in the natural order', etc.).

2. What follows is the step from 'in-itself' to 'for-itself', to ideology in its otherness, externalization: the moment epitomized by the Althusserian notion of Ideological State Apparatuses (ISA) that designate the material existence of ideology in ideological practices, rituals and institutions.[14] Religious belief, for example, is not merely, or even primarily, an inner conviction; but the Church as an institution and its rituals (prayer, baptism, confirmation, confession...) which, far from being a mere secondary externalization of the inner belief,

stand for *the very mechanisms that generate it.* When Althusser repeats, after Pascal: 'Act as if you believe, pray, kneel down, and you shall believe, faith will arrive by itself', he delineates an intricate reflective mechanism of retroactive 'auto-poetic' foundation that far exceeds the reductionist assertion of the dependence of inner belief on external behaviour. That is to say, the implicit logic of his argument is: kneel down and *you shall believe that you knelt down because of your belief* – that is, your following the ritual is an expression/effect of your inner belief; in short, the 'external' ritual performatively generates its own ideological foundation.[15]

 What we encounter here again is the 'regression' into ideology at the very point where we apparently step out of it. In this respect, the relationship between Althusser and Foucault is of special interest. The Foucauldian coun-terparts to Ideological State Apparatuses are the disciplinary procedures that operate at the level of 'micro-power' and designate the point at which *power inscribes itself into the body directly, bypassing ideology* – for that precise reason, Foucault never uses the term 'ideology' apropos of these mechanisms of micro-power. This abandoning of the problematic of ideology entails a fatal weakness of Foucault's theory. Foucault never tires of repeating how power constitutes itself 'from below', how it does not emanate from some unique summit: this very semblance of a Summit (the Monarch or some other embodiment of Sovereignty) emerges as the secondary effect of the plurality of micro-practices, of the complex network of their interrelations. However, when he is com-pelled to display the concrete mechanism of this emergence, Foucault resorts to the extremely suspect rhetoric of complexity, evoking the intricate network of lateral links, left and right, up and down . . . a clear case of patching up, since one can never arrive at Power this way – the abyss that separates micro-procedures from the spectre of Power remains unbridgeable. Althusser's advant-age over Foucault seems evident: Althusser proceeds in exactly the opposite direction – from the very outset, he conceives these micro-procedures as parts of the ISA; that is to say, as mechanisms which, in order to be operative, to 'seize' the individual, always-already presuppose the massive presence of the state, the transferential relationship of the individual towards state power, or – in Althusser's terms – towards the ideological big Other in whom the inter-pellation originates.

This Althusserian shift of emphasis from ideology 'in-itself' to its material existence in the ISA proved its fecundity in a new approach to Fascism; Wolfgang Fritz Haug's criticism of Adorno is exemplary here. Adorno refuses to treat Fascism as an ideology in the proper sense of the term – that is, as 'rational legitimization of the existing order'. So-called Fascist ideology no longer possesses the coherence of a rational construct that calls for conceptual analysis and ideologico-critical refutation; that is to say, it no longer functions as a 'lie necessarily experienced as truth' (the sign of recognition of a true ideology). 'Fascist ideology' is not taken seriously even by its promoters; its status is purely instrumental, and ultimately relies on external coercion.[16] In his response to Adorno, however, Haug[17] triumphantly demonstrates how this capitulation to the primacy of the doctrine, far from implying the 'end of ideology', asserts the founding gesture of the ideological as such: the call to unconditional subordination and to 'irrational' sacrifice. What liberal criticism (mis)perceives as Fascism's weakness is the very resort of its strength: within the Fascist horizon, the very demand for rational argumentation that should provide grounds for our acceptance of authority is denounced in advance as an index of the liberal degeneration of the true spirit of ethical sacrifice – as Haug puts it, in browsing through Mussolini's texts, one cannot avoid the uncanny feeling that Mussolini had read Althusser! The direct denunciation of the Fascist notion of the 'community-of-the-people' (*Volksgemeinschaft*) as a deceptive lure that conceals the reality of domination and exploitation fails to take note of the crucial fact that this *Volksgemeinschaft* was materialized in a series of rituals and practices (not only mass gatherings and parades, but also large-scale campaigns to help the hungry, organized sports and cultural activities for the workers, etc.) which performatively produced the effect of *Volksgemeinschaft*.[18]

3. In the next step of our reconstruction, this externalization is, as it were, 'reflected into itself': what takes place is the disintegration, self-limitation and self-dispersal of the notion of ideology. Ideology is no longer conceived as a homogeneous mechanism that guarantees social reproduction, as the 'cement' of society; it turns into a Wittgensteinian 'family' of vaguely connected and heterogeneous procedures whose reach is strictly localized. Along these lines, the critiques of the so-called Dominant Ideology Thesis (DIT) endeavour to demonstrate that an ideology either exerts an influence that is crucial, but constrained to some narrow social stratum, or its role in social reproduction is marginal. At the beginnings of capitalism, for example, the role of the Protestant ethic of hard work as an end-in-itself, and so on, was limited to the stratum of emerging capitalists, whereas workers and peasants, as well as the upper classes, continued to obey other, more traditional ethical attitudes, so that one can in no way attribute to the Protestant ethic the role of the 'cement' of the entire social edifice. Today, in late capitalism, when the expansion of the new mass media in principle, at least, enables ideology effectively to penetrate every pore of the social body, the weight of ideology as such is diminished: individuals do not act as they do primarily on account of their beliefs or ideological convictions – that is to say, the system, for the most part, bypasses ideology in its reproduction and relies on economic coercion, legal and state regulations, and so on.'[19]

Here, however, things get blurred again, since the moment we take a closer look at these allegedly extra-ideological mechanisms that regulate social reproduction, we find ourselves knee-deep in the already mentioned obscure domain in which reality is indistinguishable from ideology. What we encounter here, therefore, is the third reversal of non-ideology into ideology: all of a sudden we become aware of a For-itself of ideology at work in the very In-itself of extra-ideological actuality. First, the mechanisms of economic coercion and legal regulation always 'materialize' some propositions or beliefs that are inherently ideological (the criminal law, for example, involves a belief in the personal responsibility of the individual or the conviction that crimes are a product of social circumstances). Secondly, the form of consciousness that fits late-capitalist 'post-ideological' society – the cynical, 'sober' attitude that advocates liberal 'openness' in the matter of 'opinions' (everybody is free to believe whatever she or he wants; this concerns only his or her privacy), disregards pathetic ideological phrases, and follows only utilitarian and/or hedonistic motivations – *stricto sensu* remains an ideological attitude: it involves a series of ideological presuppositions (on the relationship between 'values' and 'real life', on personal freedom, etc.) that are necessary for the reproduction of existing social relations.

What thereby comes into sight is a third continent of ideological phenomena: neither ideology *qua* explicit doctrine, articulated convictions on the nature of man, society and the universe, nor ideology in its material existence (institutions, rituals and practices that give body to it), but the elusive network of implicit, quasi-'spontaneous' presuppositions and attitudes that form an irreducible moment of the reproduction of 'non-ideological' (economic, legal, political, sexual...) practices.[20] The Marxian notion of 'commodity fetishism' is exemplary here: it designates not a (bourgeois) theory of political economy, but a series of presuppositions that determine the structure of the very 'real' economic practice of market exchange – in theory, a capitalist clings to utilitarian nominalism, yet in his own practice (of exchange, etc.) he follows 'theological whimsies', and acts as a speculative idealist...[21] For that reason, a direct reference to extra-ideological coercion (of the market, for example) is an ideological gesture *par excellence*: the market and (mass) media are dialectically interconnected;[22] we live in a 'society of the spectacle' (Guy Debord), in which the media structure our perception of reality in advance, and render reality indistinguishable from the 'aestheticized' image of it.

The Spectre and the Real of Antagonism

Is our final outcome, therefore, the inherent impossibility of isolating a reality whose consistency is not maintained by ideological mechanisms, a reality that

does not disintegrate the moment we subtract from it its ideological component? Therein resides one of the main reasons for progressive abandonment of
the notion of ideology: this notion somehow grows 'too strong'; it begins to
embrace everything, inclusive of the very neutral, extra-ideological ground
supposed to provide the standard by means of which one can measure ideological distortion. That is to say, is not the ultimate result of discourse analysis
that the order of discourse as such is inherently 'ideological'?

Let us suppose that at some political meeting or academic conference we are
expected to pronounce some profound thoughts on the sad plight of the
homeless in our big cities, yet we have absolutely no idea of their actual
problems – the way to save face is to produce the effect of 'depth' by means
of a purely formal inversion: 'Today, one hears and reads a lot about the plight
of the homeless in our cities, about their hardship and distress. Perhaps,
however, this distress, deplorable as it may be, is ultimately just a sign of
some far deeper distress – of the fact that modern man no longer has a proper
dwelling, that he is more and more a stranger in his own world. Even if we
constructed enough new buildings to house all homeless people, the true
distress would perhaps be even greater. The essence of homelessness is the
homelessness of the essence itself; it resides in the fact that, in our world thrown
out of joint by the frenetic search for empty pleasures, there is no home, no
proper dwelling, for the truly essential dimension of man.'

This formal matrix can be applied to an infinite multitude of themes – say,
distance and proximity: 'Today, modern media can bring events from the
farthest part of our Earth, even from nearby planets, close to us in a split
second. Does not this very all-pervasive proximity, however, remove us from
the authentic dimension of human existence? Is not the essence of man more
distant from us than ever today?' Or the recurrent motif of danger: 'Today, one
hears and reads a lot about how the very survival of the human race is
threatened by the prospect of ecological catastrophe (the disappearing ozone
layer, the greenhouse effect, etc.). The true danger, however, lies elsewhere:
what is ultimately threatened is the very essence of man. As we endeavour to
prevent the impending ecological catastrophe with newer and newer technological solutions ('environment-friendly' aerosols, unleaded petrol, etc.), we
are in fact simply adding fuel to the flames, and thus aggravating the threat to
the spiritual essence of man, which cannot be reduced to a technological
animal.'

The purely formal operation which, in all these cases, brings about the effect
of depth is perhaps ideology at its purest, its 'elementary cell', whose link to the
Lacanian concept of the master-signifier is not difficult to discern: the chain of
'ordinary' signifiers registers some positive knowledge about homelessness,
whereas the master-signifier stands for 'the truly essential dimension' about

which we need not make any positive claim (for that reason, Lacan designates the Master-Signifier the 'signifier without signified'). This formal matrix bears witness in an exemplary way to the self-defeating power of a formal discourse analysis of ideology: its weakness resides in its very strength, since it is ultimately compelled to locate ideology in the gap between the 'ordinary' signifying chain and the excessive master-signifier that is part of the symbolic order as such.

Here, however, one should be careful to avoid the last trap that makes us slide into ideology under the guise of stepping out of it. That is to say, when we denounce as ideological the very attempt to draw a clear line of demarcation between ideology and actual reality, this inevitably seems to impose the conclusion that the only non-ideological position is to renounce the very notion of extra-ideological reality and accept that all we are dealing with are symbolic fictions, the plurality of discursive universes, never 'reality' – *such a quick, slick 'postmodern' solution, however, is ideology* par excellence. It all hinges on our persisting in this impossible position: although no clear line of demarcation separates ideology from reality, although ideology is already at work in everything we experience as 'reality', we must none the less maintain the tension that keeps the *critique* of ideology alive. Perhaps, following Kant, we could designate this impasse the 'antinomy of critico-ideological reason': ideology is not all; it is possible to assume a place that enables us to maintain a distance from it, *but this place from which one can denounce ideology must remain empty, it cannot be occupied by any positively determined reality* – the moment we yield to this temptation, we are back in ideology.

How are we to specify this empty place? Perhaps we should take as a starting point the thread that runs through our entire logico-narrative reconstruction of the notion of ideology: it is as if, at every stage, the same opposition, the same *undecidable* alternative Inside/Outside, repeats itself under a different exponent. First, there is the split within ideology 'in-itself': on the one hand, ideology stands for the distortion of rational argumentation and insight due to the weight of the 'pathological' external interests of power, exploitation and so on; on the other, ideology resides in the very notion of a thought not permeated by some non-transparent power strategy, of an argument that does not rely upon some non-transparent rhetorical devices.... Next, this very externality splits into an 'inner externality' (the symbolic order, i.e. the decentred discursive mechanisms that generate meaning) and an 'external externality' (the ISA and social rituals and practices that materialize ideology) – *the externality misrecognized by ideology is the externality of the 'text' itself as well as the externality of 'extra-textual' social reality*. Finally, this 'extra-textual' social reality itself is split into the institutional Exterior that dominates and regulates the life of individuals 'from above' (ISA) and ideology that is not imposed by the ISA but emerges 'spontaneously', 'from below', out of the extra–institutional activity of individuals (commodity fetishism) – to give it names, Althusser versus Lukács. This opposition between ISA and commodity fetishism – between the *materiality that always-already pertains to ideology as such* (material, effective apparatuses which give body to ideology) and *ideology that always-already pertains to materiality as such* (to the social actuality of production) – is ultimately the opposition between state and market, between the external superior agency that organizes society 'from above' and society's 'spontaneous' self-organization.

This opposition, whose first philosophical manifestation is provided by the couple of Plato and Aristotle, finds its last expression in the guise of the two modes of cynical ideology: 'consumerist', post-Protestant, late-capitalist cynicism and the cynicism that pertained to the late 'real Socialism'. Although, in both cases, the system functions only on condition that subjects maintain a cynical distance and do not 'take seriously' the 'official' values, the difference is remarkable; it turns upside down the *doxa* according to which late capitalism, as a (formally) 'free' society, relies on argumentative persuasion and free consent, 'manipulated' and fabricated as it may be; whereas Socialism resorted to the raw force of 'totalitarian' coercion. It is as if in late capitalism 'words do not count', no longer oblige: they increasingly seem to lose their performative power; whatever one says is drowned in the general indifference; the emperor is naked, and the media trumpet forth this fact, yet nobody seems really to mind – that is, people continue to act as if the emperor is not naked. . . .

Perhaps the key feature of the symbolic economy of the late 'real Socialism' was, on the contrary, the almost paranoiac *belief in the power of the Word* – the state and the ruling party reacted with utmost nervousness and panic at the slightest public criticism, as if some vague critical hints in an obscure poem published in a low-circulation literary journal, or an essay in an academic philosophical journal, possessed the potential capacity to trigger the explosion of the entire Socialist system. Incidentally, this feature renders 'real Socialism' almost sympathetic to our retrospective nostalgic view, since it bears witness to the legacy of the Enlightenment (the belief in the social efficacy of rational argumentation) that survived in it. This, perhaps, was why it was possible to undermine 'real Socialism' by means of peaceful civil society movements that operated at the level of the Word – belief in the power of the Word was the system's Achilles heel.[23]

The matrix of all these repetitions, perhaps, is the opposition between ideology as the universe of 'spontaneous' experience (*vécu*), whose grip we can break only by means of an effort of scientific reflection, and ideology as a radically non-spontaneous machine that distorts the authenticity of our life-experience from outside. That is to say, what we should always bear in mind is that, for Marx, the primordial mythological consciousness of the pre-class society out of which later ideologies grew (true to the heritage of German classicism, Marx saw the paradigm of this primordial social consciousness in Greek mythology) *is not yet ideology proper*, although (or, rather, precisely because) it is immediately *vécu*, and although it is obviously 'wrong', 'illusory' (it involves the divinization of the forces of nature, etc.), ideology proper emerges only with the division of labour and the class split, only when the 'wrong' ideas lose their 'immediate' character, and are 'elaborated' by intellectuals in order to serve (to legitimize) the existing relations of domination – in short, only when the division into Master and Servant is conjugated with the division of labour itself into intellectual and physical labour. For that precise reason, Marx refused to categorize commodity fetishism as ideology: for him, ideology was always of the state and, as Engels put it, state itself is the first ideological force. In clear contrast, Althusser conceives ideology as an immediately experienced relationship to the universe – as such, it is eternal; when, following his self-critical turn, he introduces the concept of ISA, he returns in a way to Marx: ideology does not grow out of 'life itself'; it comes into existence only in so far as society is regulated by state. (More precisely, the paradox and theoretical interest of Althusser reside in his conjugation of the two lines: in its very character of immediately experienced relationship to the universe, ideology is always-already regulated by the externality of the state and its Ideological Apparatuses.)

This tension between 'spontaneity' and organized imposition introduces a kind of reflective distance into the very heart of the notion of ideology: ideology is always, by definition, 'ideology of ideology'. Suffice it to recall the disintegration of real Socialism: Socialism was perceived as the rule of 'ideological' oppression and indoctrination, whereas the passage into democracy-capitalism was experienced as deliverance from the constraints of ideology – however, was not this very experience of 'deliverance' in the course of which political parties and the market economy were perceived as 'non-ideological', as the 'natural state of things', ideological *par excellence*?[24] Our point is that this feature is *universal*: there is no ideology that does not assert itself by means of delimiting itself from another 'mere ideology'. An individual subjected to ideology can never say for himself 'I am in ideology'; he always requires *another* corpus of *doxa* in order to distinguish his own 'true' position from it.

The first example here is provided by none other than Plato: philosophical *episteme* versus the confused *doxa* of the crowd. What about Marx? Although he may appear to fall into this trap (is not the entire *German Ideology* based on the opposition of ideological chimera and the study of 'actual life'?), things get complicated in his mature critique of political economy. That is to say, why, precisely, does Marx choose the term 'fetishism' in order to designate the 'theological whimsy' of the universe of commodities? What one should bear in mind here is that 'fetishism' is a *religious* term for (previous) 'false' idolatry as opposed to (present) true belief: for the Jews, the fetish is the Golden Calf; for a partisan of pure spirituality, fetishism designates 'primitive' superstition, the fear of ghosts and other spectral apparitions, and so on. And the point of Marx is that the commodity universe provides the necessary fetishistic supplement to the 'official' spirituality: it may well be that the 'official' ideology of our society is Christian spirituality, but its actual foundation is none the less the idolatry of the Golden Calf, money.

In short, Marx's point is that there is no spirit without spirits-ghosts, no 'pure' spirituality without the obscene spectre of 'spiritualized matter'.[25] The first to accomplish this step 'from spirit to spirits' in the guise of the critique of pure spiritual idealism, of its lifeless 'negative' nihilism, was F. W. J. Schelling, the crucial, unjustly neglected philosopher of German Idealism. In the dialogue *Clara* (1810), he drove a wedge into the simple complementary mirror-relationship between Inside and Outside, between Sprit and Body, between the ideal and the real element that together form the living totality of the Organism, by calling attention to the double surplus that 'sticks out'. On the one hand, there is the *spiritual element of corporeality*: the presence, in matter itself, of a non-material but physical element, of a subtle corpse, relatively independent of time and space, which provides the material base of our free will (animal magnetism, etc.); on the other hand, there is the *corporeal element of spirituality*: the materializations of the spirit in a kind of pseudo-stuff, in substanceless apparitions (ghosts, living dead). It is clear how these two surpluses render the logic of commodity fetishism and of the ISA: commodity fetishism involves the uncanny 'spiritualization' of the commodity-body, whereas the ISA materialize the spiritual, substanceless big Other of ideology.

In his recent book on Marx, Jacques Derrida brought into play the term 'spectre' in order to indicate this elusive pseudo-materiality that subverts the classic ontological oppositions of reality and illusion, and so on.[26] And perhaps it is here that we should look for the last resort of ideology, for the pre-ideological kernel, the formal matrix, on which are grafted various ideological formations: in the fact that there is no reality without the spectre, that the circle of reality can be closed only by means of an uncanny spectral supplement. Why, then, is there no reality without the spectre? Lacan provides a precise answer to this question: (what we experience as) reality is not the 'thing itself', it is always-already symbolized, constituted, structured by symbolic mechanisms — and the problem resides in the fact that symbolization ultimately always fails, that it never succeeds in fully 'covering' the real, that it always involves some unsettled, unredeemed symbolic debt. *This real (the part of reality that remains non-symbolized) returns in the guise of spectral apparitions.* Consequently, 'spectre' is not to be confused with 'symbolic fiction', with the fact that reality itself has the structure of a fiction, in that it is symbolically (or, as some sociologists put it, 'socially') constructed; the notions of spectre and (symbolic) fiction are co-dependent in their very incompatibility (they are 'complement-ary' in the quantum-mechanical sense). To put it simply, reality is never directly 'itself'; it presents itself only via its incomplete-failed symbolization, and spectral apparitions emerge in this very gap that for ever separates reality from the real, and on account of which reality has the character of a (symbolic) fiction: the spectre gives body to that which escapes (the symbolically struc-tured) reality.[27]

The pre-ideological 'kernel' of ideology thus consists of the *spectral apparition that fills up the hole of the Real.* This is what all the attempts to draw a clear line of separation between 'true' reality and illusion (or to ground illusion in reality) fail to take into account: if (what we experience as) 'reality' is to emerge, something has to be foreclosed from it – that is to say, 'reality', like truth, is, by definition, never 'whole'. *What the spectre conceals is not reality but its 'primordially repressed', the irrepresentable X on whose 'repression' reality itself is founded.* It may seem that we have thereby lost our way in speculative murky waters that have nothing whatsoever to do with concrete social struggles – is not the supreme example of such 'reality', however, provided by the Marxist concept of *class struggle?* The consequent thinking-out of this concept compels us to admit that there is no class struggle 'in reality': 'class struggle' designates the very antag-onism that prevents the objective (social) reality from constituting itself as a self-enclosed whole.[28]

True, according to the Marxist tradition, class struggle is the 'totalizing' principle of society; this, however, does not mean that it is a kind of ultimate guarantee authorizing us to grasp society as a rational totality ('the ultimate meaning of every social phenomenon is determined by its position within the class struggle'): the ultimate paradox of the notion of 'class struggle' is that society is 'held together' by the very antagonism, splitting, that for ever prevents its closure in a harmonious, transparent, rational Whole – by the very impediment that undermines every rational totalization. Although 'class struggle' is nowhere directly given as a positive entity, it none the less functions, *in its very absence,* as the point of reference enabling us to locate every social phenomenon – not by relating it to class struggle as its ultimate meaning ('transcendental signified'), but by conceiving it as (an)other attempt to conceal and 'patch up' the rift of class antagonism, to efface its traces. What we have here is the structural-dialectical paradox of *an effect that exists only in order to efface the causes of its existence,* an effect that in a way resists its own cause.

In other words, class struggle is 'real' in the strict Lacanian sense: a 'hitch', an impediment which gives rise to ever-new symbolizations by means of which one endeavours to integrate and domesticate it (the corporatist translation-displacement of class struggle into the organic articulation of the 'members' of the 'social body', for example), but which simultaneously condemns these endeavours to ultimate failure. Class struggle is none other than the name for the unfathomable limit that cannot be objectivized, located within the social totality, since it is itself that limit which prevents us from conceiving society as a closed totality. Or – to put it in yet another way – 'class struggle' designates the point with regard to which 'there is no metalanguage': in so far as every position within social totality is ultimately overdetermined by class struggle, no neutral place is excluded from the dynamics of class struggle from which it would be possible to locate class struggle within the social totality.

This paradoxical status of class struggle can be articulated by means of the crucial Hegelian distinction between Substance and Subject. At the level of Substance, class struggle is conditional on the 'objective' social process; it functions as the secondary indication of some more fundamental discord in this process, a discord regulated by positive mechanisms independent of class struggle ('class struggle breaks out when the relations of production are no longer in accordance with the development of the productive forces').[29] We pass to the level of Subject when we acknowledge that class struggle does not pop up at the end, as the effect of an objective process, but is always-already at work in the very heart of the objective process itself (capitalists develop means of production in order to lower the relative and absolute value of the labour force; the value of the labour force itself is not objectively given but results from the class struggle, etc.). In short, it is not possible to isolate any 'objective' social process or mechanism whose innermost logic does not involve the 'subjective' dynamics of class struggle; or – to put it differently – *the very 'peace', the absence of struggle, is already a form of struggle*, the (temporal) victory of one of the sides in the struggle. In so far as the very invisibility of class struggle ('class peace') is already an effect of class struggle – that is, of the hegemony exerted by one side in the struggle – one is tempted to compare the status of class struggle to that of the Hitchcockian MacGuffin: 'What is class struggle? – The antagonistic process that constitutes classes and determines their relationship. – But in our society there is no struggle between the classes! – You see how it functions!'[30]

This notion of class struggle *qua* antagonism enables us to contrast the real of antagonism with the complementary polarity of opposites: perhaps the reduction of antagonism to polarity is one of the elementary ideological operations. Suffice it to recall the standard New Age procedure of presupposing a kind of natural balance of cosmic opposites (reason–emotions, active–passive, intellect–intuition, consciousness–unconscious, *yin–yang*, etc.), and then of conceiving our age as the age that laid too much stress upon one of the two poles, upon the 'male principle' of activity–reason – the solution, of course, lies in re-establishing the equilibrium of the two principles. . . .

The 'progressive' tradition also bears witness to numerous attempts to conceive (sexual, class) antagonism as the coexistence of two opposed positive entities: from a certain kind of 'dogmatic' Marxism that posits 'their' bourgeois science and 'our' proletarian science side by side, to a certain kind of feminism that posits masculine discourse and feminine discourse, or 'writing' side by side. Far from being 'too extreme', these attempts are, on the contrary, not extreme enough: they presuppose as their position of enunciation a third neutral medium within which the two poles coexist; that is to say, they back down on the consequences of the fact that there is no point of convergence, no neutral ground shared by the two antagonistic sexual or class positions.[31] As far as science is concerned, science, of course, is not neutral in the sense of objective knowledge not affected by class struggle and at the disposal of all classes, yet for that very reason it is *one*; there are not two sciences, and class struggle is precisely the struggle for this one science, for who will appropriate it. It is the same with 'discourse': there are not two discourses, 'masculine' and 'feminine'; there is *one* discourse split from within by the sexual antagonism – that is to say, providing the 'terrain' on which the battle for hegemony takes place.

What is at stake here could also be formulated as the problem of the status of 'and' as a category. In Althusser 'and' functions as a precise theoretical category: when an 'and' appears in the title of some of his essays, this little word unmistakably signals the confrontation of some general ideological notion (or, more precisely, of a neutral, ambiguous notion that oscillates between its ideological actuality and its scientific potentiality) with its specification which tells us how we are to concretize this notion so that it begins to function as non-ideological, as a strict theoretical concept. 'And' thus *splits up* the ambiguous starting unity, introduces into it the difference between ideology and science.

Suffice it to mention two examples. 'Ideology *and* Ideological State Apparatuses': ISA designate the concrete network of the material conditions of existence of an ideological edifice – that is, that which ideology itself has to misrecognize in its 'normal' functioning. 'Contradiction *and* Overdetermination': in so far as the concept of overdetermination designates the undecidable complex totality *qua* the mode of existence of contradiction, it enables us to discard the idealist-teleological burden that usually weighs upon the notion of contradiction (the teleological necessity that guarantees in advance the 'sublation' of the contradiction in a higher unity).[32] Perhaps the first exemplary case of such an 'and' is Marx's famous 'freedom, equality, *and Bentham*' from *Capital*: the supplementary 'Bentham' stands for the social circumstances that provide the concrete content of the pathetic phrases on freedom and equality – commodity exchange, market bargaining, utilitarian egotism. . . . And do we not encounter a homologous conjunction in Heidegger's *Being and Time*? 'Being' designates the fundamental theme of philosophy in its abstract universality, whereas 'time' stands for the concrete horizon of the sense of being.

'And' is thus, in a sense, *tautological*: it conjoins the same content in its two modalities – first in its ideological evidence, then in the extra-ideological conditions of its existence. For that reason, no third term is needed here to designate the medium itself in which the two terms, conjoined by means of the 'and', encounter each other: this third term is already the second term itself that stands for the network (the 'medium') of the concrete existence of an ideological universality. In contrast to this dialectico-materialist 'and', the idealist-ideological 'and' functions precisely as this third term, as the common medium of the polarity or plurality of elements. Therein resides the gap that for ever separates Freud from Jung in their respective notions of libido: Jung conceives of libido as a kind of neutral energy with its concrete forms (sexual, creative, destructive libido) as its different 'metamorphoses', whereas Freud insists that libido in its concrete existence is irreducibly *sexual* – all other forms of libido are forms of 'ideological' misrecognition of this sexual content. And is not the same operation to be repeated apropos of 'man *and* woman'? Ideology compels us to assume 'humanity' as the neutral medium within which 'man' and 'woman' are posited as the two complementary poles – against this ideological evidence, one could maintain that 'woman' stands for the aspect of concrete existence and 'man' for the empty-ambiguous universality. The paradox (of a profoundly Hegelian nature) is that 'woman' – that is, the moment of specific difference – functions as the encompassing ground that accounts for the emergence of the universality of man.

This interpretation of social antagonism (class struggle) as Real, not as (part of) objective social reality, also enables us to counter the worn-out line of argumentation according to which one has to abandon the notion of ideology, since the gesture of distinguishing 'mere ideology' from 'reality' implies the epistemologically untenable 'God's view' – that is, access to objective reality as it 'truly is'. The question of the suitability of the term 'class struggle' to designate today's dominant form of antagonism is secondary here, it concerns concrete social analysis; what matters is that the very constitution of social reality involves the 'primordial repression' of an antagonism, so that the ultimate support of the critique of ideology – the extra-ideological point of reference that authorizes us to denounce the content of our immediate experience as 'ideological' – is not 'reality' but the 'repressed' real of antagonism.

In order to clarify this uncanny logic of antagonism *qua* real, let us recall the analogy between Claude Lévi-Strauss's structural approach and Einstein's theory of relativity. One usually attributes to Einstein the relativization of space with regard to the observer's point of view – that is, the cancellation of the notion of absolute space and time. The theory of relativity, however, involves its own absolute constant: the space-time interval between two events is an absolute that never varies. Space-time interval is defined as the hypotenuse of a right-angled triangle whose legs are the time and space distance between two events. One observer may be in a state of motion such that for him there is a time and a distance involved between two events; another may be in a state of motion such that his measuring devices indicate a different distance and a different time between the events, but the space-time interval between the two events does not in fact vary. *This* constant is the Lacanian Real that 'remains the same in all possible universes (of observation)'. And it is a homologous constant that we encounter in Lévi-Strauss's exemplary analysis of the spatial arrangement of buildings in an aboriginal South American village (from his *Structural Anthropology*).

The inhabitants are divided into two subgroups; when we ask an individual to draw the ground-plan of his or her village (the spatial arrangement of cottages) on a piece of paper or on sand, we obtain two quite different answers, depending on which subgroup he or she belongs to: a member of the first subgroup (let us call it 'conservative-corporatist') perceives the ground-plan of the village as circular – a ring of houses more or less symmetrically arranged around the central temple; whereas a member of the second ('revolutionary-antagonistic') sub-group perceives his or her village as two distinct clusters of houses separated by an invisible frontier.... Where is the homology with Einstein here? Lévi-Strauss's central point is that this example should in no way entice us into a cultural relativism according to which the perception of social space depends on the observer's group membership: the very splitting into the two 'relative' perceptions implies the hidden reference to a constant – not the objective, 'actual' arrangement of buildings but a traumatic kernel, a fundamental antag-onism the inhabitants of the village were not able to symbolize, to account for, to 'internalize', to come to terms with: an imbalance in social relations that pre-vented the community from stabilizing itself into a harmonious whole. The two perceptions of the ground-plan are simply two mutually exclusive endeavours to cope with this traumatic antagonism, to heal its wound via the imposition of a balanced symbolic structure. (And it is hardly necessary to add that things are exactly the same with respect to sexual difference: 'masculine' and 'feminine' are like the two configurations of houses in the Lévi-Straussian village . . .)

Common sense tells us that it is easy to rectify the bias of subjective perceptions and ascertain the 'true state of things': we hire a helicopter and photograph the village directly from above.... In this way we obtain an undistorted view of reality, yet we completely miss the real of social antagonism, the non-symbolizable traumatic kernel that found expression in the very distortions of reality, in the fantasized displacements of the 'actual' arrangement of houses. This is what Lacan has in mind when he claims that *distortion and/or dissimulation is in itself revealing*: what emerges via distortions of the accurate representation of reality is the Real – that is, the trauma around which social reality is structured. In other words, if all the inhabitants of the village were to draw the same accurate ground-plan, we would be dealing with a non-antagonistic, harmonious community. If we are to arrive at the fundamental paradox implied by the notion of commodity fetishism, however, we have to go one step further and imagine, say, two different 'actual' villages each of which realizes, in the arrangement of its dwellings, one of the two fantasized ground-plans evoked by Lévi-Strauss: in this case, the structure of social reality itself materializes an attempt to cope with the real of antagonism. 'Reality' itself, in so far as it is regulated by a symbolic fiction, conceals the real of an antagonism – and it is this Real, foreclosed from the symbolic fiction, that returns in the guise of spectral apparitions.

Such a reading of spectrality as that which fills out the unrepresentable abyss of antagonism, of the non-symbolized real, also enables us to assume a precise distance from Derrida, for whom spectrality, the apparition of the Other, provides the ultimate horizon of ethics. According to Derrida, the metaphysical ontologization of spectrality is rooted in the fact that the thought is horrified at itself, at its own founding gesture; that it draws back from the spirit convoked by this gesture. Therein resides *in nuce* his reading of Marx and the history of Marxism: the original impulse of Marx consisted in the messianic promise of Justice *qua* spectral Otherness, a promise that is only as *avenir*, yet-to-come, never as a simple *futur*, what will be; the 'totalitarian' turn of Marxism that culminated in Stalinism has its roots in the ontologization of the spectre, in the translation of the spectral Promise into a positive ontological Project.... Lacan, however, goes a step further here: *spectre as such already bears witness to a retreat, a withdrawal* – from what?

Most people are terrified when they encounter freedom, like when they encounter magic, anything inexplicable, especially the world of spirits.[33]

This proposition of Schelling can be read in two ways, depending on how we interpret the comparison – in what precise sense is freedom like a spectre? Our – Lacanian – premiss here is that 'freedom' designates the moment when the 'principle of the sufficient reason' is suspended, the moment of the *act* that breaks the 'great chain of being', of the symbolic reality in which we are embedded; consequently, it is not sufficient to say that we fear the spectre – the spectre itself already emerges out of a fear, out of our escape from something even more horrifying: freedom. When we confront the miracle of freedom, there are two ways of reacting to it:

- *Either* we 'ontologize' freedom by way of conceiving it as the terrestrial apparition of a 'higher' stratum of reality, as the miraculous, inexplicable intervention into our universe of another, supra-sensible universe that persists in its Beyond, yet is accessible to us, common mortals, only in the guise of nebulous chimera;

- *Or* we conceive this universe of Beyond, this redoubling of our terrestrial universe into another *Geisterwelt*, as an endeavour to gentrify the act of freedom, to cope with its traumatic impact – spectre is the positivization of the abyss of freedom, a void that assumes the form of quasi-being.

Therein resides the gap that separates Lacan from Derrida: our primary duty is not towards the spectre, whatever form it assumes.[34] The act of freedom *qua* real not only transgresses the limits of what we experience as 'reality', it cancels our very primordial indebtedness to the spectral Other. Here, therefore, Lacan is on the side of Marx against Derrida: in the act, we 'leave the dead to bury their dead', as Marx put it in the 'Eighteenth Brumaire of Louis Bonaparte'.

The problematic of ideology, its very elusive status as attested to by its 'postmodern' vicissitudes, has thus brought us back to Marx, to the centrality of the social antagonism ('class struggle'). As we have seen, however, this 'return to Marx' entails a radical displacement of the Marxian theoretical edifice: a gap emerges in the very heart of historical materialism – that is, the problematic of ideology has led us to the inherently incomplete, 'non-all' character of historical materialism – something must be excluded, foreclosed, if social reality is to constitute itself. To those to whom this result of ours appears far-fetched, speculative, alien to the concrete social concerns of the Marxist theory of ideology, the best answer is provided by a recent work of Étienne Balibar, who arrived at exactly the same conclusion via a concrete analysis of the vicissitudes of the notion of ideology in Marx and the history of Marxism:

The idea of a theory of ideology was only ever a *way ideally to complete historical materialism*, to 'fill a hole' in its representation of the social totality, and thus a way ideally to constitute historical materialism as a system of explanation complete in its kind, at least 'in principle'.[35]

Balibar also provides the location of this hole to be filled by the theory of ideology: it concerns social antagonism ('class struggle') as the inherent limit that traverses society and prevents it from constituting itself as a positive, complete, self-enclosed entity. It is at this precise place that psychoanalysis has to intervene (Balibar somewhat enigmatically evokes the concept of the unconscious[36]) – not, of course, in the old Freudo-Marxist manner, as the element destined to fill up the hole of historical materialism and thus to render possible its *completion*, but, on the contrary, as the theory that enables us to conceptualize this hole of historical materialism as irreducible, because it is constitutive:

The 'Marxist theory of ideology' would then be symptomatic of the permanent discomfort Marxism maintains with its own critical recognition of the class struggle. . . . *the concept of ideology* denotes no other object than that of the nontotalizable (or nonrepresentable within a unique given order) complexity of the historical process; . . . historical materialism is incomplete and incomplete in principle, not only in the temporal dimension (since it postulates the relative unpredictability of the effects of determinate causes) but also in its theoretical 'topography', since it requires the articulation of the class struggle to concepts that have a different materiality (such as the unconscious).[37]

Can psychoanalysis effectively play this key role of providing the missing support of the Marxist theory of ideology (or, more precisely, of accounting for the very lack in the Marxist theory that becomes visible apropos of the deadlocks in the theory of ideology)? The standard reproach to psychoanalysis is that, in so far as it intervenes in the domain of the social and/or political, it ultimately always ends up in some version of the theory of the 'horde' with the feared-beloved Leader at its head, who dominates the subjects via the 'organic' libidinal link of transference, of a community constituted by some primordial crime and thus held together by shared guilt.[38]

The first answer to this reproach seems obvious: was not precisely this theoretical complex – the relationship between the mass and its Leader – the blind spot in the history of Marxism, what Marxist thought was unable to conceptualize, to 'symbolize', its 'foreclosed' that subsequently returned in the Real, in the guise of the so-called Stalinist cult of personality? The theoretical, as well as practical, solution to the problem of authoritarian populism–organicism that again and again thwarts progressive political projects is conceivable today only via psychoanalytic theory. This, however, in no way entails that psychoanalysis is somehow limited in its scope to the negative gesture of delineating the libidinal economy of 'regressive' proto-totalitarian communities: in the necessary obverse of this gesture, psychoanalysis also delineates the symbolic economy of how – from time to time, at least – we are able to break the vicious circle that breeds 'totalitarian' closure. When, for example, Claude Lefort articulated the notion of 'democratic invention', he did it through a reference to the Lacanian categories of the Symbolic and the Real: 'democratic invention' consists in the assertion of the purely symbolic, empty place of Power that no 'real' subject can ever fill out.[39] One should always bear in mind that the subject of psychoanalysis is not some primordial subject of drives, but – as Lacan pointed out again and again – the modern, Cartesian subject of science. There is a crucial difference between le Bon's and Freud's 'crowd': for Freud, 'crowd' is not a primordial, archaic entity, the starting point of evolution, but an 'artificial' pathological formation whose genesis is to be displayed – the 'archaic' character of the 'crowd' is precisely the illusion to be dispelled via theoretical analysis.

Perhaps a comparison with Freud's theory of dreams could be of some help here. Freud points out that within a dream we encounter the hard kernel of the Real precisely in the guise of a 'dream within the dream' – that is to say, where the distance from reality seems redoubled. In a somewhat homologous way, we encounter the inherent limit of social reality, what has to be foreclosed if the consistent field of reality is to emerge, precisely in the guise of the problematic of ideology, of a 'superstructure', of something that appears to be a mere epiphenomenon, a mirror-reflection, of 'true' social life. We are dealing here with the paradoxical topology in which the surface ('mere ideology') is directly linked to – occupies the place of, stands in for – what is 'deeper than depth itself', more real than reality itself.

Notes

1   See Étienne Balibar, 'Racism as Universalism', in *Masses, Classes, Ideas* (New York, Routledge, 1994), pp. 198–9.
2   Renata Salecl, *The Spoils of Freedom* (London, Routledge, 1994), p. 13.
3   See Jeffrey Masson, *The Assault on Truth: Freud's Suppression of the Seduction Theory* (New York, Farrar, Straus & Giroux, 1984).
4   Jacqueline Rose, 'Where Does the Misery Come From?', in Richard Feldstein and Judith Roof (eds), *Feminism and Psychoanalysis* (Ithaca, NY, and London: Cornell University Press, 1989), pp. 25–39.
5   The very title of Rose's article – 'Where Does the Misery Come From?' – is indicative here: one of the functions of ideology is precisely to explain the 'origins of Evil', to 'objectivize'-externalize its cause, and thus to discharge us of responsibility for it.
6   For that reason, the 'epochal horizons of pre-understanding' (the big theme of hermeneutics) cannot be designated as ideology.
7   For a concise account of the theoretical consequences of this double trauma, see Theodor W. Adorno, 'Messages in a Bottle', in Žižek (ed.), *Mapping Ideology*, ch. 1.

As for the way Adorno's critique of identitarian thought announces poststructur-alist 'deconstructionism', see Peter Dews, 'Adorno, Post-Structuralism and the Critique of Identity', ibid., ch. 2.

8   In his *La Philosophie de Marx* (Paris, La Découverte, 1993), Étienne Balibar drew attention to the enigma of the complete disappearance of the notion of ideology in Marx's texts after 1850. In *The German Ideology*, the (omnipresent) notion of ideology is conceived as the chimera that supplements social production and reproduction – the conceptual opposition that serves as its background is the one between the 'actual life-process' and its distorted reflection in the heads of ideologues. Things get complicated, however, the moment Marx engages in the 'critique of political economy': what he encounters here in the guise of 'com-modity fetishism' is no longer an 'illusion' that 'reflects' reality, but an uncanny chimera at work in the very heart of the actual process of social production.

The same enigmatic eclipse may be detected in many a post-Marxist author: Ernesto Laclau, for example, after the almost inflationary use of the concept of ideology in his *Politics and Ideology* (London, Verso, 1977), totally renounces it in *Hegemony and Socialist Strategy* (co-authored with Chantal Mouffe) (London, Verso, 1985).

9   To avoid a fatal misunderstanding, one must insist that this line of succession is not to be read as a hierarchical progress, as a 'sublation' or 'suppression' of the preceding mode. When, for example, we approach ideology in the guise of Ideological State Apparatuses, this in no way entails the obsolescence or irrele-vance of the level of argumentation. Today, when official ideology is increasingly indifferent towards its own consistency, an analysis of its inherent and constitutive inconsistencies is crucial if we are to pierce the actual mode of its functioning.

10   For an exemplary presentation of the Habermasian position, see Seyla Benhabib, 'The Critique of Instrumental Reason', in Žižek (ed.), *Mapping Ideology*, ch. 3.

11   See Oswald Ducrot, *Le Dire et le dit* (Paris, Éditions de Minuit, 1986).

12   See Michel Pêcheux, 'The Mechanism of Ideological (Mis)recognition', in Žižek (ed.), *Mapping Ideology*, ch. 6. One should bear in mind here that the key source of the critique of ideological evidences in the discourse analysis is Jacques Lacan's 'The Mirror-Phase as Formative of the Function of the I' (included in ibid. ch. 4), the text that introduced the concept of recognition (*reconnaissance*) as misrecogni-tion (*méconnaissance*).

13   See Laclau, *Politics and Ideology*.

14   See Louis Althusser, 'Ideology and Ideological State Apparatuses', in Žižek (ed.), *Mapping Ideology*, ch. 5.

15   Herein resides the interconnection between the ritual that pertains to ideological State Apparatuses and the act of interpellation: when I believe that I knelt down because of my belief, I simultaneously 'recognize' myself in the call of the Other-God who dictated that I kneel down... This point was developed by Isolde Charim in her intervention 'Dressur und Verneinung' at the colloquium *Der Althusser-Effekt*, Vienna, 17–20 March 1994.

16   See Theodor W. Adorno, 'Beitrag zur Ideologienlehre', in *Gesammelte Schriften: Ideologie* (Frankfurt, Suhrkamp, 1972).

17 See Wolfgang Fritz Haug, 'Annäherung an die faschistische Modalität des Ideologischen', in *Faschismus und Ideologie*, I, Argument-Sonderband 60 (Berlin, Argument Verlag, 1980).

18 Discourse analysis and the Althusserian reconceptualization of ideology also opened up a new approach in feminist studies. Its two representative cases are Michèle Barrett's post-Marxist discourse analysis (see her 'Ideology, Politics, Hegemony: From Gramsci to Laclau and Mouffe', in Žižek (ed.), *Mapping Ideology*, ch. 11) and Richard Rorty's pragmatist deconstructionism (see his 'Feminism, Ideology and Deconstruction: A Pragmatist View', in ibid., ch. 10).

19 See Nicholas Abercrombie, Stephen Hill and Bryan Turner, 'Determinacy and Indeterminacy in the Theory of Ideology'; and Göran Therborn's critical response, 'The New Questions of Subjectivity', both in ibid., ch. 7, 8). For a general overview of the historical development of the concept of ideology that led to this self-dispersal, see Terry Eagleton, 'Ideology and its Vicissitudes in Western Marxism', ibid., ch. 9.

20 For an approach to this 'implicit' ideology, see Pierre Bourdieu and Terry Eagleton, 'Doxa and Common Life', ibid., ch. 12.

21 For the notion of ideology that structures (social) reality, see Slavoj Žižek, 'How Did Marx Invent the Symptom?', ibid., ch. 14.

22 See Fredric Jameson, 'Postmodernism and the Market', ibid., ch. 13.

23 Cynicism as a postmodern attitude is superbly exemplified by one of the key features of Robert Altman's film *Nashville*: the enigmatic status of its songs. Altman, of course, maintains a critical distance from the universe of country music that epitomizes the *bêtise* of everyday American ideology: one entirely misses the point, however, if one perceives the songs performed in the film as a mocking imitation of 'true' country music – these songs are to be taken quite 'seriously'; one simply has to enjoy them. Perhaps the ultimate enigma of postmodernism resides in this coexistence of the two inconsistent attitudes, misperceived by the usual leftist criticism of young intellectuals who, although theoretically aware of the capitalist machinery of *Kulturindustrie*, unproblematically enjoy the products of rock industry.

24 Note the case of Kieslowski: his films shot in the damp, oppressive atmosphere of late Socialism (*Decalogue*) practise an almost unheard-of critique of ('official' as well as 'dissident') ideology; whereas the moment the left Poland for the 'freedom' of France, we witness the massive intrusion of ideology (see the New Age obscurantism of *La Double Vie de Véronique*).

25 Within the domain of the Law, this opposition between *Geist* and the obscene *Geisterwelt* assumes the form of the opposition between the explicit public written Law and its superego obverse – that is, the set of unwritten-unacknowledged rules that guarantee the cohesion of a community. (As to this opposition, see ch. 3 Slavoj Žižek, *The Metastases of Enjoyment* (London, Verso, 1994), ch. 3.) Suffice it to recall the mysteriously obscene institution of fraternities-sororities on American campuses, these half-clandestine communities with their secret rules of initiation where the pleasures of sex, drinking and so on and the spirit of authority

go hand in hand; or the image of the English public school in Lindsay Anderson's *If*: . . . the terror imposed by the elder students upon the younger, who are sub-mitted to the humiliating rituals of power and sexual abuse. Professors can thus play the role of good-humoured liberals, amusing students with jokes, entering the classroom on a bicycle, and so on – the true support of power lies elsewhere, in the elder students whose acts bear witness to an indiscernible mixture of Order and its Transgression, of sexual enjoyment and the 'repressive' exercise of power. In other words, what we find here is a transgression that serves as the ultimate support of Order, an indulgence in illicit sexuality that directly grounds 'repres-sion'.

26   See Jacques Derrida, *Spectres de Marx* (Paris, Galilée, 1993).

27   This gap that separates the Real from reality is what opens up the space for *performative* in its opposition to constative. That is to say, without the surplus of the Real over reality that emerges in the guise of a spectre, symbolization would merely designate, point towards, some positive content in reality. In its most radical dimension, performative is the attempt to conjure the real, to gentrify the spectre that is the Other: 'spectre' is originally the Other as such, another subject in the abyss of his or her freedom. Lacan's classic example: by saying 'You are my wife!', I thereby oblige-constrain the Other; I endeavour to entrap her abyss into a symbolic obligation.

28   This notion of antagonism comes, of course, from Laclau and Mouffe, *Hegemony and Socialist Strategy*.

29   What gets lost in the notion of social classes *qua* positive entities that get enmeshed in struggle only from time to time is the genuinely dialectical paradox of the relationship between the universal and the particular: although the whole of history hitherto is the history of class struggle (as Marx claims at the beginning of chapter 1 of *The Communist Manifesto*), there exists (one is almost tempted to write it: ex-sists) *stricto sensu* only one class, the bourgeoisie, the capitalist class. Prior to capitalism, classes were not yet 'for themselves', not yet 'posited as such'; they did not properly exist but 'insisted' as the underlying structuring principle that found its expression in the guise of states, castes, moments of the organic social edifice, of society's 'corporate body', whereas the proletariat *stricto sensu* is no longer a class but a class that coincides with its opposite, a non-class – the historical tendency to negate class division is inscribed into its very class position.

30   For this Hitchcockian analogy I am indebted to Isolde Charim and Robert Pfaller.

31   In the case of sexual difference, the theological name for this third asexual position is 'angel'; for that reason, the question of the *sex of angels* is absolutely crucial for a materialist analysis.

32   This point was developed by Robert Pfaller in his intervention 'Zum Althusser-ianischen Nominalismus' at the colloquium *Der Althusser-Effekt*.

33   F. W. J. Schelling, 'Clara', in *Sämtliche Werke* (Stuttgart, Cotta, 1856–61), vol. 9 p. 39.

34   Or, to put this distance of ours towards Derrida in a different way: does not Derrida himself, apropos of the spectre, get caught up in the logic of conjuration?

According to Derrida, the ultimate 'source of evil' resides in the ontologization of the spectre, in the reduction of its undecidable status (with reference to the couple reality/illusion) to a 'mere appearance' opposed to some (ideal or real) full existence. Derrida's entire effort is directed into ensuring that the spectre will remain the spectre, into preventing its ontologization – is not Derrida's theory itself, therefore, a conjuration destined to preserve the spectre in the intermediate space of the living dead? Does not this lead him to repeat the classic metaphysical paradox of the conjunction of impossibility and prohibition that he himself articulated apropos of the supplement (the supplement *cannot* endanger the purity of the Origin, which is why we must *fight against it*): the spectre *cannot* be ontologized, which is why this ontologization *must not* happen, one should fight against it. . . .

35   Étienne Balibar, 'Politics and Truth: The Vacillation of Ideology, II', in *Masses, Classes, Ideas*, p. 173.

36   If it is to play this crucial role, the concept of the unconscious is to be conceived in the strictly Freudian sense, as 'trans-individual' – that is, beyond the ideological opposition of 'individual' and 'collective' unconscious: the subject's unconscious is always grounded in a transferential relationship towards the Other; it is always 'external' with regard to the subject's monadic existence.

37   Balibar, 'Politics and Truth', pp. 173–4.

38   One is usually quick to add that this structure of the community of guilt dominated by the feared-beloved paternal figure of the Leader has been faithfully reproduced in all psychoanalytic organizations, from the International Psycho-analytical Association to Lacan's *École freudienne*.

39   See Claude Lefort, *Democracy and Political Theory* (Cambridge, Polity Press, 1988).

4

Fantasy as a Political Category: A Lacanian Approach

This is an article from the *Journal for the Psychoanalysis of Culture and Society* (vol. 1:2 (Fall 1996), pp. 77–85). It explores the part played by fantasy in maintaining both the consistency of subjects and the solidarity of groups. But, paradoxically, fantasy reveals the very transgressions it affects to hide: it endeavours to suppress the scandal of the Real, but in so doing inevitably provokes the return of the repressed, which breaks out in unexpected material forms. Thus, although the scandal appears to be securely sanitized by the operations of fantasy, it is fantasy itself that produces what is scandalous. However utilitarian the object is, it never-theless contains ideological evidence, as in the example given of the variation in toilet design from country to country, which reveals in turn German thoroughness, French fastidiousness and American pragmatism.

Žižek examines four aspects of the construction of the subject. First, the subject's focus of identification does not correspond to its appearance in its own narrative; it would rather see itself from the favourable viewpoint of the ego-ideal. Fantasy enables the subject to choose from a variety of 'subject-positions', as long as none of them betrays what the fantasy is there for, to give the subject substance and thus hide its split. Second, fantasy always includes the 'impossible gaze' of the Other, which makes the subject assume that its 'substance' has been there from time imme-morial and it cannot resituate itself. Žižek illustrates the dilemma of being fixed by this timeless gaze with a pro-life parable in which aborted children live alone on an island, sadly contemplating the parents who deserted them; theirs is an 'impossible gaze' evoking endless parental guilt for their life in limbo. Thus it is always a question of where the gaze is coming from. In the operations of Mother Teresa a double 'ideological profit' can be detected: while she stopped the poor from politicizing their predicament by making them see poverty as a way to redemption, at the same time she worked on the guilt of the rich by appealing to them for charitable donations. Underlying this scenario is Calcutta pictured as a place so hopeless that all that can be done is offer charity. Third, the fantasmatic scene is not a transgression but a support. Oddly enough, the fantasy does not stage the breaking of the law, but rather the establishing of it – that is, the moment of castration. This is why fantasy 'is in its very notion close to perversion', since the pervert is always staging a total severity of the Law, wanting the Law to illumine him fully. Fourth, for fantasy to work, the everyday world has to be kept separate from the fantasy that upholds it. In David Lynch's film *Wild at Heart*, the woman is forced to bring her rape fantasy into the light of day, her humiliation being all the greater because she is robbed of this fantasmatic support after being drawn into an open consent to it, only to be rejected (a brutal failure of the seduction fantasy). The point is that subjectivity fades if the fantasy is realized, for being a subject depends on the split between its fantasmatic support and its Symbolic/Imaginary identifications. If the balance is disturbed, the subject will lose either its stake in the Real or its identification in the Symbolic.

These four features are brought to bear on the notion of 'fantasy as a political category'. In a film like *M*A*S*H* the ideology capitalizes on the enjoyment of behind-the-scenes transgressions which, far from representing a rebellion, support the system. All ideologies make this appeal to a 'trans-ideological kernel' – witness National Socialism, which encouraged an 'ecstatic aestheticized experience of community', more sinister than its attempt to politicize the whole of social life. These two false modes of promoting identification fail, because there is a gap between solidarity and alienation: too far into either ignores the split in the Law between letter and spirit, Symbolic and Real. What supports identification is the Freudo-Lacanian 'unary trait', a chance feature in the other upon which the subject founds its being – not the grand symbols of unity, but rather something particular that marks it off from them: when a 'flaw' is discovered in a leader, the unconscious complicity of the group, themselves implicated in this knowledge, strengthens its solidarity. What distinguishes one subject from another, then, is the something that the Symbolic does not recognize, the Lacanian *objet a* as the inscrutable cause of desire.

When, a couple of years ago, the disclosure of Michael Jackson's alleged 'immoral' private behaviour (his sexual games with boys under age) dealt a blow to his innocent Peter Pan image elevated above sexual and race differences (or concerns), some perspicacious commentators asked the obvious question: what's all the fuss about? Wasn't this so-called dark side of Michael Jackson all the time here for all of us to see, in the video spots that accompanied his musical releases and that were saturated with ritualized violence and obscene sexual gestures (exemplarily in the case of Thriller and Bad)? This paradox illustrates perfectly Lacan's thesis according to which 'the unconscious is outside', not hidden in any unfathomable depths – or, to quote *The X Files* motto: 'The truth is out there.'

Such a focusing on material externality proves very fruitful in the analysis of the inherent antagonisms of an ideological edifice. Do not the two opposed architectural designs of Casa del Fascio (the local headquarters of the Fascist Party), Adolfo Coppede's neo-Imperial pastiche from 1928, and Giuseppe Teragni's highly modernist transparent glass-house from 1934–6, in their simple juxtaposition, reveal the inherent contradiction of the Fascist ideological project, which simultaneously advocates a return to pre-modern organicist corporatism and the unheard-of mobilization of all social forces in the service of rapid modernization? An even better example is provided by the great projects of public buildings in the Soviet Union of the 1930s, which put on the top of a flat multi-storey office building a gigantic statue of the idealized New Man or couple. Within a couple of years, the tendency became clearly discernible to flatten even more the office building – the actual working place for the living people – so that it changed more and more into a mere pedestal for the larger-than-life statue – does this external, material feature of architectural design not render visible the 'truth' of the Stalinist ideology in which actual, living people are reduced to instruments, sacrificed as the pedestal for the spectre of the future New Man, an ideological monster that crushes under his feet actual living men? The paradox is that whereas anyone in the Soviet Union of the 1930s who might say openly that the vision of the Socialist New Man was an ideological monster squashing actual people would immediately be arrested – it was allowed, and even encouraged, to make this point via the architectural design: 'the truth is out there.' What we are thus arguing is not simply that ideology permeates also the alleged extra-ideological strata of everyday life, but that this materialization of ideology in the external materiality renders visible inherent antagonisms that the explicit formulation of ideology cannot afford to acknowledge. It is as if an ideological edifice, in order to function 'normally', must obey a kind of 'imp of perversity', and articulate its inherent antagonism in the externality of its material existence.

This externality which directly materializes ideology is also occluded as 'utility'. That is to say, in everyday life, ideology is at work, especially in the apparently innocent reference to pure utility. One should never forget that in the symbolic universe, 'utility' functions as a reflective notion: it always involves the assertion of utility as meaning. For example, a man with a Land Rover who lives in a large city owns such a car in order to signal that he leads his life under the sign of a no-nonsense, 'real life' attitude. The unsurpassed master of such analysis, of course, was Claude Lévi-Strauss, whose semiotic triangle of preparing food (raw, baked, boiled) demonstrated how food also serves as 'food for thought'. As a supplement to his brilliant work, one is tempted to propose that shit can also serve as a *matière-à-penser*: do not the three basic types of toilets form a kind of excremental correlative counterpoint to the Lévi-Straussian triangle of cooking? In a traditional German toilet, the hole in which shit disappears after we flush water is way in front, so that shit is first laid out for us to sniff at and inspect for traces of illness. In the typical French toilet, on the contrary, the hole is in the back: shit is supposed to disappear as soon as possible. Finally, the American toilet presents a kind of synthesis, a mediation between these two opposed poles – the toilet basin is full of water, so that the shit floats in it, visible, but not to be inspected. It is clear that none of these versions can be accounted for in purely utilitarian terms: a certain ideological perception of how the subject should relate to the unpleasant excrement which comes from within our body is clearly discernible in it.

Thus, while it is easy for an academic to claim at a round table that we live in a post-ideological universe – the moment he visits the rest-room after the heated discussion, he is again overtaken by ideology. The ideological invest-ment of such references to utility is attested by their dialogical character: the American toilet acquires its meaning only through its differential relation to French and German toilets. The same goes for the different ways one washes the dishes. In Denmark, for example, a detailed set of features opposes it to the way they do it in Sweden, and a close analysis soon reveals how this opposition is used to index the fundamental perception of Danish national identity, which is defined in opposition to Sweden (see Linde-Laursen, 1995). And, to reach in an even more intimate domain, do we not encounter the same semiotic triangle in the three main hair-styles of the feminine sex organ's pubic hair? The wildly grown, unkempt pubic hair indexes the hippie attitude of natural spontaneity; yuppies prefer the disciplinary procedure of a French garden (one shaves the hair on both sides close to legs, so that all that remains is a narrow band in the middle with a clear-cut shave line); and in the punk attitude, the vagina is wholly shaved and furnished with rings (usually attached to a perfor-ated clitoris). Is this not yet another version of the Lévi-Straussian semiotic triangle of 'raw' wild hair, well-kept 'baked' hair, and shaved 'boiled' hair?

One can thus see how even the most intimate attitude towards one's body is used to make an ideological statement.

How, then, does this material existence of ideology relate to our conscious convictions? Bergson emphasized how Molière's Tartuffe is funny not only on account of his hypocrisy, but because he gets caught in his own mask of hypocrisy:

He immersed himself so well into the role of a hypocrite that he played it as it were sincerely. This way and only this way he becomes funny. Without this purely material sincerity, without the attitude and speech which, through the long practice of hypocrisy, became for him a natural way to act, Tartuffe would be simply repulsive. (Bergson, 1987, p. 83)

The expression 'purely material sincerity' announces the Althusserian notion of Ideological State Apparatuses, of the external ritual that materializes ideology: the subject who maintains his distance towards the ritual is unaware of the fact that the ritual already dominates him from within. As Pascal put it, if you do not believe, kneel down, act as if you believe, and belief will come by itself. This is also what the Marxian 'commodity fetishism' is about: in his explicit self-awareness, a capitalist is a common-sense nominalist, but the 'purely material sincerity' of his deeds displays the 'theological whimsies' of the commodity universe.

Another way to put it is to say that this 'purely material sincerity' of the external ideological ritual, not the depth of the subject's inner convictions and desires, is the true locus of the fantasy that sustains an ideological edifice. The standard notion of the way fantasy works within ideology is that of a fantasy-scenario that obfuscates the true horror of a situation: instead of the full rendering of the antagonisms that traverse our society, for example, we indulge in the notion of society as an organic whole kept together by forces of solidarity and co-operation. However, here too it is much more productive to look for this notion of fantasy where one would not expect to find it, in marginal and, again, apparently purely utilitarian situations. Suffice it to recall the safety instructions prior to the take-off of an airplane. Aren't they sustained by a fantasmatic scenario of how a possible plane-crash will look? After a gentle landing on water miraculously, it is always supposed to happen on water!), each of the passengers puts on the life-jacket and, as on a beach toboggan, slides into the water and takes a swim, like a nice collective lagoon holiday experience under the guidance of an experienced swimming instructor. Is not this 'gentrifying' of a catastrophe (a nice soft landing, stewardesses in a dance-like style graciously pointing with their hands towards the 'Exit' signs) also ideology at its purest? However, the psychoanalytic notion of fantasy cannot be reduced to that of a fantasy-scenario that obfuscates the true horror of a situation. The first, rather obvious thing to add is that the relationship between fantasy and the horror of the Real that it conceals is much more ambiguous than it may seem: fantasy conceals this horror, yet at the same time it creates what it purports to conceal, its 'repressed' point of reference. Are not the images of the ultimate horrible Thing, from the deep-sea gigantic squid to the ravaging twister, fantasmatic creations *par excellence*? Furthermore, one should specify the notion of fantasy with a whole series of features.[1]

First, the answer to the question, 'How is the (fantasizing) subject inscribed into the fantasmatic narrative?', is far from obvious. Even when the subject appears in person in his own narrative, this is not automatically his point of identification. That is, he by no means necessarily 'identifies with himself'. Far more usual is the identification with the ego-ideal, with the gaze for which – the point of view from which – I, in my activity depicted in the fantasmatic narrative, appear in a likeable way. In the standard pornographic scene – a man doing 'it' to a woman – the spectator does not identify with the man who fucks the woman. Woman is as a rule asserted as the exhibitionist subject who fully enjoys doing it and being viewed by the spectator doing it, in clear contrast to the man, who is reduced to the pure, faceless instrument of woman's enjoyment. If he sometimes wears a mask, this mask does not allow every spectator to identify himself with the man doing it to her, but rather hides the fact that there is nothing to hide; that is, it emphasizes the man's desubjectivized, mechanical status. The spectator, far from identifying with the male actor, rather identifies with the Third implicit position, that of a pure gaze observing the woman who fully enjoys herself. The spectator's satisfaction is of a purely reflective nature: it derives from the awareness that a woman can find full satisfaction in phallic enjoyment.

Thus, not only does the fantasizing subject as a rule not identify with his own appearance within the fantasmatic space; even more radically, fantasy creates a multitude of 'subject-positions' among which the (observing, fantasizing) subject is free to float, to shift his identification from one to another. Here, the talk about 'multiple, dispersed subject-positions' is justified, with the proviso that these subject-positions are to be strictly distinguished from the void of the subject ($). The voyeurist sado-masochist play, for example, between Isabella Rossellini and Dennis Hopper in Lynch's *Blue Velvet* implies three 'subject-positions': it can be conceived as staged for the voyeurist in the closet secretly observing the scene (Kyle MacLachlan); for the obscene, impotent father, who, obviously aware of being observed, endeavours to project the image of his potency; and, finally, for the depressed woman herself, to draw her back into the life circuit by means of a kind of shock therapy.[2]

The second point is that fantasy always involves an impossible gaze by means of which the subject is already present at the act of his/her own conception. An exemplary case of this vicious cycle in the service of ideology is an anti-abortion fairy-tale written in the 1980s by Joze Snoj, a Slovene right-wing nationalist poet. The tale takes place on an idyllic South Sea island where the aborted children live together without their parents: although their life is nice and calm, they miss parental love, and spend their time in sad reflections on how their parents preferred a career or a luxurious holiday to them. The trick, of course, resides in the fact that the aborted children are presented as having been born, only into an alternative universe (the lone Pacific island), retaining the memory of parents who 'betrayed' them. This way, they can direct at their parents a reproachful gaze which makes them guilty.

Apropos of a fantasmatic scene, the question to be asked is thus always: for which gaze is it staged? Which narrative is it destined to support? According to some recently published documents, the British General Michael Rose, head of the UNPROFOR forces in Bosnia, and his special team of SAS operatives definitely had another 'hidden agenda' in Bosnia. Under the pretence of maintaining truce between the so-called warring factions, their secret task was to put the blame on Croats, and especially Muslims. Soon after the fall of Srebrenica, for example, Rose's operatives suddenly 'discovered' in the north of Bosnia some Serb bodies allegedly slaughtered by the Muslims; and their attempts to 'mediate' between Muslims and Croats actually inflamed the conflict between them. These diversions were intended to create the perception of the Bosnian conflict as a kind of 'tribal warfare', a civil war of everybody against everybody else in which 'all sides are equally to blame'. Instead of clear condemnation of the Serb aggression, this perception was destined to prepare the terrain for an international effort of 'pacification' which would 'reconcile the warring factions'. From a sovereign state, victim of aggression, Bosnia was suddenly transformed into a chaotic place in which 'power-mad warlords' acted out their historical traumas at the expense of innocent women and children. What lurks in the background, of course, is the pro-Serbian attitude according to which peace in Bosnia is possible only if we do not 'demonize' one side in the conflict: responsibility is to be equally distributed, with the West assuming the role of the neutral judge elevated above the local tribal conflicts. For our analysis, the key point is that General Rose's pro-Serb 'secret war' on the terrain itself was trying not to change the relation of military forces, but rather to prepare ground for a different narrative perception of the situation: 'real' military activity itself was here in the service of ideological narrativization.

The same operation is easily discernible in the abundant media reports on the 'saintly' activities of Mother Teresa in Calcutta, which clearly rely on the fantasmatic screen of the Third World. Calcutta is regularly presented as Hell on Earth, the exemplary case of the decaying Third World megalopolis, full of social decay, poverty, violence and corruption, with its residents caught in terminal apathy (facts are, of course, totally different: Calcutta is a city bursting with activity, culturally much more thriving than Bombay, with a successful local Communist government maintaining a whole network of social services). In this picture of utter gloom, Mother Teresa brings a ray of hope to the dejected with the message that poverty is to be accepted as a way to redemption, since in enduring their sad fate with silent dignity and faith the poor repeat Christ's way of the cross. The ideological profit of this operation is double: in so far as one proposes to the poor and terminally ill to look for salvation in their very suffering, Mother Teresa deters them from probing into the causes of their predicament – i.e., from politicizing their situation. At the same time, she offers the rich from the West the possibility of a kind of substitute redemption by making financial contributions to Mother Teresa's charitable activity. And, again, all this works against the background of the fantasmatic image of the Third World as Hell on Earth, as the place so utterly desolate that no political activity, only charity and compassion, can alleviate the suffering (see Hitchens, 1995).

The third point is that contrary to the common-sense notion of fantasizing as indulging in the hallucinatory realization of desires prohibited by the Law, the fantasmatic narrative does not stage the suspension-transgression of the Law, but is rather the very act of its installation, of the intervention of the cut of symbolic castration. What the fantasy endeavours to stage is ultimately the 'impossible' scene of castration. For that reason, fantasy as such is, in its very notion, close to perversion. The perverse ritual stages the act of castration, of the primordial loss that allows the subject to enter the symbolic order. Or, to put it in a more precise way: in contrast to the 'normal' subject, for whom Law functions as the agency of prohibition that regulates (the access to the object of) his desire, for the pervert, the object of his desire is the Law itself; the Law is the Ideal he is longing for, he wants to be fully acknowledged by Law, integrated into its functioning. The irony of this fact should not escape us: the pervert, this 'transgressor' *par excellence* who purports to violate all the rules of 'normal' and decent behaviour, in effect longs for the very rule of Law.[3]

At the political level, suffice it to recall the interminable search for the fantasmatic point at which German history 'took the wrong turn' which ended up in Nazism: the delayed national unification due to the dismemberment of the German empire after the Thirty Years' War; the aestheticization of politics in the Romantic reaction to Kant (the theory of Jean-Luc Nancy and Philippe Lacoue-Labarthe); the 'crisis of investiture' and the Bismarck state socialism in the second half of nineteenth century; all the way back to the report of the German tribes' resistance to Romans which allegedly already displayed the features of *Volksgemeinschaft*. Similar examples abound. When exactly, for instance, did patriarchal repression coincide with the repression and exploitation of nature? Eco-feminism provides a multitude of 'regressive' determinations of this unique fantasmatic moment of the Fall: the predominance of nineteenth-century Western capitalism; the modern Cartesian science with its objectivizing attitude towards nature; the Greek rationalist Socratic Enlightenment; the emergence of great barbarian empires; back to the passage from nomadic to agricultural civilization. And, as was pointed out by Jacques-Alain Miller, is Foucault himself also not caught in the same fantasmatic loop in his search for the moment when the Western order of sexuality emerged. He regressed further and further back from modernity, until he finally set the limit at the disintegration of the antique ethic of the 'care of the Self' into the Christian ethics of confession. The fact that the tone of Foucault's last two books on pre-Christian ethics differs thoroughly from his earlier probing into the complex of power, knowledge and sexuality – instead of his usual analyses of the material micro-practices of ideology, we get a rather standard version of the 'history of ideas' – bears witness to the fact that Foucault's Greece and Rome 'before the Fall' (into sexuality–guilt–confession) are purely fantasmatic entities.

The fourth point is that constitutive of fantasy's efficiency is the gap between the subject's everyday symbolic universe and its fantasmatic support. One of the most painful and troubling scenes from Lynch's *Wild at Heart* brings into play the tension between reality and its fantasmatic background. In a lonely motel room, Willem Dafoe exerts a rude pressure on Laura Dern: he touches and squeezes her, invading the space of her intimacy and repeating in a threatening way, 'Say fuck me!' – i.e., extorting from her a word that would signal her consent to a sexual act. The ugly, unpleasant scene drags on, and when, finally, the exhausted Laura Dern utters a barely audible 'Fuck me!', Dafoe abruptly steps away, assumes a nice, friendly smile, and cheerfully retorts: 'No, thanks, I don't have time today; but on another occasion I would do it gladly.' He has attained what he really wanted: not the act itself, just her consent to it, her symbolic humiliation. What we have here is rape in fantasy which refuses its realization in reality, and thus further humiliates its victim – the fantasy is forced out, aroused, and then abandoned, thrown upon the victim. That is to say, it is clear that Laura Dern is not simply disgusted by Dafoe's (Bobby Perou's) brutal intrusion into her intimacy: just prior to her 'Fuck me!', the camera focuses on her right hand, which she slowly spreads out, the sign of her acquiescence, the proof that he has stirred up her fantasy. The point is thus to read this scene in a Lévi-Straussian way, as an inversion of the standard scene of seduction, in which the gentle approach is followed by the brutal sexual act, after the woman, the target of the seducer's efforts, finally says 'Yes!'

One of the most repulsive racist rituals from the American Old South was to force the African-American cornered by a white gang to commit the first gesture of insult: while the African-American was held tightly by his captors, a white racist thug shoured at him, 'Spit on me! Tell me I'm scum!' and so on, in order to extort from him the 'occasion' for a brutal beating or lynching – as if the white racist wanted to set up retroactively the proper dialogical context for his violent outburst. Here we encounter the perversity of the injurious word at its purest. The proper order of succession and implication is perverted: in a mocking imitation of the 'normal' order, I compel the victim to insult me voluntarily – i.e., to assume the discursive position of the offender and thereby to justify my violent outburst. It is easy to perceive the homology with the scene from *Wild at Heart*: the point of this repulsive racist ritual is not simply that white thugs compel the well-meaning humble Uncle Tomish African-American to offend them against his will. Both parties are well aware that the besieged African-American does cultivate aggressive fantasies about his white oppressors, that he does consider them scum (in a quite justified way, considering the brutal oppression he and his race have been exposed to), and their pressure serves to awaken these fantasies, so that, when the African-American finally spits on the white thug or tells him 'You're scum!', he in a way lets go his defences, his sense of survival, and displays his true desire, cost him what it may. This is exactly like Laura Dern in *Wild at Heart* who, in saying 'Fuck me!', yields not only to external pressure but also to her fantasmatic kernel of *jouissance*. In short, the poor African-American is beaten (probably killed) for his desire.

The traumatic impact of these two scenes thus relies on the gap between the subject's everyday symbolic universe and its fantasmatic support. Let us approach this gap through another disturbing phenomenon. When attention is drawn to the fact that women often do fantasize about being handled brutally and raped, the standard answer to it is either that this is a male fantasy about women or that women only have such fantasies in so far as they have 'internalized' the patriarchal libidinal economy and endorsed their victimization. The underlying idea is that the moment we recognize this fact of day-dreaming about rape, we open the door to the male-chauvinist platitudes about how, in being raped, women only get what they secretly wanted; their shock and fear only express the fact that they were not honest enough to acknowledge this. To this commonplace, one should answer that (some) women actually may day-dream about being raped, but that this fact not only in no way legitimizes the actual rape, it makes it even more violent. Consider two women, the first, liberated and assertive, active; the other, secretly day-dreaming about being brutally handled by her partner, even raped. The crucial point is that, if both of them are raped, the rape will be much more traumatic for the second one, on account of the very fact that it will realize in 'external' social reality the 'stuff of her dreams'. Perhaps a better way to put it would be to paraphrase yet again the immortal lines of Stalin: it is impossible to say which of the two rapes would be worse. They are both worse. Rape against one's attitude, of course, is in away worse, since it violates our disposition. But on the other hand, the very fact that rape was done in accordance with our secret disposition makes it even worse.[4]

There is a gap that for ever separates the fantasmatic kernel of the subject's being from the more 'superficial' modes of his or her symbolic and/or imaginary identifications. It is never possibly for me fully to assume (in the sense of symbolic integration) the fantasmatic kernel of my being. When one approaches it too often, or when one comes too close to it, what occurs is the aphanisis of the subject: the subject loses his or her symbolic consistency, it disintegrates. And, perhaps, the forced actualization in social reality itself of the fantasmatic kernel of my being is the worst, most humiliating kind of violence, a violence which undermines the very base of my identity (of my 'self-image'). Another way to make the same point is to draw attention to the crucial fact that men who actually perform rapes do not fantasize about raping women – on the contrary, they fantasize about being gentle, about finding a loving partner; rape is rather a violent *passage à l'acte* emerging from their incapacity to find such a partner in real life.[5]

All these features allow us to approach the way fantasy functions in an ideological edifice. Let us recall Robert Altman's, *M*A*S*H*, which occupies an exceptional place: at the beginning of the director's opus, it negates its basic 'tone', so that all his later films can be read as so many attempts to surmount the ideological limitations of *M*A*S*H*. That is to say, contrary to the misleading appearance, *M*A*S*H* is a perfectly conformist film: through all their mockery of authority, practical jokes, sexual escapades and so on, the members of the *M*A*S*H* crew exemplarily perform their job, and thus present absolutely no threat to the smooth running of the military machine. No wonder the film served as the base for a long-running and definitely not 'subversive' TV series. In other words, the cliché about *M*A*S*H* as an anti-militarist film depicting the horrors of the meaningless military slaughter which can be endured only through a healthy measure of cynicism, practical jokes, laughing at the pompous official rituals and so on misses the point. This very distance is ideology. Ideological identification exerts a true hold on us precisely when we maintain an awareness that we are not fully identical to it, that there is a rich human person beneath it. The position, 'not all is ideology, beneath the ideological mask, I am also a human person', is the very form of ideology, of its 'practical efficiency'. The close analysis of even the most 'totalitarian' ideological edifice inevitably reveals that in it, not everything is 'ideology' (in the popular sense of the 'politically instrumentalized legitimization of power relations'): in every ideological edifice, there is a kind of 'trans-ideological' kernel, since, if an ideology is to become operative and effectively 'seize' individuals, it has to parasitize on and manipulate some kind of 'trans-ideological' vision that cannot be reduced to a simple instrument of legitimizing pretensions to power (notions and sentiments of solidarity, justice, belonging to a community, and so on).

Is not a kind of 'authentic' vision discernible even in Nazism (the notion of the deep solidarity that keeps together the 'community of people'), not to mention Stalinism? The point is thus not only that there is no ideology without a trans-ideological, 'authentic' kernel, but rather that it is only the reference to such a trans-ideological kernel that renders an ideology 'workable'. In one of his speeches to the Nazi crowd in Nuremberg, Hitler made a self-referential remark about how this very reunion is to be perceived: an external observer unable to experience the 'inner greatness' of the Nazi movement will see only the display of external military and political strength, while for us, members of the movement who live and breathe with it, it is infinitely more, the assertion of the inner link connecting us. Here again we encounter the reference to the extra-ideological kernel. Hitler's favourite Wagner opera was neither the overtly German *Meistersinger* nor *Lohengrin* with its call to arms to defend Germany against the Eastern hordes, but *Tristan* with its tendency to leave behind the Day – the daily life of symbolic obligations, honours, debts and so on – and to immerse oneself in the Night, to embrace ecstatically one's death. This 'aesthetic suspension of the political' (to paraphrase Kierkegaard) was at the very core of the fantasmatic background of the Nazi attitude: at stake in it was 'something more than politics', an ecstatic aestheticized experience of Community best exemplified precisely by the nightly rituals during the Nuremberg rallies. So, paradoxically, the dangerous ingredient of Nazism is not its 'utter politicization' of the entire social life, but, on the contrary, the suspension of the political via the reference to an extra-ideological kernel, much stronger than in a 'normal' democratic political order.

Therein, perhaps, resides the problem with Judith Butler's question:

Does politicization always need to overcome disidentification? What are the possibilities of politicizing disidentification, this experience of misrecognition, this uneasy sense of standing under a sign to which one does and does not belong? (1994, p. 219)

Is not, however, the attitude of the heroes of *M*A*S*H* precisely that of an active *dis*identification? Of course, one can argue that this disidentification is something entirely different from the lesbian parodic imitation/subversion of feminine codes. None the less, the point remains that the difference is the one between the two modes of *dis*identification, not between identification and its subversion. Or, to put it in a more precise way: an ideological edifice can be undermined by a too literal identification, which is why its successful functioning requires a minimum of distance toward its explicit rules. Is not an exemplary case of the subversion-through-identification provided by Jaroslav Hasek's *The Good Soldier Schwejk*, the novel whose hero causes total havoc by simply executing the orders of his superiors in an over-zealous and all too literal way? Everything hinges on the crucial fact that the Law is already split in itself, which is why an all too direct identification with it cripples its functioning.

The inevitable conclusion to be drawn from this paradox is that the feature that effectively sustains identification – the famous Freudian-Lacanian *einziger Zug*, the unary feature – is not the obvious one, the big 'official' insignia, but a small feature, even the one of taking a distance toward the official insignia. When a lesbian imitates-parodies-repeats-subverts the standard feminine code, does she not thereby, at a 'deeper' level, assert her 'true' queer identity, which requires such an ironic-subverting-parodizing attitude? A different example of the same logic is provided by the leader 'caught with his pants down': the solidarity of the group is strengthened by the subjects' common disavowal of the misfortune that laid open the leader's failure or impotence. A shared lie is an incomparably more effective bond for a group than the truth. When, in an academic department, members of the inner circle around a famous professor are aware of some flaw of his (he is addicted to drugs, a kleptomaniac, a sexual masochist pervert; he has stolen a key line of argumentation from a student; and so on), this very knowledge of the flaw – together with the willingness to disavow this knowledge – is the true nature of identification that keeps the group together.[6] One should introduce here the difference between the Lacanian S and a, between identification at the level of symbolic and/or imaginary features and its real kernel: a 'real' identification requires 'something more', some ineffable *je ne sais quoi* that transpires only through the distance toward the 'official' symbolic features.

The Duellists, Ridley Scott's extraordinary directorial début (based on a short story by Heinrich Kleist), depicts the life-long combat between two high-ranking soldiers, a true upper-class nobleman and an aspiring officer of middle-class origins. What keeps them for ever apart is the difference in the way each of them relates to the upper-class code of honour: the aspiring middle-class officer doggedly follows this code, and for that very reason generates the lasting impression of awkward ridicule, while his counterpart, the nobleman, constantly violates the explicit rules of the official code, and thereby asserts his true upper-classness. The problem of the aspiring lower-middle classes is that they

misperceive the true cause of their failure. They think they are missing something, some golden rule, so that they have to learn to follow even more closely
all the rules. What they misperceive is that the mysterious X that accounts for
the true upper-classness cannot be pin-pointed to a specific positive symbolic
feature.[7] Here, we encounter again *l'objet petit a*: when we are dealing with two
series of behaviour that cannot be distinguished by any clearly defined positive
symbolic feature, and yet the difference between the two is the unmistakable
difference between true high-classness and its clumsy imitation, that unfathomable X, the *je ne sais quoi* that accounts for this gap – in short, the object that
makes the difference where one cannot establish any positive difference – is
precisely *l'object petit a* as the unfathomable object-cause of desire. One can also
say that the Lacanian *objet petit a* is the ultimate shibboleth, the element which
accounts for the difference where no difference is perceptible. Were the Nazis
not all the time in search of a shibboleth that would allow them clearly to
identify Jews, like the humans in science-fiction films on the invasion of
mimicker aliens who are desperately searching for a tiny feature by means of
which one can identify an alien?

Notes

1 I will not consider here the three key features that I already developed elsewhere
   (see Žižek *Metastases of Enjoyment*): (1) the tension in the notion of fantasy between
   its beatific and disturbing dimensions; (2) the fact that fantasy does not simply
   realize a desire in a hallucinatory way, but rather constitutes our desire, provides its
   co-ordinates – i.e., literally 'teaches us how to desire'; (3) the fact that the desire
   staged in a fantasy is ultimately not the (fantasizing) subject's own desire but the
   desire of his/her Other: fantasy is an answer to the question, 'What am I for the
   Other? What does the Other want from me?'
2 For a more detailed analysis of this scene, see ibid., ch. 5.
3 A further point about the pervert is that since, for him, the Law is not fully
   established (the Law is his lost object of desire), he supplements this lack with an
   intricate set of regulations (see the masochist ritual). The crucial point is thus to bear
   in mind the opposition between Law and regulations (or 'rules'): the latter witness
   to the absence or suspension of Law.
4 And the same goes for the male side: a gay man who has fantasies of being
   sodomized will probably be more hurt when actually raped than a straight man.
5 Another point of ambiguity: men who rape women are either totally ignorant of
   how the victim reacts to being raped, or they force her to fake pleasure, or they find
   supplementary pleasure in her being horrified.
6 For a more detailed account of this paradox of the 'leader caught with his pants
   down', see ibid., ch. 3.

7 This unfathomable distinction between true upper-classness and the false upper-classness of the middle classes is, of course, a constant theme in the work of Pierre Bourdieu. To put it in Hegelian terms, the difference is here between the In-itself and the For-itself: upper classes lives their code 'in itself', while middle classes which consciously aspire to it relate to it 'for itself', in a reflected way, and thus spoil the effect, which has to emerge as a 'by-product'. The same goes for fashion: the aspiring middle classes doggedly follow the fashion, and thus always lag behind, while the upper classes freely violate the rules of fashion, and thus personify its trends.

References

Bergson, Henri 1937: *An Essay on Laughter*. London: Smith.

Butler, Judith 1994: *Bodies that Matter*. New York and London: Routledge.

Hitchens, Christopher 1995: *The Missionary Position*. London and New York: Verso.

Linde-Laursen, Anders 1995: Small differences – large issues. *South Atlantic Quarterly*, 94, pp. 45–73.

Žižek, Slavoj 1994: *The Metastases of Enjoyment*. London and New York: Verso.

5

Is it Possible to Traverse the Fantasy in Cyberspace?

In this essay, published for the first time, Žižek considers how an engagement with cyberspace, through the distancing it offers, can allow particular structures of fantasy to surface. This distancing from actual
experience most commonly takes the form of 'interpassivity', because
the surfer is active with the intention of rendering the 'anonymous "big
Other"' passive, so that he or she can reach the security of a narcissistic
identification, and thereby be illusorily inscribed in the Symbolic. In order
to enhance the definition of 'interpassivity', Žižek invests the term 'interactivity' with a contrary sense: the subject is passive while another actively
performs its task. In fact, active and passive are interdependent, since
society often provides an active form (such as rituals of mourning) to
give an inward passive feeling an outward expression, thereby opening
a gap between inner and outer, reality and appearance. The gap permits
the bogus performance of a ritual, and, conversely, the ritual can provoke
genuine feeling in someone going through the motions, while, as a third
alternative, the gap for the obsessional neurotic stretches between the
ritual he performs and the feeling he avoids.

This gap between feeling and expression is exploited in Žižek's prime
example of interpassivity: the Japanese electronic toy, the *tamagochi*, a
fake child/pet that needs care, captivating its carers by its imperious
demands issued through beeps and flashing lights for 'food', 'drink' and
'play', all supplied by buttons. If it is not 'fed', it 'dies', which leaves open
the possibility that it can be 'killed' by a murderous cyberwise child.

Alternatively, the *tamagochi* enables you to 'love your neighbour' without a troublesome neighbour to love, conveniently reducing a canonized virtue to a private pathological need. The *tamagochi* does not depend on any resemblance to produce its effect, but on its power to exchange signals and apparently take the initiative. However, all this activity on the part of the subject is an imaginary Symbolic strategy to keep the Other's desire at bay, rendering it passive in order to postpone the realization that *jouissance* cannot be obtained in full. The structure is similar to that of an analysis: the drive is diverted into a surrogate activity of chatter that keeps the analyst passive – until, that is, the analysand can at last assume the activity of the drive without leaning on a passivity in the analyst. Meanwhile, the analysand babbles away at the analyst, endeavouring to annul his desire and blot him out as a subject of lack, thus 'reducing him to a partial object with which one can play games – *tamagochi*, the ultimate exemplification of the Lacanian *objet a*'. This is only one step away from looking for a final mystical One with whom to commune and whose commandments we obey, God the Father himself, 'the ultimate *tamagochi*'.

In entering cyberspace, are we in search of an ultimate Symbolic, oedipally constructed, or are we going for the 'end of Oedipus'? Žižek lists four modes of engagement: (1) foreclosing Oedipus (psychotic immersion); (2) acceding to Oedipus (neurotic mediation); (3) perverting Oedipus (staging the perfection of the Law); and (4) appropriating Oedipus (playing out one's capture in the Symbolic). A first version of (1) claims that cyberspace involves the exclusion of a prohibiting agency, with a resulting dissolution in a pre-symbolic psychotic realm in which the computer incestuously absorbs the subject. The more that 'simulacra' (images beyond which nothing real can be found) are pursued, the more 'appearance' (symbolic fictions invested with visionary promise) is impaired. A second version perceives advantages in this dissolution of the patriarchal order and all that it implies, in that it visualizes an alternative to Oedipus: cyberspace rescues subjects from fixed symbolic identities, 'interpellation' into oppressive regimes, allowing them to create themselves freely beyond the constraints of binary oppositions. (2) Counter to both these versions is the notion that cyberspace, far from loosening the oedipal structure, actually strengthens it, because a real participation in a fictive mode renders more obvious the mediation by proxy of ordinary communication: the gap that exists between the Real of the subject (the 'subject of enunciation') and its symbolic identity (the 'subject of the enunciated') already requires the adoption of a persona. (3) Between the psychosis of (1) and the neurosis of (2), between foreclosure of the Law and its integration, is the pervert's computerized game: as cyberspace tries to be free of the Real, paradoxically by installing whatever laws it likes, so the 'proverbial male masochist' is precisely the one who enjoys laying down the law that forbids his own enjoyment. (4) The final option that cyberspace can provide is liberation from the enslavement of one's 'fundamental fantasy'. Here Žižek is alluding to the Freudo-Lacanian formulation of fantasy as support of the subject in its alienation, covering the failure of language to acknowledge its being: 'to traverse the fantasy' is the Lacanian version of Freud's 'working-through' – a breaking-up of the false consistency of the subject in all its morbid fixities by activating through the imagination something involuntarily created by the 'pre-synthetic imagination'. Cyberspace offers a realm of undisclosed possibilities of moving beyond Oedipus and returning, allowing for dramatic responses that preserve a minimal distance electronically safeguarded.

The four options do not, however, rule one another out, as if there were a simple choice; for cyberspace is subject to lines of force vibrating from symbolic networks of domination and resistance.

I

Recent theory of ideology and art has focused on the strange phenomenon of *interpassivity*,[1] a phenomenon that is the exact obverse of 'interactivity' in the sense of being active through another subject who does the job for me, like the Hegelian Idea manipulating human passions to achieve its Goals (the 'cunning of Reason' (*List der Vernunft*)). Perhaps the first implicit formulation of interpassivity was given by Lacan in his commentary on the role of the Chorus in Greek tragedy:

And what is a Chorus? You will be told that it's you yourselves. Or perhaps it isn't you. But that's the point. Means are involved here, emotional means. In my view, the Chorus is people who are moved.

[...] When you go to the theatre in the evening, you are preoccupied by the affairs of the day, by the pen that you lost, by the check that you will have to sign next day. You shouldn't give yourselves too much credit. Your emotions are taken charge of by the healthy order displayed on the stage. The Chorus takes care of them. The emotional commentary is done for you.... It is just sufficiently silly; it is also not without firmness; it is more or less human.

Therefore, you don't have to worry; even if you don't feel anything, the Chorus will feel in your stead. Why after all can one not imagine that the effect on you may be achieved, at least a small dose of it, even if you didn't tremble that much?[2]

In order to avoid standard contemporary examples of interpassivity like so-called canned laughter (where laughter is included in the sound-track, so that the TV set laughs for me – that is, it realizes, takes over, the spectator's very passive experience of the show), let me evoke a different example,[3] that of the collector who merely accumulates paintings or video cassettes with films, without ever having time (or true proclivity) to watch them. What matters to him is the fact that he possesses them, the awareness that they are there, all the time at his disposal. Isn't there a parallel between him and the famous Pascalian/Althusserian example of a non-believer who just has to kneel down and blindly repeat the gestures of ritual, and faith will come by itself? The point is to reinterpret the non-believer following the external ritual in the light of the logic of the collector: he does not wait for the magic moment of faith to occur – merely imitating the gestures of faith, laying the foundation for it, is enough for him. Crucial is this obsessional economy of postponing the final event – that is, of limiting oneself to merely laying the ground for it: the truly Christian statement is not 'I do not need to follow the external rituals, deep in my heart I believe and that's all that matters', but the opposite one, 'I follow the rituals of belief, but I can never be certain that I believe . . .'.

Another exemplary case of interpassivity is the embarrassing scene in which a person tells a tasteless joke and then, when nobody around him laughs, himself bursts out into a noisy laughter, repeating 'That was funny!' or something similar – that is to say, himself acting out the expected reaction of the audience. The situation here is in a way the exact opposite of that of the Greek Chorus: the Chorus feels for us, bored and preoccupied spectators unable to let ourselves go and experience the appropriate passive emotions, while here, it is the agent (the narrator of the joke) himself who also assumes the passive role, who laughs (at his own joke) instead of us, his public. The contrast is even stronger if we compare the situation with that of the canned laughter on TV: the agent who laughs instead of us (i.e., through whom we, the bored and embarrassed public, none the less laugh) is not the anonymous 'big Other' of the invisible artificial public, but the narrator of the joke himself. He does it to assure the inscription of his act into the 'big Other' the symbolic order; that is, his compulsive laughter is not dissimilar to exclamations like 'Oops!' which we feel obliged to utter when we stumble or do something stupid. The mystery of this last case is that it is also possible for another person who merely witnesses our blooper to say 'Oops!' *for us.* So, in all these examples, I am active in order to assure the passivity of an Other who stands for my true place. Interpassivity, like interactivity, thus subverts the standard opposition between activity and passivity: if in interactivity (of the 'cunning of Reason'), I am passive while being active through another, in interpassivity, I am active while being passive through another. More precisely, the term 'interactivity' is currently used in two senses: (1) *interacting with* the medium – that is, not being just a passive consumer; (2) *acting through* another agent, so that my job is done, while I sit back and remain passive, just observing the game. While the opposite of the first mode of interactivity is also a kind of 'interpassivity', the mutual passivity of two subjects, like two lovers passively observing each other and merely enjoying the other's presence, the proper notion of interpassivity aims at the reversal of the second meaning of interactivity: the distinguishing feature of interpassivity is that, in it, the subject is incessantly – frenetically even – *active*, while displacing on to another the fundamental passivity of his or her being.

Of course, being active and being passive are inextricably linked, since a passive feeling, authentic as it is, in a way acquires actuality only in so far as it is properly externalized, 'expressed' in an activity that is already socially codified (the most obvious example: in Japan, laughter signals our host's respectful embarrassment, while for us, if someone answers our query with a laugh, it rather signals aggressive disrespect . . .). This minimal gap opens up the way not only to faking authentic feelings, but also to *inducing them* by means of externally submitting to their ritualized expression (in this way, one can 'make oneself cry', etc.), so that, although it started as a fake, we end up 'really feeling it'. It is this minimal gap that is mobilized in the obsessional economy: the obsessional ritual is precisely a kind of 'empty' ritual, a ritual in which we, say, go through gestures of mourning precisely in order *not* to experience the true sorrow over the death of our fellow whose loss we are mourning. Doesn't *tamagochi*, the new Japanese toy extremely popular among children, rely on this same gap? *Tamagochi* is a virtual pet, a small round object with a screen that behaves like a child (or a dog, or a bird, or some other pet animal that *needs care*), making noises and – the key feature – posing demands on the child who owns it. When it beeps, one has to look on the screen, where the object's demand can be read – for food, drink, or whatever – and push the proper buttons beneath the screen to satisfy these demands. The object can also demand that we play with it; if it is too wild, the proper thing to do is to punish it by, again, pressing the proper buttons. Various signals (like the number of small hearts on display) even tell us the level of the object's happiness. If one fails too many times to meet these demands, the object 'dies'; it possesses only one more life, and when we fail yet another time, the object dies definitively – that is, stops functioning – so that, of course, we have to buy a new one . . . (And, incidentally, one of the common ways in which wicked children heckle their peers innocently immersed in their care for *tamagochi* is to meddle with the toy when it is briefly left unattended, provoking catastrophic consequences – for example, feeding it too much so that the virtual animal behind the screen chokes to death. *Tamagochi* is thus also breeding a number of virtual murderers among children, giving rise to the cyberspace counterpart of the sadistic child torturing a cat or a butterfly to death.[4]) Since this ultimate 'death' has caused numerous nervous breakdowns and deep traumas in the children who owned them, recent versions of *tamagochi* contain endless possibilities of resuscitation – that is, after the pet-object dies, the game is simply over, and one can start it again. This, of course, already obfuscates what was so provocative and traumatic about the original *tamagochi*: namely, the very fact that its (second or third) death was *final*, irrevocable.[5] The interesting thing here is that we are dealing with a toy, a mechanical object, that provides satisfaction precisely by behaving like a difficult child bombarding us with demands. The satisfaction is provided by our being compelled to care for the object any time it wants – that is, by fulfilling its demands. Don't we find here the ultimate exemplification of the obsessional's object, in so far as the obsessional's object of desire is the other's demand? *Tamagochi* enables us to possess an other who satisfies our desire in so far as it is reduced to a series of pure demands.

The other is thus purely virtual: no longer a true, living, intersubjective other, but an inanimate screen, a stand-in for the non-existent pet animal, which just signals the animal's demands. In other words, what we find here is a strange realization of the scene described by John Searle in his famous Chinese room mental experiment designed to prove that machines cannot think: we know that there is no 'real' partner of communication, nobody who really 'understands' the emitted demands, just a meaningless digital circuit. The uncanny enigma, of course, resides in the fact that we feel fully the appropriate emotions, although we are well aware that there is nothing beyond the screen – that is, that we are playing with signals with no referent: the game is reduced to the symbolic order, to the exchange of signals, with no referent beyond it. We can thus well imagine also a sex-*tamagochi*: a *tamagochi* bombarding us with demands like 'Kiss me! Lick me down there! Penetrate me!', to which we respond by simply pressing the appropriate buttons, and thus fulfilling our duty to enjoy, while in 'real life' we can rest calmly and have a nice lone drink. No wonder some conservative theologians in Europe have already proclaimed *tamagochi* to be the latest incarnation of Satan, in so far as, in ethical terms, 'Satan' is also a name for the solipsistic self-immersion and utter ignorance of loving compassion for my neighbour. Isn't the faked compassion and care for a digital toy infinitely more perverse than a simple, direct egoistical ignorance of others, since it somehow blurs the very difference between egoism and altruistic compassion? However, doesn't the same hold also for all kinds of inanimate objects with which children and adults play games under the condition of the fetishist disavowal ('I know very well that this is just an inanimate object, but none the less I act as if I believe this is a living being'), from children's dolls to inflatable sex-dolls with appropriate holes for penetration? Two features distinguish *tamagochi* from the usual inanimate plaything: (1) in contrast to a doll, the *tamagochi* no longer aims at imitating (as realistically as possible) the contours of what it replaces; it does not 'look like' a small baby or a naked woman or a puppet – we are dealing with a radical reduction of *imaginary* resemblance to the *symbolic* level, to the exchange of signals; that is, tamagochi is an object that merely emits demands in the form of signals, (2) In contrast to a doll, which is a passive, pliable object with which we can do whatever we want, *tamagochi* is thoroughly active; that is, the whole point of the game is that *it always has the initiative*, that the object controls the game and bombards us with demands.

This brings us back to the problem of the interpassive delegating of our innermost feelings (ultimately, our *jouissance*) to another. If, in our feelings, we always minimally imitate what a presupposed other feels – one cries and laughs when one sees one's neighbours crying or laughing – who, then, was the first link in the chain? What if there is no first link? What if delegation to a non-existent other is primordial? However, if there is no first link, then the whole chain potentially collapses, falling down like a house of cards or a series of dominoes, so that we arrive at *tamagochi*. That is, I can replace my immediate partner with a mechanical toy consisting of mere signals of my partner's emotions. The link with obsessional neurosis is crucial for the notion of interpassivity, since the key problem of the obsessional neurotic is how to postpone the encounter with *jouissance* (and thus maintain the belief in its possibility): if, instead of viewing films, I just endlessly record them on video, this postponing maintains the belief that, if or when I finally do it, this will really be 'it'. *Tamagochi* merely draws the logical conclusion from this obsessional postponing: if I never really want to encounter the Other, why bother at all with a Real Other? Isn't a machine which manipulates and fabricates substanceless signals of the Other good enough? Ultimately, the toy itself, the small round object, becomes the object of our worry, in accordance with the obsessional strategy that consists in erasing the Other (the 'real person' *qua* split/desiring subject), in reducing him or her to the partial object with which one can play games – *tamagochi*, the ultimate exemplification of the Lacanian *objet petit a*.

And, to risk the most daring hypothesis: is not the ultimate consequence of all this for a materialist that *God himself is the ultimate* tamagochi, fabricated by our unconscious and bombarding us with inexorable demands? That is, is *tamagochi* not *the* virtual entity, non-existent in itself, with whom we exchange signals and comply to its demands? Does not the non–imaginary character of *tamagochi* (which no longer endeavours to resemble the pet it stands for) hold especially for the Judaic tradition, with its prohibition on producing images of God? Again, no wonder that for some theologians tamagochi is Satan incarnate: it, as it were, lays bare the mechanism of the believer's dialogue with God, since it demonstrates how an intense, caring exchange of symbols is possible with an entity which is purely virtual – that is, which exists only as an interface simulacrum.

In other words, *tamagochi* is a machine *which allows you to satisfy your need to love your neighbour.* You have a need to indulge in care for your neighbour, a child, a pet? No problem: *tamagochi* enables you to do it without bothering your actual neighbours with your intrusive compassion – *tamagochi* can take care of this pathological need of yours. The charm of this solution resides in the fact that (what traditional ethics regarded as) the highest expression of your humanity – the compassionate need to take care of another living being – is treated as a dirty idiosyncratic pathology which should be satisfied in private, without bothering your actual fellow beings.

Tamagochi thus gives the ultimate twist to interpassivity: a purely virtual passive other that bombards us with demands and pushes us to frenetic activity to keep it satisfied – that is, calm, immobile, ultimately asleep. As every child knows, one is most profoundly satisfied when *tamagochi* leaves one alone and is 'asleep' for a couple of hours. – *Tamagochi* is thus an instrument of interpassivity in its contrast with the standard puppet-toy (a doll, a dog, etc.), which is a passive object offering itself to be manipulated (cared for, fondled, etc.) by us: we do the same with the *tamagochi*, but with the crucial difference that, in doing it, we are not following our whims, but fulfilling its demands. Does not this reference to the interpassive object also explain in what sense, for the subject-patient, the analyst is his *objet petit a*, or, more precisely, in what sense the patient wants to reduce the analyst to a kind of *tamagochi* to be kept happy by the patient's incessant seductive babble? In both cases, we are dealing with the attempt to obliterate the dimension of the Other's desire: the goal of the obsessional's fulfilling the Other's demands is to prevent the Other's desire from emerging. In the case of *tamagochi*, we have a mechanical Other which, although it incessantly emits demands, has no desire proper – this is what makes it such a perfect partner for the obsessional. And it is the same in the obsessional's dealings with his analyst: the goal of his incessant activity is to avoid or, rather, postpone indefinitely the confrontation with the abyss of the Other's desire.

The first thing to do here, of course, would be to oppose the analyst to the theatrical practice of so-called 'claques', people paid by the artist or his or her supporters to start applauding and thus organize a triumphant reception of the artist's performance. In the case of a claque, the Other is paid for staging the gesture of recognition (of the artist's endeavour) and thus satisfying his or her narcissism, while, in clear contrast to it, the patient pays the analyst for the exact opposite reason: that is, not to give direct recognition to his superficial self-perception, to frustrate his demand for recognition and narcissistic satisfaction. In the analytic treatment, true interpassivity is discernible at a more radical level. What we have in mind here is not the obvious fact that, in order to avoid confrontation with the truth of her desire, its symbolization, the patient offers *herself* as the passive object of the analyst's desire, trying to seduce him, to start a love affair with him. Interpassivity, rather, intervenes when, in the course of the cure, the subject is incessantly active, tells stories and memories, bemoans his fate, accuses the analyst, etc., endeavouring to come to terms with the trauma of 'What does the analyst want from me?', with the dark spot of the analyst's desire, while the analyst is just there, in the guise of his impassive, inert presence. The point is not just that I, the patient, am bothered and frustrated by the analyst's enigmatic silence, but, perhaps even more, that I am active precisely *in order to keep the other (analyst) silent* – that is, so that nothing will happen, so that he will not proclaim the word (or accomplish some other gesture) which will disclose the nullity of my incessant babble. This example shows very clearly how the key feature of interpassivity is that it designates not a situation in which the other replaces me, does something for me, but the opposite situation in which *I am incessantly active*, and sustain my activity by the other's passivity. For that reason, the equivalence between interpassivity and drive is none the less problematic: the whole point of the relationship between the patient and the analyst, in which the analyst is passive for the patient, is that the subject-patient remains within a transferential attitude towards the analyst – that is, that he definitely remains within the constraints of desire, bothered by the enigma of the other's desire. It is only with the conclusion of the cure (the dissolution of the transference) that I no longer need to rely on the other to be passive for me – that is, that, in order to be active, I no longer need the fantasmatic support in the scene in which I am reduced to a passive object. And it is our contention that this notion of interpassivity – that is, such uncanny situations in which I am active, while transposing on to the Other the unbearable passivity of my being – provides the key – or at least one of the keys – to the artistic potentials of the new digital media.

II

As a psychoanalytically oriented (Lacanian) philosopher, let me begin with the question one expects an analyst to raise: what are the consequences of cyberspace for Oedipus – that is, for the mode of subjectivization that psychoanalysis conceptualized as the Oedipus complex and its dissolution? The predominant *doxa* today is that cyberspace explodes, or at least potentially undermines the reign of Oedipus: it involves the 'end of Oedipus', in that what occurs in it is the passage from the structure of symbolic castration (the intervention of the Third Agency that prohibits/disturbs the incestuous dyad, and thus enables the subject's entry into the symbolic order) to some new, post-oedipal libidinal economy. Of course, the mode of perception of this 'end of Oedipus' depends on the standpoint of the theoretician. First, there are those who see in it a dystopian prospect of individuals regressing to pre-symbolic psychotic immersion, of losing the symbolic distance that sustains the minimum of critical/ reflective attitude (the idea that the computer functions as a maternal Thing that swallows the subject, who entertains an attitude of incestuous fusion towards it). In short, today, in the digitalized universe of simulation, the Imaginary overlaps the Real, at the expense of the Symbolic (Jean Baudrillard, Paul Virilio).

This position is at its strongest when it insists on the difference between appearance and simulacrum: 'appearance' has nothing in common with the postmodern notion that we are entering the era of universalized simulacra, in which reality itself becomes indistinguishable from its simulated double. The nostalgic longing for the authentic experience of being lost in the deluge of simulacra (detectable in Virilio), as well as the postmodern assertion of a Brave New World of universalized simulacra as the sign that we are finally getting rid of the metaphysical obsession with authentic Being (detectable in Vattimo), both miss the distinction between simulacrum and appearance: what gets lost in today's digital 'plague of simulations' is not the firm, true, non-simulated real, but *appearance itself.* So what is appearance? In a sentimental answer to a child asking what God's face looks like, a priest answered that, whenever the child encounters a human face radiating benevolence and goodness, whoever this face belongs to, he gets a glimpse of God's face. The truth of this sentimental platitude is that the Supra-sensible (God's face) is discernible as a momentary, fleeting appearance, a 'grimace', of an earthly face. It is *this* dimension of 'appearance' that, as it were, transubstantiates a piece of reality into something that, for a brief moment, radiates the supra-sensible Eternity that is missing in the logic of the simulacrum. In the simulacrum, which becomes indistinguishable from the real, everything is here and not other; a transcendent dimension effectively 'appears' in/through it. Here we are back at the Kantian problematic of the Sublime: in Kant's famous reading of the enthusiasm evoked by the French Revolution in the enlightened public throughout Europe, the revolutionary events functioned as a sign through which the dimension of trans-phenomenal Freedom, of a free society, *appeared.* 'Appearance' is thus the domain not simply of phenomena, but of those 'magic moments' in which another, noumenal dimension momentarily 'appears' in ('shines through') some empirical/contingent phenomenon. Therein also resides the problem with cyberspace and virtual reality: what virtual reality threatens is *not* 'reality', which is dissolved in the multiplicity of its simulacra, but, on the contrary, *appearance* itself. To put it in Lacanian terms: simulacrum is imaginary (illusion), while appearance is symbolic (fiction); when the specific dimension of symbolic appearance starts to disintegrate, the Imaginary and the Real become more and more indistinguishable. The key to today's universe of simulacra, in which the Real is less and less distinguishable from its imaginary simulation, resides in the retreat of 'symbolic efficiency'. This crucial distinction between the simulacrum (overlapping with the Real) and appearance is easily discernible in the domain of sexuality, in the guise of the distinction between pornography and seduction: pornography 'shows it all', 'real sex', and for that very reason produces mere simulacra of sexuality, while the process of seduction consists entirely in the play of appearances, hints and promises, and thereby evokes the elusive domain of the supra-sensible sublime Thing.

On the other hand, there are those who emphasize the liberating potential of cyberspace: cyberspace opens up the domain of shifting multiple sexual and social identities, at least potentially liberating us from the hold of the patriarchal Law; it, as it were, realizes in our everyday practical experience the 'deconstruction' of old metaphysical binaries ('real Self' versus 'artificial mask', etc.). In cyberspace, I am compelled to renounce any fixed symbolic identity, the legal/political fiction of a unique Self guaranteed by my place in the socio-symbolic structure. In short, according to this second version (Sandy Stone, Sherry Turkle), cyberspace announces the end of the Cartesian *cogito* as the unique 'thinking substance'. Of course, from this second point of view, the pessimistic prophets of the psychotic 'end of Oedipus' in the universe of simulacra simply betray their inability to imagine an alternative to Oedipus. What we have here is another version of the standard postmodern deconstructionist narrative, according to which, in the bad old patriarchal order, the subject's sexual identity was predetermined by his or her place and/or role within the fixed symbolic oedipal framework – the 'big Other' took care of us, and conferred on us the identity of either a 'man' or a 'woman', and the subject's ethical duty was limited to the effort to succeed in occupying the pre-ordained symbolic place (homosexuality and other 'perversions' were perceived as simply so many signs of the subject's *failure* to follow the oedipal path and thus achieving 'normal'/'mature' sexual identity). Today, however, as Foucault supposedly demonstrated, the legal/prohibitive matrix of Power that underlies the oedipal functioning of sexuality is in retreat, so that, instead of being interpellated to occupy a pre-ordained place in the socio-symbolic order, the subject has gained the freedom (or at least the promise, the prospect of freedom) to shift between different socio-symbolic sexual identities, to construct his Self as an aesthetic *oeuvre* – the motif at work from the late Foucault's notion of the 'care of the Self' up to deconstructionist feminist emphasis on the social formation of gender. It is easy to perceive how the reference to cyberspace can provide an additional impetus to this ideology of aesthetic self-creation: cyberspace delivers me from the vestiges of biological constraints and elevates my capacity to construct freely my Self, to let myself go in a multitude of shifting identities.

However, opposed to both versions of 'cyberspace as the end of Oedipus' are some rare, but none the less penetrating, theoreticians who assert the continuity of cyberspace with the oedipal mode of subjectivization.[6] Cyberspace retains the fundamental oedipal structure of an intervening Third Order which, in its very capacity as the agency of mediation/mediatization, sustains the subject's desire, while simultaneously acting as the agent of prohibition that prevents its direct, full gratification. Owing to this intervening Third, every partial gratification/satisfaction is marked by a fundamental 'This is not *that*'. The notion that cyberspace as the medium of hyper-reality suspends symbolic efficiency and brings about a false total transparency of the imaginary simulacra coinciding with the Real, while effectively expressing a certain 'spontaneous ideology of cyberspace' (to paraphrase Althusser), dissimulates the actual functioning of cyberspace, which not only continues to rely on the elementary *dispositif* of the symbolic Law, but even renders it more palpable in our everyday experience. Suffice it to recall the conditions of our surfing along in the Internet or participating in a virtual community: first, there is the gap between the 'subject of enunciation' (the anonymous X who does it, who speaks) and the 'subject of the enunciated/of the statement' (the symbolic identity that I assume in cyberspace, which can be, and in a sense always is, 'invented' – the signifier that marks my identity in cyberspace is never directly 'myself'); the same goes for the other side, for my partner(s) in cyberspace communication. Here, the undecidability is radical: I can never be sure who they are, whether they are 'really' the way they describe themselves, whether there is a 'real' person at all behind a screen-persona, whether the screen-persona is a mask for a multiplicity of persons, whether the same 'real' person possesses and manipulates more screen-personas, or whether I am simply dealing with a digitalized entity that does not stand for any 'real' person. It thus seems that cyberspace materializes directly the so-called schema L elaborated by Lacan in the early fifties to account for the structure of communication: within cyberspace, two screen-personae interact along the imaginary axis, myself (a) and its mirror-partner (a'), while, beneath it and traversing it, there is the symbolic axis of the relationship between myself as the subject of the enunciation ($) and the Other, which for ever remains an enigma beyond the 'wall of language', his or her 'Che vuoi?' for ever unanswered (he or she is sending me this message, but what is behind it? what does he or she want to achieve with it?). In short, *inter-face* means precisely that my relationship to the Other is never *face to face*, that it is always mediat(iz)ed by the interposed digital machinery that stands for the Lacanian 'big Other', the anonymous symbolic order whose structure is that of a labyrinth. I 'browse', I bounce around in this infinite space where messages circulate freely without fixed destination, while the Whole of it – this immense circuitry of 'murmurs' – remains for ever beyond the scope of my comprehension. (In this sense, one is tempted to propose the proto-Kantian notion of the 'cyberspace Sublime' as the magnitude of messages and their circuits, which even the greatest effort of my synthetic imagination cannot encompass/comprehend.) Furthermore, doesn't the a priori possibility of viruses disintegrating the virtual universe point towards the fact that, in the virtual universe as well, there is no 'Other of the Other', that this universe is a priori inconsistent, with no final guarantee of its coherent functioning? The conclusion thus seems to be that there *is* a properly 'symbolic' functioning of cyberspace: cyberspace remains 'oedipal' in the sense that, in order to circulate freely in it, one must assume a fundamental prohibition and/or alienation. Yes, in cyberspace, 'you can be whatever you want', you're free to choose a symbolic identity (screen-persona), but you must choose *one* which in a way will always betray you, which will never be fully adequate; you must accept representation in cyberspace by a signifying element that runs around in the circuitry as your stand-in. Yes, in cyberspace, 'everything is possible', but at the price of assuming a fundamental *impossibility*: you cannot circumvent the mediation of the interface, its 'bypass', which separates you (as the subject of enunciation) for ever from your symbolic stand-in.

There is, however, a sense in which 'Oedipus on-line' no longer functions as Oedipus proper. To get this break clear, one has to bear in mind Lacan's strict distinction between the Oedipus myth (the *narrative* of his parricide and incest, etc.) and the underlying purely formal structure of symbolic prohibition as the price to be paid for entry into the symbolic order: 'No!' of the father is just a stand-in for, an imaginary embodiment of, the purely formal fact that '*jouissance* is prohibited to the one who speaks as such' (Lacan). The moment my need is formulated as a symbolic demand addressed to the Other, I get involved in the twists and deadlocks of the impossibility of its full gratification (the gap opens up between every material object which satisfies my need and the unfathomable 'it' at which my desire aims; my desire becomes mediated by the desire of the Other – that is, the fundamental enigma which bothers me is 'What am I as an object of desire for the Other? What does the Other see in me that makes me (un)worthy of his or her desire?', etc., etc.). So, although cyberspace does involve a fundamental prohibition/alienation, what we encounter in it is rather the purely formal structure of symbolic prohibition, without the 'little piece of the (paternal) real' (the paternal figure) sustaining it. Does this not open the way to mediate between the two readings of cyber-space, post-oedipal and oedipal? Cyberspace is post-oedipal with regard to Oedipus *qua* mythical narrative, but not post-oedipal with regard to Oedipus *qua* the formal structure of prohibition/mediation. In other words, what is 'beyond Oedipus' (as a certain historically specified narrative/myth) is Oedipus itself *qua* purely formal structure co-substantial with the very fact of the symbolic order.[7] Paradoxically, cyberspace thus designates a potential 'relapse' into psychosis, a breakdown of the symbolic mediation, precisely in so far as it actualizes the pure structure of symbolic prohibition/mediation without the 'little piece of the real' of a figure which gives body to it.

However, clear and elucidating as it may appear, this difference between Oedipus *qua* mythical narrative and Oedipus *qua* formal structure leaves a crucial question unanswered: where does the need for the narrative supplement to the formal structure come from? Why can the formal structure not reign in its purity, without its confusing identification with an empirical 'pathological' element (the paternal figure) which gives body to it? Why can we not simply enter the symbolic order, and directly assume the loss involved in this entry? Needless to add, we encounter thereby the enigma of the prohibition of the impossible: if *jouissance* is in itself *impossible*, why do we need the superfluous gesture of formally *prohibiting* it? That is to say, the basic paradox of symbolic prohibition resides not in why a human animal accepts and 'internalizes' an 'irrational' harsh renunciation, but, quite to the contrary, in its ultimately *superfluous* character. Let us recall the small scene from Sergio Leone's *Once Upon a Time in the West*, in which Henry Fonda shoots a cheap informer, telling him that he cannot trust him – how can one trust a man who doesn't even trust his belt (he wears, to support his trousers, a belt *and* shoulderstraps)?[8] The hysterical inhibitions are somewhat like that: one acts as if the barrier/obstacle is not already in language itself; so one imposes on oneself an additional empirical prohibition (or cut or burden) – with the illusion, of course, that, if one were to circumvent *this* additional prohibition, one would get the *thing itself.* Perhaps this very illusion provides the reason for the otherwise senseless superfluous gesture of prohibiting something which is already in itself impossible. Berliners used to refer to the wall separating the eastern from the western part of the divided city till 1989 as an attempt to 'stabilize the impossible': is this not the elementary function of every wall of symbolic prohibition?[9]

This same paradox accounts also for the fundamental ambiguity of the psychoanalytic notion of transference. In Lacan, 'transference' does not designate a 'personal' relationship: transference is inherent in language as such, in the 'big Other'. Language itself is 'supposed to know'; that is, the subject speaks in so far as he or she presupposes that the big Other is complete, that the meaning of his or her utterances is guaranteed in or by the big Other. Transference, as such, is another name for what Davidson called the 'charity principle', the fundamental attitude of trust towards the Other. None the less, this trust must be supported by *le peu de réel*, by some remainder of the Real. Say, with regard to the gap between the symbolic function-place of the father and the person who occupies this function, there is no transference to the father without some 'peu de réel', some stain, some purely idiosyncratic feature which apparently prevents him from fully embodying the paternal function. In other words, our standard attitude towards a paternal figure of authority involves a fundamental misperception: usually, we say, 'In spite of his idiosyncrasies, I still believe in his authority, since he is after all my father', whereas the true relationship is the opposite one: that is, that these little idiosyncrasies guarantee that this flesh-and-blood person actually acts as the embodiment of the paternal authority – that without them, there would be no transference proper, and 'father' would remain a monstrous pure symbolic function, all-devouring and real in his very spectral invisibility.

So the only consistent answer to the question 'Why does the superfluous prohibition emerge, which merely prohibits the impossible?' is: in order to obfuscate this inherent impossibility – that is, in order to sustain the illusion that, were it not for the externally imposed prohibition, the full ('incestuous') gratification would be possible. Far from acting as the 'repressive agency preventing us gaining access to the ultimate object of desire', the function of the paternal figure is thus quite the opposite, to relieve us from the debilitating deadlock of desire, to 'maintain hope' . . . The problem with 'Oedipus on-line' is thus that what is missing in it is precisely this 'pacifying' function of the paternal figure which enables us to obfuscate the debilitating deadlock of desire – hence the strange mixture of 'everything is possible' (since there is no positive prohibiting figure) and an all-pervasive frustration and deadlock that characterizes the subject's experience of cyberspace.

III

Clinically, it is easy to categorize these three versions as psychosis, perversion and hysteria: the first version claims that cyberspace entails universalized psychosis: according to the second one, cyberspace opens up the liberating perspective of globalized multiple perversion; the third one claims that cyber-space remains within the confines of the enigmatic Other that hystericizes the subject. So which of them is the right one? One is tempted to answer: a fourth one – a perversion like the second one, but on condition that one conceptual-izes perversion in a much stricter way. That is to say, both standard reactions to cyberspace are deficient: one is 'too strong' (cyberspace as involving a break with Oedipus), while the other is 'too weak' (cyberspace as a continuation of

Oedipus by other means). In contrast to them, perversion is the position (the libidinal stance) that endeavours to provide some kind of 'proper measure in order to contain the threat of libidinal disintegration' and 'to stabilize the impossible'. However, the key point is clearly to delineate the specific intermediate status of perversion, in between psychosis and neurosis, in between the psychotic's foreclosure of the Law and the neurotic's integration into the Law. According to the standard view, the perverse scenario stages the 'disavowal of castration': perversion can be seen as a defence against the motif of 'death and sexuality', against the threat of mortality as well as the contingent imposition of sexual difference: what the pervert enacts is a universe in which, as in cartoons, a human being can survive any catastrophe, in which adult sexuality is reduced to a childish game; in which one is not forced to die or to choose one of the two sexes. As such, the pervert's universe is the universe of pure symbolic order, of the signifier's game running its course, unencumbered by the Real of human finitude.

In a first approach, it may seem that our experience of cyberspace fits perfectly this universe. Isn't cyberspace also a universe unencumbered by the inertia of the Real, constrained only by its self-imposed rules? However, according to Lacan, what this standard notion of perversion leaves out of consideration is the unique short circuit between Law and *jouissance* that characterizes the innermost structure of perversion: in contrast to the neurotic, who acknowledges the Law in order to occasionally take enjoyment in its transgressions (masturbation, theft, etc.), and thus obtains satisfaction by snatching back from the Other part of the stolen *jouissance*, the pervert directly elevates the enjoying big Other into the agency of Law. The pervert's aim is to *establish*, not to undermine, the Law: the proverbial male masochist elevates his partner, the dominatrix, into the Law-giver whose orders are to be obeyed. A pervert fully acknowledges the obscene underside of the Law, since he gains satisfaction from the very obscenity of the gesture of installing the rule of Law – that is, out of 'castration'. In the 'normal' state of things, the symbolic Law prevents access to the (incestuous) object, and thus creates the desire for it; in perversion, *it is the object itself* (say, the dominatrix in masochism), *that makes the Law*. The theoretical concept of the masochist perversion touches here the common notion of a masochist who 'enjoys being tortured by the Law': a masochist *locates enjoyment in the very agency of the Law that prohibits the access to enjoyment*. A perverse ritual thus stages the act of castration, of the primordial loss that allows the subject to enter the symbolic order, but with a specific twist: in contrast to the 'normal' subject, for whom the Law functions as the agency of prohibition that regulates (access to the object of) his desire, for the pervert, *the object of his desire is Law itself* – the Law is the Ideal he longs for, he wants to be fully acknowledged by the Law, integrated into its functioning. The irony of this should not escape us: the pervert, this 'transgressor' *par excellence* who purports to violate all the rules of 'normal', decent behaviour, effectively longs for the very rule of Law.[10] A further point regarding the pervert is that, since, for him, the Law is not fully established (the Law is his *lost* object of desire), he supplements this lack with an intricate set of *regulations* (see the masochist ritual). The crucial point is thus to bear in mind the opposition between Law and regulations (or 'rules'): the latter bear witness to the absence or suspension of Law.

So what is effectively at stake in perversion? There is an agency in New York called 'Slaves are us', which provides people who are willing to clean your apartment for free, and want to be treated rudely by the lady of the house. The agency gets the cleaners through ads (whose motto is 'Slavery is its own reward!'): most of them are highly paid executives, doctors and lawyers, who, when questioned about their motives, protest that they are sick of being in charge all the time. They immensely enjoy just being brutally ordered to do their job and shouted at, in so far as this is the only way open to them to gain access to Being. And the philosophical point not to be missed here is that masochism as the only access to Being is strictly correlative with the advent of modern Kantian subjectivity, with the subject reduced to the empty point of self-relating negativity. At this point, a brief survey of post-Cartesian philosophy is very instructive: it was haunted by the vestiges of an Other Scene at which the subject – this free, active, self-positing agent – is reduced to an object of unbearable suffering or humiliation, deprived of the dignity of his freedom.

In 'Le Prix du progrès', one of the fragments that conclude *The Dialectic of Enlightenment*, Adorno and Horkheimer quote the argumentation of the nineteenth-century French physiologist Pierre Flourens against medical anaesthesia with chloroform. Flourens claims that it can be proved that the anaesthetic works only on our memory's neuronal network. In short, while we are being butchered alive on the operating table, we feel fully the terrible pain, but later, after awakening, we do not remember it. For Adorno and Horkheimer, this, of course, is the perfect metaphor of the fate of Reason based on the repression of nature in itself: his body, the part of nature in the subject, feels fully the pain; it is only that, owing to repression, the subject does not remember it. Therein resides the perfect revenge of nature for our domination over it: unknowingly, we are our own greatest victims, butchering ourselves alive. Isn't it also possible to read this as the perfect fantasy-scenario of interpassivity, of the Other Scene in which we pay the price for our active intervention in the world? A sado-masochist willingly assumes this suffering as the access to Being.

Our second example: Kant, in a section of his *Critique of Practical Reason* mysteriously entitled 'Of the Wise Adaptation of Man's Cognitive Faculties to his Practical Vocation', answers the question of what would happen to us if we were to gain access to the noumenal domain, to Things in themselves, thus:

[I]nstead of the conflict which now the moral disposition has to wage with inclinations and in which, after some defeats, moral strength of mind may be gradually won, God and eternity in their awful majesty would stand unceasingly before our eyes. . . . Thus most actions conforming to the law would be done from fear, few would be done from hope, none from duty. The moral worth of actions, on which alone the worth of the person and even of the world depends in the eyes of supreme wisdom, would not exist at all. The conduct of man, so long as his nature remained as it is now, would be changed into mere mechanism, where, as in a puppet show, everything would gesticulate well but no life would be found in the figures.[11]

No wonder this vision of a man who, through his direct insight into the monstrosity of the divine being-in-itself, would turn into a lifeless puppet provokes such unease among commentators on Kant (usually, it is either passed over in silence or dismissed as an uncanny foreign body). What Kant delivers in it is no less than what one is tempted to call the 'Kantian fundamental fantasy', the interpassive Other Scene of freedom, of the spontaneous free agent, the scene in which the free agent is turned into a lifeless puppet at the mercy of the perverse God. Its lesson, of course, is that there is no active free agent without this fantasmatic support, without this Other Scene in which he is totally manipulated by the Other.[12] That is to say, in so far as the Kantian subject, this empty point of self-relating negativity, is none other than the Lacanian 'barred' subject of the signifier – le manque à être, lacking a support in the positive order of Being – what fantasy stages is precisely the subject's impossible being lost owing to the subject's entry into the symbolic order. No wonder, then, that the fundamental fantasy is passive, 'masochistic', reducing me to an object acted upon by others: it is as if only the experience of the utmost pain can guarantee the subject access to Being: la douleur d'exister means that I 'am' only in so far as I experience pain. For this reason, the Kantian prohibition of direct access to the noumenal domain should be reformulated: what should remain inaccessible to us is not the noumenal Real, but our fundamental fantasy itself – the moment the subject comes too close to this fantasmatic core, it loses the consistency of its existence.

This is also one of the ways of specifying the meaning of Lacan's assertion of the subject's constitutive 'decentrement': the point is not that my subjective experience is regulated by objective unconscious mechanisms that are 'decentred' with regard to my self-experience and, as such, beyond my control (a point asserted by every materialist), but rather something much more unsettling. I am deprived of even my most intimate 'subjective' experience, the way things 'really seem to me', the experience of the fundamental fantasy that constitutes and guarantees the core of my being, since I can never consciously experience it and assume it. According to the standard view, the dimension that is constitutive of subjectivity is that of the phenomenal (self-) experience – I am a subject the moment I can say to myself: 'No matter what unknown mechanism governs my acts, perceptions and thoughts, nobody can take from me what I see and feel now.' Say, when I am passionately in love, and a biochemist informs me that all my intense sentiments are just the result of biochemical processes in my body, I can answer him by clinging to the appearance: 'All that you're saying may be true, but, none the less, nothing can take from me the intensity of the passion that I am experiencing now.' Lacan's point, however, is that the psychoanalyst is the one who, precisely, *can* take this from the subject: that is, his ultimate aim is to deprive the subject of the very fundamental fantasy that regulates the universe of his (self-) experience. The Freudian 'subject of the unconscious' emerges only when a key aspect of the subject's *phenomenal* (self-)experience (his 'fundamental fantasy') becomes *inaccessible* to him – that is, is 'primordially repressed'. At its most radical, the unconscious is the *inaccessible phenomenon*, not the objective mechanism that regulates my phenomenal experience. So, in contrast to the commonplace that we are dealing with a subject the moment an entity displays signs of 'inner life' – that is, of a fantasmatic self-experience that cannot be reduced to external behaviour – one should claim that what characterizes human subjectivity proper is, rather, the gap that separates the two: the fact that fantasy, at its most elementary, becomes inaccessible to the subject; it is this inaccessibility that makes the subject 'empty' ($\emptyset$). We thus obtain a relationship that totally subverts the standard notion of the subject who directly experiences himself, his 'inner states': an 'impossible' relationship between the *empty, non-phenomenal subject* and the *phenomena that remain inaccessible to the subject* – the very relation registered by Lacan's formula of fantasy, $\emptyset \lozenge a$.

Geneticists predict that in about ten to fifteen years, they will be able to identify and manipulate each individual's exact genome (*c*.six billion genetic marks comprising the entirety of inherited 'knowledge'). Potentially, at least, each individual will thus have at his disposal the complete formula of what he or she 'objectively is'. How will this 'knowledge in the real', the fact that I will be able to locate and identify myself completely as an object in reality, affect the status of subjectivity? Will it lead to the end of human subjectivity? Lacan's answer is negative: what will continue to elude the geneticist is not my phenomenal self-experience (say, the experience of a love passion that no knowledge of the genetic and other material mechanisms determining it can take from me), but the 'objectively subjective' fundamental fantasy, the fantasmatic core inaccessible to my conscious experience. Even if science formulates the genetic formula of what I objectively am, it will still be unable to formulate my 'objectively subjective' fantasmatic identity, this objectal counterpoint to my subjectivity, which is neither subjective (experienced) nor objective.

IV

So how does all this concern cyberspace? It is often said that cyberspace opens up the domain which allows us to realize (to externalize, to stage) our innermost fantasies. By focusing on fundamental fantasy, today's artistic practices are asserting their status of art in the age of the scientific objectivization of human essence: art refers to the space of what a priori eludes the grasp of scientific objectivization. And perhaps cyberspace, with its capacity to externalize our innermost fantasies in all their inconsistency, opens up to artistic practice a unique possibility to stage, to 'act out', the fantasmatic support of our existence, up to the fundamental 'sado-masochistic' fantasy that can never be subjectivized. We are thus invited to risk the most radical experience imaginable: the encounter with our 'noumenal Self', with the Other Scene that stages the foreclosed hard core of the subject's Being. Far from enslaving us to these fantasies, and thus turning us into de-subjectivized blind puppets, it enables us to treat them in a playful way, and thus to adopt towards them a minimum of distance – in short, to achieve what Lacan calls la traversée du fantasme ('going-through, traversing the fantasy').

So let us conclude with a reference to the (in)famous last proposition of Wittgenstein's Tractatus: 'Wovon man nicht sprechen kann, darüber muss man schweigen.' This proposition renders in the most succinct way possible the paradox of the oedipal Law that prohibits something (incestuous fusion) that is already in itself impossible (and thereby gives rise to the hope that, if we remove or overcome the prohibition, the 'impossible' incest will become possible). If we are effectively to move to a region 'beyond Oedipus', Wittgenstein's proposition must be rephrased as: 'Wovon man nicht sprechen kann, darüber muss man schreiben.' There is, of course, a long tradition of conceiving art as a mode or practice of writing auguring what 'one cannot speak about' – that is, the utopian potential 'repressed' by the existing socio-symbolic network of prohibitions. There is also a long tradition of using writing as a means to communicate a declaration of love too intimate and/or too painful to be directly asserted in a face-to-face speech-act. Not only is the Internet widely used as a space for the amorous encounters of shy people; significantly, one of the anecdotes about Edison, the inventor of the telegraph, is that he himself used it to declare love and ask the hand of his secretary (being too shy to do it directly, by means of a spoken word). However, what we are aiming at is not this standard economy of using cyberspace as a place in which, since we are not directly engaged in it – that is, since we maintain a distance from it – we feel free to externalize and stage our innermost private fantasies. What we have in mind is a more radical level, the level that concerns our very fundamental fantasy as that 'wovon man nicht sprechen kann': the subject is never able to assume his or her fundamental fantasy, to recognize himself or herself in it in a performance of a speech-act: perhaps cyberspace opens up a domain in which the subject can none the less externalize/stage his or her fundamental fantasy, and thus gain a minimum of distance towards it.

In short, what we are claiming is that, in cyberspace (or through cyberspace), it is possible to accomplish what Lacan calls an authentic act, which consists in a gesture that disturbs ('traverses') the subject's fundamental fantasy. For Lacan, a gesture counts as an act only in so far as it disturbs (unhinges) this most radical level of the subject's consistency, the level that is even more fundamental than the subject's basic symbolic identification(s). The first negative consequence of this proposition, of course, is that we should reject the common-sense notion that indulging in cyberspace is by definition not an act, since we dwell in a virtual universe of simulacra instead of engaging ourselves with the 'real thing'. For Lacan, fantasy is not simply a work of imagination as opposed to hard reality – that is, a product of our mind that obfuscates our direct approach to reality, our ability to 'perceive things the way they really are'. With regard to the basic opposition between reality and imagination, fantasy is not simply on the side of imagination; fantasy is, rather, the little piece of imagination by which we gain access to reality – the frame that guarantees our access to reality, our 'sense of reality' (when our fundamental fantasy is shattered, we experience the 'loss of reality').[13] For this reason, 'traversing the fantasy' has absolutely nothing to do with a sobering act of dispelling the fantasies that obfuscate our clear perception of the real state of things, or with a reflective act of acquiring a critical distance from the ruminations of our imagination (getting rid of false superstitions, etc.). The paradoxical point is, rather, that fantasy intervenes (serves as a support) precisely when we draw the line of distinction between what is merely our imagination and what 'really exists out there'. 'Traversing the fantasy', on the contrary, involves our *over-identification* with the domain of imagination: in it, through it, we break the constraints of the fantasy and enter the terrifying, violent domain of pre-synthetic imagination, the domain in which *disjecta membra* float around, not yet unified and 'domesticated' by the intervention of a homogenizing fantasmatic frame. This, perhaps, is what playing in cyberspace enables us to do; if we follow it to the end, if we immerse ourselves in it without restraint, if we externalize in it our imagination in its very inconsistency, the very fantasmatic frame that guarantees the consistency of our (self-) experience can, perhaps, be undermined.

This, however, in no way implies that inducing us to 'traverse the fantasy' is an automatic effect of our immersion into cyberspace. What one should do here is, rather, to accomplish a Hegelian reversal of epistemological obstacle into ontological deadlock: what if it is wrong and misleading to ask directly which of the four versions of the libidinal/symbolic economy of cyberspace that we outlined is the 'correct' one (psychotic suspension of the Oedipus complex; the continuation of the Oedipus complex by other means; the perverse staging of the Law; traversing the fantasy)? What if these four versions are the four possibilities opened up by cyberspace technology, so that, ultimately, the choice is ours, the stake in a politico-ideological struggle? How cyberspace will affect us is not directly inscribed into its technological properties; rather, it hinges on the network of socio-symbolic relations (of power and domination, etc.) which always-already overdetermine the way cyberspace affects us.

Notes

1 See Robert Pfaller's intervention at the symposium *Die Dinge lachen an unserer Stelle*, Linz (Austria), 8–10 October, 1996. For a more detailed elaboration of interpassivity, see Žižek, *The Plague of Fantasies*, ch. 3.

2 Jacques Lacan, *The Ethics of Psychoanalysis* (London, Routledge, 1992), p. 252.

3 Borrowed from Robert Pfaller.

4 Another amusing detail is what often happens when the toy 'awakens' in the middle of the night, demanding immediate attention: the child wants the toy to be taken care of properly; however, since he or she is too tired to get up and do it, he or she awakens his or her parents and demands that they do what the toy demands (feed it, etc.). We are thus dealing with the double structure of delegation: the parent, who does not take the game seriously, has to occupy him or herself with feeding the purely virtual, non-existent animal in the middle of the night, while the child, the only one who takes the game seriously, continues his or her sound sleep . . . No wonder, then, that there are already web sites for parents, telling them how to deal with *tamagochis* on behalf of their children.

5 There are, of course, already burial sites for the dead *tamagochis*.

6 See Jerry Aline Flieger, 'Oedipus On-Line?', *Pretexts* 1/6 (July 1997), pp. 81–94.

7 Is this not confirmed by a reference to Lacan's development itself: first, in his early *Complexes familiaux* (1938), Lacan historicized Oedipus (as a specific family structure); later, however, he elaborated the underlying formal prohibitional structure of the symbolic order, which can be actualized in a set of different historical shapes.

8 I owe this example to Alain Abelhauser, Paris.

9 To put it in a slightly different way: what is crucial here is the distinction between lack/void (the impossibility which is operative already at the level of *drive*) and symbolic Law/Interdiction which founds the dialectic of *desire*: 'Oedipus complex' (the imposition of the symbolic Law) is ultimately *the operator of the transformation of drive into desire.*

10 For a closer elaboration of the structure of perversion, see Žižek, *Plague of Fantasies*, ch. 1.

11 Immanuel Kant, *Critique of Practical Reason* (New York, Macmillan, 1956), pp. 152–3.

12 What Hegel does is to 'traverse' this fantasy by demonstrating its function of filling in the pre-ontological abyss of freedom – i.e. of reconstituting the positive scene in which the subject is inserted into a positive noumenal order. In other words, for Hegel, Kant's vision is meaningless and inconsistent, since it secretly reintroduces the ontologically fully constituted divine totality, i.e. a world conceived *only* as Substance, *not* also as Subject.

13 Our ideological experience today is structured by a series of oppositions which stake out the terrain and the terms of the big debates: simulacrum versus reality, globalization versus maintaining particular identities, fantasy versus reality, etc. Each of these oppositions is false, obfuscating the true one. For example, globalization and the resuscitation of particular ethnic, religious, etc. identities are two sides of the same process: what is effectively threatened by globalization is, paradoxically, the proper dimension of universality co-substantial with subjectivization. Along the same lines, simulacrum and real ultimately coincide, so that what is ultimately threatened by the reign of digital and other simulacra is not the 'real reality', but the very dimension of appearance which is the locus of subjectivity. And, again, along the same lines, far from obfuscating true reality, fantasy is that which constitutes it: the true opposition is that between fantasy and imagination in the radical sense of the violent pre-synthetic gesture of exploding the ontological consistency of Being, a gesture which is another name for the subject.

Part II

Woman

6

Otto Weininger, or 'Woman doesn't Exist'

This chapter was first published in *New Formations* (vol. 23 (1994), pp. 97–113). It brings into mutual implication two aspects of late capitalism: the fanatical violence active within ideologies and the representations of woman in modern culture are explored for the operations of an ambiguous enjoyment.

Žižek goes to Otto Weininger's *Sex and Character*, enlisting him as an unlikely ally for Lacan. While Weininger is ostensibly writing in support of the dominant sexist ideology of his time, at the same time he reveals contradictions within the subject. In particular, Weininger claims that it is man's sinful Fall into sexuality that creates a determinate place for woman, such that she has no subjectivity of her own; she exists only in the desire for phallic enjoyment, which gives her no active part to play. By this detour he comes to the Lacanian conclusion that woman 'therefore does not exist'. Her passivity encourages man to love his own ideal in her, thereby betraying his ethical responsibility. Here Weininger gets near to the truth of courtly love, with man becoming impotent and woman a mere screen, a set-up in which, having neither recognition nor freedom, she produces hysterical symptoms. This again points forward to Lacan, who identifies in woman 'the symptom of man'. In this way Weininger attributes to her a constitutive negativity, and thereby fails to see in his characterization of woman as 'the infinite craving of Nothing for Something' the ontological predicament of all subjects, their struggling to place their substantial being within the Symbolic. For Lacan, the idea of woman as an enigma persists in the fantasy of the 'eternal feminine', and this induces in woman a masquerade as her only option, beneath which lies, not the 'true woman', but her unsignifiable void.

Every subject suffers from an 'insurmountable gap' between its being and its symbolic definition. Žižek turns to Kant, who asserted the impossibility of ever knowing what 'I' am that thinks, unlike Descartes, who believed he had wrested something substantial out of the dubious Real with his notion of *res cogitans*, 'the thing that thinks'. Weininger's low opinion of woman springs from a deeper universal doubt, the inability to confront the emptiness within the subject. The subject no longer has the light of reason at its core, as the Enlightenment would have it, but rather, in Hegel's words, 'the night of the world', the indeterminate origin of the Symbolic itself. As a telling legacy of this dark origin, there is the problematic of the relation of the Universal (the 'common' term) to the Particular (the 'singular' thing). Far from the Universal providing the Particular with its identity, there is always a failure of fit, a surplus that renders the attempt futile. This failure emerges in the relation of the family to the state, which, for Hegel, turns the woman into the cynical defender of the former against the latter, and which, for Žižek, is what establishes the traditional ideology of, on the one hand, within the family, man as Adventurer and woman as Mother, and, on the other, within the state, man as Ethical Hero and woman as Whore.

It is what Lacan calls the 'phallic function' (the castration performed by the Symbolic) that keeps phallic enjoyment from invading the desexualized ethical field. To achieve this enjoyment, we have, paradoxically, to renounce it, to accept castration by entering the ethical field, which allows love to emerge as a gratuitous effect, an 'unforeseeable answer of the Real'. What may thus result in the relation between the sexes is the asymmetrical structure such that, to the degree that the man pursues some publicly admirable goal which distracts him from the sexual path, the woman, in her belief that he is doing it for her, is drawn to love the man, a relation that is the converse of courtly love.

This antagonistic structure between the sexes finds a parallel in Kant's philosophy in the form of his mathematical and dynamical antinomies, which follow out the impossibility of applying strict definition to what in the former are parts of a continuum and in the latter the relations of cause and effect. It is the structure of these antinomies that can be found in Lacan's sexuation formulas. On the feminine side, although part of woman remains within the phallic function, she has a supplementary *jouissance* (the overflow of her continuum); while, on the masculine side, the universality of the phallic function cannot avoid the postulation of an exception (the primal father who escapes castration). Thus there is

no neat opposition between the sexes, no underlying ontological difference: it is rather that there is one entity, a subject, riven by internal
antagonisms in two radically different ways. This imbalance ensures
that, as Lacan has it, 'there is no sexual relationship': that is, there can
be no final symbolic resolution that can harmonize the relation of the
sexes. Hence, Weininger's anti-feminism is turned on its head: instead of
woman being wholly at the mercy of the phallic, it is man who is under
the phallic injunction. Woman, from the inconsistency of her place in the
structure, is able to find non-phallic enjoyment.

'Let us hope that the public will not deem it unworthy of a philosopher and
beneath him to concern himself with coitus...' (237).[1] This statement could
be taken as a motto to Weininger's work: he elevated sexual difference and the
sexual relationship to the central theme of philosophy. The price he paid for it
was terrible: suicide at 24, only months after his great book *Sex and Character*
came out. Why?

The first thing that strikes us about Weininger is the unmitigated *authenticity*
of his writing. We are not dealing with an 'objective' theory; the writer is
utterly, unreservedly *engaged* in his subject-matter. It is by no accident that, in
the first decades of our century, *Sex and Character* headed the reading lists of
troubled adolescents: it provided an answer to all the questions that tormented
their stormy inner lives. It is easy to denigrate this answer as a combination of
contemporary anti-feminist and anti-Semitic prejudices, with some rather
shallow philosophical commonplaces mixed in. But what gets lost in such a
dismissal is the effect of *recognition* brought about by the reading of Weininger:
it was as if he 'called by name' all that the 'official' discourse silently presupposed, not daring to pronounce publicly. In short, Weininger hauled into the
light of the day the 'sexist' fantasmatic support of the dominant ideology.

'Woman is Only and Thoroughly Sexual'

For Weininger, sexual difference is grounded in the very ontological opposition of subject and object, of active spirit and passive matter. Woman is a
passive, impressionable object, which means that she is entirely dominated by
sexuality:

Woman is only and thoroughly sexual, since her sexuality extends to her entire body
and is in certain places, to put it in physical terms, only more dense than in others – *she
is sexually affected and penetrated* by every thing – always and on the entire surface of her
body. What we usually call coitus is merely a special case of the highest intensity....

Fatherhood is for that reason a miserable deception: we have always to share it with innumerable other things and people . . . An entity which can be at every point sexually penetrated by all things can also get pregnant everywhere and by all things; *mother is in herself a receptacle*. In her, all things are alive, since physiologically everything acts upon her and forms her child. (258–9)

(Here we already encounter the source of all Weininger's difficulties: namely: his confounding of phallic enjoyment with the feminine Other enjoyment: the latter is not centred on the phallus and bombards the body from all directions. Weininger's entire theoretical edifice hinges on the possibility of reducing the Other enjoyment to the phallic enjoyment.) For that reason, 'the idea of pairing is the only conception that has positive worth for women. . . . Pairing is the supreme good for the woman; she seeks to effect it always and everywhere. Her personal sexuality is only a special case of this universal, generalized impersonal instinct' (260). This universality is to be conceptualized in two ways. First, coitus colours with its specific tonality woman's entire activity. Woman is not capable of a pure spiritual attitude, she cannot aim at truth for the sake of truth itself, at the fulfilment of duty for the sake of duty; she cannot sustain a disinterested contemplation of beauty. When she seems to assume such a spiritual attitude, a closer observation never fails to discern a 'pathological' sexual interest lurking in the background (a woman speaks the truth in order to make an impression on man and thus facilitate her seduction of him, etc.). Even suicide *qua* absolute act act is accomplished with narcissistic-pathological considerations: 'such suicides are accompanied practically always by thoughts of other people, what they will think, how they will mourn over them, how grieved – or angry – they will be' (286). It goes without saying that the same holds even more strongly in the case of love, which always conceals the motive for sexual intercourse: woman is never capable of pure, disinterested admiration of the beloved person. Furthermore, for a woman, the idea of coitus is the only way to overcome her egoism, the only ethical idea available to her – 'ethical' in the sense of expressing an ideal towards which woman strives, irrespective of her particular 'pathological' interest:

Her wish for the activity of her own sexual life is her strongest impulse, but it is only a special case of her deep, her only vital interest, the interest that sexual unions shall take place; the wish that as much of it as possible shall occur, in all cases, places, and times. (257–258)

Coitus is therefore the only case apropos of which woman is capable of formulating her own version of the universal ethical imperative: 'Act so that your activity will contribute to the realization of the infinite idea of general pairing.' In contrast to woman, who is thoroughly dominated by sexuality, by the notion of coitus, man, in his relationship to woman, is split between the mutually exclusive poles of sexual coveting and erotic love:

Love and desire are two unlike, mutually exclusive, opposing conditions, and during the time a man really loves, the thought of physical union with the object of his love is insupportable. . . . The more erotic a man is the less he will be troubled with his sexuality, and vice versa. . . . there is only 'platonic' love, because any other so-called love belongs to the kingdom of the senses. (239–40)

If, however, by the very nature of woman, the scope of her interest is limited to coitus, where does woman's beauty come from? How can she function as an object of purely spiritual love? Here Weininger draws a radical conclusion: the nature of woman's beauty is 'performative'; namely, it is man's love that creates woman's beauty:

The love bestowed by the man is the standard of what is beautiful and what is hateful in woman. The conditions are quite different in aesthetics from those in logic or ethics. In logic there is an abstract truth that is the standard of thought; in ethics there is an ideal good that furnishes the criterion of what ought to be done . . . In aesthetics beauty is created by love . . . *All beauty is really more a projection, an emanation of the requirements of love*; and so the beauty of woman is not apart from love, it is not an objective to which love is directed, but woman's beauty is the love of man; they are not two things, but one and the same thing. (242)

A further, inevitable conclusion is that man's love for a woman – his very 'spiritual', 'pure' love, as opposed to sexual longing – is a thoroughly *narcissistic* phenomenon: in his love of a woman, man loves only himself, his own ideal image. Man is well aware of the gap that for ever separates his miserable reality from this ideal, so he projects, transfers, it on to another, on to the idealized woman. This is why love is 'blind': it hinges on the illusion that the idea we are striving for is already realized in the other, in the object of love:

In love, man is only loving himself. Not his empirical self, not the weaknesses and vulgarities, not the failings and smallnesses which he outwardly exhibits; but all that he wants to be, all that he ought to be, his truest, deepest, intelligible nature, free from all fetters of necessity, from all taint of earth. . . . *He projects his ideal of an absolutely worthy existence, the ideal that he is unable to isolate within himself, upon another human being, and this act, and this alone, is none other than love and the significance of love.* (243–4)

No less than hate, love is therefore a phenomenon of cowardice, an easy way out: in hate, we externalize and transfer on to the other the evil that dwells in ourselves, thereby avoiding any confrontation with it; whereas in love, instead of taking pains to realize our spiritual essence, we project this essence upon the other as an already realized state of being. On this account, love is cowardly and treacherous, not only in relationship to man himself, but also and above all in relationship to its object – it disregards utterly the object's (woman's) true nature, and uses it only as a kind of empty projection screen:

Love of a woman is possible only when it does not consider her real qualities, and so is able to replace the actual psychical reality by a different and quite imaginary reality. The attempt to realise one's ideal in a woman, instead of the woman herself, is a necessary destruction of the empirical personality of the woman. And so the attempt is cruel to the woman; it is the egoism of love that disregards the woman, and cares nothing for her real inner life . . . Love is murder. (249)

(Here Weininger, of course, speaks aloud the hidden truth of the idealized figure of the Lady in the courtly love.) The key enigma of love is therefore: why does man choose *woman* as the idealized object in which he (mis)perceives the realization of his spiritual essence? Why does he project his *salvation* upon the very being responsible for his *fall*, since, as we have already seen, man is split between his spiritual-ethical essence and the sexual longing aroused in him by woman's standing invitation to sexual intercourse? The only way to solve this enigma is to accept that man's relationship towards woman as object of erotic love and his relationship towards woman as object of sexual coveting are both 'performative'. Strictly speaking, woman is not the *cause* of man's fall: it is man's fall into sexuality that itself creates woman, confering existence upon her:

It is only when man accepts his own sexuality, denies the absolute in him, turns to the lower, that he gives woman existence. When man became sexual he formed woman. That woman is at all has happened simply because man has accepted his sexuality. Woman is merely the result of this affirmation; she is sexuality itself. . . . Therefore woman's one object must be to keep man sexual. . . . she has but one purpose, that of continuing the guilt of man, for she would disappear the moment man had overcome his sexuality. *Woman is the sin of man.* (298–9)

The normal relationship between cause and effect is here inverted: *woman is not the cause of man's Fall, but its consequence.* For that reason, one need not fight woman actively, since the possesses no positive ontological consistency at all: '*Woman therefore does not exist*' (302). For woman to cease to exist, it is enough for man to overcome the sexual urge in himself. We can see, now, precisely why man has chosen woman as the object of his love: the unbearable fault of creating woman by way of acknowledging his sexuality weighs heavily upon him. Love is but a cowardly, hypocritical attempt by man to compensate for his guilt towards woman:

The crime man has committed in creating woman, and still commits in assenting to her purpose, he excuses to woman by his eroticism. . . . Woman is nothing but man's expression and projection of his own sexuality. Every man creates himself a woman, in which he embodies himself and his own guilt. But woman is not herself guilty; she is made so by the guilt of others, and everything for which woman is blamed should be laid at man's door. *Love strives to cover guilt, instead of conquering it*; it elevates woman instead of nullifying her.(300)

Woman's existence bears witness to the fact that man 'compromised his desire', that he betrayed his true nature as an autonomous ethical subject by giving way to sexuality. Consequently, her true nature consists of the boundless craving for sexual intercourse, an expression of how the phallus 'entirely – although often only unconsciously – dominates woman's entire life'. On account of this constitutive submission to the phallus, woman is heteronomous in the strict Kantian sense, unfree, at the mercy of external Fate:

The male organ is to a woman the Id whose name she doesn't know; her destiny resides in it, something she cannot escape from. For that reason, she does not like to see a naked man and she never expresses a need to see him: she feels she is lost at that moment. The phallus *thus deprives woman completely and irrevocably of her freedom*. (269) Woman is not free: ultimately, the urge to be raped by man in one or another way always prevails in her; woman is governed by the phallus. (274)

Consequently, when a woman resists her sexual urge and is ashamed of it, she suppresses her true nature. Internalizing male spiritual values can go so far as to shove awareness of a woman's true nature out of her consciousness – however, this nature fights back violently, returning in the guise of hysterical symptoms. What the hysterical woman experiences as a foreign, evil and immoral urge is thus simply her innermost nature, her subordination to the phallus. The ultimate proof of woman's amoral character is that the more she desperately endeavours to assume male spiritual values, the more hysterical she becomes. When a woman acts in accordance with moral precepts, she does so in a heteronomous way, out of fear of the male master or in efforts to fascinate him: woman's autonomy is feigned, it is an externally imposed imitation of autonomy. When she speaks the truth, she does so not out of true veracity, but in order to impress man, to seduce him in a more refined way: 'So that woman always lies, even if, objectively, she speaks the truth' (287). Herein resides the '*ontological* untruthfulness of woman'; that is, in this sense, woman's 'love for truth is only a special *case of her mendaciousness*' (291). The highest insight a woman can achieve is an obscure premonition of her constitutive enslavement, which leads her to strive for salvation through self-annihilation.

To the reader acquainted with Lacan's theory of feminine sexuality, it is not difficult to discern in this brief outline a whole series of Lacan's fundamental propositions. Can't we see in Weininger's 'Woman therefore does not exist' the herald of Lacan's *La femme n'existe pas*? The notion that woman gives body to man's fault, that her very existence hinges on man's betrayal of his spiritual-ethical posture – does not this notion present a variation of Lacan's thesis on 'woman as a symptom of man'? (According to Lacan, the symptom as a compromise-formation bears witness to how the subject *cèder sur son désir*.) When Weininger insists that woman can never be fully integrated into the spiritual universe of Truth, Good and Beauty, since this universe remains for her a heteronomous order externally imposed upon her, doesn't he point towards Lacan's assertion that woman is not fully integrated into the symbolic order? And, finally, as to the motif of woman's total subordination to the phallus (in contrast to man, who is only partially submitted to its rule): Lacan's 'formulas of sexuation', don't they also assert that no part of woman is excepted from the phallic function, whereas the masculine position involves an exception, an X *not* submitted to the phallic function?

The Feminine 'Night of the World'

Unfortunately, a closer examination soon unsettles this apparent homology, without thoroughly devalorizing it. The great merit of Weininger, which must be taken into account by feminism, is his complete break from the ideological problematic of 'woman's enigma', of feminity *qua* secret that supposedly eludes the rational, discursive universe. The assertion 'Women does not exist' in no way refers to an ineffable feminine essence beyond the domain of discursive existence: *what does not exist is this very unattainable beyond*. In short, by playing upon the somewhat worn-out Hegelian formula, we can say that the 'enigma of woman' ultimately conceals that there is nothing to conceal? What Weininger fails to accomplish is a Hegelian reflective reversal of *recognizing in this 'nothing' the very negativity that defines the notion of the subject*. Let us recall here the well-known joke about a Jew and a Pole, in which the Jew extracts money from the Pole under the pretext of imparting to him the secret of how Jews succeed in extracting from people their very last penny.[3] Weininger's violent anti-feminist outburst – 'There is no feminine secret at all, behind the mask of the Enigma, there is simply nothing!' – remains at the level of the Pole's fury that springs up when he finally grasps how the Jew, by endlessly postponing the final revelation, was merely extracting more and more money from him; what Weininger fails to perform is a gesture that would correspond to the Jew's answer to the Pole's outburst: 'Well, now you see how we, the Jews, extract money from people...', namely, a gesture that would reinterpret, reinscribe, the failure as a success – something like 'See, this nothingness behind the mask is the very absolute negativity on account of which woman is the subject *par excellence*, not a limited object opposed to the force of subjectivity!'

The status of this nothing can be explained by means of the Lacanian distinction between the subject of the enunciation and the subject of the enunciated. Far from being dismissible as a meaningless paradox, the statement 'I don't exist' can acquire an authentic existential weight in so far as it signals the contraction of the subject into the empty vanishing point of enunciation that precedes every imaginary or symbolic identification: I can easily find myself excluded from the intersubjective symbolic network, so that I lack the identificatory feature which would enable me to declare victoriously, 'That's me!' That is to say, in a sense far from simply metaphorical, 'I am' only what I am for the others, in so far as I am inscribed into the network of the big Other, in so far as I possess a social-symbolic existence – outside of such an inscribed existence I am nothing, nothing but the vanishing point of 'I think', avoid of any positive content. However, 'It's me who thinks' is already an answer to the question 'Who is the one who thinks?'; that is, it already accounts for a minimal positive identity of the thinking subject. Lacan's point here is that an unsurmountable gap separates forever what I am 'in the real' from the symbolic mandate that procures my social identity: the primordial ontological fact is the void, the abyss on account of which I am inaccessible to myself in my capacity as a real substance, or, to quote Kant's unique formulation from his *Critique of Pure Reason*, on account of which I never get to know what I am as 'I or he or it (the Thing) which thinks (*Ich, oder Er, oder Es (das Ding), welches denkt)*'. Every symbolic identity that I acquire is ultimately nothing but a supplementary feature whose function is to fill out this void. This pure void of subjectivity, this empty form of 'transcendental apperception', has to be distinguished from the Cartesian *cogito* which remains a *res cogitans*, a little piece of substantial reality miraculously saved from the destructive force of universal doubt: it was only with Kant that the distinction was made between the empty form of 'I think' and the thinking substance, the 'thing which thinks'.

Here, then, Weininger falls short: when, in his ontological interpretation of woman's seduction of man as the 'infinite craving of Nothing for Something', he conceives of woman as *object*. In this endeavour of nothing to become something, he fails to recognize *the very striving of the subject for a substantial support*. Or, in so far as the subject is a 'being-of-language', Weininger fails to recognize in this striving the constitutive motion of the subject *qua* void, lack of the signifier, that is, the striving of a hole, a missing link in the signifying chain, for a signifying representative. In other words, far from expressing the subject's fear of a 'pathological' stain, of the positivity of an inert object, Weininger's aversion to woman bears witness to the fear of the most radical dimension of subjectivity itself: of the Void which 'is' the subject. In a manuscript for the Jena *Realphilosphie* of 1805–6, Hegel characterized this experience of pure Self *qua* 'abstract negativity', this 'eclipse of (constituted) reality', this contraction-into-self of the subject, as the 'night of the world':

The human being is this night, this empty nothing, that contains everything in its simplicity – an unending wealth of many representations, images, of which none belongs to him – or which are not present. This night, the inner of nature, that exists here – pure self – in phantasmagorical representations, is night all around it, in which here shoots a bloody head – there another white ghastly apparition, suddenly here before it, and just so disappears. One catches sight of this night when one looks human beings in the eye – into a night that becomes awful.[4]

And the symbolic order, the universe of the word, *logos*, can emerge only from the experience of this abyss. As Hegel puts it, this inwardness of the pure self 'must enter also into existence, become an object, oppose itself to this innerness to be external; return to being. This is language as name-giving power. . . . Through the name the object as individual entity is born out of the I.'[5] What we must be careful not to miss here is how Hegel's break with the Enlightenment tradition can be discerned in the reversal of the very metaphor for the subject: the subject is no longer the light of reason opposed to the non-transparent, impenetrable stuff (of nature, tradition . . .); his very kernel the gesture which opens up the space for the light of logos, is absolute negativity *qua* 'night of the world'. And what are Weininger's infamous 'henids – the confused feminine representations that did not yet achieve the clarity of the Word, the self-identity of notion – if not the very 'phantasmagorical representations' mentioned by Hegel, that is, the fantasy-formations that emerge where the word fails, since their function is precisely to fill out the void of this failure? Herein resides the paradox of Weininger's anti-feminism: far from being a result of his obscurantist anti-Enlightenment attitude, his anti-feminism attests to his adherence to the ideal of the Enlightenment, to his avoidance of the abyss of pure subjectivity.[6]

The same goes for Weininger's notorious anti-Semitism, which also cannot obliterate its indebtedness to the Enlightenment – notwithstanding Weininger's ethical voluntarism, the fact remains that his principal philosophical reference is Kant, the philosopher of the Enlightenment *par excellence* (this link between anti-Semitism and a certain kind of Enlightenment thinking was already suggested by Adorno and Horkheimer in their *Dialectic of Enlightenment*). At the most fundamental level, anti-Semitism does not associate

Jews with corruption as a positive feature, but rather with shapelessness itself; that is, with the lack of a definite, delimited ethnic disposition. In this vein, Alfred Rosenberg, Hitler's chief ideologue, asserted that all European nations possess a well-defined 'spiritual shape' (*Gestalt*) which gives expression to their ethnic character — and this 'spiritual shape' is precisely what is missing in Jews. And — again — is not this very 'shapelessness' (*Gestaltlosigkeit*) the constitutive feature of subjectivity; does not subjectivity by definition transcend every positive spiritual shape? It should be clear, now, in what precise way anti-Semitism and Fascist corporatism form the two sides of one and the same coin. In its repudiation of Judaeo-democratic 'abstract universalism', as opposed to the notion of society *qua* harmonious organic form in which every individual and every class has its own well-defined place, corporatism is inspired by the very insight that many a democrat prefers to shirk: *only an entity that is in itself hindered, dislocated — that is, one that lacks its 'proper place', that is by definition 'out of joint' — can immediately refer to universality as such.*

Or, to ask in terms of the relationship between the universal and the particular: how does the particular participate in the universal? According to the traditional ontology, the universal guarantees to the particular its identity: particular objects participate in their universal genus in so far as they 'truly are what they are': namely, as far as they realize or fit their notion. A table, for example, participates in the notion of table in so far as it is 'truly a table'. Here universality remains a 'mute', indifferent feature connecting particular entities, an in-itself that is not posited as such. The particular does not relate to the universal as such. This is in contrast to the subject *qua* 'self-consciousness', who participates in the universal precisely and only in so far as his identity is truncated, marked by a lack; in so far as he is not fully 'what he is' — this is what Hegel has in mind when he speaks of 'negative universality'. Let us recall an exemplary case from political dialectics: when does some particular (ethnic, sexual, religious, etc.) minority make an appeal to the universal? Precisely when the existing framework of social relations fails to satisfy the minority's needs and prevents it from realizing its potential. At this precise point, the minority is compelled to ground its demands in the universal and universally acknowledged principles, claiming that its members are prevented from participating in education, job opportunities, free expression, public political activity, to the same extent as others.

An exemplary case of this for-itself of the universal, that is, of the dialecticized relationship towards the universal, is offered by the infamous claim of Malcolm X that *white man as such is evil*. The meaning of this pronouncement is not that all whites are evil, but rather that, on account of the wrongs committed by white men against black people, evil pertains to the very universal notion of a white man. However, this does not prevent me, a singular white man, from becoming 'good' by achieving awareness of the evil that defines the very substance of my being, and by fully assuming this guilt and working to overcome it. (The same goes for the Christian notion of the sinfulness inscribed in the very core of human nature in so far as we are all 'sons of Adam': the way to salvation lies in reflectively assuming this guilt.) Let us quote here Ernesto Laclau's apposite formulation (thoroughly Hegelian, notwithstanding Laclau's declared anti-Hegelianism):

> ... the universal is part of my identity insofar as I am penetrated by a constitutive lack – that is, insofar as my differential identity has failed in its process of constitution. The universal emerges out of the particular not as some principle underlying and explaining it, but as an incomplete horizon suturing a dislocated particular identity.[7]

In this precise sense 'the universal is the symbol of a missing fullness'.[8] I can relate to the universal as such only in so far as my particular identity is thwarted, 'dislocated', only in so far as some impediment prevents me from 'becoming what I already am'. And, as we already pointed out, proof *per negationem* is provided by the interconnection of the two features that distinguish Fascist corporatism: its obsession with the image of society as an organic community whose every constituent is supposed to 'occupy its proper place' and its pathological resistance to abstract universality as a force of social disintegration – that is, to the idea that an individual can directly, irrespective of his or her place within the social organism, participate in the Universal (the idea, for example, that I possess inalienable rights simply as a human being, not only in my capacity of a member of a certain class or corporation).

Beyond Phallus

The paradox of Weininger is that he is at his closest to feminism precisely where he appears to be more anti-feminist than the 'official' ideology. That is to say, in opposition to this ideology, Weininger denies even the (limited) ethical value of mother, the pillar of the family, and reformulates the traditional splitting: man is divided into autonomous spiritual attitude and phallic sexuality (fall into heteronomy); woman is divided into her 'true nature' (which consists of her very lack of a proper nature – she 'is' nothing but the craving for man; she exits only in so far as she attracts his gaze) and heteronomous, externally imposed, morality. If, however, we recognize in the ontological void of the woman the very void that defines subjectivity, this double division changes into Lacan's 'formulas of sexuation'. Woman's division is of a hysterical nature, it assumes the form of the *inconsistency* of her desire: 'I demand of you to refuse my demand, since this is not *that*' (Lacan). When, for example, Wagner's Kundry seduces Parsifal, she actually wants him to resist her advances – this obstruction, this sabotage of her own intent, does it not testify to a dimension in her which resists the domination of the phallus? (Weininger himself speaks of an obscure longing in woman for deliverance, for shaking off the yoke of the phallus through self-annihilation.) The male dread of woman, which so deeply branded the *Zeitgeist* at the turn of the century, from Edvard Munch and August Strindberg up to Franz Kafka, thus reveals itself as the dread of feminine inconsistency: feminine hysteria, which trau-matized these men (and which also marked the birthplace of psychoanalysis), confronted them with an inconsistent multitude of masks (a hysterical woman immediately moves from desperate pleas to cruel, vulgar derision and so on). What causes such uneasiness is the impossibility of discerning behind the masks a consistent subject manipulating them: behind the multiple layers of masks is nothing, or, at the most, nothing but the shapeless, mucus stuff of the life-substance. Suffice it to mention Edvard Munch's encounter with hysteria, which left such a deep mark upon him. In 1893 Munch was in love with the beautiful daughter of an Oslo wine-merchant. She clung to him, but he was afraid of such a tie and anxious about his work, so he left her. One stormy night a sailing-boat came to fetch him: the report was that the young woman was on the point of death and wanted to speak to him for the last time. Munch was deeply moved and without question went to her place, where he found her lying on a bed between two lit candles. But when he approached her bed, she rose and started to laugh: the whole scene was nothing but a hoax. Munch turned and started to leave; at that point, she threatened to shoot herself if he left her; and drawing a revolver, she pointed it at her breast. When Munch bent to wrench the weapon away, convinced that this too was only part of the game, the gun went off and wounded him in the hand...[9] Here we encounter hysterical theatre at its purest: the subject is caught in a masquerade in which what appears to be deadly serious reveals itself as fraud (dying), and what appears to be an empty gesture reveals itself as deadly serious (the threat of suicide). The panic that seizes the (male) subject confronting this theatre expresses a dread that behind the many masks, which fall away from each other like the layers of an onion, here is nothing, no ultimate feminine secret.

Here, however, we must avoid a fatal misunderstanding. In so far as these hysterical masks are the way for a woman to captivate the male gaze, the inevitable conclusion seems to be that the feminine secret inaccessible to the male phallic economy – the 'eternally Feminine /*das ewig Weibliche/*' (Goethe) beyond symbolic masks – consists of the feminine substance that eludes the reign of 'phallogocentrism'. The complementary conclusion is that, in so far as there is nothing behind the masks, woman is wholly subordinated to the phallus. According to Lacan, however, the exact opposite is true: the presymbolic 'eternally Feminine' is a retroactive patriarchal fantasy – that is, the exception which grounds the reign of the phallus (the same as with the anthropological notion of an original matriarchal paradise, which was ruined by the fall into patriarchal civilization and which, from Bachofen onwards, firmly supports patriarchal ideology, since it relies on the notion of teleological evolution from matriarchy to patriarchy). It is thus the very lack of any exception to the phallus that renders the feminine libidinal economy inconsistent, hysterical, and thereby undermines the reign of the phallus. When, therefore, as Weininger puts it, woman is 'coited by every object', this very boundless extension of phallus undermines phallus as the principle of the universal and its founding exception.

Lacan's 'Subversion of the subject...' ends with the ambiguous 'I won't go any further here'.[10] Ambiguous, since it can be taken to imply that, later, somewhere else, Lacan *will* 'go further'. This lure enticed some feminist critics of Lacan to reproach him for coming to a halt at the very point he should accomplish the decisive step beyond Freud's phallocentrism: although Lacan does talk about feminine *jouissance* eluding the phallic domain, he conceives of it as an ineffable 'dark continent' separated from (the male) discourse by a frontier impossible to trespass. For feminists like Irigaray or Kristeva, this refusal to trespass the frontier, this 'I won't go any further here', signals the continued tabooing of women; what they want is to 'go further': namely, to deploy the contours of a 'feminine discourse' beyond the 'phallic' symbolic order. Why does this operation that, from the standpoint of common sense, cannot but appear fully justified, miss its mark? In traditional terms, the limit that defines woman is not epistemological but ontological: *beyond it there is nothing*. 'Feminine' is the structure of the limit as such, a limit that *precedes* what may or may not lie in its beyond: all that we perceive in this beyond (the eternal feminine, for example) are our own fantasy projections. Woman *qua* enigma is a spectre generated by the inconsistent surface of multiple masks – the secret of 'Secret' itself is the inconsistency of the surface. And the Lacanian name for this inconsistency of the surface (for the convoluted topological space like the Moebius strip) is simply *the subject*.

In the case of man, on the contrary, the split is, as it were, externalized: man escapes the inconsistency of his desire by establishing a line of separation between the domain of the phallus – that is, sexual enjoyment, the relationship to a sexual partner – and the non-phallic – that is, the domain of ethical goals, of non-sexual 'public' activity (exception). Encountered here is the paradox of 'states that are essentially by-products': man subordinates his relationship to a woman to the domain of ethical goals (when forced to choose between woman and ethical duty – in the guise of professional obligation, he immediately opts for duty), yet he is simultaneously aware that only a relationship to a woman can bring him genuine 'happiness' or personal fulfilment. His 'wager' is that woman will be most effectively seduced precisely when he does not subordinate all his activity to her – what she will be unable to resist is her fascination with his 'public' activity, her secret awareness that he is actually doing it for her. What we have here is the inverted libidinal economy of *courtly love*: in courtly love I directly devote myself to the Lady, I posit my serving her as my supreme duty, and for that reason woman remains a cold, indifferent, capricious despot, an 'inhuman partner' (Lacan) with whom the sexual relationship is neither possible nor really desirable, whereas here I render the sexual relationship possible precisely by *not* positing it as my explicit goal . . .

This paradox emerges in almost every melodrama that interprets the man's readiness to sacrifice his beloved for the (public) cause as the supreme proof of his love for her: namely, of how 'she is everything to him'. The sublime moment of recognition occurs when the woman finally realizes that the man has left her for the sake of his love for her. An interesting variation on this theme is offered by Minnelli's version of *The Four Riders of the Apocalypse*: Glenn Ford plays Julio, a wealthy Argentinian who leads a merry life in Paris during the German occupation, socializing with German officers, and living with the beautiful wife of an absent leader of the Resistance (Ingrid Thulin). Although the woman is passionately in love with Julio, she is uneasy that the man she is living with is a weakling, taking refuge in private pleasures, whereas the husband whom she left for her lover is a true hero. Suddenly this entire scenario is exposed as masquerade: in an emergency, Julio is urgently contacted by a man whom she knows to be part of the Resistance, so she guesses that Julio was feigning to be a man of pleasure in order to socialize with German high officers and thereby gain access to precious information about the enemy. Formally, Julio betrayed her love, yet in spite of this betrayal she lets him go forward into the last, probably suicidal action: she is well aware that, in a deeper sense, he is doing it for her, in order to become worthy of her love . . .

What Lacan designates as the 'phallic function' is this very splitting between the domain of phallic enjoyment and the desexualized 'public' field that eludes it; that is, *'phallic' is this self-limitation of the phallus, this positing of an exception*. In this precise sense the phallus is the signifier of castration: 'symbolic castration' is ultimately another name for the paradox of 'states that are essentially by-products': *if we are to achieve fulfilment through phallic enjoyment, we must renounce it as our explicit goal*. In other words, true love can emerge only within a relationship of 'partnership' that is animated by a different, non-sexual goal (see the novels of Marguerite Duras). Love is an unforeseeable answer of the Real: it (can) emerge(s) 'out of nowhere' only when we renounce any attempt to direct and control its course. (Here, of course, as with every instance of the Real, opposites coincide: love is at the same time the foreseeable product of an absolute mechanism – as evidenced by the absolutely predictable character of transferential love in psychoanalysis. This love is produced 'automatically' by the very analytical situation, irrespective of the actual characteristics of the analyst. In this precise sense the analyst is the *object petit a* and not another subject: because of its 'automatic' character, transferential love dispenses with the illusion that we fall in love on account of the beloved person's positive properties, namely on account of what he or she is 'in reality'. We fall in love with the analyst *qua* the formal place in the structure, devoid of 'human features', not with a flesh-and-blood person.[11]

The 'Formulas of Sexuation'

Apropos of these two asymmetric antinomies of symbolization (the 'masculine' side that involves the universality of the phallic function grounded in an exception; the 'feminine' side that involves a 'non-all' field which, for that very reason, contains no exception to the phallic function) a question imposes itself with a kind of self-evidence: what constitutes the link that connects these two purely logical antinomies with the opposition of female and male, which, however symbolically mediated and culturally conditioned, remains an obvious biological fact? The answer to this question is: *there is no link*. What we experience as 'sexuality' is precisely the effect of the contingent act of 'grafting' the fundamental deadlock of symbolization on to the biological opposition of male and female. The answer to the question: isn't this link between the two logical paradoxes of universalization and sexuality illicit? is therefore: *that's precisely Lacan's point*. What Lacan does is simply to transpose this 'illicit' character from the epistemological level to the ontological level: sexuality itself, what we experience as the highest, most intense assertion of our being, is a *bricolage*, a montage of two heterogeneous elements. Herein resides Lacan's 'deconstruction' of sexuality.

This parasitic 'grafting' of the symbolic deadlock on to animal coupling undermines the instinctual rhythm of animal coupling, and confers on it an indelible brand of failure: 'there is no sexual relationship'; every relation of the two sexes can take place only against the background of a fundamental impossibility. This 'graft' is radically contingent in the sense that it hinges on the homology between the penis in the male and the fact that, in the 'masculine' formulas, we are dealing with the exception that grounds universality: the short circuit between the two changes the penis into a material support of the phallic signifier, the signifier of symbolic castration. How, then, on a closer look, are the 'masculine' and the 'feminine' side structured?

A standard example of a 'non-all' field is provided by the Marxist notion of class struggle: every position we assume towards the class struggle, inclusive of a theoretical one, is already a moment of the class struggle, it involves 'taking sides' in it, which is why there is no impartial objective standpoint enabling us to delinerate class struggle. In this precise sense, 'class struggle doesn't exist', since 'there is no element eluding it' − we cannot apprehend it 'as such', what we are dealing with are always the partial effects whose absent cause is the class struggle.[12] Let us, however, turn to a more aetheric example, that of philosophy. A quick glance at any manual of philosophy makes it clear how every universal, all-encompassing notion of philosophy is rooted in a particular philosophy, how it involves the standpoint of a particular philosophy. There is no neutral notion of philosophy to be divided into analytical philosophy, hermeneutic philosophy, etc.; every particular philosophy encompasses itself and (its view on) all other philosophies. Or, as Hegel put it in his *Lessons on the History of Philosophy*, every epochal philosophy is in a way the whole of philosophy; it is not a subdivision of the whole but this whole itself apprehended in a specific modality. What we have here is thus not a simple reduction of the universal to the particular, but rather a kind of *surplus* of the universal: no single universal encompasses the entire particular content, since each particular has *its own* universal − that is, contains a specific perspective on the entire field.

And the masculine position designates precisely the endeavour to resolve this impasse of 'too many universals' by way of excluding *one* paradoxical particular; this exceptional particular immediately gives body to the universal as such and simultaneously negates its constitutive feature. *This is how Universal 'as such', in its opposition to particular content, comes to exist.* An exemplary case of it is the figure of the Lady in the courtly love that belongs thoroughly to the masculine symbolic economy. In the figure of the Lady, woman *qua* sexual object reaches existence − yet at the price of being posited as the inaccessible thing: that is, desexualized, transformed into an object that, precisely in so far as it gives body to sexuality as such, renders the masculine subject impotent.[13]

A few years ago, *Mad* published a series of caricatures exemplifying the four possible levels at which a subject can relate to a symbolic norm adopted in his community. Let us limit ourselves to the norm of fashion. At the lowest level are the poor, whose attitude towards fashion is indifferent − their sole aim is simply to avoid looking shabby, to maintain a standard of decency. Next are the lower middle classes, who desperately strive to follow fashion; however, owing to financial constraint, they always come 'too late' and wear what was fashionable a season ago. The upper middle classes, who actually can afford the latest fashion, do not yet represent the highest level: above them are the trend-setting rich, who are again (as was already the case with the lowest level) indifferent towards fashion, but for a very different reason – they have no external norm to comply with, since they themselves set the norm. What they wear *is the fashion*. Of special significance to the theory of the signifier is this fourth and last level, which, as a kind of paradoxical surplus, supplements the perfect compliance with the latest fashion. This level involves a kind of reflective reversal of the preceding one: as to content, the last two levels are exactly the same, the difference between them is of a purely formal nature – the trend-setting rich are dressed the same as the upper middle classes, but not for the same reason: that is, not because they want to follow the latest fashion, but simply because whatever they wear *is* the latest fashion. We encounter the same four levels apropos of legal power: beyond those who are indifferent to laws, those who break laws while remaining integrated into the system of law and order, and those who stick strictly to the letter of the law, there are those at the very top whose acts are always in accordance with the law, not because they obediently follow the law but because their activity *determines* what is law in a performative way – what(ever) they do simply *is* the law (the king in an absolute monarchy, for example). This point of inversion is the exception that founds the universal.

Hegel's thesis that every genus has only one species, the other species being the genus itself, aims at the same paradoxical point of inversion. When, for example, we say 'Rich people are poor people with money', this definition is not reversible – we cannot say 'Poor people are rich people without money'. We do not have a neutral genus 'people', divided into its two species, 'poor people' and 'rich people': the genus is 'poor people' to whom we must add the *differentia specifica* (money) in order to obtain its species, 'rich people'. Psychoanalysis conceives of the sexual difference in a somewhat homologous way: 'Woman is a castrated man.' Here, also, the proposition cannot be inverted into 'Man is woman with phallus'. However, it would be wrong to conclude from this that man *qua* male possesses a kind of ontological priority. The properly Hegelian paradox is that *the 'cut' of the specific difference is constitutive of the genus itself*. In other words, castration defines the genus of man; the '*neutral*' universality of man unmarked with castration is already an index of the disavowal of castration.

Lacan's achievement is here to conceive of the sexual difference at the transcendental level in the strict Kantian sense of the term – that is, without reference to any 'pathological' empirical content. At the same time, his definition of sexual difference avoids the pitfall of 'essentialism' by conceiving of the 'essence' of each of the two sexual positions as a specific form of inconsistency, of antagonism. The 'essence of woman' is not some positive entity but an impasse, a deadlock that prevents her from 'becoming woman'. This is why the parallel between Lacan's 'formulas of sexuation' and Kant's antinomies of pure reason is fully justified: in Lacan, 'masculine' or 'feminine' is not a predicate providing positive information about the subject – that is, designating some of its phenomenal properties; it is, rather, a case of what Kant conceives of as a purely negative determination which merely designates, registers, a certain limit; more precisely: a specific modality of how the subject failed in his or her bid for identity which would constitute him or her as an object within phenomenal reality. Lacan is on that account as far as possible from the notion of sexual difference as the relationship of two opposite poles which supplement each other and together form the whole of man: 'masculine' and 'feminine' are not the two species of the genus of man but, rather, the two modes of the subject's *failure* to achieve the full identity of man. 'Man' and 'woman' together do not form a whole, since *each of them is already in itself a failed whole.*

It should also be clear, now, why Lacan's conceptualization of sexual difference avoids the trap of the infamous 'binary logic': in it, 'masculine' and 'feminine' are not opposed in the guise of a series of contrary predicates (active/passive, cause/effect, reason/sentiment); 'masculine' and 'feminine', rather, involve a different modality of the very antagonist relationship between these opposites. 'Man' is not a cause of the woman-effect, but a specific modality of the relationship between cause and effect (the linear succession of causes and effects with an excepted unique element, the last cause), in contrast to 'woman', who implies a different modality (a kind of convoluted 'interaction' where the cause functions as an effect of its own effects). Within the domain of sexual pleasures proper, masculine economy tends to be 'teleological', centred on phallic orgasm *qua* pleasure *par excellence*, whereas feminine economy involves a dispersed network of particular pleasures that are not organized around some teleological central principle. The result of it is that 'masculine' and 'feminine' are not two positive substantial entities, but two different modalities of one and the same entity: in order to 'feminize' a masculine discourse, it suffices to change, sometimes in a barely perceptive way, its specific 'tonality'.

It is here that Foucauldian 'constructionists' and Lacan part ways: for the 'constructionists', sex is not a natural given but a *bricolage*, an artificial unification of heterogeneous discursive practices, whereas Lacan rejects this view without returning to naïve substantialism. For him, sexual difference is not a discursive, symbolic construction; instead, it emerges at the very point of the failure of symbolization: we are sexed beings because symbolization always runs up against its own inherent impossibility. What is at stake here is not that 'actual', 'concrete' sexual beings can never fully fit the symbolic construction of 'man' or 'woman': the point is rather that this symbolic construction itself supplements a certain fundamental deadlock. In short, *if it were possible to symbolize sexual difference, we would not have two sexes but only one.* 'Male' and 'female' are not two complementary parts of the whole, they are two (failed) attempts to symbolize this whole.

The ultimate result of our reading of Weininger is thus a paradoxical, yet inevitable inversion of the anti-feminist ideological dispositive espoused by Weininger himself, according to which women are wholly submitted to phallic enjoyment, whereas men have access to the de-sexualized domain of ethical goals beyond the phallus: it is man who is wholly submitted to the phallus (since positing an exception is the way to maintain the universal domination of the phallus), whereas it is woman who, through the inconsistency of her desire, attains the domain 'beyond the phallus'. Only woman has access to the Other (non-phallic) enjoyment.

The traumatic element that Weininger absolutely refused to acknowledge, although it followed from his own work, was this inherent reversal of his 'official' position: woman, not man, can reach 'beyond the phallus'. Weininger, rather, opted for suicide, for this sole example of a successful repression, a repression without the return of the repressed. By means of his suicide, Weininger confirmed two things: that somewhere 'deep in himself', in his unconscious, *he knew it*, and, simultaneously, that this knowledge was for him absolutely unbearable. The choice for him was neither 'life or death' nor 'money or death', but rather 'knowledge or death'. That death was the only possible escape from this knowledge bears witness to the unquestionable *authenticity* of his subjective position. For that reason, Weininger is still worth reading.

Notes

1   Numbers in parentheses refer to the pages of the – extremely unreliable – English translation of Sex and Character. Authorized translation from the 6th German edition (Lndon, Heinemann; G. P Putnam's & Sons, New York, Emphasis in quoted extracts is Žižek's.

2   The infamous 'enigma of the East' follows the same logic as the 'enigma of the Woman', which is why the first step in breaking with Eurocentrism must be to repeat *mutatis mutandis* Lacan's 'Woman doesn't exist' and to assert that 'the Orient doesn't exist'.

3   For an interpretation of this joke, see Slavoj Žižek, *The Sublime Object of Ideology*, (London, Verso, 1989), ch. 2.

4   Quoted from Donald Phillip Verene, *Hegel's Recollection* (Albany, NY, Suny Press, 1985), pp. 7–8.

5   Ibid., p. 8.

6   The link between *La femme n'existe pas* and her status of a pure subject can also be ascertained through reference to Kant.

7   Ernesto Laclau, 'Universalism, Particularism, and the Question of Identity', *October* 61. (1992), pp. 83–94, at p. 89.

8   Ibid.

9   See J. P. Hodin, *Edvard Munch* (London, Thames and Hudson, 1972), pp. 88–9.

10 Jacques Lacan, *Ecrits: A Selection* (New York, Norton, 1977), p. 324.

11 The automatism of love is set in motion when some contingent, ultimately indifferent, (libidinal) object finds itself occupying a pre-given fantasy-place. This role of fantasy in the automatic emergence of love hinges on the fact that 'there is no sexual relationship', no universal formula or matrix guaranteeing a harmonious sexual relationship with the partner: on account of the lack of this universal formula, every individual has to invent a fantasy of their own.

12 In the Stalinist discursive universe, on the contrary, class struggle *does* exist, since there is an exception to it: technics and language are conceived of as neutral instruments at the disposal of everybody and as such external to class struggle.

13 One of the privileged ways of maintaining the fiction of woman's existence as the exception that immediately gives body to the universals is the operatic aria: its climatic moment when the soprano 'puts herself entirely into the voice'. At this moment, one can briefly entertain the illusion that the woman 'has it in herself', *object petit a*, the voice-object, the cause of desire, and, consequently, that she exists.

7

Courtly Love, or Woman as Thing

This is a chapter from *The Metastases of Enjoyment* (1994, pp. 89–112). Here Žižek argues that courtly love, far from being out of date, has a structure which can still be detected in sexual relations today. Since the masochistic couple came into theoretical focus in the late nineteenth century, we have been the better able to understand 'the libidinal economy of courtly love'. For an analysis of its 'masochistic theatre', he turns to Lacan, who regards the Lady not as sublime object, but as universal ideal emptied of all substance – a remote impassive figure who imposes arbitrary tasks. This matches the relation of knight to master, but with an additional perverse twist, that the tasks imposed are sometimes curiously at odds with her putative spirituality. The courtly lover's narcissistic illusion conceals from him the traumatic strangeness of 'the Freudian Thing'.

Another way in which courtly love betrays its link with masochism is its emphasis on strict performance of codes. Masochism is to be distinguished from sadism in that it is a contract between two parties, in which the supposed victim is giving the orders, unlike sadism, in which the torment is uncontrolled. This makes the masochistic scene essentially theatrical, the violence 'endlessly repeated as an interrupted gesture'. This high theatre of the masochistic performance no more disrupts everyday reality than the masochist's instructions to the dominatrix prevent the game from proceeding. Here is a parallel to the Symbolic *per se*, in that the scene has to be played with a straight face, because it is the playing as such that counts, not any supposed reality behind the mask. When, however, the dominant partner becomes sickened of being no more than a lay figure in the masochist's scenario, 'an object-instrument of the other's *jouissance*', he may revoke the contract with a hysterical act of violence. Similarly, the sadist may try to justify the excess of his violence by claiming that the victim is a masochist who is making him into her slave.

The fascination of the Lady in courtly love is usually attributed to her inaccessibility; but in the Lacanian reading, the obstacle that makes her inaccessible is of the subject's own creation, for the reason that the courtly lover cannot confront the impossibility of what he seeks. The Lady becomes a substitute for what he pursues, thus allowing him to set up the obstacle that keeps her at a safe distance, enforcing a detour, a theme that recurs in the films of Louis Buñuel in the artificial impediments set up for desire. The Thing can be seen only in a distorted form, in an 'anamorphosis', never directly; a direct view would destroy the illusion and leave nothing. This structure falls within Lacan's view of sublimation, the raising of an object 'to the dignity of the Thing': the sublime Lady-object (a 'concrete maternal object of need') is produced by the endless skirting of the target (the 'unserviceable Thing'). The same paradox of detour is discernible in the phallic signifier, as it stands both for the immediacy of *jouissance* and for its refusal (castration), so that *jouissance* can be reached only through the endless succession of symbolic desires. Thus the very agency that entices us to search for enjoyment induces us to renounce it.

Here Žižek finds an analogy with a characteristic of Western philosophy: namely, the urge to raise some specific feature of a theory to the dignity of a general explanation, such as Marx taking production to be the foundational principle of the whole system of distribution, exchange, consumption and production, or J. L. Austin, making the performative mode into the genus for both species of statement, constative and per-formative. In contrast, Heidegger's notion of 'ontological difference' implies that whatever is chosen as the ground of explanation of a totality cannot encompass the Real. By the same token, the Lady is a name for the Real that continually evades the grasp, a negative feature that functions as a positive one. She is pursued precisely because she is forbidden, illustrating the notion of 'the imp of the perverse' (Edgar Allan Poe) as something done with no motive other than that it is prohibited, hence, a kind of subverted Kantian choice that has no 'pathological' motive.

The wish to ensure that the Real evades his grasp characterizes the lover's ordeal, of which Žižek produces a series of exemplifications: the seducer who betrays a virtual Kantian imperative in *Les Liaisons danger-euses*, the indirections of the letters in *Cyrano de Bergerac*, the cata-strophic effect of provoking the fantasy in *Wild at Heart*, and the *film noir* as producing in the *femme fatale* a latter-day version of the Lady, issuing arbitrary commands to her hard-boiled suitor, while remaining out of reach as the possession of the paternal gangster-boss. As a final variation of the courtly love dilemma, and a possible resolution thereof, the black male transvestite in *The Crying Game* is structurally in the position of the Lady through the distance maintained by her unknowing lover. The crux of the film occurs when the lover discovers 'something' where he expected 'nothing', a reversal of the Freudian shock. Where courtly love fails, the possibility of 'real' love emerges: the lover is ultimately able to move from loving her for something in her more than herself – that is, as object – to seeing 'her' as a subject of lack.

The survival of the courtly love structure testifies to the continuing male attempt to compensate for his reduction of the woman to a mere vehicle for his fantasy. In turn the woman comes to inhabit this fantasy as her 'femininity' – thus deprived of her own particularity as woman – which leads to a symmetrical view of the sexes. If sexual difference always retains a Real that cannot be symbolized, lovers are fated to settle for a relationship that is also a 'non-relationship', in that each partner is not wholly subject, but intersects with the Thing.

Why talk about courtly love (*l'amour courtois*) today, in an age of permissiveness when the sexual encounter is often nothing more than a 'quickie' in some dark corner of an office? The impression that courtly love is out of date, long superseded by modern manners, is a lure blinding us to how the logic of courtly love still defines the parameters within which the two sexes relate to each other. This claim, however, in no way implies an evolutionary model through which courtly love would provide the elementary matrix out of which we generate its later, more complex variations. Our thesis is, instead, that history has to be read retroactively: the anatomy of man offers the key to the anatomy of the ape, as Marx put it. It is only with the emergence of masochism, of the masochist couple, towards the end of the last century that we can now grasp the libidinal economy of courtly love.

The Masochistic Theatre of Courtly Love

The first trap to be avoided apropos of courtly love is the erroneous notion of the Lady as the sublime object: as a rule, one evokes here the process of spiritualization, the shift from raw sensual coveting to elevated spiritual longing. The Lady is thus perceived as a kind of spiritual guide into the higher sphere of religious ecstasy, in the sense of Dante's Beatrice. In contrast to this notion, Lacan emphasizes a series of features which belie such a spiritualization: true, the Lady in courtly love loses concrete features and is addressed as an abstract ideal, so that 'writers have noted that all the poets seem to be addressing the same person. . . . In this poetic field the feminine object is emptied of all real substance.'[1] However, this abstract character of the Lady has nothing to do with spiritual purification; rather, it points towards the abstraction that pertains to a cold, distanced, inhuman partner – the Lady is by no means a warm, compassionate, understanding fellow-creature:

By means of a form of sublimation specific to art, poetic creation consists in positing an object I can only describe as terrifying, an inhuman partner.
    The Lady is never characterized for any of her real, concrete virtues, for her wisdom, her prudence, or even her competence. If she is described as wise, it is only because she embodies an immaterial wisdom or because she represents its functions more than she exercises them. On the contrary, she is as arbitrary as possible in the tests she imposes on her servant.[2]

The knight's relationship to the Lady is thus the relationship of the subject-bondsman, vassal, to his feudal Master-Sovereign, who subjects him to senseless, outrageous, impossible, arbitrary, capricious ordeals. It is precisely in order to emphasize the non-spiritual nature of these ordeals that Lacan quotes a poem about a Lady who demanded that her servant literally lick her arse: the poem consists of the poet's complaints about the bad smells that await him down there (one knows the sad state of personal hygiene in the Middle Ages), about the imminent danger that, as he is fulfilling his duty, the Lady will urinate on his head. . . . The Lady is thus as far as possible from any kind of purified spirituality: she functions as an inhuman partner in the sense of a radical Otherness which is wholly incommensurable with our needs and desires; as such, she is simultaneously a kind of automaton, a machine which utters meaningless demands at random.

    This coincidence of absolute, inscrutable Otherness and pure machine is what confers on the Lady her uncanny, monstrous character – the Lady is the Other which is not our 'fellow-creature'; that is to say, she is someone with whom no relationship of empathy is possible. This traumatic Otherness is what Lacan designates by means of the Freudian term *das Ding*, 'the Thing' – the Real that 'always returns to its place',[3] the hard kernel that resists symbolization. The idealization of the Lady, her elevation to a spiritual, ethereal ideal, is therefore to be conceived of as a strictly secondary phenomenon: it is a narcissistic projection whose function is to render her traumatic dimension invisible. In this precise and limited sense, Lacan concedes that 'the element of idealizing exaltation that is expressly sought out in the ideology of courtly love has certainly been demonstrated; it is fundamentally narcissistic in character'.[4] Deprived of every real substance, the Lady functions as a mirror on to which the subject projects his narcissistic ideal. In other words – those of Christina Rossetti, whose sonnet 'In an Artist's Studio' speaks of Dante Gabriel Rossetti's relationship to Elizabeth Siddal, his Lady – the Lady appears 'not as she is, but as she fills his dream'.[5] For Lacan, however, the crucial accent lies elsewhere:

> The mirror may on occasion imply the mechanisms of narcissism, and especially the dimension of destruction or aggression that we will encounter subsequently. But it also fulfills another role, a role as limit. It is that which cannot be crossed. And the only organization in which it participates is that of the inaccessibility of the object.[6]

Thus, before we embrace the commonplaces about how the Lady in courtly love has nothing to do with actual women, how she stands for the man's narcissistic projection which involves the mortification of the flesh-and-blood woman, we have to answer this question: where does that empty surface come from, that cold, neutral screen which opens up the space for possible projections? That is to say, if men are to project on to the mirror their narcissistic ideal, the mute mirror-surface must already be there. This surface functions as a kind of 'black hole' in reality, as a limit whose Beyond is inaccessible.

The next crucial feature of courtly love is that it is thoroughly a matter of courtesy and etiquette; it has nothing to do with some elementary passion overflowing all barriers, immune to all social rules. We are dealing with a strict fictional formula, with a social game of 'as if', where a man pretends that his sweetheart is the inaccessible Lady. And it is precisely this feature which enables us to establish a link between courtly love and a phenomenon which, at first, seems to have nothing whatsoever to do with it: namely, masochism, as a specific form of perversion articulated for the first time in the middle of the last century in the literary works and life-practice of Sacher-Masoch. In his celebrated study of masochism,[7] Gilles Deleuze demonstrates that masochism is not to be conceived of as a simple symmetrical inversion of sadism. The sadist and his victim never form a complementary 'sado-masochist' couple. Among those features evoked by Deleuze to prove the asymmetry between sadism and masochism, the crucial one is the opposition of the modalities of negation. In sadism we encounter direct negation, violent destruction and tormenting, whereas in masochism negation assumes the form of disavowal – that is, of feigning, of an 'as if' which suspends reality.

Closely depending on this first opposition is the opposition of institution and contract. Sadism follows the logic of institution, of institutional power tormenting its victim and taking pleasure in the victim's helpless resistance. More precisely, sadism is at work in the obscene, superego underside that necessarily redoubles and accompanies, as its shadow, the 'public' Law. Masochism, contrary, is made to the measure of the victim: it is the victim (the serv. the masochistic relationship) who initiates a contract with the Master (won authorizing her to humiliate him in any way she considers appropriate (wi the terms defined by the contract) and binding himself to act 'according to the whims of the sovereign lady', as Sacher-Masoch put it. It is the servant, therefore, who writes the screenplay – that is, who actually pulls the strings and dictates the activity of the woman (*dominatrix*): he stages his own servitude.[8] One further differential feature is that masochism, in contrast to sadism, is inherently theatrical: violence is for the most part feigned, and even when it is 'real', it functions as a component of a scene, as part of a theatrical performance. Furthermore, violence is never carried out, brought to its conclusion; it always remains suspended, as the endless repeating of an interrupted gesture.

It is precisely this logic of disavowal which enables us to grasp the fundamental paradox of the masochistic attitude. That is to say, how does the typical masochistic scene look? The man-Servant establishes in a cold, businesslike way the terms of the contract with the woman-Master: what she is to do to him, what scene is to be rehearsed endlessly, what dress she is to wear, how far she is to go in the direction of real, physical torture (how severely she is to whip him, in what precise way she is to enchain him, where she is to stamp him with the tips of her high heels, etc.). When they finally pass over to the masochistic game proper, the masochist constantly maintains a kind of reflective distance; he never really gives way to his feelings or fully abandons himself to the game; in the midst of the game, he can suddenly assume the stance of a stage director, giving precise instructions (put more pressure on that point, repeat that movement, . . .), *without thereby in the least 'destroying the illusion'*. Once the game is over, the masochist again adopts the attitude of a respectful bourgeois and starts to talk with the Sovereign Lady in a matter-of-fact, businesslike way: 'Thank you for your favour. Same time next week?', and so on. What is of crucial importance here is the total self-externalization of the masochist's most intimate passion: the most intimate desires become objects of contract and composed negotiation. The nature of the masochistic theatre is therefore thoroughly 'non-psychological': the surrealistic passionate masochistic game, which suspends social reality, none the less fits easily into that everyday reality.[9]

For this reason, the phenomenon of masochism exemplifies in its purest form what Lacan had in mind when he insisted again and again that psychoanalysis is not psychology. Masochism confronts us with the paradox of the symbolic order *qua* the order of 'fictions': there is more truth in the mask we wear, in the game we play, in the 'fiction' we obey and follow, than in what is concealed beneath the mask. The very kernel of the masochist's being is externalized in the staged game towards which he maintains his constant distance. And the Real of violence breaks out precisely when the masochist is hystericized – when the subject refuses the role of an object-instrument of the enjoyment of his Other, when he is horrified at the prospect of being reduced in the eyes of the Other to *objet a*; in order to escape this deadlock, he resorts to *passage à l'acte*, to the 'irrational' violence aimed at the other. Towards the end of P. D. James's *A Taste for Death*, the murderer describes the circumstances of the crime, and lets it be known that the factor which resolved his indecision and pushed him towards the act (the murder) was the attitude of the victim (Sir Paul Berowne):

'He wanted to die, God rot him, he wanted it! He practically asked for it. He could have tried to stop me, pleaded, argued, put up a fight. He could have begged for mercy, "No, please don't do it. Please!" That's all I wanted from him. Just that one word. . . . He looked at me with such contempt. . . . He knew then. Of course he knew. And I wouldn't have done it, not if he'd spoken to me as if I were even half-human.'[10]

'He didn't even look surprised. He was supposed to be terrified. He was supposed to prevent it from happening. . . . He just looked at me as if he were saying "So it's you. How strange that it has to be you." As if I had no choice. Just an instrument. Mindless. But I did have a choice. And so did he. Christ, he could have stopped me. Why didn't he stop me?'[11]

Several days before his death, Sir Paul Berowne experienced an 'inner breakdown' resembling symbolic death: he stepped down as a Government Minister and cut all his principal 'human ties', assuming thereby the 'excremental' position of a saint, of *objet petit a*, which precludes any intersubjective relationship of empathy. This attitude was what the murderer found unbearable: he approached his victim as $, a split subject – that is to say, he wanted to kill him, yet he was simultaneously waiting for a sign of fear, of resistance, from the victim, a sign which would prevent the murderer from accomplishing the act. The victim, however, did not give any such sign, which would have subjectivized the murderer, acknowledging him as a (divided) subject. Sir Paul's attitude of non-resistance, of indifferent provocation, objectivized the murderer, reducing him to an instrument of the Other's will, and so left him with no choice. In short, what compelled the murderer to act was the experience of having his desire to kill the victim coincide with the victim's death drive.

This coincidence recalls the way a male hysterical 'sadist' justifies his beating of a woman: 'Why does she make me do it? She really wants me to hurt her, she compels me to beat her so that she can enjoy it – *so I'll beat her black and blue and teach her what it really means to provoke me!*' What we encounter here is a kind of loop in which the (mis)perceived effect of the brutal act upon the victim retroactively legitimizes the act: I set out to beat a woman and when, at the very point where I think that I thoroughly dominate her, I notice that I am actually her slave – since she wants the beating and provoked me to deliver it – I get really mad and beat her...[12]

The Courtly 'Imp of the Perverse'

How, on closer examination, are we to conceptualize the inaccessibility of the Lady-Object in courtly love? The principal mistake to avoid is reducing this inaccessibility to the simple dialectic of desire and prohibition according to which we covet the forbidden fruit precisely in so far as it is forbidden – or, to quote Freud's classic formulation:

[T]he psychical value of erotic needs is reduced as soon as their satisfaction becomes easy. An obstacle is required in order to heighten libido; and where natural resistances to satisfaction have not been sufficient men have at all times erected conventional ones so as to be able to enjoy love.[13]

Within this perspective, courtly love appears as simply the most radical strategy for elevating the value of the object by putting up conventional obstacles to its attainability. When, in his seminar *Encore*, Lacan provides the most succinct formulation of the paradox of courtly love, he says something that is apparently similar, yet fundamentally different: 'A very refined manner to supplant the absence of the sexual relationship is by feigning that it is us who put the obstacle in its way.'[14] The point, therefore, is not simply that we set up additional conventional hindrances in order to heighten the value of the object: *external hindrances that thwart our access to the object are there precisely to create the illusion that without them, the object would be directly accessible* – what such hindrances thereby conceal is the inherent impossibility of attaining the object. The place of the Lady-Thing is originally empty: she functions as a kind of 'black hole' around which the subject's desire is structured. The space of desire is bent like space in the theory of relativity; the only way to reach the Object-Lady is indirectly, in a devious, meandering way – proceeding straight on ensures that we miss the target. This is what Lacan has in mind when, apropos of courtly love, he evokes 'the meaning we must attribute to the negotiation of the detour in the psychic economy':

The detour in the psyche isn't always designed to regulate the commerce between whatever is organized in the domain of the pleasure principle and whatever presents itself as the structure of reality. There are also detours and obstacles which are organized so as to make the domain of the vacuole stand out as such . . . The techniques involved in courtly love – and they are precise enough to allow us to perceive what might on occasion become fact, what is properly speaking of the sexual order in the inspiration of this eroticism – are techniques of holding back, of suspension, of *amor interruptus*. The stages courtly love lays down previous to what is mysteriously referred to as *le don de merci*, 'the gift of mercy' – although we don't know exactly what it meant – are expressed more or less in terms that Freud uses in his *Three Essays* as belonging to the sphere of foreplay.[15]

For that reason, Lacan accentuates the motif of anamorphosis (in his Seminar on the Ethics of Psychoanalysis, the title of the chapter on courtly love is 'Courtly Love as Anamorphosis'): the Object can be perceived only when it is viewed from the side, in a partial, distorted form, as its own shadow – if we cast a direct glance at it we see nothing, a mere void. In a homologous way, we could speak of temporal anamorphosis: the Object is attainable only by way of an incessant postponement, as its absent point of reference. The Object, therefore, is literally something that is created – whose place is encircled – through a network of detours, approximations and near-misses. It is here that *sublimation* sets in – sublimation in the Lacanian sense of the elevation of an object into the dignity of the Thing: 'sublimation' occurs when an object, part of everyday reality, finds itself at the place of the impossible Thing. Herein resides the function of those artificial obstacles that suddenly hinder our access to some ordinary object: they elevate the object into a stand-in for the Thing. This is how the impossible changes into the prohibited: by way of the short circuit between the Thing and some positive object rendered inaccessible through artificial obstacles.

The tradition of Lady as the inaccessible object is alive and well in our century – in surrealism, for example. Suffice it to recall Luis Buñuel's *The Obscure Object of Desire*, in which a woman, through a series of absurd tricks, postpones again and again the final moment of sexual reunion with her aged lover (when, for example, the man finally gets her into bed, he discovers beneath her nightgown an old-fashioned corset with numerous buckles which are impossible to undo . . .). The charm of the film lies in this very nonsensical short circuit between the fundamental, metaphysical Limit and some trivial empirical impediment. Here we find the logic of courtly love and of sublimation at its purest: some common, everyday object or act becomes inaccessible or impossible to accomplish once it finds itself in the position of the Thing – although the thing should be easily within reach, the entire universe has somehow been adjusted to produce, again and again, an unfathomable contingency blocking access to the object. Buñuel himself was quite aware of this paradoxical logic: in his autobiography he speaks of 'the non-explainable impossibility of the fulfilment of a simple desire', and a whole series of films offers variations on this motif: in *The Criminal Life of Archibaldo de la Cruz* the hero wants to accomplish a simple murder, but all his attempts fail; in *The Exterminating Angel*, after a party, a group of rich people cannot cross the threshold and leave the house; in *The Discreet Charm of the Bourgeoisie* two couples want to dine together, but unexpected complications always prevent the fulfilment of this simple wish . . .

It should be clear, now, what determines the difference with regard to the usual dialectic of desire and prohibition: the aim of the prohibition is not to 'raise the price' of an object by rendering access to it more difficult, but to raise this object itself to the level of the Thing, of the 'black hole', around which desire is organized. For that reason, Lacan is quite justified in inverting the usual formula of sublimation, which involves shifting the libido from an object that satisfies some concrete, material need to an object that has no apparent connection to this need: for example, destructive literary criticism becomes sublimated aggressivity; scientific research into the human body becomes sublimated voyeurism; and so on. What Lacan means by sublimation, on the contrary, is shifting the libido from the void of the 'unserviceable' Thing to some concrete, material object of need that assumes a sublime quality the moment it occupies the place of the Thing.[16]

What the paradox of the Lady in courtly love ultimately amounts to is thus the paradox of *detour*: our 'official' desire is that we want to sleep with the Lady; whereas in truth, there is nothing we fear more than a Lady who might generously yield to this wish of ours – what we truly expect and want from the Lady is simply yet another new ordeal, yet one more postponement.

It is against this background that one must conceive of the often mentioned, yet no less often misunderstood, 'phallic' value of the woman in Lacan – his equation Woman = Phallus. That is to say, precisely the same paradox characterizes the phallic signifier *qua* signifier of castration. 'Castration means that *jouissance* must be refused, so that it can be reached on the inverted ladder of the Law of desire.'[17] How is this 'economic paradox' feasible, how can the machinery of desire be 'set in motion' – that is to say, how can the subject be made to renounce enjoyment not for another, higher Cause but simply in order to gain access to it? Or – to quote Hegel's formulation of the same paradox – how is it that we can attain identity only by losing it? There is only one solution to this problem: the phallus, the signifier of enjoyment, had simultaneously to be the signifier of 'castration', that is to say, *one and the same signifier had to signify enjoyment as well as its loss*. In this way, it becomes possible that the very agency which entices us to search for enjoyment induces us to renounce it.[18]

Back to the Lady: are we, therefore, justified in conceiving of the Lady as the personification of the Western metaphysical passion, as an exorbitant, almost parodical example of metaphysical hubris, of the elevation of a particular entity or feature into the Ground of all being? On closer examination, what constitutes this metaphysical, or simply philosophical, hubris? Let us take what might appear to be a surprising example. In Marx, the specifically *philosophical* dimension is at work when he points out that production, one of the four moments of the totality of production, distribution, exchange and consumption, is simultaneously the encompassing totality of the four moments, conferring its specific colour on that totality. (Hegel made the same point in asserting that every genus has two species, itself and its species – that is to say, the genus is always one of its own species.) The 'philosophical' or 'metaphysical' is this very 'absolutization', this elevation of a particular moment of the totality into its Ground, this hubris which 'disrupts' the harmony of a balanced whole.

Let us mention two approaches to language: that of John L. Austin and that of Oswald Ducrot. Why is it legitimate to treat their work as 'philosophy'? Austin's division of all verbs into performatives and constatives is not yet philosophy proper: we enter the domain of philosophy with his 'unbalanced', 'excessive' hypothesis that every proposition, including a constative, *already is a performative* – that the performative, as one of the two moments of the Whole, simultaneously *is* the Whole. The same goes for Oswald Ducrot's thesis that every predicate possesses, over and above its informative value, an argumentative value. We remain within the domain of positive science as long as we simply endeavour to discern in each predicate the level of information and the level of argumentation – that is, the specific modality of how certain information 'fits' some argumentative attitude. We enter philosophy with the 'excessive' hypothesis that *the predicate as such, including its informative content, is nothing but a condensed argumentative attitude*, so that we can never 'distil' from it its 'pure' informative content, untainted by some argumentative attitude. Here, of course, we encounter the paradox of 'non-all': the fact that 'no aspect of a predicate's content remains unaffected by some argumentative attitude' does not authorize us to draw the seemingly obvious universal conclusion that 'the entire content of a predicate is argumentative' – the elusive surplus that persists, although it cannot be pinned down anywhere, is the Lacanian Real.

This, perhaps, offers another way of considering Heidegger's 'ontological difference': as the distance that always yawns between the (specific feature, elevated into the) Ground of the totality and the Real which eludes this Ground, which itself cannot be 'Grounded' in it. That is to say, 'non-metaphysical' is not a 'balanced' totality devoid of any hubris, a totality (or, in more Heideggerian terms: the Whole of entities) in which no particular aspect or entity is elevated into its Ground. The domain of entities gains its consistency from its sup-posited Ground, so that 'non-metaphysics' can only be an insight into the difference between Ground and the elusive Real which – although its positive content ('reality') is grounded in the Ground – none the less eludes and undermines the reign of the Ground.

And now, back to the Lady again: this is why the Lady is *not* another name for the metaphysical Ground, but, on the contrary, one of the names for the self-retracting Real which, in a way, grounds the Ground itself. And in so far as one of the names for the metaphysical Ground of all entities is 'supreme Good', the Lady *qua* Thing can also be designated as the embodiment of radical Evil, of the Evil that Edgar Allan Poe, in two of his stories, 'The Black Cat' and 'The Imp of the Perverse', called the 'spirit of perverseness':

Of this spirit philosophy takes no account. Yet I am not more sure that my soul lives, than I am that perverseness is one of the primitive impulses of the human heart.... Who has not, a hundred times, found himself committing a vile or a stupid action, for no other reason than because he knows he should *not*? Have we not a perpetual inclination, in the teeth of our best judgment, to violate that which is *Law*, merely because we understand it to be such? ('The Black Cat')

It is, in fact, a *mobile* without motive, a motive not *motiviert*. Through its promptings we act without comprehensible object; or, if this shall be understood as a contradiction in terms, we may so far modify the proposition as to say, that through its promptings we act, for the reason that we should *not*. In theory, no reason can be more unreasonable; but, in fact, there is none more strong.... I am not more certain that I breathe, than that the assurance of the wrong or error of any action is often the one unconquerable *force* which impels us, and alone impels us to its prosecution. Nor will this over-whelming tendency to do wrong for the wrong's sake, admit of analysis, or resolution into ulterior elements. It is a radical, a primitive impulse – elementary. ('The Imp of the Perverse')

The affinity of crime as an unmotivated *acte gratuit* to art is a standard topic of Romantic theory (the Romantic cult of the artist comprises the notion of the artist *qua* criminal): it is deeply significant that Poe's formulas ('a *mobile* without motive, a motive not *motiviert*') immediately recall Kant's determinations of the aesthetic experience ('purposefulness without purpose', etc.). What we must not overlook here is the crucial fact that this command – 'You must because you are not allowed to!', that is to say, a purely negative grounding of an act accomplished only because it is prohibited – is possible only within the differential symbolic order in which negative determination as such has a positive reach – in which the very *absence* of a feature functions as a *positive feature*. Poe's 'imp of the perverse' therefore marks the point at which the motivation of an act, as it were, cuts off its external link to empirical objects and grounds itself solely in the immanent circle of self-reference – in short, Poe's 'imp' corresponds to the point of freedom in the strict Kantian sense.

This reference to Kant is far from accidental. According to Kant, the faculty of desiring does not possess a transcendental status, since it is wholly dependent upon pathological objects and motivations. Lacan, on the contrary, aims to demonstrate the transcendental status of this faculty – that is, the possibility of formulating a motivation for our desire that is totally independent of pathology (such a non-pathological object-cause of desire is the Lacanian *objet petit a*). Poe's 'imp of the perverse' offers us an immediate example of such a pure motivation: when I accomplish an act 'only because it is prohibited', I remain within the universal-symbolic domain, without reference to any empirical-contingent object – that is to say, I accomplish what is *stricto sensu* a non-pathological act. Here, then, Kant miscalculated his wager: by cleansing the domain of ethics of pathological motivations, he wanted to extirpate the very possibility of doing Evil in the guise of Good; what he actually did was to open up a new domain of Evil far more uncanny than the usual 'pathological' Evil.

Exemplifications

From the thirteenth century to modern times, we encounter numerous variations on this matrix of courtly love. In *Les Liaisons dangereuses*, for example, the relationship between the Marquise de Montreuil and Valmont is clearly the relationship between a capricious Lady and her servant. The paradox here turns on the nature of the task the servant must perform in order to earn the promised gesture of Mercy: he must seduce other ladies. His Ordeal requires that, even at the height of passion, he maintain a cold distance towards his victims: in the very moment of triumph, he must humiliate them by abandoning them without reason, thereby proving his fidelity to the Lady. Things get complicated when Valmont falls in love with one of his victims (Présidente de Tourvel) and thereby 'betrays his Duty': the Marquise is quite justified in dismissing his excuse (the famous 'c'est pas ma faute': it's beyond my control, it's the way things are . . .) as beneath Valmont's dignity, as a miserable recourse to a 'pathological' state of things (in the Kantian sense of the term).

The Marquise's reaction to Valmont's 'betrayal' is thus strictly ethical: Valmont's excuse is exactly the same as the excuse invoked by moral weaklings when they fail to perform their duty – 'I just couldn't help it, such is my nature, I'm simply not strong enough . . .'. Her message to Valmont recalls Kant's motto 'Du kannst, denn du sollst!' (You can, because you must!). For that reason, the punishment imposed by the Marquise on Valmont is quite appropriate: in renouncing the Présidente de Tourvel, he must have recourse to exactly the same words – that is, he must compose a letter to her, explaining to her that 'it's not his fault' if his passion for her has expired, it's simply the way things are. . . .

Another variation on the matrix of courtly love emerges in the story of Cyrano de Bergerac and Roxane. Ashamed of his obscene natural deformity (his too-long nose), Cyrano has not dared to confess his love to the beautiful Roxane; so he interposes between himself and her a good-looking young soldier, conferring on him the role of proxy through whom he expresses his desire. As befits a capricious Lady, Roxane demands that her lover articulate his love in elegant poetic terms; the unfortunate simple-minded young soldier is not up to the task, so Cyrano hastens to his assistance, writing passionate love-letters for the soldier from the battlefield. The dénouement takes place in two stages, tragic and melodramatic. Roxane tells the soldier that she does not love his beautiful body alone; she loves his refined soul even more: she is so deeply moved by his letters that she would continue to love him even if his body were to become mutilated and ugly. The soldier shudders at these words: he realizes that Roxane does not love him as he really is but as the author of his letters – in other words, she unknowingly loves Cyrano. Unable to endure this humiliation, he rushes suicidally into an attack and dies. Roxane enters a cloister, where she has regular visits from Cyrano, who keeps her informed about the social life of Paris. During one of these visits Roxane asks him to read aloud the last letter of her dead lover. The melodramatic moment now sets in: Roxane suddenly notices that Cyrano does not read the letter, he recites it – thereby proving that he is its true author. Deeply shaken, she recognizes in this crippled merry-maker her true love. But it is already too late: Cyrano has come to this meeting mortally wounded. . . .

The reverse variation on the same motif is at work in a short love scene from Truffaut's *La Nuit américaine* (*Day for Night*). When, on the drive from the hotel to the studio, a car tyre blows, the assistant cameraman and the script-girl find themselves alone on a lake shore. The assistant, who has pursued the girl for a long time, seizes the opportunity and bursts into a pathetic speech about how much he desires her and how much it would mean to him if, now that they are alone, she were to consent to a quick sexual encounter; the girl simply says 'Yes, why not?' and starts to unbutton her trousers. . . . This non-sublime gesture, of course, totally bewilders the seducer, who conceived of her as the unattainable Lady: he can only stammer 'How do you mean? Just like that?' What this scene has in common with the scene from *Wild at Heart* (and what sets it within the matrix of courtly love) is the unexpected gesture of refusal: the man's response to the woman's 'Yes!', obtained by long, arduous effort, is to refuse the act.

We encounter a more refined variation on the matrix of courtly love in Eric Rohmer's *Ma Nuit chez Maud*: courtly love provides the only logic that can account for the hero's lie at the end. The central part of the film depicts the night that the hero and his friend Maud spend together; they talk long into the small hours and even sleep in the same bed, but the sexual act does not take place, owing to the hero's indecision – he is unable to seize the opportunity, obsessed as he is by the mysterious blonde woman whom he saw the evening before in a church. Although he does not yet know who she is, he has already decided to marry her (i.e. the blonde is his Lady). The final scene takes place several years later. The hero, now happily married to the blonde, encounters Maud on a beach; when his wife asks him who this unknown woman is, the hero tells a lie – apparently to his detriment; he informs his wife that Maud was his last love adventure before marriage. Why this lie? Because the truth could have aroused the suspicion that Maud also occupied the place of the Lady, with whom a brief, non-committal sexual encounter is not possible – precisely by telling a lie to his wife, by claiming that he did have sex with Maud, he assures her that Maud was not his Lady, but just a passing friend.

The definitive version of courtly love in recent decades, of course, arrives in the figure of the *femme fatale* in *film noir*: the traumatic Woman-Thing who, through her greedy and capricious demands, brings ruin to the *hard-boiled* hero. The key role is played here by the third person (as a rule the gangster-boss) to whom the *femme fatale* 'legally' belongs: his presence renders her inaccessible, and thus confers on the hero's relationship with her the mark of transgression. By means of his involvement with her, the hero betrays the paternal figure who is also his boss (in *The Glass Key, Killers, Criss-Cross, Out of the Past*, etc.).

This link between the courtly Lady and the *femme fatale* from the *noir* universe may appear surprising: is not the *femme fatale* in *film noir* the very opposite of the noble sovereign Lady to whom the knight vows service? Is not the hard-boiled hero ashamed of the attraction he feels for her; doesn't he hate her (and himself) for loving her; doesn't he experience his love for her as a betrayal of his true self? However, if we bear in mind the original traumatic impact of the Lady, not its secondary idealization, the connection is clear: like the Lady, the *femme fatale* is an 'inhuman partner', a traumatic Object with whom no relationship is possible, an apathetic void imposing senseless, arbitrary ordeals.[19]

From the Courtly Game to *The Crying Game*

The key to the extraordinary and unexpected success of Neil Jordan's *The Crying Game* is perhaps the ultimate variation that it delivers on the motif of courtly love. Let us recall the outlines of the story: Fergus, a member of the

IRA guarding a captured black British soldier, develops friendly links with him; the soldier asks him, in the event of his liquidation, to pay a visit to his girl-friend, Dil, a hairdresser in a London suburb, and to give her his last regards. After the death of the soldier, Fergus withdraws from the IRA, moves to London, finds a job as a bricklayer and pays a visit to the soldier's love, a beautiful black woman. He falls in love with her, but Dil maintains an ambiguous ironic, sovereign distance towards him. Finally, she gives way to his advances; but before they go to bed together, she leaves for a brief moment, returning in a transparent nightgown; while casting a covetous glance at her body, Fergus suddenly perceives her penis – 'she' is a transvestite. Sickened, he crudely pushes her away. Shaken and wet with tears, Dil tells him that she thought he knew all the time how things stood (in his obsession with her, the hero – as well as the public – did not notice a host of tell-tale details, including the fact that the bar where they usually met was a meeting-place for transvestites). This scene of the failed sexual encounter is structured as the exact inversion of the scene referred to by Freud as the primordial trauma of fetishism: the child's gaze, sliding down the naked female body towards the sexual organ, is shocked to find nothing where one expects to see something (a penis) – in the case of *The Crying Game*, the shock is caused when the eye finds *something* where it expected *nothing*.

After this painful revelation, the relationship between the two is reversed: now it turns out that Dil is passionately in love with Fergus, although she knows her love is impossible. From a capricious and ironic sovereign Lady she changes into the pathetic figure of a delicate, sensitive boy who is desperately in love. It is only at this point that true love emerges, love as a metaphor in the precise Lacanian sense:[20] we witness the sublime moment when *eromenos* (the loved one) changes into *erastes* (the loving one) by stretching out her hand and 'returning love'. This moment designates the 'miracle' of love, the moment of the 'answer of the Real'; as such, it perhaps enables us to grasp what Lacan has in mind when he insists that the subject itself has the status of an 'answer of the Real'. That is to say, up to this reversal the loved one has the status of an object: he is loved on account of something that is 'in him more than himself' and that he is unaware of – I can never answer the question 'What am I as an object for the other? What does the other see in me that causes his love?' We thus confront an asymmetry – not only the asymmetry between subject and object, but asymmetry in a far more radical sense of a discord between what the lover sees in the loved one and what the loved one knows himself to be.

Here we find the inescapable deadlock that defines the position of the loved one: the other sees something in me and wants something from me, but I cannot give him what I do not possess – or, as Lacan puts it, there is no relationship between what the loved one possesses and what the loving one lacks. The only way for the loved one to escape this deadlock is to stretch out his hand towards the loving one and to 'return love' – that is, to exchange, in a metaphorical gesture, his status as the loved one for the status of the loving one. This reversal designates the point of subjectivization: the object of love changes into the subject the moment it answers the call of love. And it is only by way of this reversal that a genuine love emerges: I am truly in love not when I am simply fascinated by the *agalma* in the other, but when I experience the other, the object of love, as frail and lost, as lacking 'it', and my love none the less survives this loss.

We must be especially attentive here so that we do not miss the point of this reversal: although we now have two loving subjects instead of the initial duality of the loving one and the loved one, the asymmetry persists, since it was the object itself that, as it were, confessed to its lack by means of its subjectivization. Something deeply embarrassing and truly scandalous abides in this reversal by means of which the mysterious, fascinating, elusive object of love discloses its deadlock, and thus acquires the status of another subject.

We encounter the same reversal in horror stories: is not the most sublime moment in Mary Shelley's *Frankenstein* the moment of the monster's subjectivization – the moment when the monster-object (who has been continually described as a ruthless killing machine) starts talking in the first person, revealing his miserable, pitiful existence? It is deeply symptomatic that all the films based on Shelley's *Frankenstein* have avoided this gesture of subjectivization. And perhaps, in courtly love itself, the long-awaited moment of highest fulfilment, when the Lady renders *Gnade*, mercy, to her servant, is not the Lady's surrender, her consent to the sexual act, nor some mysterious rite of initiation, but simply a sign of love on the part of the Lady, the 'miracle' that the Object answered, stretching its hand out towards the supplicant.[21]

So, back to *The Crying Game*: Dil is now ready to do anything for Fergus, and he is more and more moved and fascinated by the absolute, unconditional character of her love for him, so that he overcomes his aversion and continues to console her. At the end, when the IRA again tries to involve him in a terrorist act, he even sacrifices himself for Dil and assumes responsibility for a killing she committed. The last scene of the film takes place in the prison where she visits him, again dressed up as a provocatively seductive woman, so that every man in the visiting room is aroused by her looks. Although Fergus has to endure more than four thousand days of prison – they count them up together – she cheerfully pledges to wait for him and visit him regularly. . . . The external impediment – the glass partition in the prison preventing any physical contact – is here the exact equivalent to the obstacle in courtly love that renders the object inaccessible; it thereby accounts for the absolute, unconditional character of this love in spite of its inherent impossibility – that is, in spite of the fact that their love will never be consummated, since he is a 'straight' heterosexual and she is a homosexual transvestite. In his introduction to the published screenplay, Jordan points out that

the story ended with a kind of happiness. I say a kind of happiness, because it involved the separation of a prison cell and other more profound separations, of racial, national, and sexual identity. But for the lovers, it was the irony of what divided them that allowed them to smile. So perhaps there is hope for our divisions yet.[22]

Is not the division – the unsurmountable barrier – that allows for a smile the most concise mechanism of courtly love? What we have here is an 'impossible' love which will never be consummated, which can be realized only as a feigned spectacle intended to fascinate the gaze of the spectators present, or as an endlessly postponed expectation; this love is absolute precisely in so far as it transgresses not only the barriers of class, religion and race, but also the ultimate barrier of sexual orientation, of sexual identification. Herein resides the film's paradox and, at the same time, its irresistible charm: far from denouncing heterosexual love as a product of male repression, it renders the precise circumstances in which this love can today retain its absolute, unconditional character.

The Crying Game Goes East

This reading of The Crying Game immediately brings to mind one of the standard reproaches to Lacanian theory: in all his talk about feminine inconsistency and so on, Lacan speaks about woman only as she appears or is mirrored in male discourse, about her distorted reflection in a medium that is foreign to her, never about woman as she is in herself: to Lacan, as earlier to Freud, feminine sexuality remains a 'dark continent'. In answer to this reproach, we must emphatically assert that if the fundamental Hegelian paradox of reflexivity remains in force anywhere, it is here: the remove, the step back, from woman-in-herself to how woman qua absent Cause distorts male discourse brings us much closer to the 'feminine essence' than a direct approach. That is to say, is not 'woman' ultimately just the name for a distortion or inflection of the male discourse? Is not the spectre of 'woman-in-herself', far from being the active cause of this distortion, rather its reified-fetishized effect?

All these questions are implicitly addressed by M. Butterfly (directed by David Cronenberg, script by David Henry Hwang from his own play), a film whose subtitle could well have been 'The Crying Game' Goes to China.

The first feature of this film that strikes the eye is the utter 'improbability' of its narrative: without the information (given in the credits) that the story is based on true events, nobody would take it seriously. During the Great Cultural Revolution, a minor French diplomat in Beijing (Jeremy Irons) falls in love with a Chinese opera singer who sings some Puccini arias at a reception for foreigners (John Lone). His courting leads to a lasting love relationship; the singer, who is to him the fatal love object (with reference to Puccini's opera, he affectionately calls her 'my butterfly'), apparently becomes pregnant, and produces a child. While their affair is going on, she induces him to spy for China, claiming that this is the only way the Chinese authorities will tolerate their association. After a professional failure, the diplomat is transferred to Paris, where he is assigned to the minor post of diplomatic courier. Soon afterwards, his love joins him there and tells him that if he will carry on spying for China, the Chinese authorities will allow 'their' child to join them. When, finally, French security discovers his spying activities and they are both arrested, it turns out that 'she' is not a woman at all, but a man – in his Eurocentric ignorance, the hero did not know that in Chinese opera, female roles are sung by men.

It is here that the story stretches the limits of our credulity: how was it that the hero, in their long years of consummated love, did not see that he was dealing with a man? The singer incessantly evoked the Chinese sense of shame, s/he never undressed, they had (unbeknownst to him, anal) sex discreetly, s/he sitting on his lap ... in short, what he mistook for the shyness of the Oriental woman was, on 'her' side, a deft manipulation destined to conceal the fact that 'she' was not a woman at all. The choice of the music that obsesses the hero is crucial here: the famous aria 'Un bel did, vedremo' from *Madama Butterfly*, perhaps the most expressive example of Puccini's gesture that is the very opposite of bashful self-concealment – the obscenely candid self-exposure of the (feminine) subject that always borders upon *kitsch*. The subject pathetically professes what she is and what she wants, she lays bare her most intimate and frail dreams – a confession which, of course, reaches its apogee in the desire to die (in 'Un bel di, vedremo', Madama Butterfly imagines the scene of Pinkerton's return: at first, she will not answer his call, 'in part for fun and in part not to die at the first encounter' (*per non morir al primo incontro*)).

From what we have just said, it may seem that the hero's tragic blunder consists in projecting his fantasy-image on to an inadequate object – that is to say, in mistaking a real person for his fantasy-image of the love object, the Oriental woman of the Madama Butterfly type. However, things are definitely more complex. The key scene of the film occurs after the trial, when the hero and his Chinese partner, now in an ordinary man's suit, find themselves alone in the closed compartment of a police car on their way to prison. The Chinese takes off his clothes and offers himself naked to the hero, desperately proclaiming his availability: 'Here I am, your butterfly!' He proposes himself as what he is outside the hero's fantasy-frame of a mysterious Oriental woman. At this crucial moment, the hero retracts: he avoids his lover's eyes and rejects the offer. It is here that he gives up his desire, and is thereby marked by an indelible guilt: he betrays the true love that aims at the real kernel of the object beneath the phantasmic layers. That is to say, the paradox resides in the fact that although he loved the Chinese without any underhand thoughts while the Chinese manipulated his love on behalf of the Chinese secret service, it now becomes obvious that the Chinese's love was in some sense purer and far more authentic. Or, as John le Carré put it in *A Perfect Spy*: 'Love is whatever you can still betray.'

As every reader of 'true' spy adventures knows very well, a large number of cases in which a woman has seduced a man out of duty, in order to extract from him some vital piece of information (or vice versa), end with a happy marriage – far from dispelling the mirage of love, the disclosure of the deceitful manipulation that brought the lovers together only strengthened their bond. To put it in Deleuzian terms: we are dealing here with a split between the 'depth' of reality, the intermixture of bodies in which the other is the instrument I mercilessly exploit, in which love itself and sexuality are reduced to means manipulated for politico-military purposes, and the level of love *qua* pure surface event. Manipulation at the level of bodily reality renders all the more manifest love *qua* surface event, *qua* effect irreducible to its bodily support.[23]

The painful final scene of the film conveys the hero's full recognition of his guilt.[24] In prison, the hero stages a performance for his vulgar and noisy fellow-prisoners: dressed as Madama Butterfly (a Japanese kimono, heavily made-up face) and accompanied by excerpts from Puccini's opera, he retells his story; at the very climax of 'Un bel di, vedremo', he cuts his throat with a razor and collapses dead. This scene of a man performing public suicide dressed as a woman has a long and respectable history: suffice it to mention Hitchcock's *Murder!* (1930), in which the murderer Handel Fane, dressed as a female trapeze artist, hangs himself in front of a packed house after finishing his number. In *M. Butterfly*, as in *Murder!* this act is of a strictly ethical nature: in both cases the hero stages a psychotic identification with his love object, with his *sinthome* (synthetic formation of the non-existent woman, 'Butterfly') – that is, he 'regresses' from the object-choice to an immediate identification with the object; the only way out of the insoluble deadlock of this identification is suicide *qua* the ultimate *passage à l'acte*. By his suicidal act the hero makes up for his guilt, for his rejection of the object when the object was offered to him outside the fantasy-frame.

Here, of course, the old objection again awaits us: ultimately, does not *M. Butterfly* offer a tragi-comic confused bundle of male fantasies about women, not a true relationship with a woman? The entire action of the film takes place among men. Does not the grotesque incredibility of the plot simultaneously mask and point towards the fact that what we are dealing with is a case of homosexual love for the transvestite? The film is simply dishonest, and refuses to acknowledge this obvious fact. This 'elucidation', however, fails to address the true enigma of *M. Butterfly* (and of *The Crying Game*): how can a hopeless love between the hero and his partner, a man dressed up as a woman, realize the notion of heterosexual love far more 'authentically' than a 'normal' relationship with a woman?

How, then, are we to interpret this perseverance of the matrix of courtly love? It bears witness to a certain deadlock in contemporary feminism. True, the courtly image of man serving his Lady is a semblance that conceals the actuality of male domination; true, the masochist's theatre is a private *mise en scène* designed to recompense the guilt contracted by man's social domination; true, the elevation of woman to the sublime object of love equals her debasement into the passive stuff or screen for the narcissistic projection of the male ego-ideal, and so on. Lacan himself points out how, in the very epoch of courtly love, the actual social standing of women as objects of exchange in male power-plays was probably at its lowest. However, this very semblance of man serving his Lady provides women with the fantasy-substance of their identity whose effects are real: it provides them with all the features that constitute so-called femininity and define woman not as she is in her *jouissance féminine*, but as she refers to herself with regard to her (potential) relationship to man, as an object of his desire. From this fantasy-structure springs the near-panic reaction – not only of men, but also of many a woman – to a feminism that wants to deprive woman of her very 'femininity'. By opposing 'patriarchal domination', women simultaneously undermine the fantasy-support of their own 'feminine' identity.

The problem is that once the relationship between the two sexes is conceived of as a symmetrical, reciprocal, voluntary partnership or contract, the fantasy-matrix which first emerged in courtly love remains in power. Why? In so far as sexual difference is a Real that resists symbolization, the sexual relationship is condemned to remain an asymmetrical non-relationship in which the Other, our partner, prior to being a subject, is a Thing, an 'inhuman partner'; as such, the sexual relationship cannot be transposed into a symmetrical relationship between pure subjects. The bourgeois principle of contract between equal subjects can be applied to sexuality only in the form of the *perverse* – masochistic – contract in which, paradoxically, the very form of balanced contract serves to establish a relationship of domination. It is no accident that in the so-called alternative sexual practices ('sado-masochistic' lesbian and gay couples) the Master-and-Slave relationship re-emerges with a vengeance, including all the ingredients of the masochistic theatre. In other words, we are far from inventing a new 'formula' capable of replacing the matrix of courtly love.

For that reason, it is misleading to read *The Crying Game* as an anti-political tale of escape into privacy – that is to say, as a variation on the theme of a revolutionary who, disillusioned by the cruelty of the political power-play, discovers sexual love as the sole field of personal realization, of authentic existential fulfilment. Politically, the film remains faithful to the Irish cause, which functions as its inherent background. The paradox is that in the very sphere of privacy where the hero hoped to find a safe haven, he is compelled to accomplish an even more vertiginous revolution in his most intimate personal attitudes. Thus *The Crying Game* eludes the usual ideological dilemma of 'privacy as the island of authenticity, exempt from political power-play' versus 'sexuality as yet another domain of political activity': it renders visible the *antagonistic* complicity between public political activity and personal sexual subversion, the antagonism that is already at work in Sade, who demanded a sexual revolution as the ultimate accomplishment of the political revolution. In short, the subtitle of *The Crying Game* could have been 'Irishmen, yet another effort, if you want to become republicans!'

Notes

1 Jacques Lacan, *The Ethics of Psychoanalysis* (London, Routledge, 1992), p. 149.
2 Ibid., p. 150; translation modified.
3 Is not Lacan's definition of the Real as that which always returns to its place 'pre-Einsteinian' and, as such, de-valorized by the relativization of space with regard to the observer's point of view – that is, by the cancellation of the notion of absolute space and time? However, the theory of relativity involves its own absolute constant: the space-time interval between two events is an absolute that never varies. Space-time interval is defined as the hypotenuse of a right-angled triangle whose legs are the time and space distance between the two events. One observer may be in a state of motion such that for him there is a time and a distance involved between the two events; another may be in a state of motion such that his measuring devices indicate a different distance and a different time between the events, but the space-time interval between them does not vary. *This* constant is the Lacanian Real that 'remains the same in all possible universes'.
4 Lacan, *Ethics of Psychoanalysis*, p. 151.
5 It is clear, therefore, that it would be a fateful mistake to identify the Lady in courtly love, this unconditional ideal of the Woman, with woman in so far as she is not

submitted to phallic enjoyment: the opposition of everyday, 'tamed' woman, with whom sexual relationship may appear possible, and the Lady *qua* 'inhuman partner' has nothing whatsoever to do with the opposition of woman submitted to phallic signifier and woman *qua* bearer of the Other enjoyment. The Lady is the projection of man's narcissistic Ideal, her figure emerges as the result of the masochistic pact by way of which woman accepts the role of *dominatrix* in the theatre staged by man. For that reason, Rossetti's *Beata Beatrix*, for example, is not to be perceived as the figuration of the Other enjoyment: as with Isolde's love-death in Wagner's *Tristan*, we are dealing with *man's* fantasy.

6   Lacan, *Ethics of Psychoanalysis*, p. 151.

7   Gilles Deleuze, 'Coldness and Cruelty', in *Masochism* (New York, Zone Press, 1991).

8   For that reason lesbian sado-masochism is far more subversive than the usual 'soft' lesbianism, which elevates tender relationships between women in contrast to aggressive-phallic male penetration: although the content of lesbian sado-maso-chism imitates 'aggressive' phallic heterosexuality, this content is subverted by the very contractual form.

9   Here the logic is the same as in the 'non-psychological' universe of *Twin Peaks*, in which we encounter two main types of people: 'normal', everyday people (based on soap-opera clichés) and 'crazy' eccentrics (the lady with a log, etc.); the uncanny quality of the *Twin Peaks* universe hinges on the fact that the relationship between these two groups follows the rules of 'normal' communication: 'normal' people are not at all amazed or outraged by the strange behaviour of the eccentrics; they accept them as part of their daily routine.

10   P. D. James, *A Taste for Death* (London and Boston, Faber & Faber, 1986), p. 439.

11   Ibid., p. 440.

12   An exemplary case of the inverse constellation – of the gaze *qua objet* a hystericiz-ing the other – is provided by Robert Montgomery's *Lady in the Lake*, a film whose interest consists in its very failure. The point of view of the hard-boiled detective to which we are confined via a continuous subjective camera in no way arouses in us, the spectators, the impression that we are actually watching the events through the eyes of the person shown by the camera in the prologue or the epilogue (the only 'objective shots' in the film) or when it confronts a mirror. Even when Marlowe 'sees himself in the mirror', the spectator does not accept that the face he sees, the eyes on it, is the point of view of the camera. When the camera drags on in its clumsy, slow way, it seems, rather, that the point of view is that of a living dead from Romero's *Night of the Living Dead* (the same association is further encouraged by the Christmas choral music, very unusual for a *film noir*). More precisely, it is as if the camera is positioned next to or closely behind Marlowe and somehow looks over his back, imitating the virtual gaze of his shadow, of his 'undead' sublime double. There is no double to be seen next to Marlowe, since this double, what is in Marlowe 'more than himself', is the gaze itself as the Lacanian *objet petit a* that does not have a specular image. (The voice that runs a commentary on the story belongs to this gaze, not to Marlowe *qua*

diegetic person.) This object-gaze is the cause of the desire of women who, all the time, turn towards it (i.e. look into the camera): it lays them bare in an obscene way – or, in other words, it hystericizes them by simultaneously attracting and repelling them. It is on account of this objectivization of the gaze that *The Lady in the Lake* is not a *film noir*: the essential feature of a *film noir* proper is that the point of view of the narration is that of a *subject*.

13 Sigmund Freud, 'On the Universal Tendency to Debasement in the Sphere of Love' (1912), in James Strachey (ed.), *The Standard Edition of the Complete Psychological Works of Sigmund Freud*, vol. 11 (London, Hogarth Press and the Institute of Psycho-Analysis, 1986), p. 187.

14 Jacques Lacan, *Le Séminaire, livre XX: Encore* (Paris, Éditions du Seuil, 1975), p. 65.

15 Lacan, *Ethics of Psychoanalysis*, p. 152.

16 '. . . par une inversion de l'usage du terme de sublimation, j'ai le droit de dire que nous voyons ici la déviation quant au but se faire en sens inverse de l'objet d'un besoin' (Jacques Lacan, *Le Séminaire, livre VIII: Le transfert* (Paris, Éditions du Seuil, 1991), p. 250). The same goes for every object which functions as a sign of love: its use is suspended; it changes into a means of the articulation of the demand for love.

17 Jacques Lacan, *Écrits: A Selection* (New York, Norton, 1977), p. 324. The first to formulate this 'economic paradox of castration' in the domain of philosophy was Kant. One of the standard reproaches to Kant is that he was a contradictory thinker who got stuck half-way: on the one hand *already* within the new universe of democratic rights (*égaliberté*, to use Étienne Balibar's term), on the other hand *still* caught in the paradigm of man's subordination to some superior Law (imperative). However, Lacan's formula of fetishism (a fraction with *a* above minus phi of castration) enables us to grasp the co-dependence of these two allegedly opposed aspects. The crucial feature that distinguishes the democratic field of *égaliberté* from the pre-bourgeois field of traditional authority is the potential *infinity* of rights: rights are never fully realized or even explicitly formulated, since we are dealing with an unending process of continually articulating new rights. On that account, the status of rights in the modern democratic universe is that of *objet petit a*, of an evasive object-cause of desire. Where does this feature come from? Only one consistent answer is possible: *rights are (potentially) infinite because the renunciation upon which they are based is also infinite*. The notion of a radical, 'infinite' renunciation as the price the individual must pay for his entry into the social-symbolic universe – that is to say, the notion of a 'discontent in civilization', of an irreducible antagonism between man's 'true nature' and the social order – emerged only with the modern democratic universe. Previously, within the field of traditional authority, 'sociability', a propensity for subordination to authority and for aligning oneself with some community, was conceived of as an integral part of the very 'nature' of man *qua zöon politikon*. (This, of course, does not mean that this renunciation – 'symbolic castration', in psychoanalytic terms – was not, implicitly, at work from the very beginning: we are dealing here with the logic of retroactivity where things 'become what they

always-already were': the modern bourgeois universe of Rights made visible a renunciation that was *always-already* there.) And the infinite domain of rights arises precisely as a kind of 'compensation': it is what we *get in exchange* for the infinite renunciation as the price we had to pay for our entry into society.

18 This paradox of castration also offers the key to the function of perversion, to its constitutive loop: the pervert is a subject who directly assumes the paradox of desire and inflicts pain, in order to enable enjoyment, who introduces schism in order to enable reunion, and so on. And, incidentally, theology resorts to obscure talk about the 'inscrutable divine mystery' precisely at the point where it would otherwise be compelled to acknowledge the perverse nature of God: 'the ways of the Lord are mysterious', which usually means that when misfortune pursues us everywhere, we must presuppose that he plunged us into misery in order to force us to take the opportunity to achieve spiritual salvation. . . .

19 Films that transpose the *noir* matrix into another genre (science fiction, musical comedy, etc.) often exhibit some crucial ingredient of the *noir* universe more patently than the *noir* proper. When, for example, in *Who Framed Roger Rabbit?*, Jessica Rabbit, a cartoon character, answers the reproach of her corruption with 'I'm not bad, I was just drawn that way!', she thereby displays the truth about *femme fatale* as a male fantasy – that is, as a creature whose contours are drawn by man.

20 See chapters 3 and 4 of Lacan, *Le Séminaire, livre VIII: Le transfert.*

21 This moment when the object of fascination subjectivizes itself and stretches out its hand is the magical moment of crossing the frontier that separates the fantasy-space from 'ordinary' reality: it is as if, at this moment, the object that otherwise belongs to another, sublime space intervenes in 'ordinary' reality. Suffice it to recall a scene from *Possessed*, Clarence Brown's early Hollywood melodrama with Joan Crawford. Crawford, a poor small-town girl, stares amazed at the luxurious private train that slowly passes in front of her at the local railway station; through the windows of the carriages she sees the rich life going on in the illuminated inside – dancing couples, cooks preparing dinner and so on. The crucial feature of the scene is that we, the spectators, together with Crawford, perceive the train as a magic, immaterial apparition from another world. When the last carriage passes by, the train comes to a halt, and we see on the observation deck a good-natured drunkard with a glass of champagne in his hand, which stretches over the railing towards Crawford – as if, for a brief moment, the fantasy-space intervened in reality. . . .

22 *A Neil Jordan Reader* (New York, Vintage Books, 1993), pp. xii–xiii. The question to be raised here is also that of inserting *The Crying Game* into the series of Jordan's other films: are not the earlier *Mona Lisa* and *Miracle* variations on the same motif? In all three cases, the relationship between the hero and the enigmatic woman he is obsessed with is doomed to fail – because she is a lesbian, because she is the hero's mother, because she is not a 'she' at all but a transvestite. Jordan thus provides a veritable matrix of the impossibilities of sexual relationship.

23 As for this Deleuzian opposition of surface event and bodily depth, see Žižek, *Metastases of Enjoyment*, ch. 5.

24 At this point the film differs from 'reality': the 'true' hero is still alive and rotting in a French prison.

8

There is No Sexual Relationship

This essay is in a collection entitled *Gaze and Voice as Love Objects*, edited by Renata Salecl and Slavoj Žižek (1996, pp. 208–49). Lacan's dictum 'There is no sexual relationship' asserts that there is a constitutive antagonism in the relationship of man and woman that love endeavours to erase. Fulfilment is blocked by the fascination for what Freud called 'partial objects', relics of the primordial attachment to the mother (the breast, faeces, phallus). Lacan adds to Freud's list the gaze and the voice, which become the most powerful of the love objects and which entice the subject to attempt to reach the Real in the other, culminating in struggles for domination and/or acts of sacrifice.

In this essay Žižek focuses on the impossibility of the sexual relationship through an exploration of Wagner's operas and the films of Kieslowski and Sautet. In particular, he addresses the theme of sacrifice, that of self or other. Wagner's *The Ring* and a number of his other operas have as a central concern the sacrifice of a passionate love. In Žižek's view this takes three forms, corresponding to Kierkegaard's three 'stages' of existence – the aesthetic, the ethical and the religious – each arriving at a different outcome. (1) For Kierkegaard, the aesthetic (feeling) stage is one in which a spontaneous pursuit of delight ends in 'an abyss of nothingness', which finds a form in *Tristan und Isolde*, where the lovers are immersed in their passion, finding a solution in sacrifice, a dissolution in death, the *Liebestod*. (2) The ethical stage is one in which the subject allows itself to be guided by universal rule, thus accepting the sacrifice of spontaneous passion in the performance of duty, as in *Die Meistersinger von Nürnberg*, where Hans Sachs yields Eva to Walther in an act of creative sublimation. (3) The religious level is reached when the subject performs a complete renunciation, expecting no return, not even in the form of a sublimation, as in *Parsifal*, where there is a total denial of passion.

These stages correspond to three versions of the impossibility of the sexual relation: as the demands of the sacrifice increase, the prohibitions of the Law, far from becoming stronger, grow weaker and enjoyment increases. In the aesthetic, the blind pursuit of passion results in the object being lost altogether; in the ethical, some enjoyment is gained through what the Law allows; in the religious, enjoyment is at its most intense in the abject mortification of the courtly lover, subjected to boundless demands from his Lady, as if Law and Thing were now identical – a promise of the Real forever beyond his reach.

This paradox of 'radical ascetic renunciation' coinciding with 'intense erotic fulfilment' Žižek locates first in *Tristan* and then, in its most extreme form, in *Parsifal*, where the Law that prohibits (Parsifal) and the Thing that suffers (Amfortas) are set in absolute opposition. Wagner cannot bridge this gulf between the ethical world of contract and the aesthetic one of feeling (*jouissance*). Thus *Parsifal* is not to be seen as the 'religious' apotheosis of sacrifice, but rather, with Nietzsche, as a decadent acting-out of the hysterical attitude, where Law and desire remain in conflict. Klingsor's castle as the mythical representative of uncontrolled enjoyment and the Grail community as a total rejection of it are both alike in their incestuous fixation, and the only figure to go back and forth the boundary between them, the woman Kundry, ends up dead. Hence, there is no compromise between Real and Symbolic, which makes the resolution in Parsifal a psychotic closure.

Žižek traces the political aspect of Wagner to the same structure of opposition. Although Wagner rejected the German Idealist hope of harmonizing love and Law, he still harked back to an ideal of organicist unity which he saw as having been destroyed by the invasion of the economics of capitalist exchange. Since Wotan's law is based on the notion of contract, so, by Wagner's logic, it inevitably brings about its own decline. Wagner identified the evils of contract with the Jew and the possibility of redemption either with an ascetic figure like Parsifal or with an incestuous couple like Siegmund and Sieglinde, whose love is not based on exchange. When the immortal passion has to face the deadly refusals of the Symbolic, a sacrifice is called for, not of a scapegoat, but of the self. In this light, Elsa's fateful question in *Lohengrin* can be seen as enabling her lover to find his true creative destiny at the expense of her own love. The self-sacrifice is inevitable, not because of the socio-political, but because of the structural impossibility of the sexual relation, the Real of love being recalcitrant to symbolic definition. The 'death drive' (so called by Freud), as that which goes beyond an economy of pleasure and seeks its own annihilation, marks the deadlock between the symbolic contract and the traumatic kernel of the Real. In ideology this impossibility is presented either as a property of 'human nature' or as the outcome of the social or both. The figure of Wotan is made to show the acceptance of this impossibility in that he has to will the necessity of his own death (the ring to be returned to the Rhine). This process enacts what Lacan calls 'the second death' (the 'first' being the biological one), the subject's consent within the Symbolic that it is implicated in the definition of its own death.

Žižek finds the same deadlock present in two different guises in films by Kieslowski and Sautet. The deadlock takes the form of two extremes of failure to confront the antagonism between Real and Symbolic, one arising out of loving too much, the other out of loving not at all. Both films resist what Freud called the 'tendency to debasement in the sphere of love' by a male refusal to consummate the sexual relationship, but the two refusals are contraries. In the Kieslowski film the one who loves, Tomek, wants 'nothing' in return for his love – no debasement of love, 'elevating the woman to the dignity of the Thing'; in the Sautet film, the one who is loved, Stephan, lacks 'nothing' – there is no debasement because he cannot love, not having achieved a separation from the Thing. In the former, there is Tomek's excess of idealization in the Symbolic; in the latter, Stephan's withdrawal into the Real – like Parsifal allowing the one who loves him to be redeemed. Both films, like Wagner's operas, testify to the impossibility of the sexual relationship.

One of the enigmas of Richard Wagner's *Ring* concerns the motif usually designated as that of 'renunciation': this motif is first heard in scene 1 of *Das Rheingold*, when, answering Alberich's query, Woglinde discloses that 'nur wer der Minne Macht versagt' (only the one who renounces the power of love) can take possession of the gold; the 'renunciation' motif is then repeated approximately twenty times, most noticeably toward the end of Act I of *Die Walküre*, at the moment of the most triumphant assertion of love between Siegmund and Sieglinde – just prior to his pulling out the sword from the tree trunk, Siegmund sings it: 'Heiligster Minne höchste Not' (Holiest love's deepest need).[1] Why, then, does the same motif stand first for the renunciation of love, then for its most intense assertion? Claude Lévi-Strauss[2] provided the hitherto most consistent answer. According to his reading, the central problem of the *Ring* is the constitutive imbalance of the (social) exchange. Wotan – the very 'god of contracts' supposed to safeguard exchanges – again and again engages in attempts to break the self-imposed bond of his own rules and to get 'something for nothing'; in contrast to him, Alberich is more honest: he exchanges something (love) for something else (power), thereby obeying the fundamental symbolic law according to which 'you can't have it all': that is, you can have what you possess only on the basis of a previous renunciation. The problem with Siegmund, Wotan's offspring, is that, like his father, he again 'wants it all', power (the sword) *and* love, refusing to enter the circle of social exchange. In so far as exchange (of women) is grounded in the prohibition of incest, it is quite logical that Siegmund and Sieglinde form an incestuous couple – and the motif of renunciation is here to remind us that this incestuous combination of power and love must end in a catastrophe.

This Lévi-Straussian analysis must be supplemented by a self-referential twist: the choice of power doesn't only involve the loss of love (and vice versa), it also leads to the truncation or outright loss of power itself. The outcome of Alberich's choice of power is that he ends up as a powerless dwarf: the lesson of his downfall is that in order to have power, we have to limit its exercise, to acknowledge our subordination to some higher power that invests us with a limited amount of power. The outright choice of love is even more suicidal: in order for the love to survive, one has to resist yielding to its immediate urge and to subordinate it to the necessities of social exchange via the prohibition of incest. In short, the impediment that prevents the full realization of love is internal, so the solution to the enigma of the motif of renunciation is to treat the two lines as two fragments of the complete sentence that was distorted by the 'dreamwork', that is, rendered unreadable by being split into two – the solution is to reconstitute the complete proposition: 'Love's deepest need is to renounce its own power.' The ultimate proof of a true (absolute, 'incestuous') love is that the lovers split, renounce the full consummation of their relationship – if the lovers were to remain together, they would either die or turn into an ordinary everyday bourgeois couple – 'I can't love you unless I give you up,' to quote Edith Wharton.[3] From a certain perspective, Wagner's entire opus is nothing but a variation on this theme: from *The Flying Dutchman* to the *Ring*, fulfilment goes awry, and can be achieved only in death. For that reason, Nietzsche was right in conceiving *Meistersinger* as complementary to *Tristan:* if one is to survive in the everyday world of social reality, one has to renounce the absolute claim of love, which is precisely what Hans Sachs does, thereby enabling the only semblance of a *happy end* in Wagner. By adding to this list *Parsifal*, one obtains three versions of redemption, which follow the logic of the Kierkegaardian triad of the aesthetic, the ethical and the religious. *Tristan* gives body to the aesthetic solution: refusing to compromise one's desire, one goes to the end and willingly embraces death. *Meistersinger* counters it with the ethical solution: true redemption resides not in following the immortal pattern to its self-destructive conclusion; one should rather learn to overcome it via creative sublimation and to return, in a mood of wise resignation, to the 'daily' life of symbolic obligations. In *Parsifal*, finally, the passion can no longer be overcome via its reintegration to society in which it survives in a gentrified form: one has to deny it thoroughly.

The mention of Kierkegaard was by no means accidental: it was precisely Kierkegaard who provided the hitherto most elaborated account of why 'love's deepest need is to renounce its own power'. In all three Kierkegaardian 'stages', – aesthetic, ethical and religious – the same sacrificial gesture is at work, each time in a different 'power/potential' (in Schelling's sense of the term). The religious sacrifice is a matter of course (suffice it to recall Abraham's readiness to sacrifice Isaac, Kierkegaard's supreme example), so we should concentrate on the renunciation that pertains to the 'ethical' and the 'aesthetic'.

The ethical stage is defined by the sacrifice of the immediate consumption of life, of our yielding to the fleeting moment, in the name of some higher universal norm. In the domain of erotics, one of the most refined examples of this renunciation is provided by Mozart's *Così fan tutte*. If Mozart's *Don Giovanni* embodies the aesthetic (as developed by Kierkegaard himself in his detailed analysis of the opera in *Either/Or*), the lesson of *Così fan tutte* is ethical – why? The point of *Così* is that the love that unites the two couples at the beginning of the opera is no less 'artificial', mechanically brought about, than the second falling in love of the sisters with the exchanged partners dressed up as Albanian officers that results from the manipulations of the philosopher Alfonso – in both cases, we are dealing with a mechanism that the subjects follow in a blind, puppet-like way. Therein consists the Hegelian 'negation of negation': first, we perceive the 'artificial' love, the product of Alfonso's manipulations, as opposed to the initial 'authentic' love; then, all of a sudden, we become aware that there is actually no difference between the two – the original love is no less 'artificial' than the second. So, since one love counts as much as the other, the couples can return to their initial marital arrangements. This is what Hegel has in mind when he claims that, in the course of a dialectical process, the immediate starting point proves itself to be something already mediated – that is, its own self-negation: in the end, we ascertain that we always-already were what we wanted to become, the only difference being that this 'always-already' changes its modality from in-itself into for-itself.[4] Ethical is in this sense the domain of repetition *qua* symbolic: if, in the aesthetic, one endeavours to capture the moment in its uniqueness, in the ethical a thing only becomes what it is through its repetition.[5]

In the aesthetic stage, the seducer works on an innocent girl whom he considers worthy of his efforts, but at a crucial moment, just prior to his triumph – that is, when for all practical purposes her surrender is already won and the fruits of his labour have only to be reaped – he has not only to renounce the realization of the sexual act but, over and above, to induce *her* to drop him (by putting on the mask of a despicable person and thus arousing her disgust).[6] Why this renunciation? The realization of the process of seduction in the sexual act renders visible the goal the seducer was striving at in all its transience and vulgarity, so the only way to avoid this horror of radical 'desublimation' is to stop short of it, thereby keeping awake the dream of what *might have* happened – by losing his love in time, the seducer gains her for eternity.[7] One must be careful here not to miss the point: the 'desublimation' one tries to avoid by renouncing the act does *not* reside in the experience of how realization always falls short of the ideal we were striving for – that is, of the gap that for ever separates the ideal from its realization – in it; it is rather the ideal itself that loses its power, that changes into repugnant slime – the ideal is, as it were, undermined 'from within'; when we approach it too closely, it changes into its opposite.[8]

In all three 'stages', the same gesture of sacrifice is at work in a different 'power/potential': what shifts from the one to the other is the locus of impossibility. That is to say, one is tempted to claim that the triad aesthetic–ethical–religious provides the matrix for the three versions of the impossibility of sexual relationship. What one would expect here is that, with the 'progression' (or, rather, leap) from one to the next stage, the pressure of prohibition and/or impossibility gets stronger: in the aesthetic, one is free to 'seize the day', to yield to enjoyment without any restraints; in the ethical, enjoyment is admitted, but on condition that it remains within the confines of the Law (marriage), that is, in an aseptic, 'gentrified' form that suspends its fatal charm; in the religious, finally, there is no enjoyment, just the most radical, 'irrational' renunciation for which we get nothing in return (Abraham's readiness to sacrifice Issac). However, this clear picture of progressive renunciation immediately gets blurred by the uncanny resemblance, noticed by many a sagacious commentator, between Abraham's sacrifice of Isaac (which, of course, belongs to the religious) and Kierkegaard's own renunciation to Regina (which belongs to the aesthetic dialectics of seduction). On a closer look, one can thus ascertain that, contrary to our expectations, the prohibition (or rather inhibition) *loosens* with the leap from one to the next stage: in the aesthetic, the object is completely lost, beyond our reach, owing to the inherent instability of this level (in the very gesture of our trying to lay our hands on the fleeting moment of pleasure, it slips between our fingers); in the ethical, enjoyment is already rendered possible in a stable, regular form via the mediation of the Law; and, finally, in the religious . . . what is the religious mode of erotics, if its aesthetic mode is seduction and its ethical mode marriage? Is it at all meaningful to speak of a religious mode of erotics in the precise Kierkegaardian sense of the term? The point of Lacan is that this, precisely, is the role of *courtly love*: the Lady in courtly love suspends the ethical level of universal symbolic obligations and bombards us with totally arbitrary ordeals in a way that is homologous to the religious suspension of the ethical; her ordeals are on a par with God's ordering Abraham to slaughter his son Isaac. And, contrary to first appearance, that sacrifice reaches here its apogee; it is only here that, finally, we confront the Other *qua* Thing that gives body to the excess of enjoyment over mere pleasure. If an aesthetic endeavour to seize the full moment ends in fiasco and utter loss, paradoxically, religious renunciation, the elevation of the Lady into an untouchable and unattainable object, leads to the trance of enjoyment that transgresses the limits of Law.

And is not this extreme point at which radical ascetic renunciation para-doxically coincides with the most intense erotic fulfilment the very topic of Wagner's *Tristan*? One can also see why Nietzsche was right in claiming that *Parsifal* is Wagner's most decadent work and the antithesis to *Tristan*. In *Parsifal*, normal, everyday life totally disappears as a point of reference – what remains is the opposition between hysterically over-excited chromaticism and asexual purity, the ultimate denial of passion.[9] *Parsifal* thus offers a kind of spectral decomposition of *Tristan*: in it, the immortal longing of the two lovers, sexualized and simultaneously spiritualized to extremes, is decomposed into its two constituents, sexual chromatic excitation and the spiritual purity beyond the cycle of life. Amfortas and Parsifal, the suffering king who cannot die and the innocent 'pure fool' beyond desire, are the two ingredients that, when brought together, give us Tristan.

We can see, now, how we are to interpret Wagner: the 'meaning' of *Tristan* becomes visible when we establish the connection between it and the two other music dramas (in short, when we apply to it the structural interpretation of myths elaborated by Lévi-Strauss, himself a great Wagnerian).[10] What really matters is not the pseudo-problem of which of the three solutions reflects Wagner's 'true' position (did he really believe in the redemptive power of the orgasmic *Liebestod*? did he resign himself to the necessity of returning to the everyday world of symbolic obligations?), but the formal matrix that generates these three versions of redemption. What effectively defines Wagner's position is this underlying problematic, the unstable relationship between the 'ethical' universe of social-symbolic obligations ('contracts'), the overwhelming sexual passion that threatens to dissolve social links (the 'aesthetic'), and the spiritualized self-denial of the will (the 'religious'). Each of the three operas is an attempt to compress this triangle into the opposition between two elements: between the spiritualized sexual passion and the socio-symbolic universe in *Tristan*, between sexual passion and the spiritual sublimation of socialized art in *Meistersinger*, between sexualized life and pure ascetic spiritualism in *Parsifal*. Each of these three solutions relies on a specific musical mode which predominates in it: the chromaticism of *Tristan*, the choral aspect of *Meistersinger*, the contrast between chromaticism and static diatonics of *Parsifal*.

In *Parsifal*, 'love's deepest need' to renounce its own power thus finds its ultimate formulation: sexual passion itself contains a secret longing for its radical self-denial, which only brings peace and redemption. This self-impediment inherent to the dynamics of love transpires in the deadlock of hysteria, this modern phenomenon *par excellence*, and it was, again, already Nietzsche who claimed that the problems Wagner presents on the stage are 'all of them problems of hysterics – the convulsive nature of his affects, his over-excited sensibility, his taste that required ever stronger spices, his instability which he dressed up as principles'.[11] The first move in interpreting Wagner's hysteria should be therefore to 'translate Wagner into reality, into the modern – let us be even crueller – into the bourgeois':[12] 'All of Wagner's heroines, without exception, as soon as they are stripped of their heroic skin, become almost indistinguishable from Madame Bovary!'[13] This experience is known to every perceptive spectator of Wagner: is the dance of the Flower Maidens in Act II of *Parsifal* not a cabaret performance from a high-class nineteenth-century brothel? Is Act II of *The Twilight of the Gods* not a bourgeois farce on the deceived housewife and the humiliated, impotent husband?

[. . .]

Concerning the political, the debate usually centres on the change in the ending of *The Twilight of the Gods*: from Feuerbach to Schopenhauer, from the revolutionary assertion of new humanity delivered from the oppressive rule of gods and finally free to enjoy love to the reactionary resignation and disavowal of the very will to life – in a paradigmatic case of ideological mystification, Wagner inflates the defeat of the revolution and his betrayal of the revolutionary ideals into the end of the world itself. . . . However, on a closer look, it soon becomes clear that the true state of things rather resembles the good old Soviet joke on Rabinovitch: Did he really win a car in the lottery? In principle, yes, only it wasn't car but a bicycle; besides, he didn't win it, it was stolen from him. . . . So the standard explanation for the changed ending of *The Twilight of the Gods* is also in principle true, only that the ending we actually have is closer to the original one (people, common mortals, do survive and just stare as mute witnesses at the cosmic catastrophe of the gods); furthermore, the early revolutionary Wagner is definitely more proto-Fascist than the late one – his 'revolution' looks rather like the restitution of the organic unity of the people who, led by the prince, have swept away the rule of money embodied in Jews. . . .

The true problem lies elsewhere. In his *Ring*, Wagner addresses the fundamental ethico-political question of German Idealism: how is it possible to unite love and Law? In contrast to German Idealists whose political vision involved the hope of a reconciliation between the assertion of authentic intersubjective bonds of love and the demands of the objective social order of contracts and laws, Wagner is no longer prone to accept this solution. His apprehension articulates itself in the opposition between Wotan and Alberich, between contractual, symbolic authority and the spectral, invisible Master: Wotan is a figure of symbolic authority; he is the 'god of contracts'; his will is bound by the Word, by the symbolic pact (the giant Fasolt tells him, 'What you are, / you are through contracts only'),[14] whereas Alberich is an all-powerful (because invisible) agent not bound by any law:

> Nibelungs all,
> bow down to Alberich!
> He is everywhere,
> watching you! . . .
> You must work for him,
> though you cannot see him!
> When you don't think he's there,
> You'd better expect him!
> You're subject to him for ever![15]

Wagner's crucial insight is, of course, that this opposition is inherent in Wotan himself: the very gesture of establishing the rule of law contains the seeds of its ruin – why? Wagner is here guided by a perception that was given different theoretical articulations by Marx, Lacan and Derrida: equivalent exchange is a deceptive mirage – what it conceals is the very excess on which it is grounded. The domain of contracts, of giving and receiving something in return, is sustained by a paradoxical gesture that provides in its very capacity of withholding a kind of generative lack, a withdrawal that opens up space, a lack which acts as a surplus. This gesture can be conceptualized as the Derridean gift, the primordial *Yes!* of our openness to dissemination, or as the primordial loss, the Lacanian 'symbolic castration'. (In Wagner's mythical space, this violent gesture of grounding the domain of legal exchange is depicted as Wotan's tearing out of the World Ash-Tree, from which he then cuts his spear and inscribes on it runes containing the laws; this act is followed by a whole series of similar gestures: Alberich's snatching the gold, Siegmund's pulling out the sword. . . .) Wagner is thus well aware that the very balance of exchange is grounded on the disturbance of the primordial balance, on a traumatic loss, an 'out-of-joint', which opens up the space of social exchange. However, at this crucial point, the critique of exchange becomes ambivalent: it either endeavours to assert the primordial *Yes!*, the irreducible excess of the openness toward the Otherness that cannot be restricted to the field of balanced exchange, of its 'closed economy'; or it aims at restoring the primordial balance prior to this excessive gesture. Wagner's rejection of (the society of) exchange, which is the basis of his anti-Semitism, amounts to an attempt to regain the pre-lapsarian balance. Nowhere is this more obvious than in his sexual politics, which asserts the incestuous link against the exogamic exchange of women: Sieglinde and Siegmund, the 'good' incestuous couple, against Sieglinde and Hunding, the 'bad' couple based on exchange; Brünnhilde and Siegfried against two further couples based on exchange (Brünnhilde and Günther, Gutrune and Siegfried) . . .

In dealing with Wagner's anti-Semitism, we should always bear in mind that the opposition of German true spirit versus the Jewish principle is not the original one: there is a third term, modernity, the reign of exchange, of the dissolution of organic links, of modern industry and individuality – the theme of exchange and contracts is *the* central theme of the *Ring*. Wagner's attitude toward modernity is not simply negative but, much more, ambiguous: he wants to enjoy its fruits, while avoiding its disintegrative effects – in short, Wagner wants to have his cake and eat it. For that reason, he needs a Jew: so that, first, modernity – this abstract, impersonal process – is given a human face, is identified with concrete, palpable features; then, in a second move, by rejecting the Jew who gives body to all that is disintegrated in modernity, we can retain its fruits. In short, anti-Semitism does not stand for anti-modernism as such, but for an attempt to combine modernity with social corporatism, which is characteristic of conservative revolutionaries. So, since the rule of Law, the society of 'contracts', is founded on an act of illegitimate violence, Law not only has to betray love, but also has to violate its own highest principles: 'The purpose of their [the gods'] higher world order is moral consciousness: but they are tainted by the very injustice they hunt down; from the depths of Nibelheim [where Alberich lives] the consciousness of their guilt echoes back threateningly.'[16]

[. . .]

In order to grasp how Wagner is able to use sexual relationship as the paradigm for authentic political order, one has only to bear in mind the way, according to him, man and woman complement each other. Woman is the all-embracing unity, the ground that bears man, yet precisely as such she has, in her positive, empirical existence, to be subordinated to the 'formative power' of man. For that reason, the elevation of and subordination to the essential Woman goes hand in hand with the exploitation of, and the domination over, actual flesh-and-blood women. Suffice it to recall here Schelling's notion of the highest freedom as the state in which activity and passivity, being-active and being-acted-upon, harmoniously overlap. Schelling gives here a specific twist to the distinction between *Vernunft* and *Verstand*, reason and understanding, which plays a crucial role in German idealism: '*Vernunft* is nothing else than *Verstand* in its subordination to the highest, the soul.'[17] *Verstand* is the intellect as active, as the power of active seizing and deciding by means of which one asserts himself as a fully autonomous subject; however, one reaches one's acme when one turns one's very subjectivity into the predicate of an ever higher power (in the mathematical sense of the term) – that is, when one, as it were, yields to the Other, 'depersonalizes' one's most intense activity and performs it as if some other, higher power is acting through him or her, using him or her as its medium – like an artist who, in the highest frenzy of creativity, experiences himself as a medium through which the impersonal spirit expresses itself. What is crucial is the explicit sexual connotation of this highest form of freedom: feminization (adoption of a passive attitude toward the transcendent absolute) serves as the inherent support of masculine assertion. It is therefore clearly wrong to interpret the Wagnerian elevation of the feminine as a protest against the male universe of contracts and brutal exercise of power, as the utopian vision of a new life beyond aggressive modern subjectivity: the reference to the eternal Feminine toward which the male subject adopts a passive attitude is the ultimate metaphysical support of the worldly aggressive attitude – and, incidentally, the same goes for the contemporary New Age assertion of the (feminine) Goddess.

The political use of this notion is thus easy to grasp: in an authentic political order, the prince (*der Fürst*), to whom Wagner refers even in his revolutionary period as the one to head the revolution, is to behave toward his people like the man to his feminine ground: his very subordination to the transcendent notion of the people (the fact that he adopts a feminine attitude toward the people and merely serves it, brings forth its deepest interests) legitimizes him in acting as the 'formative power' and exerting full authority over empirically existing, actual people. It is this organic, sexualized relationship between the prince and his people that the modern society of egotistic mechanical links and profit-oriented contracts threatens to disrupt. . . . The same notion of harmonious sexual relationship also serves as the ultimate phantasmatic support of the notion of 'music drama'. Wagner described music as a means to an end in drama, and drama as a 'musical deed made visible': how are we to resolve this paradox of drama as a function of music and music a function of drama?

Wagner resorts again to the matrix of sexual relationship: music is Woman made fecund by the male word, so that the subordination of music to word equals the subordination of the background to the figure, of woman to man. On that account, music is doubly inscribed. It is the Schopenhauerian 'Thing', the direct vibration of our true inner life, the ground which 'embraces drama in itself', since the latter is merely its external, phenomenal manifestation. However, Wagner is as far as possible from any notion of absolute music – drama is the 'formative motive' of music, so that music in its positive, determinate existence has to serve as a means to render present the dramatic stage action; it can actualize, self-realize, itself only as the musical envelope of the stage action.[18]

What danger is Wagner trying to avoid by means of this sexualization of the relationship between drama and music? In his *Opera and Drama*, he himself provides the key: '[E]ach art tends toward an indefinite extension of its power... [T]his tendency leads it finally to its limit... [I]t would not know how to pass this limit without running the risk of losing itself in the incomprehensible, the bizarre, and the absurd.' On that account, 'each art demands, as soon as it reaches the limits of its power, to give a hand to the neighbouring art.'[19] This 'refusal to transgress' is what is ultimately at stake in the project of *Gesamtkunstwerk*: each art

is ordered by a sort of law of the 'passage to the limit': but if it tries to move beyond this limit, and this will be exactly the enterprise of modern art (Wagner sees things very clearly), it is threatened with absurdity and inanity.

The dialectical confrontation of the individual arts in the 'total work of art' is consequently a means of containing excess and safeguarding meaning.[20]

This Wagnerian 'conservative revolution', which unites music and drama in the *Gesamtkunstwerk*, in order to prevent the two elements from following their inherent logic and thus stepping over the threshold of true modernism, is at work as far away as Hollywood, where the most daring atonal music is fully acceptable in so far as it accompanies a scene of madness or violence – that is, in so far as it serves to illustrate some clearly defined psychological state or realist action. This mention of Hollywood is by no means accidental, since Wagner's music is intimately related to it. What I have in mind here are not so much John Williams's scores for the big-budget science-fiction and fantasy films of the seventies and eighties, which provide merely a series of pseudo-Wagnerian effects, but rather the so-called Hollywood classicism, which exerted its hegemony from mid-thirties till mid-fifties (in the films of Max Steiner, Franz Waxman, Miklos Rosza, etc.). This 'Hollywood classicism' is characterized by the following main features:

– the invisibility of the apparatus that produces music – that is, the displacement of the music into an imaginary 'invisible pit', correlative to the Wagnerian 'hidden orchestra': the music that accompanies the screen action emanates from a kind of atemporal non-localized present;
– emotions translated by music (as in Wagner, not only direct emotional reactions of the persons on the screen but also emotional under-currents these persons are not aware of – music can announce the birth of fatal love in what the future lovers experience as an insignificant, passing encounter . . .);
– 'narrative cueing': the unending melody with its leitmotifs accentuates narration and provides for its continuity and unity.[21]

My hypothesis is that Hollywood classicism was an attempt to resolve a deadlock that was similar to that of the pre–Wagnerian opera. Exemplary here is the credits sequence of Fritz Lang's *Testament des Dr. Mabuse*, in which the noisy, spectacular music gradually changes into the rhythmic buzz of vibrating machines – a passage reminiscent of the music accompanying Wotan's and Loge's descent into Niebelheim in *Rheingold*, with its intermingling of the rhythmic beat of the instruments and the sound of hammering. The late twenties and early thirties thus provide a series of attempts to 'inscribe music into the movement of life – of the collective, physical life – and, simultaneously, to extract from reality its own latent symphony',[22] predominantly in the form of the so-called symphony of the city, of the celebration of industrious city life, with its incessant buzzing of the machines and the noise of the human crowd, which are elevated into the direct presentation of the fundamental rhythm of the metaphysical life itself. (This 'rhythm of life itself' returns much later, in the guise of the obscene, uncanny pulsation of the life substance, in some of the films of David Lynch (*Blue Velvet, Dune, Elephant Man*).)

There is, however, one element that resists inclusion in this 'symphony of life': *speech*, not a song or a poetic declamation but precisely speech in its capacity as 'natural' conversation. In order to accommodate this element, the rhythmic continuum of noise and music gradually withdraws into the background, so that cinema is more and more centred on speech accompanied by an unending melody that provides its emotional and/or mythical context. What takes place is the shift of accent from a dynamic, assertive, clearly articulated rhythm to a lyrical chromaticism of unending melody that serves as the elusive complex background to the naturalized speech and action. The price for the naturalization of the action on the screen is thus the displacement of the mythical dimension on to the anti-naturalist lyricism of the musical score: the musical score is clearly subordinated to the naturalist screen action, illustrating and accompanying it; yet precisely as such, it 'denaturalizes' it, serves as the means of its stylization, confers on it its mythical dimension.

Music is thus simultaneously *more* present (ideally the spectator is submerged in it all the time, relying on it for the proper emotional attitude toward the screen action) and *less* present (the spectator's attention is not focused on the musical score; music just provides the invisible emotional, mythical, etc. frame for what goes on on the screen). Is all this not strictly homologous to the way the Wagnerian orchestral melody 'weaves the immense background to the events from reminiscences and fleeting allusions'? So,

the orchestral store of mythic motives – those of the ring, Valhalla, Erda, the gods' downfall, contracts and the curse – connects the events now taking place to their primeval premises and origins. . . . If there is any danger of the divine myth fading in significance beside the heroic drama, because it does not take physical shape on the stage, the music restores it – and the overall context of the cycle – to its rightful dramatic place.[23]

As is well known, Flaubert's main stylistic device was the so-called *style indirect libre*, in which propositions immediately 'objectivize' the feelings and attitudes of the persons – and does Wagner's use of leitmotifs not amount to a kind of musical *style indirect libre?* The problem, of course, was that Wagner's attempt to synchronize music and poetry was doomed to fail: what we get instead of their organic harmony is a paradoxical double surplus. 'Too much theatre' (for the partisans of absolute music, who bemoan the fact that Wagner effectively reduces music to an illustration or a psychological commentary of the stage action) seems to invert continually into 'too much music' (which, as the all-present background, overflows everything, so that we, the spectators, are submerged in it). Both domains are furthermore split from within: music oscillates between timeless mythical monumentalism and modern 'hystericity'; drama oscillates between traditional monumental heroism and relapses into bourgeois vulgarity. Either the heroic stage action lags behind, and is belied by the chromatic modernity of the musical texture, or the stage action strikes us as modern-bourgeois, sometimes even bordering on naturalism, in contrast to the timeless-mythical monumentalism of the music. However, although one is therefore tempted to agree with Dahlhaus that the notion of music drama is a 'metaphor for unresolved problems' rather than their solution, one should be quick to add that the above-mentioned inconsistencies and gaps in the realization of the concept of music drama in no way impinge on the artistic impact of Wagner's work, but are precisely the most reliable index of its authenticity – nowhere is Wagner more authentic than when the chromatic musical texture renders manifest the 'hysterical' foundation and background of the heroic stage action, or when the modern bourgeois features of the stage action reveal the concrete socio-historical foundation of the music's mythical monumentalism:

hysterical chromaticism and mythical timelessness are unitary in so far as they present the two facets of the dissolution of everyday realism. As Adorno would have put it, the artistic truth of Wagner resides in the very contradictions brought about by the realization of his project.

This non-contemporaneity of music and words (the dramatic plot) designates the way the impossibility of sexual relationship is inscribed into the very notion of the music drama. Nietzsche was the first to discern this crack in the edifice of the music drama when he emphasized how, in Wagner, music loses its auto-nomous structure and is turned into a means to render and accentuate melo-dramatic stage action: 'Wagner was *not* a musician by instinct. He showed this by abandoning all lawfulness and . . . all style in music in order to turn it into what he required, theatrical rhetoric, a means of expression, of underscoring gestures, of suggestion, of the psychologically picturesque.'[24] The unmelodic chromaticism of the Wagnerian music, its lack of a firmly erected inner structure, intoxicates, hypnotizes, seduces, excites our nerves, overwhelms us; its unique mixture of sentimentality and empty pomposity, of artificiality and brutality, reduces the public to the passive attitude of the feminine hysteric. The inherent obverse of this over-excited universe of hysteria is the longing for 'redemption', for the pacification that, within this hysterical perspective, can only be imagined in the guise of a saintly, life-denying, asexual, aseptic-anaemic figure – Christ, Parsifal. The hysterical search for shocking effects and the longing for eternal peace are thus strictly co-dependent: in modern decadence, the authentic *vita activa* dissolves into the empty shell of superficial excitations and the denial of the will, the stepping out of the cycle of life. It is the music of *Tristan* that gives the purest expression to the inherent link between hysterical chromaticism and the longing for death: chromaticism allows for no pacification, no dissolution of the tension, in social reality – only death, only the very annihilation of the life process, brings peace and redemption. In *Parsifal*, this tension is externalized into, on the one hand, Klingsor with his magic castle, a new edition of *Venusberg*, a decadent *paradis artificiel*, full of Oriental perfumes, and, on the other hand, Parsifal himself, the apathetic saint who shares with his hysterical counterpart oversensitivity and an inability to endure the passions and struggles of real life. The immobility of space exempted from the flow of time, the refuge in the self-enclosed Grail community, which stands for Wagner's negation of modernity and its discon-tents, is a modernist myth *par excellence*, and as such is no less modernist than over-excited chromaticism. As has been pointed out already by Adorno, what is so modern about *Parsifal* is not only the chromaticism of Kundry and Amfortas's suffering, but also the static diatonics of the Grail community that endeavours to negate it.

The very form of *Parsifal* (musical as well as dramatic) thus belies its ideological project of androgynous reconciliation: its two spheres, Klingsor's castle and the temple of the Grail – or, musically: chromaticism and diatonics – remain side by side in their irreconcilable opposition. The universe of *Parsifal* is 'incestuous' to extremes precisely in so far as it involves the refusal of any exchange between its two spheres: Kundry, the element circulating between the two, has to drop dead at the end. Klingsor's castle stands for the asocial excess of incestuous enjoyment; the temple of the Grail, its sterile counterpoint, is no less asocial in its incestuous rejection of any mingling with the Otherness. The two domains are thus opposed as surplus and lack: luxuriant, putrefying abundance versus ascetic purity. No wonder Wagner entertained the notion that the Montségur castle, the mysterious seat of the Cathars, was the possible location of the temple of the Grail: according to the Cathars, sexuality as such should be abandoned since all sexual intercourse is incestuous. The disappearance of 'normal' secular social life in *Parsifal* is therefore unavoidable: society is based on (linguistic, sexual, economic) exchange. In *Parsifal*, surplus and lack remain side by side; they are not united on the base of the paradoxical gesture that provides in its very withholding. This disappearance of the domain of (social) exchange bears witness to the dimension of psychosis: *Parsifal* stages a psychotic resolution of the deadlock of hysteria. For that reason, far from signalling castration, Parsifal's renunciation of the sexual urge stands for its most forceful denial: Parsifal rejects the loss involved in the act of man's opening up to the other-woman.

[. . .]

Nietzsche's last written text, finished at Christmas 1888, a few days before his final mental collapse, is *Nietzsche contra Wagner*, a collection of passages from his older writings destined to prove that Nietzsche's sudden violent rejection of Wagner is not inspired by sudden malice, but presents a logical outcome of his entire work. And it is as if Nietzsche stumbled here, as if he wasn't able to delimit himself clearly from the neurosis called Wagner – what we encounter here is the old topic of *cogito and madness*. Modern philosophy in its entirety can be read as a desperate endeavour to draw a clear line separating the transcendental philosopher from the madman (Descartes: how do I know I'm not hallucinating reality? Kant: how to delimit metaphysical speculation from Swedenborgian hallucinatory rambling?, etc.). Along the same lines, Nietzsche's problem is: how do I know I'm not just another Wagnerian, another victim of hysterical hallucinations? It is as if Wagner was Nietzsche's symptom: the element Nietzsche desperately needed in order for his thought to retain its minimal coherence by way of projecting into it all that he found so despicable in himself – the attempt to cut off all links with Wagner thus necessarily ended in his final breakdown.

Why, then, did Nietzsche's delimitation fail? It would be easy, all too easy, to focus on the clearly sexualized character of Nietzsche's scorn for Wagner: Nietzsche perceives in Wagner the lack of an erect, assertive, firm male attitude – instead of the clearly structured rhythmic and melodic edifice, his music indulges in the 'feminized' attitude of passively submerging into the shapeless ocean of feeling. . . This femininity scorned by Nietzsche is the 'eternal Feminine', the phantasmatic support of the actual subordination of women; paradoxically, Nietzsche's scorn for Wagner's 'feminization' of music is thus much closer to feminism that the Wagnerian elevation of woman as man's redeemer. So the failure of Nietzsche's delimitation from Wagner is not the failure of the male subject's attempt to delimit himself from the feminine. The problem with Nietzsche's rejection of Wagner's hysteria resides elsewhere. Contrary to the deceptive appearance according to which Nietzche and Freud share a common ground (they both seem to conceive hysteria as resulting from the suppression of the healthy life substance by an anaemic moralism), it is *Freud contra Nietzsche* that is appropriate here: for Freud, hysteria is not based on the decadent denial of life power; the hysterical subject is rather a kind of *symptom* of the Master – what he renders palpable is the primordial deadlock that pertains to the dimension of subjectivity as such, and which is concealed by the posture of the Master. Freud's name for this deadlock, for this authentic kernel of the hysterical theatre that eludes Nietzsche's grasp and undermines from within *vita activa*, is *death drive*.

For Freud, the death drive is not merely a decadent reactive formation – a secondary self-denial of the originally assertive will to power, the weakness of the will, its escape from life, disguised as heroism – but the innermost radical possibility of a human being. When one says 'death drive and Wagner', the first association is, of course, Schopenhauer, Wagner's principal reference for the redemptive quality of the longing for death. Our thesis, however, is that the way the longing for death effectively functions within Wagner's universe is much closer to the Freudian notion of 'death drive'. The death drive is not to be confused with the 'Nirvana principle', the striving to escape the life cycle of generation and corruption and to achieve the ultimate equilibrium, the release from tensions: what the death drive strives to annihilate is not this biological cycle of generation and corruption, but rather the symbolic order, the order of the symbolic pact that regulates social exchange and sustains debts, honours, obligations.[25] The death drive is thus to be conceived against the background of the opposition between 'day' and 'night' as it is formulated in *Tristan*: the opposition between the 'daily' social life of symbolic obligations, honours, contracts, debts, and its 'nightly' obverse, an immortal, indestructible passion that threatens to dissolve this network of symbolic obligations. One should bear in mind how sensitive Wagner was to the borderline that separates the realm of the symbolic from what is excluded from it: the deadly passion defines itself against the everyday public universe of symbolic obligations. Therein resides the effect of the love potion in *Tristan*: it is in its capacity of the 'drink of death' that it acts as the 'drink of love' – the two lovers mistake it for the drink of death and, thinking that they are now on the brink of death, delivered from ordinary social obligations, feel free to acknowledge their passion. This immortal passion does not stand for biological life beyond the socio-symbolic universe: in it, carnal passion and pure spirituality paradoxically coincide. That is, we are dealing with a kind of 'denaturalization' of the natural instinct that inflates it into an immortal passion raised to the level of the absolute, so that no actual, real object can ever fully satisfy it.

More precisely, there is a dimension of life that the death drive wills to annihilate, but this dimension is not the simple biological life; it has rather to be located in the uncanny domain that Lacan called 'between the two deaths'. In order to elucidate this notion, let us recall the other big enigma of the *Ring*: since the gold – the ring – is finally returned to Rhine, why do the gods none the less perish? We are obviously dealing with *two* deaths: a biologically necessary demise and a 'second death', the fact that the subject died in peace, with his accounts settled, with no symbolic debt haunting his memory. Wagner himself changed the text concerning this crucial point: in the first version of Erda's warning in the final scene of *Rheingold*, the gods will perish if the gold is not returned to the Rhine; whereas in the final version, they will perish anyway; the point is merely that prior to their demise, the gold should be returned to the Rhine, so that they will die properly and avoid the 'irretrievable dark perdition'. . . . What we encounter in this uncanny space between the two deaths is the palpitation of a life substance that cannot ever perish, like Amfortas's wound in *Parsifal*. Suffice it to recall Leni Riefenstahl, who, in her unending search for the ultimate life substance, focused her attention first on the Nazis, then on an African tribe whose male members allegedly display true masculine vitality, and finally on deep-sea animals – as if it was only here, in this fascinating crawling of primitive life-forms, that she finally encountered her true object. This underwater life seems indestructible, like Leni herself: what we fear when we are following reports on how, well into her nineties, she is engaged in diving in order to make a documentary on deep-sea life, is that she will never die – our unconscious fantasy is definitely that she is immortal . . . It is crucial to conceive the notion of death drive against the background of this 'second death', as the will to abolish the indestructible palpitation of life beyond death (of the Dutchman, of Kundry and Amfortas), not as the will to negate the immediate biological life cycle. After Parsifal succeeds in annihilating the 'pathological' sexual urge in himself, this precisely opens up his eyes for the innocent charm of the immediate natural life cycle (the magic of Good Friday). So, back to Wotan, who wants to shed his guilt in order to die properly, in peace, and thus to avoid the fate of an undead monster, who, unable to find peace even in death, haunts common mortals – this is what Brünnhilde has in mind when, at the very end of *The Twilight of the Gods*, after returning the ring to the Rhine-maidens, she says: 'Rest, rest now, you god!' (Ruhe, ruhe, du Gott!)

This notion of the 'second death' enables us to locate properly Wagner's claim that Wotan rises to the tragic height of willing his own downfall: 'This is everything we have to learn from the history of mankind: to will the inevitable and to carry it out oneself.'[26] Wagner's precise formulation is to be taken literally, in all its paradoxicality – if something is already in itself inevitable, why should we then actively will it and work toward its occurrence, one might ask? This paradox, central to the symbolic order, is the obverse of the paradox of prohibiting something impossible (incest, for example), which can be discerned in Wittgenstein's famous 'What one cannot speak about, thereof one should be silent' – if it is in any case impossible to say anything about it, why add the superfluous prohibition? The fear that one would nevertheless say something about it is strictly homologous to the fear that what is necessary will not occur without our active assistance. The ultimate proof that we are not dealing here with futile logical games is the existential predicament of pre-destination: the ideological reference that sustained the extraordinary explosion of activity in early capitalism was the Protestant notion of predestination. That is to say, contrary to the common notion according to which, if everything is decided in advance, why bother at all, it was the very awareness that their fate is already sealed up that propelled the subjects into frantic activity. The same goes for Stalinism: the most intense mobilization of the society's productive effort was sustained by the awareness that the people are merely realizing inexorable historical necessity....

[...]

However, Wotan's gesture of willing his own destruction in order to shed his guilt, and Tristan and Isolde embracing their disappearance into the abyss of nothingness as the climatic fulfilment of their love, these two exemplary cases of the Wagnerian death drive, are to be supplemented by a third one, that of Brünnhilde, this 'suffering, self-sacrificing woman' who 'becomes at last the true, conscious redeemer'.[27] She also wills her annihilation, but not as a desperate means to compensate for her guilt – she wills it as an act of love destined to redeem the beloved man, or, as Wagner himself put it in a letter to Liszt:

The love of a tender woman has made me happy; she dared to throw herself into a sea of suffering and agony so that she should be able to say to me 'I love you!' No one who does not know all her tenderness can judge how much she had to suffer. We were spared nothing – but as a consequence I am redeemed and she is blessedly happy because she is aware of it.[28]

Once again, we should descend here from the mythic heights into the everyday bourgeois reality: woman is aware of the fact that, by means of her suffering which remains invisible to the public eye, of her renunciation for the beloved man and/or her renunciation to him (the two are always dialectically inter-connected, since, in the phantasmatic logic of the Western ideology of love, it is for the sake of her man that the woman must renounce him), she rendered possible man's redemption, his public social triumph – like la Traviata, who abandons her lover and thus enables his reintegration into the social order; like the young wife in Edith Wharton's *The Age of Innocence*, who knows of her husband's secret adulterous passion, but feigns ignorance in order to save their marriage. Examples are here innumerable, and one is tempted to claim that – like Eurydice, who, by sacrificing herself – that is, by intentionally provoking Orpheus into turning his gaze toward her and thus sending her back to Hades – delivers his creativity and sets him free to pursue his poetic mission. Elsa also intentionally asks the fateful question, and thereby delivers Lohengrin, whose true desire, of course, is to remain the lone artist sublimating his suffering into his creativity. We can see here the link between the death drive and creative sublimation, which provides the co-ordinates for the gesture of feminine self-sacrifice, this constant object of Wagner's dreams: by way of giving up her partner, the woman effectively redeems him – that is, compels him to take the path of creative sublimation and work the raw stuff of the failed real sexual encounter into the myth of absolute love.[29] What one should do, therefore, is read Wagner's *Tristan* the way Goethe explained his *Werther:* by way of writing the book, the young Goethe symbolically acted out his infatuation, and brought it to its logical conclusion (suicide); this way, he relieved himself of the unbearable tension, and was able to return to his everyday existence. The work of art acts here as the phantasmatic supplement: its enactment of the fully consummated sexual relationship supports the compromise we make in our actual social life – in *Tristan*, Wagner erected a monument to Mathilde Wesendonck and to his immortal love for her, so that, in reality, he was able to get over his infatuation and return to normal bourgeois life.[30]

The conclusion to be drawn is not that the death drive is merely a mask in the guise of which the male Master mystifies his political betrayal or his male chauvinist attitude toward women: it simultaneously points toward the trau-matic kernel of the Real, which underlies the pompous ideological mask of guilt or of feminine sacrifice. The extent to which, in today's social theory, the motif of sacrifice is automatically translated into that of scapegoating is deeply suspicious: the Other into whom we project our own disavowed, repressed content is sacrificed, so that, through the destruction of the Other, we purify ourselves. However, the true enigma of the sacrifice does not reside in the magic efficiency of scapegoating, of sacrificing a substitute other, but rather in the readiness of the subject effectively to sacrifice *himself/herself* for the cause. This disturbing fact that somebody is ready to put at stake everything, including his life, is what makes the so-called fundamentalist fanaticism so shocking in the eyes of our late-capitalist sensitivity used to reason in the categories of utilitarian calculus: one desperately endeavours to 'explain it away' by providing some kind of psycho-pathological or socio-pathological account of it (collective madness, the strange workings of a mind that hasn't yet progressed to the Western notions of rational choice and individual freedom, etc.). It is as if the good old Hegelian dialectics of Master and Slave is repeated here, with the West behaving like the slave who dares not embrace fully the radical negativity and put everything at stake. In this sense, every ideology relies on some kernel of the Real (the readiness to make the ultimate sacrifice, the fear of death), which cannot be interpreted away as the outcome of ideological manipulation, of the 'false consciousness' due to the social situation of the subject. *Mutatis mutandis*, it is homologous with sexual relationship: its fulfilment is not impossible because political and social circumstances forbid it; the impossibility is rather inherent, it comes first, and the 'externalization' of the Real of this inherent impediment into a secondary obstacle ('social repression') serves to maintain the phantasm that, without these obstacles, the object would have been accessible. What Freud called the 'death drive' is the impediment inherent in the drive that for ever prevents its fulfilment; and, perhaps, the primordial gesture of ideology is not only that of elevating a limitation grounded in concrete historical circumstances into an a priori of human existence, but also that of explaining away a structural impediment as the result of unfortunate concrete circumstances.

A critique of ideology has thus to proceed in two moves. First, of course, it has to follow Jameson's well-known injunction 'Historicize!', and to discern in an apparently universal unchangeable limitation the ideological 'reification' and absolutization of a certain contingent historical constellation – what presents itself as a 'metaphysical' longing for death can have its roots in the foreboding of the ruling class that its days are running out; what presents itself as an eternal condition of love (the inherent necessity to renounce its fulfilment) can well be grounded in the contingent historical conditions of the bourgeois patriarchal symbolic economy within which love is allocated to the domain of 'private' as opposed to the 'public'; and so on. The second move then, in a kind of reflective turn, compels us to conceive this explanatory reference to concrete historical circumstances itself as a 'false', ideological attempt to circumvent the traumatic kernel of the Real (the death drive, the non-existence of sexual relationship), to explain it away and thus render invisible its structural necessity. Apropos of Wagner, a critical analysis of the Wagnerian longing for redemption in death has thus to avoid two pitfalls: it isn't enough to refuse to take at its face value the ideological coating of the sacrificial gesture and to discern in the metaphysical will to self-destruction displayed by Wotan and Brünnhilde an overblown mystified expression of contingent historical circumstances; at a more radical level, one should at the same time demarcate the contours of the kernel of the Real, of the 'death drive', which sustains the will to destruction in its specific ideological coating.

[. . .]

This Wagnerian reference remains crucial even today, at a time when the process Freud tried to encapsulate in the title of his article 'On the Universal Tendency to Debasement in the Sphere of Love' seems to be approaching its climax. Two recent films, Kieslowski's *Short Film on Love* and Sautet's *A Heart in Winter*, endeavour to counter this 'tendency to debasement' by rendering a male gesture of rejection, of refusal to engage in sexual commerce; however, as we shall see, the scope of the two gestures is almost exactly opposed.

There is an unexpected formal homology between the two central instalments (5 and 6) of Kieslowski's *Decalogue, A Short Film on Killing* and *A Short Film on Love*: in both cases, we are dealing with a failed metaphorical reversal-substitution. The second act, instead of accomplishing a successful 'sublation' (*Aufhebung*) of the first act (by way of compensating for its damage and re-establishing the lost balance), actually makes things worse by ending up as a *repetition* of the first act. In 'Killing', a young unemployed man commits the brutal and meaningless murder of a taxi-driver; the second part then renders in painful detail the trial and the execution of the murderer. This rendering of the machinery of law at work is so disturbing because it registers the *failure of the 'metaphor of Law'*, that is, of the metaphoric substitution of the punishment for the crime: the punishment is experienced not as just retribution that undoes the harm brought about by the crime, but rather as its uncanny repetition – the act of punishment is somehow tainted by an additional obscenity that makes it a travesty, an obscene repetition, of the original crime in the guise of law. *A Short Film on Love* is also a film about a failed metaphoric substitution, the substitution (of the beloved for the loving one) that, according to Lacan, defines love. From his bedroom in a large, dreary, concrete apartment block, Tomek, a young postal clerk, each evening and night peeps on Maria Magdalena [*sic*], a mature, sexually attractive, and promiscuous woman who lives in the same block, across from Tomek's backyard. His activity is not limited to passively observing her sexual prowess in dealing with her numerous lovers; step by step, he intervenes in her life, sending her false notices of money orders so that she will come to his window in the post office, calling plumbers to her apartment in the middle of her love-making, and so on. When, finally, he gathers courage, contacts her and discloses that he is the source of her recent nuisances, her curiosity is aroused. She entices him into a humiliating sexual game that ends in his attempted suicide. After his return from hospital, their respective roles are reversed: stirred by her guilt, she 'stretches out her hand', constantly observes his window from her apartment, endeavours frantically to attract his attention, in order to make him come to her again and to offer him her apologies, whereas he now ignores her. In short, the metaphor of love fails: when the beloved object turns into the loving one, she is no longer loved.

A closer analysis renders visible a fundamental ambiguity that pertains to this film, an ambiguity that becomes fully visible in the crucial difference between the two versions of the *Short Film on Love*, the original sixty-minute television version and the ninety-minute version for release in movie theatres. The longer version ends up in a kind of Catholic reconciliation and compassion (with Maria sitting by Tomek's bed, silently holding his hand, the implication of it being that a kind of spiritual contact has taken place between the two, beyond the self-destructive dialectic of sexuality), whereas in the television version, their encounter remains failed, non-synchronized. In this precise sense, *A Short Film on Love* is the stage of a 'class struggle' in art, the battle-ground of the two lines, the irreconciled 'materialist' and the spiritualist 'idealist', in dealing with the fundamental deadlock of love. When, upon their becoming acquainted, Maria asks Tomek what he effectively wants from her, a mere kiss, a little tenderness, or a full sexual act, his resolute answer is 'nothing'. This 'nothing', of course, is the unmistakable index of true love: Tomek is not to be satisfied with any positive content or act (going to bed with him, for example) by means of which Maria could reciprocate his love. What he wants her to offer in return is the very 'nothingness' in her, what is 'in her more than herself' – not something that she possesses but precisely what she does *not* have, the return of love itself. In response to his unconditional demand of love, Maria arouses him by offering her sexual services to him, so that, inexperienced as he is, he reaches orgasm before intercourse proper takes place, and then, triumphantly, tells him: 'Now you see, this is all love is really about! Go and wash yourself in the bathroom!' This gesture of offering herself, her body, to him, effectively amounts to an act of utter rejection and/or humilia-tion: what she accomplished therewith is radical desublimation – that is, she renders palpable the gap that separates the void of the Thing from the physio-logical functioning of sexual intercourse. This humiliation, this experience of the gap between the 'nothingness' of the true object of love and the desubl-imated bodily sexual mechanism, is more than he can stand: utterly ashamed, he runs out of her apartment and cuts his veins. What follows thereupon is a shift of perspective from his to her point of view, so that, in a sense, his suicide *does* succeed – that is, he totally obliterates himself as the narrative point of view. And, as we already hinted, at this point, the two versions differ: the longer one takes a Catholic turn, and suggests the possibility of a compassionate solidarity beyond carnal passions, of a spiritual communion that can fill out the void of the inherent impossibility of a sexual relationship, whereas in the shorter version, the deadlock remains unresolved.[31]

On a closer look, one is compelled to state that the crucial metaphoric substitution in *A Short Film on Love* actually runs contrary to the standard substitution by means of which the loved one changes into the loving one – that is, solves the impasse of not knowing what the other (the loving one) sees in him by returning love: the true enigma of the film is Tomek's change from the loving one into the object of Maria's love. So how does he succeed in substituting his position of the loving one with the position of the beloved? How does he capture Maria's desire? The answer, of course, resides in the very purity and absolute intensity of his love: he acts as the pure $, the subject whose desire is so burning that it cannot be translated into any concrete demand – this very intensity, because of which his desire can only express itself in the guise of a refusal of any demand ('I want nothing from you'), is what makes him irresistible. This second metaphoric substitution is not simply symmetrical to the first one: their difference hinges on the opposition of 'to have' and 'to be'. In the first case, we are in the dimension of *having* (the loved one doesn't know what he *has* in himself that makes him worthy of the other's love, so, in order to escape this deadlock, he returns love), whereas in the second case, the loving *is* (becomes) the beloved object on account of the sheer intensity of his love.[32]

What one has to reject here is the notion that Tomek's love for Maria is authentic and pure, spiritual, elevated above vulgar sensuality, whereas Maria, disturbed by this purity, intends to humiliate him and later changes her attitude out of a feeling of guilt. It is, on the contrary, Tomek's love that is fundamentally false, a narcissistic attitude of idealization whose necessary obverse is a barely conceived lethal dimension. That is to say, *A Short Film on Love* should be read against the background of *slasher* films, in which a man observes and harasses a woman who traumatizes him, finally attacking her with a knife: it is a kind of introverted *slasher* in which the man, instead of striking at the woman, deals a blow to himself.[33] The reason his love for Maria is not genuine does not reside in its 'impure' character: the murderous burst of self-inflicted violence is the inherent obverse of its very 'purity'. This inauthenticity of his love is corroborated by his inability to undergo the experience of desublimation, of the splitting between the woman *qua* impossible-idealized Thing and the flesh-and-blood woman who offers herself to him – that is, by the way this experience sets in motion the murderous *passage à l'acte*: the measure of true love is precisely the capacity to withstand such a splitting. Maria's love for him, in contrast, is fully authentic: from the moment Tomek tells her he wants nothing from her, true love – which, as Lacan points out, is always a love returned – is here, and her humiliation of Tomek is merely a desperate attempt to disavow this fact.

Our second example, Claude Sautet's *A Heart in Winter* ('Un Coeur en hiver'), a film on the deadlocks of love from the same period, tells the story of a love triangle with two high-class violin-makers and Camille, a young, beautiful and charismatic violin-player. When Camille starts to live with one of them, she thereby perturbs the well-established routine of their professional relationship. Gradually, with the help of his ambiguous, active-passive co-operation, she falls in love with the other partner, Stephan; however, when, in a passionate outburst, she declares her love and offers herself to him, Stephan calmly explains to her that it's all a misunderstanding – maybe he was flirting a little with her, but he definitely does not love her. Stephan's character is rather enigmatic: the point is not that Camille isn't his true love, but rather that he simply feels no need for love – there is no place for love in his psychological universe. This incapacity to love accounts for the kind of inner peace and completion irradiated by his personality: unperturbed by any emotional turmoils, profoundly *apathetic*, he is able to devote himself fully to his craft. In other words, far from being a person whose mask of normal social functioning conceals madness, Stephan is a person who, although to an outside view he may appear 'abnormal', possesses an inherent norm, measure, completeness. We are dealing here with a variation on the Lacanian motif of 'non-all': what, in a way, makes him more 'complete' and harmonious than 'normal' people – that is, what makes him a person who, in a way, lacks nothing – is the very aspect that appears from the outside as his deficiency or even psychic mutilation. In other words, the trap one has to avoid in analysing Sautet's film is the search for any kind of 'psychological' background or foundation that would account for Stephan's incapacity to love: there is no need here for any 'psychoanalytical' reference to sexual frustrations, childhood traumas and so on. When, in the course of the film, Stephan himself evokes the possibility of such an explanation, he obviously indulges in an irony homologous to that of a neo-Nazi skinhead who is always quick to provide a socio-psychological explanation of his violence against foreigners. Stephan is an *empty* subject: beneath the surface of his acts there is no plenitude of 'pathological' content, no secret desires and anxieties. One is tempted to draw a comparison between Stephan and Wagner's Parsifal: when, alone with Camille in his car, Stephan utters his final 'Je ne vois aime pas,' is he not a contemporary Parsifal who, by not giving way to the woman's advances, redeems her (enables her to pursue her artistic career)?[34]

We are thus already deep in the murky Wagnerian waters of the implacable antagonism between man's ethical 'vocation', which commits him to the full deployment of his creative potential, and his (sexual) relationship with a woman: what a woman effectively wants from a man is the hidden kernel of his being; she feels envy and hatred toward the mysterious ingredient beyond her reach that accounts for his creative genius, so she wants to snatch it from him and destroy it. Even prior to *Parsifal*, Wagner provided the first clear articulation of this discord in his earlier *Lohengrin*, the opera centred on the theme of the forbidden question – that is, on the paradox of self-destructive female curiosity. A nameless hero saves Elsa von Brabant and marries her, but enjoins her not to ask him who he is or what his name is – as soon as she does so, he will be obliged to leave her. Unable to resist temptation, Elsa asks him the fateful question; so Lohengrin tells her that he is a knight of the Grail, the son of Parsifal from the castle of Montsalvat, and then departs on a swan, while the unfortunate Elsa falls dead. Although both in *Lohengrin* and in *Parsifal* the hero is split between the Grail *qua* pre-genital 'partial object' and the love of a woman, the two operas differ with regard to a crucial feature: in *Lohengrin*, the hero continues to yearn for a happy sexual relationship (when, at the opera's end, he bids his fare-well to Elsa, he is full of romantic mourning for the lost opportunity of at least one happy year of marital life with her), whereas in *Parsifal*, the hero unambiguously and with no remorse rejects the woman (Kundry) as his sexual partner.[35]

In what, then, on a closer look, consists the discord that corrupts the relationship between Elsa and Lohengrin? It may appear that *Lohengrin* is just another variation on the old theme of a prince who, in order to make sure that his future bride will love him for himself, not because of his symbolic title, first wants to arouse her love dressed up as a servant or a messenger. However, the enigma of *Lohengrin* resides elsewhere: why can he exert his *power* only in so far as his name remains *unknown* – that is, only in so far as he is not inscribed in the 'big Other' of the intersubjective public space, so that he has to withdraw the moment his symbolic identity is publicly revealed? What we are dealing with is thus the opposition between master-signifier and *a*, the 'incastratable' object that can exert its efficiency only *qua* concealed: the misunderstanding between Elsa and Lohengrin resides in the fact that Elsa perceives Lohengrin as the traditional figure of symbolic authority, whereas he functions as a spectral apparition that cannot sustain its disclosure in the public symbolic medium.

And, back to *A Heart in Winter*, is Stephan also not an object that cannot bear its symbolic revelation? Is his subjective position, like that of Parsifal, not also marked by a radical *indifference*: namely, indifference toward the *desire of the Other*? Stephan is a subject who is simply not 'gnawed' by the desire of the Other, by the enigma of 'Che vuoi?' of what the Other wants from me – and since (Lacan *dixit*) desire as such is the desire of the Other, one is compelled to draw the inevitable conclusion that Stephan, strictly speaking, is not a desiring subject, that he simply does not dwell in the dimension of desire. Therein resides the uncanny 'cold' of his character, its 'flatness', the absence of any enigmatic depth. On that account, Stephan is incapable not only of love but even of common friendship, which always involves a minimum of empathy: he is able, without any hesitation, to deliver a lethal injection to his elder friend-teacher, a kind of paternal surrogate, thereby putting an end to the meaningless agony of his mortal illness. Is not this indifference toward the Other's desire strictly equivalent to what Lacan designates as 'subjective destitution'?

We can see, now, in what, precisely, resides the difference between *A Short Film on Love* and *A Heart in Winter*. In both films, we encounter a man's 'I want nothing', which puts an obstacle in the way of sexual intercourse; that is, both Tomek and Stephan turn down the woman's proposal, but this rejection has a totally different meaning in each case. In *Love*, we are dealing with 'I want nothing' of the *desire* that aims at the *objet a* in the other: the true meaning of this 'I want nothing' is 'I want you absolutely, in the very kernel of your being, in the void that constitutes the elusive vortex of your subjectivity, and I am not ready to exchange it for any substitute in the guise of some positive (sexual) service'. With regard to Kierkegaard, this means that Kieslowski remains within the religious: at a level more fundamental than the Catholic communion of souls in the longer version of the film, Tomek's attitude is religious; his 'I want nothing' is a desperate attempt to counteract the 'debasement in the sphere of love' by way of elevating the woman to the dignity of a Thing. Sautet's Stephan, in contrast, confronts us with something incomparably more uncanny: what we have here is a man who 'wants nothing' because he simply lacks nothing: he is not 'gnawed' by the enigma of the Other's desire; he is fundamentally indifferent toward *objet a*, the object-cause of desire; his subjectivity is not organized around a traumatic excess of the surplus enjoyment. Why not? There is only one answer possible: *because he himself occupies the place of this object*. In short, the opposition between Tomek and Stephan is the opposition between $\$$ and *a*, between the pure subject of desire and the 'saint', somebody who has undergone 'subjective destitution' and thereby turned into the pure being of a drive beyond desire.

Notes

All English translations have been made by the author, with the exception of those cited in the notes.

1 A detail to be noted is that, in both cases, this motif announces an act of a homologous nature: an element is torn out from its 'natural' place where it was resting – the gold from the bottom of Rhine, the sword from the tree trunk.

2 See Claude Lévi-Strauss, 'A Note on the Tetralogy', in *The View from Afar*, trans. Claire Jacobson (Chicago, University of Chicago Press, 1985), pp. 235–9.

3 Edith Wharton, *The Age of Innocence* (Harmondsworth, Penguin, 1974), p. 146.

4 See also Mladen Dolar's 'At First Sight', in *Gaze and Voice*, ch. 5. It should be a surprise only to those who cling to the standard textbook image of Hegel's 'panlogicism' that an exemplary case of a homologous Hegelian reversal is found in the work of Jeremy Bentham. In accordance with his utilitarian economy, Bentham always tends to replace the 'thing itself' with its (less costly) appearance, provided that the effect is the same – what counts is only the effect. So, in the case of punishment, the only thing that effectively counts is the deterrent, inhibitory effect that the spectacle of punishment achieves in potential future criminals – wouldn't it then be far more economical to replace real punishment with its appearance, with a pure staging? Bentham none the less opts for real punishment; yet his argument in favour of it is far more refined than one would expect from him and possesses a properly Hegelian allure: what ultimately counts is only appearance – i.e. how things appear, the effect of their appearance – and it is for that very reason that 'real' punishment is to be preferred to a faked staging – reality is in a sense *the best, the most effective, appearance of itself.*

5 The closest Hollywood got to the properly *ethical* notion of repetition was in the series of so-called comedies of remarriage from the late thirties and early forties: their point is that it is only the second marriage among the same partners that brings forth an authentic, mature intersubjective link (see Stanley Cavell's *In Pursuit of Happiness* (Cambridge, Mass., Harvard University Press, 1981). Incidentally, the interest of Mike Nichols's *Heartburn* (with Meryl Streep and Jack Nicholson) is that it provides, as it were, the negative of the comedies of remarriage: it is literally a 'comedy of re-divorce'; i.e. the first divorce of the couple remains within the confines of a narcissistic love game, it is only with the second divorce that the symbolic bond that united the partners is effectively dissolved.

6 A homologous self-sacrificing gesture of dirtying one's image in the eyes of the beloved in order to save him for morality is found in Michael Curtiz's *Angels with Dirty Faces* (1938), in which James Cagney plays a charismatic Brooklyn gangster admired by a group of slum boys. When he is finally caught and sentenced to the electric chair, he is, of course, not afraid to die, and intends to turn his execution into a display of his heroic defiance of death. However, on the eve of the execution, a priest who is aware of the redeeming qualities beneath Cagney's tough act, visits him in his cell, and begs him to pretend next morning that he is dying in fear – in

this way, he will render a last service to society; i.e. instead of remaining an idol in the eyes of the kids, he will serve them as an example of how crime doesn't pay and will thus promote their reintegration into society. On his way to the electric chair, Cagney casts a quick glance toward the journalists who witness the execution, and, when he is sure of being observed, he starts to feign panic, to cry and shout that he doesn't want to die . . . Next day, when the boys read in a newspaper the report of Cagney's cowardly death, their world falls apart, they are deeply shattered and depressed: they have lost their hero, their ideal ego, the point of identification – and are thereby saved for the morality. Henry Staten (in a private communication) pointed out that this scene stages perfectly Nietzsche's notion of the 'decadent', 'nihilistic' character of common morality, which is founded on the renunciation of assertive life energy. Here we have the Lacanian distinction between morals and ethics: Cagney's final act is moral, yet definitely unethical. Incidentally, notwithstanding the superficial analogy, Cagney's act is wholly incommensurable with the profoundly *ethical* gesture of Barbara Stanwyck at the end of *Stella Dallas*, where she also puts on the image of a vulgar debauchee in order to enable her daughter to drop her and enter high-society married life without remorse.

7   This paradox can also be explained against the background of the dialectical short circuit between possibility and actuality: the moment the conquest (of a woman by her seducer) becomes effectively possible, he has to withdraw; i.e. the possibility as such already counts as success. Therein resides a common feature of the psychic economy: often, deep satisfaction is provided by the mere awareness that we *could have* done something that we desired (slept with a passionately desired sexual partner, taken revenge on a long-time enemy, etc.) – as if the realization of this possibility would somehow spoil the purity of our success. . . . And is not the extreme example of this logic a possibility that counts as actuality – i.e. which, as a possibility, exerts actual effects – the Cold War paradox of the 'mad' logic of nuclear armament: the possession and further development of nuclear arms were perceived as the supreme guarantee that they would never be used: since each side knows that the other also possesses the means to annihilate, both sides are aware that any use of nuclear arms will inevitably lead to mutual self-destruction. In short, the greater the threat of the catastrophe, the greater the certainty that this threat will not be actualized. . . . Far from bearing witness to a kind of Cold War 'perversion' of our rationality, this 'madness' simply renders palpable a feature constitutive of the symbolic order as such.

8   From the Nietzschean–Deleuzian perspective, this inherent impossibility, this hindrance that prevents us from consummating the process of seduction, of course, bears witness to the 'nihilistic' perversion of our life force: force loses its purely assertive character and becomes infected by negativity, by the split between what it *can* do, conceived in itself, and what it actually accomplishes within the complex network of relations with other forces – it changes into a pure capacity that can never fully actualize itself. . . . For Lacan, on the contrary, this very splitting between possibility and actuality, i.e., the fact that possibility as such already counts as effective, which is why its actualization is experienced as anti-climactic – in short,

this structure of 'symbolic castration' – provides the basic, constitutive feature of the symbolic order.

9   One is tempted to claim that the triad of *Tristan, Meistersinger* and *Parsifal* repeats at a different level (in a higher 'potency') the triad of *The Flying Dutchman, Tannhäuser* and *Lohengrin*.

10 One is tempted to suggest that the same procedure can also throw a new, more appropriate light on Bertolt Brecht, this great anti-Wagnerian: the key to Brecht's *Jasager*, which also advocates the subject's radical self-sacrifice, is to read it together with its two later versions (*Neinsager, Jasager II*) as the three possible variations allowed by the same underlying matrix.

11 Friedrich Nietzsche, 'The Case of Wagner', in *The Birth of Tragedy; and, The Case of Wagner*, trans. Walter Kaufmann (New York, Vintage, 1967), p. 166.

12 Ibid., p. 175.

13 Ibid., p. 176.

14 Richard Wagner, *The Ring of the Nibelung*, trans. Andrew Porter (New York, Norton, 1977), p. 24.

15 Ibid., p. 40.

16 Carl Dahlhaus, *Richard Wagner's Music Dramas*, trans. Mary Whittall (Cambridge, Cambridge University Press, 1979), p. 97.

17 F. W. J. Schelling, *Sämtliche Werke*, ed. K. F. A. Schelling (Stuttgart, Cotta, 1856–61), vol. 7, p. 472.

18 See Dahlhaus, *Richard Wagner's Music Dramas*, pp. 5–6.

19 Philippe Lacoue-Labarthe, *Musica Ficta*, trans. Felicia McCarren (Stanford, Calif., Stanford University Press, 1994), p. II.

20 Ibid., p. 12.

21 We rely here on Michel Chion, *La Musique au cinema* (Paris, Fayard, 1995), and Claudia Gorbman, *Unheard Melodies: Narrative Film Music* (Bloomington, Ind., British Film Institute and Indiana University Press, 1987).

22 Chion, *La Musique*, p. 105.

23 Dahlhaus, *Richard Wagner's Musical Dramas*, p. 135.

24 Nietzsche, 'Case of Wagner', pp. 172–3.

25 See Jacques Lacan, *The Ethics of Psychoanalysis*, trans. Dennis Porter (New York, Routledge, 1992), pp. 210–14.

26 William O. Cord, *An Introduction to Richard Wagner's 'Der Ring des Nibelingen'* (Athens: Ohio University Press, 1983), p. 125.

27 Deryck Cooke, *I Saw the World End* (Oxford, Oxford University Press, 1979), pp. 16–17.

28 Robert Donington, *Wagner's 'Ring' and its Symbols* (London, Faber & Faber, 1990), p. 265.

29 We can see, now, in what consists the crucial difference between the *Ring* and *Parsifal*: in the *Ring*, knowledge is not yet accessible to 'the pure fool' Siegfried – he has to die so that Brünnhilde, the woman, can become knowing ('dass wissend wird ein Weib'); whereas in *Parsifal*, the hero himself, the pure fool, becomes knowing ('des reinsten Wissens Macht, dem zagen Toren gab'). Syberberg was

thus fully justified, in his film version of *Parsifal*, in turning Parsifal into a woman after his conversion: the moment he gains access to knowledge, Parsifal effectively occupies the 'feminine' position of Brünnhilde.

30 At the opposite end, Wagner composed *Parsifal*, this hymn to the radical rejection of the sexual drive, in order to be able to pursue his affair with Judith Gautier, the real-life model of Kundry.

31 For a Lacanian reading of *A Short Film on Love*, see Roland Chemana, 'La Passion selon Tomek', in *Éléments lacaniens pour une psychanalyse au quotidien* (Paris, Le Discours Psychanalytique, 1994), pp. 363–6. Incidentally, the two versions of *A Short Film on Love* offer an exemplary case of how, by way of merely rearranging or leaving out part of the material, one can radically change its entire scope; or, as Lacan put it, interpretation is in its most fundamental dimension an act of scansion, of establishing the proper syntax, not an act of bringing to light the 'repressed' meaning. Perhaps an even more illuminating example is provided by the finale of Moussorgsky's *Boris Godunov*: according to the composer's original idea, the death of Tsar Boris is the penultimate scene, so that the opera concludes with the scene of the crowd hailing the new Tsar Dimitry and the saintly beggar-fool predicting hard times for Russia. Rimsky-Korsakov, however, who put the opera into its final shape, was worried about the weak dramatic impact of the original finale, and changed the order of the last two scenes, so that the version we all know ends, as befits tragedy, with the death of its hero. It is clear that, beneath the purely theatrical question of 'dramatic impact', there lurks the far more fundamental question of interpretation: Rimsky-Korsakov reinscribes *Boris* into the traditional hero-centred framework, whereas the original version 'decentres' it and asserts the acephal 'crowd' as the opera's true hero. A simple decision about the order of scenes thus involves an interpretative act of far-reaching consequences: it is really a decision about inserting (or not) the opera into the traditional hero narrative.

32 There is a homology worthy of notice between this reversal of the metaphor of love and the final reversal in Delmer Daves's psychological western from the late fifties, *3.10 to Yuma*. The film tells the story of a poor farmer (Van Heflin) who, for 200 dollars that he needs badly in order to save his cattle from drought, accepts the job of escorting a bandit with a high price on his head (Glenn Ford) from the hotel where he is held to the train that will take him to prison in Yuma. What we have, of course, is a classic story of an ethical ordeal; throughout the film, it seems that the person submitted to the ordeal is the farmer himself, exposed as he is to temptations in the style of the (undeservedly) more famous *High Noon*: all those who promised him help abandon him when they discover that the hotel is surrounded by the gang sworn to save their boss; the imprisoned bandit himself alternately threatens the farmer and tries to bribe him, etc. The last scene, however, in retrospect totally changes our perception of the film: close by the train, which is already leaving the station, the bandit and the farmer find them-selves face to face with the entire gang waiting for the right moment to shoot the farmer and thus free their boss. At this tense moment, when the situation seems hopeless for the farmer, the bandit suddenly turns to him and tells him 'Trust me!

Let's jump together on the wagon!' In short, the one effectively under an ordeal was the bandit himself, the apparent agent of temptation: at the end, he is overcome by the farmer's integrity and sacrifices his own freedom for him.

33   The notion of *A Short Film on Love* as an inverted slasher was suggested to me by Paul Villemen. Incidentally, the basic matrix of slasher films is contained in the paradox of the *objet petit a* elaborated by Lacan in the last chapter of his *Seminar* XI: 'I love you, but, because inexplicably I love in you something more than you – the *objet petit a* – I mutilate you' (Jacques Lacan, *The Four Fundamental Concepts of Psycho-Analysis*, trans. Alan Sheridan (Harmondsworth, Penguin, 1979), p. 268).

34   What our reading of the film did not take into account is, of course, the fact that the woman (Camille) is an *object of exchange* between the two men: is it not that the two man fight their own battle through her, the one betraying his partnership with the other by entering into a relationship with her, the other taking his revenge for this betrayal by seducing her in his turn? For that reason, he can reject her the moment his seduction succeeds and she offers herself to him – she has no inherent 'use value' for Stephan; the only point of seducing her was to deliver a message to his (male) partner. Such a reading, which introduces the motif of latent homosexuality and male bonding, adequate as it is at its own level, none the less fails to provide a satisfactory account of Stephan's gesture of rejection.

35   In *The Flying Dutchman*, too, the hero is divided between a damned-sacred object (his ship) and the woman whose sacrifice can bring about his redemption. However, in contrast to Lohengrin, the angelic hero, the Dutchman is a damned sinner; the vocal expression of this opposition is, of course, that between tenor and baritone.

9

Death and the Maiden

In this new, previously unpublished essay Žižek considers three films, in each of which a woman carries to extremes a devotion to a man threatened by death. All are cautionary tales in which the patriarchal definition of woman is subjected to a *reductio ad absurdum*, demonstrating a structure in the woman of respectively perversion, hysteria and psychosis. In each case her apparent goodness leads to an extraordinary sacrifice, which is simultaneously cancelled out by the pathological nature of the excess.

The first film, *Dead Man Walking*, is about loving one's neighbour to excess: Christian love is carried to an extreme, disclosing a pathology of perversion. The two central figures, one a religious sister, the other a criminal awaiting execution for rape and murder, provoke a situation whereby the woman becomes obsessed with the man's crime to the extent that she comes 'to accept this neighbour in the very Evil of his *jouissance*'. As an indirect result, the man is able to meet his execution by feeding on her false compassion. In the second film, *Leaving Las Vegas*, the central figure is a prostitute, who similarly identifies with the *jouissance* of the man, an alcoholic determined to end his life. The woman devotes herself to his free ethical choice to the point of being unable to act on her compassion to save him. Her satisfaction in resisting this temptation to do good is bound up with a masochistic fantasy of making her desire wholly subservient to his. Thus she is hysterically divided between her passion for his single-minded cause and her 'humanity'. In this case too, since the man achieves his self-destructive end, the woman's goodness is entrapped in a self-cancelling sacrifice.

The third film, *Breaking the Waves*, also about a self-cancelling good-ness, reverses the pattern of the previous two films, in that it is now the woman who is compulsively driven to her own annihilation. In this case a simple young woman, devoutly Protestant, prays to God to give her back her intensely loved, newly married husband from his job on an oil-rig. When he is brought back after an accident, paralysed from the waist down, she takes this as 'an answer of the Real', a sign from God that extremes of sacrifice are called for to offset the fulfilment of her wish. This throws her into a continual cycle of masochistic acts of humiliation, starting with acceding to her husband's perverse request that she prosti-tute herself in order to feed his fantasies and ending with her self-induced destruction when none of her sacrifices appear to work. Although a femin-ist reading of the film might have it that the woman is totally entrapped within the patriarchal ideology, in that she gives up her own *jouissance* to serve the man's perverse desire, a closer analysis reveals another economy. Lacan's theory of sexual difference, as encoded in his 'sexuation' formulas, postulates for the woman a *jouissance* supplementary to a phallic one (on this point see 'How Not to Read Lacan's Formulas of Sexuation', in Žižek, *Indivisible Remainder*, pp. 155–65). This divides woman, since 'not all' of her is bent on responding to the fantasy of the man by means of the lure of an enigmatic masquerade. The notion of masquerade implies that the woman can be more subject than man, aware that her self-representation, far from being a mask concealing the 'inner person', is where her life is lived. Whereas the man stupidly believes in his substantiality and innate worthiness over and above the Symbolic, the woman knows the insubstan-tiality of the masquerade and hence the status of the subject as hysterical. In *Breaking the Waves* the woman sacrifices this lure, and devotes herself totally to the phallic prescription of fantasy, which has the inverse effect of threatening the phallic economy, now denied the illusion of a secret that is for ever beyond its grasp. The woman's attempt to provoke an 'answer from the Real' hopes to effect a closure of the lack in the Symbolic, in order that she may be finally absorbed in an ecstatic *jouissance*, and this betrays a psychotic structure.

Žižek examines the formal devices of the film to consider the question of whether the film itself is psychotic – that is to say, whether it gets off off on the woman's pathology. He discerns a clash between the film's pseudo-documentary style and its quasi-romantic narrative, which the director sees as nothing but an aesthetic strategy. But it turns out that this opposition in the form is curiously matched in the content through its depiction of a de-subjectified puritanical zeal of the Protestant commun-ity as against an over-subjectified presentation of the woman's aspiration. The apotheosis staged at the end of the film, in which the heroine's sacrifice achieves the desired end after all, seems to leave us stranded with a postmodernist lack of 'ironic or cynical distance'.

The three films stage three versions of 'Death and the Maiden': in each case a woman encounters a man who lives in the domain 'between two deaths', fatally marked by the Symbolic while still suspended in the Real of life; in each situation the woman sacrifices herself to what she perceives to be the Good. Žižek's final question touches on the moral to be derived for the sexual relation.

Three recent films which focus on the deadlock of feminine Goodness and sacrifice (Mike Figgis's *Leaving Las Vegas* (*LLV*), Tim Robbins's *Dead Man Walking* (*DMW*), and Lars von Trier's *Breaking the Waves* (*BW*)) provide a kind of matrix of the three modes for a woman to approach the very limit of the *act*: hysterical, perverse and psychotic.

The first two, *Leaving Las Vegas* and *Dead Man Walking*, are effectively two complementary films and should be read together, like the two versions of the same myth in Lévi-Strauss. In both cases, a woman, as it were, fights for the soul of the man destined to die at the film's end: in *LLV*, we have a prostitute and a loser who decided to drink himself to death; in *DMW*, a religious sister and a convicted rapist and killer. In both cases, there is a Third to whom the woman addresses her plight: the absent psychoanalyst in *LLV*, God himself in *DMW*. The man is in both cases a 'living dead', close to his death and thus in the state 'between the two deaths', already tainted with death while still alive; the best description of Ben (Nicholas Cage) in *LLV* is precisely the title of the other film – he is effectively a 'dead man walking'. In both cases, we move at the very border of ideological recuperation: will Sera, the hooker with a heart of gold (Elisabeth Shue), redeem her man and prevent him from realizing his suicidal intention? Will Sister Helen (Susan Sarandon) discover the heart of gold in the brutal rapist and murderer (Sean Penn)? Neither of the two films gives way to this *temptation of Goodness*: Sera sticks to her ethical contract with Ben, who accepted her invitation to move to her place and stay with her on the condition that she will never, ever, ask him to stop drinking; Sister Helen does not discover any inherent Goodness in Sean Penn – he is not delivered, but remains a repulsive rapist.

DMW is effectively a film about the ultimate limits of the Christian 'love for thy neighbour': in loving the lowest scum, you get caught in the 'imp of perversity', which resides in sympathizing with the murderer and rapist not *in spite of* or *irrespective of* his repulsiveness, but *because of it*. This is the reason why Sister Helen is so desperate to display her compassion also to the parents of the victims – to 'depathologize' her compassion with the murderer. The obverse of this ambiguity is the film's ambiguous stance towards capital punishment: it is far too simple to read *DMW* as the condemnation of capital punishment, since it is only the proximity of his own death which induces the murderer to assume his hideous act in a gesture of subjectivization. The final scene of execution, full of Christological associations (the dying Penn is presented as the crucified Christ), is in a way even more nauseous and troubling than the original crime: we know who was responsible for the crime, while our satisfaction in the punishment is spoiled by the fact that the responsibility for it is anonymous, dispersed, assumed by the big Other of the Institution. The flashbacks to the scene of the original crime, which intersect with the execution, thus work both ways: on the one hand, they emphasize the parallel between the two events, changing the execution into an obscene repetition of the crime (as in Kieslowski's *Short Film on Killing*); on the other hand, the full rendering of the horror of the crime serves as an argument that the harsh punishment is justified and deserved. So, far from being a vehicle for political correctness, *DMW* draws attention to its deadlock: when we trespass a certain limit of compassion, we enter a shadowy domain in which compassion turns into perversion, in which the concern for the criminal overshadows the suffering of his victim, in which the execution of the Law assumes the features of an obscene ritual. This deadlock is rooted in the inherent limitation of the attitude of 'love for thy neighbour' which tends to reduce the neighbour to a 'fellow' and to obfuscate the traumatic kernel of the other's *jouissance*: in her fearless heroism, Sister Helen endeavours to go to the end in the 'love for her neighbour' and to accept this neighbour in the very Evil of his *jouissance*.[1]

LLV turns around this dispositif of *DMW*: the compassionate woman is a whore, not a nun; she does not try to 'understand' the man bent on dying, but simply *accepts* his suicidal decision. This suicidal decision is an autonomous ethical act which should not be reduced to the effect of some external trauma (when questioned about the causes of his suicidal disposition, Ben says that he does not know if his wife left him because of his drinking or if he started to drink because his wife left him...). We are not dealing here merely with passive despair and depression, but with a liberating act of decision: cynical as this may sound, *LLV* is fundamentally a bright film, a film about suicide as the only successful act. There is effectively something uncanny in a man who fully wants to die, not as a pathetic spectacular gesture, but as a fundamental decision endorsed by his whole being. Suffice it to recall the famous case of Gary Gilmore, who murdered two men after a quarrel with his girlfriend, and then was executed by firing squad in Utah in 1977 – against the desperate pleas and advice of his brother, of his lawyers, of the humanitarian groups opposed to the death penalty, he wrote a petition to the governor demanding that he be executed. No wonder that this example, which profoundly shatters the humanitarian foundations of the opponents of the death penalty, caused such unease, and led Norman Mailer to novelize it in his *The Executioner's Song* (1979). Gilmore's brother, who passionately wanted him to stay alive, wrote in his *Shot in the Heart* (1994):

> When you are arguing with somebody who is hell-bent on dying, you realize that if you lose the argument, there is no more chance for further argument, that you will have seen that person for the last time.... You can't argue with the disease that takes your loved one or yourself, or the car accident or the killer that snuffs out a life without warning. But a man who *wants* to die...

So, to put it in Alain Badiou's terms,[2] one is tempted to conceive *LLV* as a film centred on an ethical *event*: the abyssal founding event is Ben's suicidal decision; the final act which will realize the event is suicide itself, his death; and the film is about (Sera's, not Ben's) endeavour to maintain *fidelity* to this Event. The interest of the film thus resides in the conflict between the ethical stance of fidelity to the Event and Sera's Goodness; that is, paradoxically, her Goodness (the tendency to want to save Ben from his self-destructive path) is presented as a *temptation to be resisted*.[3] (When, for a brief moment, Sera *does* give way to the 'elementary human compassion' and tries to convince Ben to go and see a doctor, this is presented as a clear case of compromising one's ethical stance.)

But is not the notion of a woman who assists her man in going to the end in his suicidal project and doesn't endeavour to stop him a *male fantasy* at its purest? Does not the film's final scene – Ben's death in the course of the sexual act which finally takes place, the literal realization of the proverbial coincidence of death and orgasm – also indicate that we are in the domain of fantasy? (Significantly, this sexual act is thoroughly desexualized, turned into an act of pure Christian communion.) Is another of the film's key scenes in which, in a desert resort, Sera sits astride Ben and, taking the bottle of tequila from him, begins to drink it down, the way he does, then undresses herself, tips the drink onto her face and breasts and leans over him, while he kisses and licks her body soaked in alcohol – is this scene not a drunkard's dream come true? (The dreamlike quality of this scene is confirmed by the way its smooth run is all of a sudden interrupted by Ben's loud, brutal fall. This fall clearly signals the intervention of reality that disturbs the dream...) However, at a deeper level, it is Ben himself who is Sera's fantasy: the fantasized ideal partner of a hysteric, a partner who fascinates her by means of his utter devotion to the death drive: the film should also be read as the realization of the masochist fantasy of a hysteric. (This double, fantasmatic mirroring is signalled in a dialogue between Sera and Ben: after she saves him from an embarrassing situation in a casino, he tells her that he thinks she is his guardian angel, more a drunkard's apparition than a real person, to which she responds that she is also using him.) So, although *LLV* may appear to be an exemplary case of Holly-wood psychological realism, its basic constellation is the same as that of the lovers' couples in Wagner's operas, where each partner is a mirage of the other: already in *The Flying Dutchman*, the Dutchman is Senta's dream realized, and vice versa; Senta is the girl about whom the Dutchman was dreaming during the long centuries of his wandering around the ocean . . .

This reference to Wagner enables us to explain what the death drive is, the utter ambiguity of this notion. Far from standing for the simple opposite of life – that is, for a tendency towards self-obliteration – the fundamental paradox of the psychoanalytic notion of the death drive is that it is the Freudian name for immortality: the death drive points towards the uncanny unconditional thrust that insists 'beyond (biological) life and death', beyond the cycle of generation and corruption. For that reason, the ultimate embodiment of the death drive is precisely the so-called undead in horror fiction: the 'living dead', indestructible monstrous entities that return again and again from their death.

From their first paradigmatic case, the Flying Dutchman, the predicament of the Wagnerian heroes is that, at some time in the past, they have committed some unspeakable evil deed, so that they are condemned to pay the price for it, not by death, but by being condemned to a life of eternal suffering, of help-lessly wandering around, unable to fulfil their symbolic function. Where is the death drive here? It does *not* reside in a simple longing to die, to find peace in death, but in a desperate endeavour to escape the clutches of their 'undead' eternal life, of their horrible wandering around in guilt and pain. The final passing away of the Wagnerian hero (the death of the Dutchman, Wotan, Tristan, Amfortas) is therefore the moment of their *liberation* from the clutches of the ultimate horror of the undead eternal life. Tristan in Act III is not so desperate because of his fear of dying: what makes him so desperate is that, without Isolde, he *cannot* die and is condemned to eternal longing – he anxiously awaits her arrival so as to be able to die. The prospect he dreads is not that of dying without Isolde (the standard complaint of a lover), but rather that of endless life without her . . . We can see now in what precise sense the Freudian death drive is to be opposed to Heidegger's *Sein-zum-Tode*, 'being-towards-death': for Lacan, the death drive does not relate to the finitude of our contingent temporal existence, but designates the endeavour to escape the dimension that traditional metaphysics designated as that of *immortality*, the indestructible life that insists beyond death.

How does Ben arouse Sera's love? By means of his thorough surrender to the death drive: although he loves her, he is not ready to revoke his suicidal decision out of consideration for her, for the sake of his love for her. What we have here is thus the extreme version of the musician's melodramas in which a woman's love is aroused by the very fact that the man, although deeply in love with her, is not ready to renounce his musical vocation for her – the woman is reduced to the mute witness of man's drive.[4] *LLV* retroactively demonstrates that the passionate (scientific, musical, political . . .) vocation on account of which, in the standard melodrama, the man cannot wholly surrender to the beloved woman, and which simultaneously renders his attraction irresistible, is the mask, the form of appearance, of the death drive. Of course, Sera accepts Ben's self-destructive drinking only because she herself is already on the path of self-destruction (engaged in a masochistic relationship with a Lithuanian pimp who punishes her for not bringing home enough money by cutting her thighs with a razor). Although caught in a self-destructive vicious cycle of her own, Sera none the less retains her subjectivity and is thus the point of our – the spectators' – hysterical identification: Ben is 'convincing' only because (and in so far as) we perceive him through Sera, through her 'humanity', through her mixture of apprehension and acceptance.

Lars von Trier's *Breaking the Waves*, another film about the inherent deadlocks of Goodness,[5] inverts the matrix common to *DMW* and *LLV*: in it, it is the woman, not the man, who is under the sway of the death drive and eventually meets death in an act of exchange. The film is set during the 1970s in a small Presbyterian community on the west coast of Scotland. Bess, a simple-minded, deeply religious local girl, marries Jan, a hearty oil-rig worker, courting the disapproval of the village elders. After the sexual ecstasy of their honeymoon, Bess can't bear having Jan return to the rigs, so she begs God to return Jan to her, saying that in exchange for his return, she would put up with any trial of her faith. Soon afterwards, as if in answer to her prayers, Jan effectively returns, but paralysed from the neck down due to an accident on the oil-rig. Confined to his hospital bed, Jan tells Bess she must make love to other men and describe her experiences to him in detail – this way, she will keep awake his will to life: although she will be doing the act physically with other men, the true sex will occur in their conversation . . . When, after her first successful adventure, Jan's condition improves slightly, Bess dolls herself up as a vulgar prostitute and starts to consort with men in spite of warnings from her mother that she will be cast out of the church. After a series of ups and downs in her perverse pact with Jan (his occasional bouts of depression when he declares that he wants to die; her near-lynching by local kids, then being consigned to a mental hospital and escaping), she is informed that Jan is dying. Interpreting this as a sign that she is not doing enough for him, she returns to an off-shore ship where she was once cut by a sadistic sailor and barely escaped, well aware of what she can expect there. She is brutally beaten and, when brought to the hospital and informed that Jan is no better, dies in despair. At the coroner's inquest, the doctor who earlier took care of her testifies that her true disease was Goodness itself. After she is none the less denied the proper funeral service, Jan (now miraculously able to walk) and his friends steal her body and launch it to rest out at sea. Later, they are woken up by the sound of church bells resounding miraculously from high above the oil-rig. . .

This final shot of the film – the bells high in the sky – is to be conceived of as the psychotic 'answer of the Real': the hallucinatory return in the Real of the divine *jouissance*, whose foreclosure from the Symbolic is signalled by the absence of the bells from the church tower (throughout the film we hear complaints about the removal of the bells from the local church). This last answer of the Real concludes the long series of exchanges and acts by proxy which follow the Fall from paradisal *jouissance*. That is to say, in the first part of the film, during her brief marital happiness, Bess fully enjoys sex with her husband in an absolutely innocent sense (all the talk in some reviews of the film about her sexual repression is totally misplaced); it is this very excessive attachment of hers to him which induces her to commit her original sin: unable to accept separation from Jan, she gets violent fits of impotent fury and rage, and then, in a desperate prayer, offers God the first symbolic exchange – she is ready to renounce anything, to suffer any deprivation or humiliation, if only Jan is brought back to her. . . When, as in an answer to her entreaty, Jan effectively returns, but completely paralyzed from the neck down, Bess reads his accident as the first 'answer of the Real', as God's price for the realization of her unconditional wish. From this point onwards, throughout the film, she reads even the tiniest fluctuations in his humour and health as signs addressed to her: when he falls back into depression, it is because she did not sacrifice herself enough for him, etc. Consequently, when, towards the film's end, Jan seems to approach the final coma, she decides to accomplish the ultimate act of exchange and visits the sadist sailor again, who, as she is well aware, will beat her to death – and indeed, after Bess dies, Jan miraculously regains his ability to walk. This denouement, of course, is purely fantasmatic: Jan's miraculous healing is the answer of the Real to her absolute sacrifice; that is, it is literally *over her dead body* that he rises up again.

Sex with strangers is for Bess a humiliating and excruciating experience, and this very pain confirms her belief that she is engaged in a properly religious act of sacrifice, doing it for the love of her neighbour, to alleviate his pain, to enable him to enjoy by proxy. (One of the critics quite appropriately remarked that *BW* does for God and sexuality what *Babette's Feast* does for God and food . . .) It is thus easy to discern in her acts the contours of what Lacan defined as the modern, post-classical tragedy:[6] the highest sacrifice of love is not to remain pure, intact, for the absent (or impotent) lover, but to *sin* for him, to besmirch oneself for him. This is clearly signalled when, alone in the church, Bess tells God that, on account of what she is doing for Jan, she is going to hell. 'Whom do you want to save?' comes the divine reply, 'Jan, or yourself?' In short, to save Jan, Bess accepts to betray HERSELF. The highest sacrifice of love is to accept freely and willingly the role of the other through which the subject enjoys: not to suffer for the other, but to enjoy for him. The price she pays for this is complete alienation: her *jouissance* is now in words, not in things – not in the bodily sexual activity itself, but in her verbal report of her exploits to the crippled Jan ... Here, of course, the obvious reproach imposes itself: is *BW* thus not the utmost 'male chauvinist' film celebrating and elevating into a sublime act of sacrifice the role which is forcefully imposed on women in patriarchal societies (that of serving as the support of male masturbatory fantasies): Bess is completely alienated in the male phallic economy, sacrificing her *jouissance* for the sake of her crippled partner's mental masturbation.

However, at a closer look, things become more complex. According to the standard version of Lacanian theory, the 'non-all' (*pas-tout*) of woman means that not all of a woman is caught up in phallic *jouissance*: she is always split between a part of her which accepts the role of a seductive masquerade aimed at fascinating the man, attracting the male gaze, and another part of her which resists being drawn into the dialectic of (male) desire, a mysterious *jouissance* beyond the phallus, about which nothing can be said ... The first thing to add to this standard version is that the *allusion to some unfathomable mysterious ingredient behind the mask is constitutive of the feminine seductive masquerade*: the way woman seduces and transfixes the male gaze is precisely by adopting the role of the Enigma embodied, as if her whole appearance is a lure, a veil concealing some unspeakable secret. In other words, the very notion of a 'feminine secret', of some mysterious *jouissance* which eludes the male gaze, is constitutive of the phallic spectacle of seduction – the first lesson of feminine seduction is that In-itself is always For-us, for the very Other whose grasp it eludes (as Hegel pointed out in his critique of the Kantian Thing-in-itself): inherent in the phallic economy is the reference to some mysterious X which remains for ever out of its reach.[7] In what, then, *does* the feminine *jouissance* 'beyond the phallus' consist? Perhaps the radical attitude of Bess in *BW* provides an answer: she undermines the phallic economy and enters the domain of *jouissance feminine* by way of her very unconditional surrender to it, by way of renouncing every remnant of the inaccessible 'feminine mystique', of some secret Beyond which allegedly eludes the male phallic grasp. Bess thus inverts the terms of phallic seduction in which a woman assumes the appearance of Mystery: Bess's sacrifice is unconditional, there is nothing Beyond, and this very absolute immanence undermines the phallic economy – deprived of its 'inherent transgression' (of the fantasizing about some mysterious Beyond avoiding its grasp), the phallic economy disintegrates. *BW* is subversive on account of its very 'over-orthodox', excessive realization of the fantasy of the feminine sacrifice for the male *jouissance*.

It is thus crucial to bear in mind the radical dissymmetry between the respective positions of Bess and Jan: Jan's *jouissance* remains phallic (a masturbatory *jouissance* supported by the fantasies of and about the Other); he acts as a kind of libidinal vampire feeding on the other's fantasies to sustain the flow of his phallic *jouissance*; while Bess's position is that of feeding him voluntarily with the blood of fantasies. The dissymmetry resides in the fact that Jan's request that Bess should have sex with other men and report on it to him is in itself ambiguous: apart from the obvious reading (to provide him with fantasies which will make his crippled life bearable for him), it can also be read as a self-sacrificing act of extreme goodness – what if he does it because he is aware that otherwise she will lead a chaste life to the end? Asking her to have sex with other men is thus a stratagem destined to *prevent* her from sacrificing herself – that is, to entice her to enjoy sex by way of providing her with a rationale which justifies it (she is really doing this just to please him...). The film indicates that, at the beginning, Jan finds himself in the predicament of the Wagnerian hero: wanting, but unable, to die; so he enjoins Bess to have sex with other men and report on it to him as a supreme altruistic act gradually, however, he gets caught up in it, and effectively enjoys it more and more, so that what began as a gesture of excessive goodness turns into perverse enjoyment – that Jan is aware of this trap he got entangled in is clear from his conversation with the priest towards the end of the film, when he confesses to him that he is evil, overwhelmed by bad thoughts...Jan's trajectory thus goes from initial goodness towards the neighbour to her perverse exploitation – with the underlying lesson that excessive goodness necessarily ends up in this way. In short, *Breaking the Waves* could be read as the inversion of the standard metaphysical opposition between pure mind and dirty body: (Jan's) dirty mind versus (Bess's) pure body.

Bess is thus the figure of pure, absolute Faith which transcends (or, rather, suspends) the very gap between the big Other and *jouissance*, between the Symbolic and the Real: the price to be paid for such immediate coincidence of religious Faith and sexual *jouissance* is psychosis. Is, then, the film itself psychotic? How can one render palatable such a direct story about miracles today, in our cynical postmodern era? The key to *Breaking the Waves* is provided by the tension between the narrative and the way it is shot, between content and form. Three features of the form cannot escape the attentive spectator: (1) the nervous, jerky hand-held camera shots, with the visible grains on the screen, as if we are watching an enlarged home movie shot on video; (2) the breaks and overlappings in the continuity (shots which follow each other often imply a time break or render the same event from a different viewpoint; furthermore, the camera pans from speaker to speaker, rather than cutting away as in a proper studio production); (3) there is no musical accompaniment (except in the case of the long static tableaux introducing each of the seven segments of the film: these tableaux are accompanied by excerpts from the big hits of Elton John, David Bowie, etc. from the time the story is supposed to take place). These features lend the film a kind of hystericized, amateurish intensity, reminding one of the famous early Cassavetes films,[8] creating a sense of immediacy, of eavesdropping on the characters before the camera person has had a chance to edit the film, thereby prettying it up. At the level of form, the film relates to the standard professional film like home-made amateur pornography to professional pornography. (Significantly, the only exceptions are the already mentioned, overtly kitschy, romantic, static countryside tableaux with a title introducing each of the episodes; these shots, composed with the greatest professional care, are a kind of stand-in for the romantic content at the level of the form – and, significantly, as if to counter this romantic effect, it is only here that we hear modern rock music from the period the narrative takes place.)

The group of European directors led by von Trier himself recently published an anti-Hollywood manifesto that enumerates a series of rules to be followed by European independent cinema production: no special effects, no post-production manipulations, hand-held camera, no big budget, etc. Although *Breaking the Waves* already follows most of these rules, it does so as part of a specific cinematic strategy that exploits the antagonism between form and content: we do not get a narrative content that would seem to fit these rules (contemporary bleak realist narrative), but, on the contrary, an extremely romantic narrative, the utmost opposite of the content implied by these formal rules. In other words, all these formal procedures (hand-held camera, violation of continuity rules, etc.) are not to be taken at their face value: they are not yet fetishized in an autonomous, self-sufficient procedure, but part of a complex of dialectic mediation. (The adequate analogy would be the one with the artists who use specific 'radical' modernist procedures – atonal music, abstract form-alist painting – as part of a global project that still follows pre-modernist late romanticist aims.) Von Trier himself emphasized that, if the film had been shot in a 'direct' melodramatic-passionate way as seems to fit its content,

it would have been far too suffocating. You would not have been able to stand it. What we've done is to take a style and put it over the story like a filter. Like encoding a television signal, when you pay in order to see a film: here we are encoding a signal for the film, which the viewer will later ensure they decode. The raw, documentary style which I've laid over the film and which actually annuls and contests it, means that we accept the story as it is.[9]

Therein resides the paradox: the only way for the spectator to 'accept the story as it is' is to encode it in a form which 'annuls and contests it' – that is, to submit it to a kind of dream-work. Furthermore, the paradox, which should not escape us, is that von Trier's procedure is the exact opposite of the usual melodramatic procedure in which the repressed kernel of the narrative returns in the excess of the form: the expressive pathos of music, the ridiculous sentimentality of acting, etc. Here, the narrative itself is ridiculously romantic, pathetic, excessive, and the form understates (instead of accentuating) the excessive pathos of the content. The key to the film is thus provided by this antagonism between the ultra-romantic content of Belief and the pseudo-documentary form – their relationship is thoroughly ambiguous. As von Trier himself emphasizes, it is not simply that the form undermines the content: it is precisely by means of the 'sober' distance towards the content that the film renders it 'palatable', that it prevents the content from appearing ridiculous (the same as in conversation, where a passionate declaration of love which would appear ridiculous if announced directly can pass if coated in the protective shield of irony). And, furthermore, is not the same antagonism discernible within the content itself, in the guise of the tension between the ascetic Presbyterian religious community, caught in a religious ritual from which every trace of *jouissance* has been evacuated (the evacuation signalled by the removal of the church bells), and the authentic personal relationship to God grounded in intense *jouissance*: what if the appearance of the strict opposition between the dry orthodox Letter of ritual (which regulates life in the Protestant community) and the living Spirit of true belief beyond dogma (of Bess) is misleading? What if, in the same way that the excessively romantic narrative is palpable only through the lens of pseudo-documentary camera form, pure authentic belief is palpable only against the background of, or filtered by, the closed orthodox religious community? Here, however, the problems with the film begin: today, the predominant form of subjectivity is not identification with a closed, orthodox, religious community (against which one could then rebel), but the 'open', permissive subject avoiding any fixed obligations – the paradox is that, in a way, both poles in *Breaking the Waves* are on the *same side* against this predominant form of subjectivity. In a society in which, more and more, since there is no God (Law), *nothing is prohibited*, the film establishes a fundamental Prohibition which opens up the space for authentic Transgression. The problem of the film is that this third term, the predominant form of subjectivity today, is simply missing in it: Trier reduces the conflict to that between tradition (Church as Institution) and postmodernity (miracle), and the properly modern dimension disappears. This dimension, of course, is present, but only in its immediate material aspect (in the guise of oil-rigs and platforms, the ultimate form of today's exploitation of nature) – it is suspended at the level of its subjective impact.

A comparison with Tarkovsky imposes itself here. Both Tarkovsky and Trier rely on the tension between narrative content and cinematic texture: if we are to discern the ultimate point of their film, narrative analysis of what seems to go on in the diegetic reality does not suffice; that is, one has to include the specific density and weight of the cinematic écriture that enters in a dialectic opposition of enabling and simultaneously hindering its narrative content. In Trier, the key feature of this texture is the pseudo-documentary, raw grain, hand-held camera, amateurish montage style that undermines the hyper-pathetic narrative line (and is this style not that of cinematic modernism *par excellence*? So one can claim that the modernity which is excluded/bypassed in the narrative content of *BW* returns in the very film's form – form is the 'return of the repressed' of its content). In Tarkovsky, the key feature of the texture is the density and weight of the material dimension of earth and water, which also grounds the specific relationship towards time that 'drags on', indefinitely, following its line, which bypasses the pure narrative logic.

It is thus all too easy to read Bess as the latest incarnation of the figure of the naïve, authentic, feminine believer dismissed by her constrained orthodox environs as a promiscuous madwoman. The film should rather be read as a meditation on the difficulty – impossibility even – of Belief today: of belief in miracles, inclusive of the miracle of cinema itself. It doesn't escape the usual fate of 'returns to authentic belief': the pure Belief inverts itself into just another aesthetic game. As to the final appearance of the bells high in the sky, a possible reading of *BW* could claim that this, precisely, is the point at which the film slides into religious obscurantism. That is to say, it seems possible to argue that the film should end with the death of Bess and Jan's subsequent regained ability to walk: this way, we would be dealing with an undecidable Pascalian wager, a 'crazy' reliance on divine Will which reads in contingent events 'answers of the Real', and which is sustained in the purity of its belief by the very fact that it cannot be 'objectively verified' (as in Jansenist theology, which emphasizes that miracles appear as such only to those who already believe in them – to neutral observers, they necessarily appear as meaningless coincidences and contingencies). If this were the case, *BW*'s ultimate message would be that 'each of us has a beatific vision of Paradise and Redemption inside of him-or herself, without any guarantee in external reality' . . . However, what *BW* accomplishes is similar to the well-known genre of paranoiac stories in which the *idée fixe* turns out to be true, not a mere hero's hallucination: it finishes with a brutal, unexpected, factual confirmation of Bess's faith, somewhat like Henry James's *Turn of the Screw* rewritten in such a way that, at the end, we get an objective confirmation that the devilish figures which appear were 'real', not just the governess's hysterical hallucination.

At this precise point, one should introduce the distinction between modernism and postmodernism: if there were no direct miracle, no bells in the sky, the film would be a typical modernist work about the tragic deadlock of absolute faith; the last minutes, when the miracle *does* occur, are a kind of postmodernist appendix to the otherwise tragic modernist existential drama of Faith. That is to say, what characterizes postmodernism is precisely that one can return to a pre-modern 'enchanted universe' in which miracles effectively do occur, as an aesthetic spectacle, without 'really believing it', but also without any ironic or cynical distance. The ending of *BW* is thus to be perceived in the same way that one should accept those 'magic' moments in David Lynch, in which persons (who otherwise often stand for utter corruption) are suddenly transported by a religious vision of an angelic bliss. In *Blue Velvet*, for example, Laura Dern unexpectedly starts to report to Kyle MacLachlan on her vision of a bleak universe suddenly filled by robins and their singing, to the accompaniment of religious organ music – it is crucial *not* to take this scene of innocent bliss with a cynical distance. Of course, in the last scene of *Blue Velvet*, we see a robin cruelly holding in her beak a dead bug, thus establishing the connection with the traumatic shot, from the film's beginning, of the camera approaching the earth and rendering the disgusting crawl of life – but, again, as in pre-Raphaelite paintings, Edenic bliss and disgust at life's corruption are the two sides of the same coin, so it would be wrong to read this last shot as an ironic undermining of Dern's ecstatic description of the robin as the embodiment of pure goodness. Is the supreme case of this radical ambiguity not Laura Palmer in *Twin Peaks*, an extremely licentious girl engaging in promiscuous sex and drugs, but none the less elevated to the status of redeemed innocence after her martyr's death? In the final scene of *Fire Walk With Me*, the movie prequel to the *Twin Peaks* series, after the famous shot of her body wrapped in white plastic, we see her in the mysterious Red Lodge – this Zone of *Twin Peaks* – sitting on a chair, with Agent Cooper standing by her with his hand on her shoulder, benevolently smiling as if to comfort her. After some moments of anxious perplexity, she gradually relaxes and starts to laugh, with a laughter mixed with tears; the laughter gets more and more buoyant, until the vision of an angel appears in the air in front of her. Ridiculous and kitschy as this scene may appear, one should insist again that, when the brutally raped and murdered Laura Palmer is redeemed, changed into a happily smiling figure looking at the angelic vision of herself, there is absolutely no irony involved. What is absolutely crucial about *BW*'s last shot of bells, therefore, is that the point of view of the camera is from above – that is, God's own point of view, the same as in Hitchcock's *Birds*, where we have the famous shot of Bodega Bay from above (are the birds which enter the frame not strictly homologous to the bells in Trier?). However, this homologous resort to the God's-eye point of view only makes the difference clearer: in Hitchcock, it is the malevolent indifference of the obscene superego divinity to human affairs, while in Trier, it is the benevolent, reconciliatory aspect of the Real of divine *Jouissance*.

All three films, *DMW*, *LLV* and *BW*, thus approach the limit of Goodness, stretching Goodness beyond a certain limit, at which it turns into (or, rather, coincides with) its opposite: Sister Helen's excessive compassion for the repulsive murderer stretches 'love for a neighbour' into perverse fascination; Sera's fidelity to Ben's suicidal decision radicalizes the proverbial hooker's sympathy into the acceptance of the other in so far as he acts against his best interest; Bess's goodness induces her to enact the extravagant symbolic exchange which involves accepting extreme humiliation and violent death. The three films thus form a kind of triad, indexed also by the three feminine positions with regard to men: a (perverse) religious, a (hysteric) prostitute, a (psychotic) married woman. They also render three variations on the theme of 'death and the maiden' – all three men whom the women confront are in a way 'living dead', dwelling in the domain 'between the two deaths': Sister Helen is confronted with a man condemned to death and awaiting execution; Sera a man who has himself decided to kill himself and is drinking himself to death: Bess a man who is totally crippled. So how do we get a 'normal' married woman? In other words, the standard Victorian male chauvinist wisdom according to which the only way for a woman to remain sane (i.e. to avoid hysteric outbursts or perverse debauchery) is to get married has to be turned around: the true question is: how is it possible for a woman to be married without falling into psychosis? The answer is, of course, by accepting the partner's (husband's) castration – that is, the fact that the partner merely *has* the phallus, but *is* not phallus itself. One is only allowed to fantasize about Another Man who would be phallus itself, while the consequences of actually encountering such a man are catastrophic, as is attested by the psychotic fate of Bess.

Notes

1   Incidentally, the status of this *jouissance* is radically ambiguous: it stands for the Sameness in which 'my' overlaps with 'other's' – i.e. the ex-timate kernel of Otherness in my very heart. For that reason, the standard formula according to which I 'project' into the Other who simultaneously fascinates and repels me my own unacknowledged/misrecognized *jouissance* (as in the white man's proverbial fascination with the African-American's potency) obfuscates the fact that *jouissance* is never simply 'mine' in the first place. The obligation to 'recognize in the Other's *jouissance* the projection of my own misrecognized *jouissance*' introduces a mirror relationship between two *jouissances* which is wholly inappropriate.

2   See Alain Badiou, *L'Être et l'évenement* (Paris, Seuil, 1988).
3   Crucial with regard to this split in Sera is the scene in which she offers Ben as a gift a small metallic container for drink: he is for a brief moment perplexed, unsure of what this gift amounts to. There is no 'correct' reading: all three possible readings (it's a small flask, drink moderately in order to survive; I love you absolutely, I accept you as you are, drink . . . ; drink yourself to death, drop dead!) must be retained, since the indiscernible character of this gesture which epitomizes the opaque mystery of a gift is the whole point of the scene.
4   Of special interest here is the inversion of the standard gender roles: usually, it is the woman who is under the spell of the death drive, while the man desperately tries to 'awaken' her, to drag her back from her lethargy into the circuit of engaged life.
5   'I wanted to do a film about goodness': ('Naked Miracles', interview with Lars von Trier, *Sight and Sound* 6 (1996), pp. 10–14, at p. 12).
6   See Jacques Lacan, *Seminar VIII: Le transfert* (Paris, Éditions du Seuil, 1988), pp. 317–21.
7   For a more detailed account of this aspect of the feminine masquerade, see Slavoj Žižek, *The Indivisible Remainder* (London, Verso, 1996), ch. 2.
8   John Cassavetes' *Faces* is interesting already at the purely formal level, with regard to the way camera positions and movements break the standard Hollywood procedure of the 'American' shot (showing persons in a dialogue from above their waists): in *Faces*, the camera approaches the actors a little bit too much, usually focusing only on their faces and part of their shoulders, and it is this intrusive overproximity which gives rise to a kind of unpleasant, uncanny effect of 'desublimation', rendering the subjects 'disgusting', showing in detail the hysterical contortions of their faces.
9   'Naked Miracles', p. 12.

Part III
Philosophy

10

Hegel's 'Logic of Essence' as a Theory of Ideology

This extract is from *Tarrying with the Negative: Kant, Hegel, and the Critique of Ideology* (1993, pp. 140–61). In this book Žižek proposes a new anatomy of ideology through a rereading of the German Idealist philosophers, rejecting, for its refusal to 'tarry with the negative' (Hegel), the postmodern dismissal of the subject as a mere epiphenomenon of discourse. In this extract the Hegelian essence of an object, its 'bundle' of defining properties governed by logical necessity, is counterposed to the spontaneity of the free subject who names the object and thus selects those properties to define it in the first place. The synthesis of this dialectic between necessity and freedom is resolved not by the effacement of their opposition but by a tarrying with their negativity.

'To tarry with the negative' is thus to retain and absorb the contradiction rather than abolish it, as, for instance, that between 'ground' and 'conditions' – ground being the essence of a thing and conditions the circumstances that bring the thing about – two opposing factors that have to be combined without losing their antagonism. A harmonizing dialectical synthesis that leads to an evolutionary advance is herewith declined inasmuch as this implies an inevitable move from an 'In-itself' to a 'For-itself', from brute objectivity to self-reflectivity. But because the 'In-itself' is already 'for-us', any potential (the ground) has to be realized on the stage of external circumstances (the conditions). For Hegel, the only way of arriving at essences is for the subject to test its claims in the world until it is deprived of all obstacles and its delusions vanish, rather like, as Žižek points out, Lacan's earlier conception of analysis, where the analyst's non-intervention, his 'passivity', allows the patient to discover that it is not external obstacles that stand in its way but its own 'inherent inauthenticity'.

The question, then, is how the subject comes to accept the inner and outer necessities of essence in what is a contingent, incalculable act. Perhaps it would be simpler if, as Kant maintains, the notion of necessary existence were dropped altogether, and existence in 'reality' were confined to representations that are actually filled out by 'intuition', by contingent phenomenal experience. This claim stimulates Hegel to the counter-claim that the concept of an object has an effect upon its existence, so that we can finally know the object-as-existent only when we have related it to itself 'through the detour' of its properties. In the same way, in Lacanian analysis the interpretation of all the aspects of a symptom (the imaginary 'object' constructed out of the Real) directly re-creates the symptom (as the new object recognized within the Symbolic). This subjective appropriation of the object's defining properties, the active presupposition of them, avoids the 'vicious circle of ground and conditions,' since it does not place one as prior to the other; similarly, in the ideology of national identity, a patriotic subject does not list all the hallmarks of his nation (the conditions) in order to derive his national identity (the ground) from them, but rather presupposes himself and his nation as already constituted by them. Hence this 'return of the thing to itself' is tautological, because it requires, through the act of naming, the apparent redundancy of positing an existent ground that upholds all the conditions. This empty presupposition that marks the act of naming is what Lacan has identified as precipitating the signifier's 'fall' into the signified, the *point de capiton* ('upholstery button') that fastens the word down on to existence – a similar structure (an empty presupposition) to that of the anti-Semitic figure of the Jew, who is named not merely for negative and contradictory attributes but also just for being a 'Jew'.

For Hegel, the act of naming is precisely the point at which freedom enters the system of necessity: freedom is not a humble recognition of the logical rigidity of the system of essences (Spinoza), but a creative act of constructing necessary entities out of the material found. This act of counting up to *one* adds nothing to what is before it, but is nevertheless the 'empty gesture' that distinguishes symbolization. At the same time, there is the impression that a hard immutable core lies beyond all the properties that make up a thing, as if there were one intelligible X underneath all the phenomenal features, precisely what characterizes ideology. This view of naming corresponds to a central tenet of Idealism: that the act of knowing creates the object, from which Hegel derives the view that the necessity established by this act is no more than an appearance. Necessity is neither discovered by a retrospective view nor projected by some fiat of a purely autonomous subject, since the former puts subjects at the mercy of the external, and the latter of the internal. Instead of being a puppet of necessity, the subject exists within an 'absolute unrest of becoming', against the pressure of which emerges the Lacanian *object a*, a substitute for the being that for ever eludes the subject, that 'remainder of matter' that the Symbolic endlessly and hopelessly pursues.

For Hegel, the actuality of freedom requires a distinction between the notion of a 'mere' possibility, a false presupposition, and a 'true' one that could emerge into actuality. The first implies an incapacity to act, the second, the capacity of acting otherwise, even when our free attempts have failed in their object – which matches Kant's claim that freedom is characterized by this real possibility. The same link between possibility and actuality occurs in the Lacanian 'symbolic castration', where it is the threat of castration that takes effect, rather than its actuality, with the result that we become subjects the very moment that this possibility takes on an actuality of its own. Similarly, the phallus, unlike the fetish, is never actualized; to the extent that it imaginarily signifies the possibility of all future meanings, it also symbolically signifies its opposite, the lack in the Other. This actual possibility is also present in Hegel's idea of the 'Lord's' power over the 'Bondsman': the Lord's power is never realized in full, working like the threat of castration, while he himself appears free from castration, illicitly filling the lack in the Other, an ideological illusion which (created from an active presupposition) maintains his position as master.

From 'In-itself' to 'For-itself'

Let us stop here and abstain from discerning the same matrix up to the end of the second part of *Logic*; suffice it to ascertain that the fundamental antagonism of the entire logic of essence is the antagonism between *ground* and *conditions*, between the inner essence ('true nature') of a thing and the external circumstances which render possible the realization of this essence: that is, the impossibility of reaching a common measure between these two dimensions, of co-ordinating them in a 'higher-order synthesis'. (It is only in the third part of *Logic*, the 'subjective logic' of Notion, that this incommensurability is surpassed.) Therein consists the alternative between positing and external reflection: do people create the world they live in from within themselves, autonomously, or does their activity result from external circumstances? Philosophical common sense would here impose the compromise of a 'proper measure': true, we have the possibility of choice, we can realize our freely conceived projects, but only within the framework of tradition, of the inherited circumstances which delineate our field of choices; or, as Marx put it in his 'Eighteenth Brumaire of Louis Bonaparte': 'Men make their own history; but they do not make it just as they please; they do not make it under circumstances chosen by themselves, but under circumstances directly encountered, given and transmitted from the past.'[1]

However, it is precisely such a 'dialectical synthesis' that Hegel declines. The whole point of his argument is that we have no way of drawing a line between the two aspects: every inner potential can be translated (its form can be converted) into an external condition, and vice versa. In short, what Hegel does here is something very precise: he undermines the usual notion of the relationship between the inner potentials of a thing and the external conditions which render (im) possible the realization of these potentials, by *positing between these two sides the sign of equality*. The consequences are far more radical than they appear; they concern above all the radically anti-evolutionary character of Hegel's philosophy, as exemplified in the notional couple *in-itself / for-itself*. This couple is usually taken as the supreme proof of Hegel's trust in evolutionary progress (the development from 'In-itself' into 'For-itself'); yet a closer look dispels this phantom of Evolution. The 'in-itself' in its opposition to 'for-self' means at one and the same time (1) what exists only potentially, as an inner possibility, contrary to the actuality wherein a possibility has externalized and realized itself, *and* (2) actuality itself in the sense of external, immediate, 'raw' objectivity which is still opposed to subjective mediation, which is not yet internalized, rendered conscious; in this sense, the 'In-itself' is actuality in so far as it has not yet reached its Notion.

The simultaneous reading of these two aspects undermines the usual idea of dialectical progress as a gradual realization of the object's inner potentials, as its spontaneous self-development. Hegel is here quite outspoken and explicit: the inner potentials of the self-development of an object and the pressure exerted on it by an external force are *strictly correlative*; they form the two parts of the same conjunction. In other words, the potentiality of the object must also be present in its external actuality, under the form of heteronomous coercion. For example (the example here is of Hegel himself), to say that a pupil at the beginning of the process of education is somebody who potentially knows, somebody who, in the course of his development, will realize his creative potentials, *equals saying* that these inner potentials must be present from the very beginning in external actuality as the authority of the Master who exerts pressure upon his pupil. Today, one can add to this the sadly famous case of the working class *qua* revolutionary subject: to affirm that the working class is 'in-itself', potentially, a revolutionary subject, equals the assertion that this potentiality must already be actualized in the Party, which knows in advance about the revolutionary mission, and therefore exerts pressure upon the working class, guiding it toward the realization of its potentials. Thus, the 'leading role' of the Party is legitimized; it is thus its right to 'educate' the working class in accordance with its potentials, to 'implant' in this class its historical mission.

We can see, now, why Hegel is as far as possible from the evolutionist notion of the progressive development of in-itself into for-itself: the category of 'in-itself' is strictly correlative to 'for-us' – that is, for some consciousness external to the thing-in-itself. To say that a clod of clay is 'in-itself' a pot equals saying that this pot is already present in the mind of the craftsman who will impose the form of pot on the clay. The current way of saying 'under the right conditions the pupil will realize his potentials' is thus deceptive: when, in excuse of his *failure* to realize his potentials, we insist that 'he would have realized them, if only the conditions had been right', we commit thereby an error of cynicism worthy of Brecht's famous lines from *The Threepenny Opera*: 'We would be good instead of being so rude, if only the circumstances were not of this kind!' For Hegel, external circumstances are not an impediment to realizing inner potentials, but on the contrary *the very arena in which the true nature of these inner potentials is to be tested*: are such potentials true potentials or just vain illusions about what might have happened? Or, to put it in Spinozian terms: 'positing reflection' observes things as they are in their eternal essence, *sub specie aeternitatis*, whereas 'external reflection' observes them *sub specie durationis*, in their dependence on a series of contingent external circumstances. Here, everything hinges on *how* Hegel overcomes 'external reflection'. If his aim were simply to reduce the externality of contingent conditions to the self-mediation of the inner essence-ground (the usual notion of 'Hegel's idealism'), then Hegel's philosophy would truly be a mere 'dynamized Spinozism'. But what does Hegel actually do?

Let us approach this problem via Lacan: in what precise sense can we maintain that Lacan of the late forties and early fifties was a Hegelian? In order to get a clear idea of his Hegelianism, it suffices to take a closer look at how he conceives the analyst's 'passivity' in the psychoanalytical cure. Since 'the actual is rational', the analyst does not have to force his interpretations upon the analysand; all he has to do is clear the way for the analysand to arrive at his own truth by means of a mere punctuation of his speech. This is what Hegel has in mind when he speaks of the 'cunning of reason': the analyst does not seek to undermine the analysand's self-deceit, his attitude of the 'Beautiful Soul', by way of directly confronting him with the 'true state of things', but by way of giving him a free rein, of removing all obstacles that may serve as an excuse, thus compelling him to reveal 'the stuff he is actually made of '. In this precise sense, 'the actual is rational': our – the Hegelian philosopher's – trust in the inherent rationality of the actual means that actuality provides the only testing-ground for the reasonableness of the subject's claims; that is, the moment the subject is bereft of external obstacles which can be blamed for his failure, his subjective position will collapse on account of its inherent inauthenticity. What we have here is a kind of cynicized Heideggerianism: since the object is in itself inconsistent, since what allows it to retain the appearance of consistency is the very external hindrance which allegedly restrains its inner potentials, the most effective way to destroy it, to bring about its collapse, is precisely to renounce any claims of domination, to remove all hindrances and to 'let it be'; that is, to leave the field open for the free deployment of its potentials.[2]

However, does the Hegelian notion of the 'cunning of reason' not entail a 'regression' to the pre-Kantian rationalist metaphysics? It is a philosophical commonplace to oppose here Kant's critique of the ontological proof of God's existence to Hegel's reaffirmation of it, and to quote Hegel's reaffirmation as the supreme proof of Hegel's return to the domain of classical metaphysics. The story goes somewhat like this: Kant demonstrated that existence is not a predicate, since, at the level of predicates which define the notional content of a thing, there is absolutely no difference between 100 actual thalers and a mere notion of 100 thalers – and, *mutatis mutandis*, the same holds for the notion of God. Furthermore, one is even tempted to see in Kant's position a kind of prefiguration of the Lacanian eccentricity of the Real with reference to the Symbolic: existence is real in so far as it is irreducible to the network of notional-symbolic determinations. Nevertheless, this commonplace has to be rejected thoroughly.

Kant's actual line of argumentation is far more refined; he proceeds in two basic steps (see *Critique of Practical Reason*, A 584–603). First, he demonstrates that there is still a hidden if-clause at work in the ontological proof of God's existence: true, 'God' does designate a being whose existence is implied in its very notion; but we still must presuppose that such a being exists (i.e., all that the ontological proof actually demonstrates is that, *if* God exists, he exists necessarily), so that it remains possible that there is simply no such being whose notion would entail existence. An atheist would even quote such a nature of God as an argument *against* his existence: there is no God precisely because one cannot imagine in a consistent way a being whose notion would entail existence. Kant's next step aims at the same point: the only legitimate use of the term 'existence' is to designate the phenomenal reality of the objects of possible experience; however, *the difference between Reason and Intuition is constitutive of reality*: the subject accepts that something 'exists in reality' only in so far as its representation is filled out by the contingent, empirical content provided by intuition – that is, only in so far as the subject is passively affected by senses. Existence is not a predicate – that is, part of the notion of an object – precisely because, in order to pass from the notion to actual existence, one has to add the passive element of intuition. For that reason, the notion of 'necessary existence' is self-contradictory – *every existence is by definition contingent.*[3]

What is Hegel's answer to all this? Hegel in no way returns to traditional metaphysics: he refutes Kant within the horizon opened up by Kant himself. He, so to speak, approaches the problem from the opposite end: how does the 'coming-to-notion' (*zum-Begriff-kommen*) affect the existence of the object in question? When a thing 'reaches its notion', what impact does this have on its existence? To clarify this question, let us recall an example which confirms Lacan's thesis that Marxism is not a 'world-view':[4] namely, the idea that the proletariat becomes an *actual* revolutionary subject by way of integrating the *knowledge* of its historical role:[5] historical materialism is not a neutral 'objective knowledge' of historical development, since it is an act of self-knowledge of a historical subject; as such, it implies the proletarian subjective position. In other words, the 'knowledge' proper to historical materialism is self-referential: it changes its 'object'. It is only via the act of knowledge that the object becomes what it truly 'is'. So, the rise of 'class consciousness' produces the effect in the existence of its 'object' (proletariat) by way of changing it into an actual revolutionary subject. And is it not the same with psychoanalysis? Does the interpretation of a symptom not constitute a direct intervention of the Symbolic in the Real; does it not offer an example of how the word can affect the Real of the symptom? And, on the other hand, does not such an efficacy of the Symbolic presuppose entities whose existence literally hinges on a certain non-knowledge: the moment knowledge is assumed (through interpretation), existence disintegrates? Existence is here not one of the predicates of a Thing, but designates the way the Thing relates to its predicates, more precisely: the way the Thing *is related to itself* by means of (through the detour of) its predicates-properties.[6] When a proletarian becomes aware of his 'historical role', *none of his actual predicates changes; what changes is just the way he relates to them, and this change in the relationship to predicates radically affects his existence.*

To designate this awareness of 'historical role', traditional Marxism makes use of the Hegelian couple 'In-itself/For-itself': by way of arriving at its 'class consciousness', the proletariat changes from a 'class-in-itself' to a 'class-for-itself'. The dialectic at work here is that of a *failed encounter*: the passage to 'For-itself', to the Notion, involves the loss of existence. Nowhere is this failed encounter more obvious than in a passionate love affair: its 'In-itself' occurs when I simply yield to the passion, unaware of what is happening to me; afterwards, when the affair is over, *aufgehoben* in my recollection, it becomes 'For-itself' – I retroactively become aware of what I had, of what I lost. This awareness of what I lost gives birth to the fantasy of the impossible conjunction

of being and knowledge ('if only I could have known how happy I was . . .').
But is the Hegelian 'In-and-for-itself' (*An-und-Für-sich*) really such an impossible conjunction, the fantasy of a moment when I am happy and I know it? Is it
not rather the unmasking of the illusion of the 'external reflection' that still
pertains to 'for-itself': the illusion that, in the past, I actually *was* happy without
knowing it – that is, the insight into how 'happiness' by definition comes to be
retroactively, by means of the experience of its loss?

This illusion of the external reflection can be further exemplified by *Billy
Bathgate*, the movie based upon E. L. Doctorow's novel. The film is fundamentally a failure, and the impression it arouses is that what we see is a pale,
distorted reflection of a far superior literary source. There is, however, an
unpleasant surprise in store for those who, after seeing the movie, set to read
the novel: the novel is far closer to the insipid happy end (in it, Billy pockets
the hidden wealth of Dutch Schultz); numerous delicate details which the
spectator unacquainted with the novel experiences as fragments happily not
lost in the impoverishing process of transposition to cinema, fragments that
miraculously survived the shipwreck, actually turn out to be added by the
script-writer. In short, the 'superior' novel evoked by the film's failure is not
the pre-existent actual novel upon which the film is based, but a retroactive
chimera aroused by the film itself.[7]

Ground versus Conditions

This conceptual background allows us to reformulate the vicious circle of
ground and conditions. Let us recall the usual mode of explaining outbreaks
of racism, which invokes the categorical couple of ground and conditions
circumstances: one conceives of racism (or, more generally, so-called outbreaks
of irrational mass sadism) as a latent psychic disposition, a kind of Jungian
archetype which comes forth under certain conditions (social instability and
crisis, etc.). From this point of view, the racist disposition is the 'ground', and
current political struggles the 'circumstances', the conditions of its effectuation.
However, what counts as ground and what counts as conditions are ultimately
contingent and exchangeable, so that one can easily accomplish the Marxist
reversal of the above-mentioned psychologist perspective, and conceive the
present political struggle as the only true determining ground. In the present
civil war in ex-Yugoslavia, for example, the 'ground' of Serbian aggression is
not to be sought in any primitive Balkan warrior archetypes, but in the struggle
for power in post-Communist Serbia (the survival of the old Communist state
apparatus). The status of eventual Serbian bellicose dispositions and other
similar archetypes (the 'Croatian genocidal character', the 'perennial tradition

of ethnic hatreds in the Balkans', etc.) is precisely that of the conditions/ circumstances in which the power struggle realizes itself. The 'bellicose dispositions' are precisely that: that is, latent dispositions which are actualized, drawn forth from their shadowy half-existence by the recent political struggle *qua* their determining ground. One is thus fully justified in saying that 'what is at stake in the Yugoslav civil war are not archaic ethnic conflicts: these perennial hatreds are inflamed only on account of their function in the recent political struggle'.[8]

How, then, are we to eschew this mess, this exchangeability of ground and circumstances? Let us take another example: *Renaissance* – that is, the rediscovery ('rebirth') of antiquity which exerted a crucial influence on the break with the medieval way of life in the fifteenth century. The first, obvious explanation is that the influence of the newly discovered antique tradition brought about the dissolution of the medieval 'paradigm'. Here, however, a question immediately pops up: why did antiquity begin to exert its influence at precisely that moment, and not earlier or later? The answer that offers itself, of course, is that owing to the dissolution of medieval social links, a new *Zeitgeist* emerged which made us responsive to antiquity; something must have changed in 'us' so that we became able to perceive antiquity not as a pagan kingdom of sin, but as the model to be adopted. That's all very well, but we still remain locked in a vicious circle, since this new *Zeitgeist* itself took shape precisely through the discovery of antique texts as well as fragments of classical architecture and sculpture. In a way, everything was already there, in the external circumstances; the new *Zeitgeist* formed itself through the influence of antiquity, which enabled Renaissance thought to shatter the medieval chains; yet, for this influence of antiquity to be felt, the new *Zeitgeist* must already have been active. The only way out of this impasse is therefore the intervention, at a certain point, of a tautological gesture: the new *Zeitgeist* had to constitute itself by literally *presupposing itself in its exteriority*, in its external conditions (in antiquity). In other words, it was not sufficient for the new *Zeitgeist* retroactively to posit these external conditions (the antique tradition) as 'its own'; it had to (presup)pose itself as already present in these conditions. *The return to external conditions (to antiquity) had to coincide with the return to the foundation, to the 'thing itself', to the ground.* (This is precisely how the Renaissance conceived itself: as the return to the Greek and Roman foundations of our Western civilization.) We do not thus have an inner ground the actualization of which depends on external circumstances; the external relation of presupposing (ground presupposes conditions, and vice versa) is surpassed in a pure tautological gesture by means of which the thing *presupposes itself*. This tautological gesture is 'empty' in the precise sense that it does not contribute anything new; it only retroactively ascertains that the thing in question *is already present in its conditions* – that is, that the totality of these conditions *is* the actuality of the thing. Such an empty gesture provides us with the most elementary definition of the *symbolic* act.

Here we see the fundamental paradox of 'rediscovering tradition' at work in the constitution of national identity: a nation finds its sense of self-identity by means of such a tautological gesture – that is, by way of discovering itself as already present in its tradition. Consequently, the mechanism of the 'redis-covery of national tradition' cannot be reduced to the 'positing of presupposi-tions' in the sense of the retroactive positing of conditions as 'ours'. The point is rather that, in the very act of returning to its (external) conditions, *the (national) thing returns to itself*. The return to conditions is experienced as the 'return to our true roots'.

The Tautological 'Return of the Thing to Itself'

Although 'really existing socialism' has already receded into a distance which confers upon it the nostalgic magic of a postmodern lost object, some of us still recall a well-known joke about what socialism is: a social system that is the dialectical synthesis of all previous history. From the prehistoric classless society it took primitivism, from antiquity slave labour, from medieval feudalism ruthless domination, from capitalism exploitation, *and from socialism the name*. This is what the Hegelian tautological gesture of the 'return of the thing to itself' is all about: one must include along with the definition of the object its name. That is to say, after we decompose an object into its ingredients, we look in vain in them for some specific feature which holds together this multitude and makes of it a unique, self-identical thing. As to its properties and ingre-dients, a thing is wholly 'outside itself', in its external conditions; every positive feature is already present in the circumstances which are not yet this thing. The supplementary operation which produces from this bundle a unique, self-identical thing is the purely symbolic, tautological gesture of positing these external conditions as the conditions-components of the thing and, simultaneously, of presupposing the existence of ground which holds together this multitude of conditions.

And, to throw our Lacanian cards on the table, this tautological 'return of the thing to itself' which renders forth the concrete structure of self-identity is what Lacan designates as the *point de capiton*, the 'quilting point' at which the signifier 'falls into' the signified (as in the above-mentioned joke on socialism, where the name itself functions as part of the designated thing). Let us recall an example from popular culture: the killer-shark in Spielberg's *Jaws*. A direct search for the shark's ideological meaning evokes nothing but misguided questions: does it symbolize the threat of the Third World to America epitom-ized by the archetypal small town? Is it the symbol of the exploitative nature of capitalism itself (Fidel Castro's interpretation)? Does it stand for the untamed nature which threatens to disrupt the routine of our daily lives? In order to avoid this lure, we have to shift our perspective radically: the daily life of the common man is dominated by an inconsistent multitude of fears (he can become the victim of big business manipulations; Third World immigrants seem to intrude into his small orderly universe; unruly nature can destroy his home; etc.), and the accomplishment of *Jaws* consists in an act of purely formal conversion which provides a common 'container' for all these free-floating, inconsistent fears by way of anchoring them, 'reifying' them, in the figure of the shark.[9] Consequently, the function of the fascinating presence of the shark is precisely to *block* any further enquiry into the social meaning (social media-tion) of those phenomena that arouse fear in the common man. To say that the murderous shark 'symbolizes' the above-mentioned series of fears is to say too much and not enough at the same time. It does not symbolize them, since it literally annuls them by itself occupying the place of the object of fear. It is therefore 'more' than a symbol: it becomes the feared 'thing itself'. Yet, the shark is decidedly less than a symbol, since it does not point toward the symbolized content, but rather blocks access to it, renders it invisible. In this way, it is homologous with the anti-Semitic figure of the Jew: 'Jew' is the explanation offered by anti-Semitism for the multiple fears experienced by the 'common man' in an epoch of dissolving social links (inflation, unemployment, corruption, moral degradation) – behind all these phenomena lies the invisible hand of the 'Jewish plot'. The crucial point here, again, is that the designation *'Jew' does not add any new content*: the entire content is already present in the external conditions (crisis, moral degeneration . . .); the name 'Jew' is only the supplementary feature which accomplishes a kind of transubstantiation, chan-ging all these elements into so many manifestations of the same *ground*, the 'Jewish plot'. Paraphrasing the joke on socialism, one could say that anti-Semitism takes from the economy unemployment and inflation, from politics parliamentary corruption and intrigue, from morality its own degeneration, from art 'incomprehensible' avant-gardism, *and from the Jew the name*. This name enables us to recognize behind the multitude of external conditions the activity of the same *ground*.

Here we also find at work the dialectic of contingency and necessity: as to their content, they fully coincide (in both cases, the only positive content is the series of conditions that form part of our actual life experience: economic crisis, political chaos, the dissolution of ethical links . . .); the passage of contingency into necessity is an act of purely formal conversion, the gesture of adding a *name* which confers upon the contingent series the mark of necessity, thereby transforming it into the expression of some hidden ground (the 'Jewish plot'). This is also how later – at the very end of the 'logic of essence' – we pass from absolute necessity to freedom. To comprehend properly this passage, one has to renounce thoroughly the standard notion of 'freedom as comprehended necessity' (after getting rid of the illusions of free will, one can recognize and freely accept one's place in the network of causes and their effects). Hegel's point is, on the contrary, that *it is only the subject's (free) act of 'dotting the i' which retroactively installs necessity*, so that the very act by means of which the subject recognizes (and thus constitutes) necessity is the supreme act of freedom and as such the self-suppression of necessity. *Voilà pourquoi Hegel n'est pas spinoziste*: on account of this tautological gesture of retroactive performativity. So 'performativity' in no way designates the power of freely 'creating' the designated content ('words mean what we want them to mean,' etc.): the 'quilting' only structures the material which is found, externally imposed. The act of naming is 'performative' only and precisely in so far as *it is always-already part of the definition of the signified content.*[10]

This is how Hegel resolves the deadlock of positing and external reflection, the vicious circle of positing the presuppositions and of enumerating the presuppositions of the posited content: by means of the tautological return-upon-itself of the thing in its very external presuppositions. And the same tautological gesture is already at work in Kant's analytic of pure reason: the synthesis of the multitude of sensations in the representation of the object which belongs to 'reality' implies an empty surplus: that is, the positing of an X as the unknown substratum of the perceived phenomenal sensations. Suffice it to quote Findlay's precise formulation:

We always refer appearances to a Transcendental Object, an X, of which we, however, know nothing, but which is none the less the objective correlate of the synthetic acts inseparable from thinking self-consciousness. The Transcendental Object, thus conceived, can be called a Noumenon or thing of thought (*Gedankending*). But the reference to such a thing of thought does not, strictly speaking, use the categories, but is something like *an empty synthetic gesture* in which nothing objective is really put before us.[11]

The transcendental object is thus the very opposite of the *Ding-an-sich*: it is 'empty' in so far as it is devoid of any 'objective' content. That is to say, to obtain its notion, one has to abstract from the sensible object its entire sensible content: that is, all sensations by means of which the subject is affected by *Ding*. The empty X which remains is *the pure objective correlate/effect of the subject's autonomous-spontaneous synthetic activity*. To put it paradoxically: the transcendental object is the 'in-itself' in so far as it is for the subject, posited by it; it is pure 'positedness' of an indeterminate X. This 'empty synthetic gesture' – which adds to the thing nothing positive, no new sensible feature, and yet, in its very capacity of an empty gesture, constitutes it, makes it into an object – is the act of *symbolization* in its most elementary form, at its zero-level. On the first page of his book, Findlay points out that the transcendental object '*is not for Kant different* from the object or objects which appear to the senses and which we can judge about and know... but it is the *same* object or objects conceived in respect of certain intrinsically unapparent features, and which is in such respects incapable of being judged about or known'.[12]

This X, this irrepresentable surplus which adds itself to the series of sensible features, is precisely the 'thing-of-thought' (*Gedankending*): it bears witness to the fact that the object's unity does not reside within it, but is the result of the subject's synthetic activity. (As with Hegel, where the act of formal conversion inverts the chain of conditions into the unconditional Thing, founded in itself.) Let us briefly return to anti-Semitism, to the 'synthetic act of apperception' which, out of the multitude of (imagined) features of Jews, constructs the anti-Semitic figure of 'Jew'. To pass for a true anti-Semite, it is not enough to claim that we oppose Jews because they are exploitative, greedy intriguers. That is, it is not sufficient for the signifier 'Jew' to designate this series of specific, positive features; one has to accomplish the crucial step further by saying 'they are like that (exploitative, greedy...) *because* they are Jews'. The 'transcendental object' of Jewishness is precisely that elusive X which 'makes a Jew into a Jew', and for which we look in vain among his positive properties. This act of pure formal conversion – that is, the 'synthetic act' of uniting the series of positive features in the signifier 'Jew' and thereby transforming them into so many manifestations of the 'Jewishness' *qua* their hidden ground – *brings about the appearance of an objectal surplus*, of a mysterious X which is 'in Jew more than Jew': in other words, of the transcendental object.[13] In the very text of Kant's *Critique of Pure Reason*, this void of the synthetic gesture is indicated by an exception in the use of the pair constitutive / regulative:[14] in general, 'constitutive' principles serve to construct objective reality, whereas 'regulative' principles are merely subjective maxims which guide reason without giving access to positive knowledge. However, when he speaks of existence (*Dasein*), Kant makes use of the pair constitutive / regulative in the midst of the very domain of the constitutive, by way of linking it to the couple mathematical / dynamical: 'In the application of pure conceptions of understanding to possible experience, the employment of their synthesis is either *mathematical* or *dynamical*; for it is concerned partly with the mere *intuition* of an appearance in general, partly with its *existence*' (B 199).

In what precise sense, then, are dynamical principles 'merely regulative principles, and [are] distinguished from the mathematical, which are constitutive

(B 223)? The principles of the mathematical use of categories refer to the intuited phenomenal content (to phenomenal properties of the thing); it is only the dynamical principles of synthesis which guarantee that the content of our representations refers to some objective existence, independent of the flux of perceiving consciousness. How, then, are we to explain the paradox of making objective existence dependent not on 'constitutive' but on 'regulative' principles? Let us return, for the last time, to the anti-Semitic figure of the Jew. Mathematical synthesis can only gather together phenomenal properties attributed to the Jew (greediness, intriguing spirit, etc.); then dynamical synthesis accomplishes the reversal by means of which this series of properties is posited as the manifestation of an inaccessible X, 'Jewishness' – that is to say, of something *real*, really existing. At work here are regulative principles, since dynamical synthesis is not limited to phenomenal features, but refers them to their underlying-unknowable substratum, to the transcendental object; in this precise sense, the existence of 'Jew' as irreducible to the series of predicates – that is, his existence as pure positing (*Setzung*) of the transcendental object *qua* substratum of phenomenal predicates, hinges on dynamical synthesis. In Lacanian terms, dynamical synthesis posits the existence of an X as the transphenomenal 'hard kernel of being' beyond predicates (which is why the hatred of Jews does not concern their phenomenal properties but aims at their hidden 'kernel of being') – a new proof of how 'reason' is at work in the very heart of 'understanding', in the most elementary positing of an object as 'really existing'. It is therefore deeply significant that, throughout the subdivision on the second analogy of experience, Kant consistently uses the word *Objekt* (designating an intelligible entity) and not *Gegenstand* (designating a simple phenomenal entity): the external, objective existence achieved by the synthetic use of dynamic regulative principles is 'intelligible', not empirical-intuitive; that is, it adds to the intuitive-sensible features of the object an intelligible, non-sensible X, and thus makes an object out of it.

In this precise sense Hegel remains within Kant's fundamental framework. That is to say, in what resides the fundamental paradox of Kant's transcendentalism? Kant's initial problem is the following one: given that my senses bombard me with a confused multitude of representations, how am I to distinguish, in this flux, between mere 'subjective' representations and objects that exist independently of the flux of representations? The answer: my representations acquire 'objective status' via transcendental synthesis which changes them into the objects of experience. What I experience as 'objective' existence, the very 'hard kernel' of the object beneath the ever-changing phenomenal fluctuations, independent of the flux of my consciousness, thus results from my (the subject's) own 'spontaneous' synthetic activity. And, *mutatis mutandis*, Hegel says the same thing: the establishment of absolute necessity equals its self-cancellation; that is, it designates the act of freedom which retroactively 'posits' something as necessary.

The 'Absolute Unrest of Becoming'

The trouble with contingency resides in its uncertain status: is it ontological – that is, are things *in themselves* contingent – or is it epistemological – that is, is contingency merely an expression of the fact that *we do not know* the complete chain of causes which brought about the allegedly 'contingent' phenomenon? Hegel undermines the common supposition of this alternative, namely, the external relationship of being and knowledge: the notion of 'reality' as something that is simply given, that exists 'out there', prior and external to the process of knowledge; the difference between the ontological and the epistemological version is only that, in the first case, contingency is part of this reality itself, whereas in the second case, reality is wholly determined by necessity. In contrast to both these versions, Hegel affirms the basic thesis of speculative idealism: the process of knowledge – that is, our comprehending the object – is not something external to the object, but inherently determines its status (as Kant puts it, the conditions of possibility of our experience are also the conditions of possibility of the objects of experience). In other words, contingency does express the incompleteness of our knowledge, but *this incompleteness also ontologically defines the object of knowledge itself* – it bears witness to the fact that the object itself is not yet ontologically 'realized', fully actual. The merely epistemological status of contingency is thus invalidated, without us falling back into ontological *naïveté*: behind the appearance of contingency there is no hidden, not-yet-known necessity, but *only the necessity of the very appearance that, behind superficial contingency, there is an underlying substantial necessity* – as in the case of anti-Semitism, where the ultimate appearance is the very appearance of the underlying necessity: that is, the appearance that, behind the series of actual features (unemployment, moral disintegration . . .), there is the hidden necessity of the 'Jewish plot'. Therein consists the Hegelian inversion of 'external' into 'absolute' reflection: in external reflection, appearance is the elusive surface concealing its hidden necessity, whereas in absolute reflection, appearance is the appearance of this very (unknown) Necessity behind contingency. Or, to make use of an even more 'Hegelian' speculative formulation, if contingency is an appearance concealing some hidden necessity, then this necessity is *stricto sensu an appearance of itself*.

This inherent antagonism of the relationship between contingency and necessity offers an exemplary case of the Hegelian triad: first the 'naïve' ontological conception which locates the difference in things themselves (some events are in themselves contingent, others necessary), then the attitude of 'external reflection' which conceives of this difference as purely epistemo-logical – that is, dependent upon the incompleteness of our knowledge (we experience as 'contingent' an even when the complete causal chain that produced it remains beyond our grasp), and, finally – what? What is the third term besides the seemingly exhaustive choice between ontology and epistemology? *The very relationship between possibility* (qua *subjective seizing of actuality*) *and actuality* (qua *the object of conceptual seizing*). Both contingency and necessity are categories which express the dialectical unity of actual and possible; they are to be distinguished only in so far as contingency designates this unity conceived in the mode of subjectivity, of the 'absolute unrest' of becoming, of the split between subject and object, and 'necessity' this same content conceived in the mode of objectivity, of determinate being, of the identity of subject and object, of the rest of the Result.[15] In short, we are again at the category of pure *formal conversion*; the change concerns only the modality of form: 'This *absolute unrest* of the *becoming* of these two determinations is *contingency*. But just because each immediately turns into its opposite, equally in this other it simply *unites with itself*, and this identity of both, of one in the other, is *necessity*.'[16]

Hegel's counter-position here was adopted by Kierkegaard, in his notion of the two different modalities of observing a process: from the standpoint of 'becoming' and from the standpoint of 'being'.[17] 'After the fact', history can always be read as a process governed by laws – that is, as a meaningful succession of stages; however, in so far as we are history's agents, embedded, caught in the process, the situation appears – at least at the turning-points when 'something is happening' – open, undecidable, far from the exposition of an underlying necessity. We must bear in mind here the lesson on the mediation of the subjective attitude with objectivity: we cannot reduce one perspective to another by claiming, for example, that the 'true' picture is that of necessity discovered by the 'backward view', that freedom is just an illusion of the immediate agents who overlook how their activity is a small wheel within the large causal mechanism; or, conversely, by embracing a kind of Sartrean existentialist perspective and affirming the subject's ultimate autonomy and freedom, conceiving the appearance of determinism as the later 'practico-inert' objectivization of the subject's spontaneous praxis. In both cases, the onto-logical unity of the universe is saved, whether in the form of substantial necessity pulling the strings behind the subject's back, or in the form of the subject's autonomous activity 'objectivizing' itself in substantial unity. What gets lost is the ontological scandal of the ultimate *undecidability* between the two choices. Here Hegel is far more subversive than Kierkegaard, who escapes the deadlock by giving preference to possibility over actuality, and thus announces the Bergsonian notion of actuality *qua* mechanical congelation of the life-process.[18]

In this undecidability lies the ultimate ambiguity of Hegel's philosophy, the index of an impossibility by way of which it 'touches the real': how are we to conceive of the dialectical re-collection?[19] Is it a retroactive glance enabling us to discern the contours of inner necessity, where the view immersed in the events can only perceive an interplay of accidents – that is, as the 'sublation' (*Aufhebung*) of this interplay of accidents in underlying logical necessity? Or is it, on the contrary, a glance enabling us to resuscitate the openness of the situation, its 'possibility', its irreducible contingency, in what afterwards, from objective distance, appears as a necessary objective process? And does not this undecidability bring us back to our starting point: is not this ambiguity again the way sexual difference is inscribed into the very core of Hegel's logic?

In so far as the relationship between contingency and necessity is that of becoming and being, it is legitimate to conceive of *objet a*, this pure semblance, as a kind of 'anticipation' of being from the perspective of becoming. That is to say, Hegel conceives of matter as correlative to incomplete form: that is, to form which still is a 'mere form', a mere anticipation of itself *qua* complete form. In this precise sense, it can be said that object a designates that remainder of matter which bears witness to the fact that form did not yet fully realize itself, that it did not become actual as the concrete determination of the object, that it remains a mere anticipation of itself. The spatial anamorphosis has to be supplemented here by the temporal anamorphosis (what is anticipation if not a temporal anamorphosis in which we produce an image of the object distorted by the hasty, overtaking glance?). Spatially, *a* is an object whose proper contours are discernible only if we glimpse it askance; it is for ever indiscernible to the straightforward look.[20] Temporally, it is an object which exists only *qua* anticipated or lost, only in the modality of not-yet or not-anymore, never in the 'now' of a pure, undivided present. Kant's transcendental object (his term for *a*) is therefore a kind of *mirage* which gives body to the inequality of the form to itself, not an index of the surplus of the material in-itself over form.

What we encounter here is again the ultimate ambiguity of Hegel. According to the standard *doxa*, the telos of the dialectical process is the absolute form that abolishes any material surplus. If, however, this is truly the case with Hegel, how are we to account for the fact that the Result effectively throws us back into the whirlpool, that it is nothing but the totality of the route we had to travel in order to arrive at the Result? In other words, is not a kind of leap from 'not-yet' to 'always-already' constitutive of the Hegelian dialectics: we endeavour to approach the Goal (the absolute form devoid of any matter), when, all of a sudden, we establish that all the time we were already there? Is not the crucial shift in a dialectical process the reversal of anticipation – not into its fulfilment, but – into retroaction? If, therefore, the fulfilment never occurs in the Present, does this not testify to the irreducible status of *objet a*?

Actuality of the Possible

The ontological background of this leap from 'not-yet' to 'always-already' is a kind of 'trading of places' between possibility and actuality: possibility itself, in its very opposition to actuality, possesses an actuality of its own – in what precise sense? Hegel always insists on the absolute primacy of actuality: true, the search for the 'conditions of possibility' abstracts from the actual, calls it into question, in order to (re)constitute it on a rational basis; yet in all these ruminations actuality is presupposed as something given. In other words, nothing is stranger to Hegel than Leibnizian speculation about the multitude of possible worlds out of which the Creator picks out the best: speculation on possible universes always takes place against the background of the hard fact of actual existence. On the other hand, there is always something traumatic about the raw factuality of what we encounter as 'actual'; actuality is always marked by an indelible brand of the (Real as) 'impossible'. The shift from actuality to possibility, the suspension of actuality through enquiry into its possibility, is therefore ultimately an endeavour to avoid the trauma of the Real: that is, to integrate the real by means of conceiving it as something that is meaningful within our symbolic universe.[21]

Of course, this squaring of the circle of possible and actual (i.e., first the suspension of actuality and then its derivation from the conceptual possibility) never works out, as proved by the very category of contingency: 'contingency' designates an actual content in so far as it cannot be wholly grounded in its conceptual conditions of possibility. According to philosophical common sense, contingency and necessity are the two modalities of actuality: something actual is necessary in so far as its contrary is not possible; it is contingent in so far as its contrary is also possible (in so far as things could also have turned out otherwise). The problem, however, resides in the inherent antagonism that pertains to the notion of possibility: possibility designates something 'possible' in the sense of being able to actualize itself, as well as something 'merely possible' as opposed to being actual. This inner split finds its clearest expression perhaps in the diametrically opposed roles played by the notion of possibility in moral argumentation. On the one hand, we have the 'empty possibility', the external excuse of the weak: 'If I really wanted to, I could have . . . (stopped smoking, etc.).' In challenging this claim, Hegel again and again points out how the true nature of a possibility (is it a true possibility or a mere empty presumption?) is confirmed only by way of its actualization: the only effective proof that you really can do something is simply to do it. On the other hand, the possibility of acting differently exerts pressure on us in the guise of the 'voice of conscience': when I offer the usual excuses ('I did all that was possible, there was no choice'), the superego voice keeps gnawing at me, 'No, you could have done more!' This is what Kant has in mind when he insists that freedom is actual already as possibility: when I gave way to pathological impulses and did not carry out my duty, the *actuality* of my freedom is attested to by my awareness of how I *could have* acted otherwise.[22] And this is also what Hegel aims at when maintaining that the actual (*das Wirkliche*) is not the same as that which simply exists (*das Bestehende*): my conscience pricks me when my act (of giving way to pathological impulses) was not 'actual', did not express my true moral nature; this difference exerts pressure on me in the guise of 'conscience'.

One can discern the same logic behind the recent revival of the conspiracy theory (Oliver Stone's *JFK*): who was behind Kennedy's murder? The ideological cathexis of this revival is clear: Kennedy's murder acquired such traumatic dimensions retroactively, from the later experience of the Vietnam War, of the Nixon administration's cynical corruption, of the revolt of the sixties that opened up the gap between the young generation and the establishment. This later experience transformed Kennedy into a person who, had he remained alive, would have spared us Vietnam, the gap separating the sixties generation from the establishment, etc. (What the conspiracy theory 'represses', of course, is the painful fact of Kennedy's *impotence*: Kennedy himself would not have been able to prevent the emergence of this gap.) The conspiracy theory thus keeps alive the dream of another America, different from the one we came to know in the seventies and eighties.[23]

Hegel's position with regard to the relationship of possibility and actuality is thus very refined and precise: possibility is simultaneously less and more than what its notion implies; conceived in its abstract opposition to actuality, it is a 'mere possibility', and, as such, it coincides with its opposite, with impossibility. On another level, however, possibility already possesses a certain actuality *in its very capacity of possibility*, which is why any further demand for its actualization is superfluous. In this sense, Hegel points out that the idea of freedom realizes itself through a series of failures: every particular attempt to realize freedom may fail; from its point of view, freedom remains an empty possibility; but the very continuous striving of freedom to realize itself bears witness to its 'actuality' – that is, to the fact that freedom is not a 'mere notion', but manifests a tendency that pertains to the very essence of reality. On the other hand, the supreme case of 'mere possibility' is the Hegelian 'abstract universal'; what I have in mind here is the well-known paradox of the relationship between universal judgement and judgement of existence in the classical Aristotelian syllogism: judgement of existence implies the existence of its subject, whereas universal judgement can also be true even if its subject does not exist, since it concerns only the notion of the subject. If, for example, one says 'At least one man is (or: some men are) mortal', this judgement is true only if at least one man exists; if, on the contrary, one says 'A unicorn has only one horn', this judgement remains true even if there are no unicorns, since it concerns solely the immanent determination of the notion of 'unicorn'. Far from its relevance being limited to pure theoretical ruminations, this gap between the Universal and the Particular has palpable material effects – in politics, for example. According to the results of a public opinion poll in the autumn of 1991, in the choice between Bush and a non-specified Democratic candidate, the non-specified Democrat would win easily; however, in the choice between Bush and any concrete, individual Democrat, provided with face and name (Kerry, Cuomo . . .), Bush would have an easy win. In short, the Democrat in general wins over Bush, whereas Bush wins over any concrete Democrat. To the misfortune of the Democrats, there was no 'Democrat in general'.[24]

The status of possibility, while different from that of actuality, is thus not simply deficient with regard to it. *Possibility as such exerts actual effects which disappear as soon as it 'actualizes' itself.* Such a 'short circuit' between possibility and actuality is at work in the Lacanian notion of 'symbolic castration': the so-called castration anxiety cannot be reduced to the psychological fact that, upon perceiving the absence of the penis in woman, man becomes afraid that 'he also might lose it'.[25] 'Castration anxiety' rather designates the precise moment at which the possibility of castration takes precedence over its actuality: that is, the moment at which the very possibility of castration, its mere threat, produces actual effects in our psychic economy. This threat as it were 'castrates' us, branding us with an irreducible loss. And it is this same 'short circuit' between possibility and actuality which defines the very notion of power: power is *actually* exerted only in the guise of a *potential* threat – that is, only in so far as it does not strike fully but 'keeps itself in reserve'.[26] Suffice it to recall the logic of paternal authority: the moment a father loses control and displays his full power (starts to shout, to beat a child), we necessarily perceive this display as impotent rage: that is, as an index of its very opposite. In this precise sense, symbolic authority always, by definition, hinges on an irreducible potentiality possibility, on the actuality effectivity that pertains to possibility *qua* possibility: we leave behind the 'raw', pre-symbolic Real and enter the symbolic universe the moment possibility acquires actuality of its own. (This paradox is at work in the Hegelian struggle for recognition between the (future) Lord and Bondsman: to say that the impasse of their struggle is resolved by way of the Lord's *symbolic* victory and the Bondsman's *symbolic* death equals saying that the mere *possibility* of victory is sufficient. The symbolic pact at work in their struggle enables them to stop before the actual physical destruction, and to accept the possibility of victory as its actuality). The Master's potential threat is far worse than his actual display of power. This is what Bentham counts on in his fantasy-matrix of Panopticon: the fact that the Other – the gaze in the central observing tower – *can* watch me; my radical uncertainty as to whether I am being observed or not at any precise moment gives rise to an anxiety far greater than that aroused by the awareness that I am actually observed. This surplus of what is 'in the possibility more than a mere possibility' and which gets lost in its actualization is *the real qua impossible.*[27]

It is precisely on account of this potential character of his power that a Master is always, by definition, an impostor: that is, somebody who illegitimately occupies the place of the lack in the Other (the symbolic order). In other words, the emergence of the figure of the Master is of a strictly *metonymical* nature: a Master never fully 'measures up to its notion', to Death *qua* 'absolute Master' (Hegel). He remains for ever the 'metonymy of Death'; his whole consistency hinges upon the deferral, the keeping-in-reserve, of a force that he falsely claims to possess.[28] It would be wrong, however, to conclude – from the fact that anyone who occupies the place of the Master is an impostor and a clown – that the perceived imperfections of the Master subvert his authority. The whole artifice of 'playing a Master' consists in knowing how to use this very gap (between the 'notion' of the Master and its empirical bearer) to our advantage: the way for a Master to strengthen his authority is precisely to present himself as 'human like the rest of us', full of little weaknesses, a person with whom it is quite possible to 'talk normally' when he is not compelled to give voice to authority. At a different level, this dialectic was widely exploited by the Catholic Church, which was always ready to condone small infringements if they stabilized the reign of Law: prostitution, pornography, etc., are sins; yet not only can they be pardoned, they can be commended if they help preserve marriage: better a periodic visit to a brothel than divorce.[29]

This primacy of possibility over actuality enables us also to articulate the difference between the phallic signifier and the fetish. This difference may seem elusive since, in both cases, we have to do with a 'reflective' element which supplements a primordial lack (the fetish fills out the void of the missing maternal phallus; the phallus is the signifier of the very lack of the signifier). However, as the signifier of pure possibility, the phallus is never fully actualized (i.e. it is the empty signifier which, although devoid of any determinate, positive meaning, stands for the potentiality of any possible future meaning); whereas a fetish always claims an actual status (i.e. it pretends actually to substitute for the maternal phallus). In other words, in so far as a fetish is an element that fills in the lack of (the maternal) phallus, the most concise definition of the phallic signifier is that it is a *fetish of itself*: phallus *qua* '*signifier of castration*' as it were gives body to *its own lack*.

Notes

1 Karl Marx, 'Eighteenth Brumaire of Louis Bonaparte', in Karl Marx and Friedrich Engels, *Collected Works* (London, Lawrence and Wishart, 1975), vol. 2, p. 103.

2 In his reference to the Hegelian Beautiful Soul, Lacan makes a deeply significant mistake by condensing two different 'figures of consciousness': he speaks of the *Beautiful Soul* who, in the name of her *Law of the Heart*, rebels against the injustices of the world (see, e.g., *Écrits: A Selection*, trans. Alan Sheridan (London, Tavistock Publications, 1977), p. 80). With Hegel, however, the 'Beautiful Soul' and the 'Law of the Heart' are two quite distinct figures: the first designates *the hysterical* attitude of deploring the wicked ways of the world while actively participating in their reproduction (Lacan is quite justified to apply it to Dora, Freud's exemplary case of hysteria); the 'Law of the Heart and the Frenzy of Self-Conceit', on the other hand, clearly refer to a *psychotic* attitude – to a self-proclaimed Saviour who imagines his inner Law to be the Law of everybody, and is therefore compelled, in order to explain why the 'world' (his social environs) does not follow his precepts, to resort to paranoiac constructions, to some plot of dark forces (like the Enlightened rebel who blames the reactionary clergy's propagating of superstitions for the failure of his efforts to win the support of the people). Lacan's slip is all the more mysterious for the fact that this difference between Beautiful Soul and the Law of the Heart can be perfectly formulated by means of the categories elaborated by Lacan himself: the hysterical Beautiful Soul clearly locates itself within the big Other, and it functions as a demand to the Other within an intersubjective field, whereas the psychotic clinging to the Law of one's Heart involves precisely a rejection, a suspension, of what Hegel referred to as the 'spiritual substance'.

3 Existence in the sense of empirical reality is thus the very opposite of the Lacanian Real: precisely in so far as God does not 'exist' *qua* part of experimental, empirical reality, he belongs to the Real.

4 Lacan, *Le Séminaire, livre xx: Encore* (Paris, Éditions du Seuil, 1975), p. 32.

5 This point was articulated in all its philosophical weight by Georg Lukács in his *History and Class Consciousness* (London, New Left Books, 1969).

6 That Kant himself already had a premonition of this link between existence and self-relating is attested to by the fact that, in the *Critique of Pure Reason*, he conferred on dynamical synthesis (which concerns also existence, not only predicates) regulative character.

7 The role of fantasy in perversion and in neurosis offers an exemplary case of this passage of in-itself into for-itself at work in the psychoanalytic clinic. A pervert immediately 'lives' his fantasy, stages it, which is why he does not entertain toward it a 'reflected' relationship; he does not relate toward it *qua* fantasy. In Hegelian terms: fantasy is not 'posited' as such, it is simply his in-itself. The fantasy of a hysteric, on the other hand, is also a perverse fantasy, but the difference consists not only in the fact that a hysteric relates to it in a reflected, 'mediated' way – *vulgari eloquentia*, that he 'only fantasizes about what a pervert is actually doing'. The

crucial point is rather that, within the hysterical economy, fantasy acquires a different function, becomes part of a delicate intersubjective game: by means of fantasy, a hysteric conceals his or her anxiety, at the same time offering it as a lure to the other for whom the hysterical theatre is staged.

8 This exchangeability could be further exemplified by the ambiguity as to the precise causal status of trauma in psychoanalytic theory: on the one hand, one is fully justified in isolating the 'original trauma' as the ultimate ground which triggered the chain reaction the final result of which is the pathological formation (the symptom); on the other hand, in order for event X to function as 'traumatic' in the first place, the subject's symbolic universe had already to have been structured in a certain way.

9 See Fredric Jameson, 'Reification and Utopia in Mass Culture', in *Signatures of the Visible* (New York, Routledge, 1991).

10 In this precise sense Lacan conceives the master signifier as an 'empty' signifier, a signifier without signified: an empty container which rearranges the previously given content. The signifier 'Jew' does not add any new signified (all its positive signified content is derived from the previously given elements which have nothing whatsoever to do with Jews as such); it just 'converts' them into an expression of Jewishness *qua* ground. One of the consequences to be drawn from it is that, in endeavouring to provide an answer to the question 'Why were precisely Jews picked out to play the scapegoat role in anti-Semitic ideology?', we might easily succumb to the very trap of anti-Semitism, looking for some mysterious feature in them that as it were predestined them for that role: the fact that Jews who were chosen for the role of the 'Jew' ultimately *is* contingent – as is pointed out by the well-known anti-anti-Semitic joke: 'Jews and cyclists are responsible for all our troubles. – Why cyclists? – WHY JEWS?'

11 J. N. Findlay, *Kant and the Transcendental Object* (Oxford, Clarendon Press, 1981), p. 187.

12 Ibid., p. 1.

13 Here, we must be attentive to how a simple symmetrical inversion brings about an asymmetrical, irreversible, non-specular result. That is to say, when the statement 'the Jew is exploitative, intriguing, dirty, lascivious...' is reversed into 'he is exploitative, intriguing, dirty, lascivious..., *because he is Jewish*', we do not state the same content in another way. Something new is produced thereby, the *objet petit a*, that which is 'in Jew more than the Jew himself' and on account of which the Jew is what he phenomenally is. This is what the Hegelian 'return of the thing to itself in its conditions' amounts to: the thing returns to itself when we recognize in its conditions (properties) the effects of a transcendent Ground.

14 As to this exception, see Monique David-Menard, *La Folie dans la raison pure* (Paris, Vrin, 1991), pp. 154–5.

15 This irreducible antagonism of being and becoming thus also provides the matrix for Hegel's solution of the Kantian enigma of the Thing-in-itself: *the Thing-in-itself is in the modality of 'being' what the subject is in the modality of 'becoming'*.

16 *Hegel's Science of Logic* (Atlantic Heights, NJ, Humanities Press International, 1989), p. 545. What we encounter in the tetrad *actuality–possibility–contingency–*

necessity is thus the repetition, on a higher, more concrete, level, of the initial tetrad of *being–nothing–becoming–determinate being*: contingency is the 'passing' of possibility into actuality, whereas necessity designates their stable unity.

17 See ch. 5 of Žižek, *For They Know Not What They Do*, and ch. 3 of Žižek, *Enjoy Your Symptom!*

18 This Kierkegaardian opposition of 'becoming' and 'being' perhaps lurks in the background of Heidegger's recurrent figure apropos of the ontological difference, viz., the tautological verbalization of the substantive: 'worlding of the world', etc. 'Worlding of the world' designates precisely 'world in its becoming', in its possibility, which is not to be conceived as a deficient mode of actuality: ontological difference is the difference between (ontic) actuality and its (ontological) possibility: i.e., that surplus of possibility which gets lost the moment possibility actualizes itself. On another level, the 'ordering of the [political] order' could be said to designate the 'open' process of the formation of a new order, the 'unrest of becoming' (epitomized, in the case of Rumania, by the hole in the centre of the flag, previously occupied by the red star, the Communist symbol) which disappears, becomes invisible, the moment a new order is established via the emergence of a new master-signifier.

19 This undecidability also pertains to Hegel's *Phenomenology of Spirit*: one has only to bear in mind that its close, absolute knowledge coincides with the starting-point of *Logic*, the point without presuppositions, the point of absolute *non-knowledge* in which all one is capable of expressing is the empty being, the form of nothingness. The path of *Phenomenology* thus appears as what it is: *a process of forgetting* – i.e., the very opposite of the gradual, progressive 'remembering' of the Spirit's entire history. *Phenomenology* functions as the 'introduction' to the 'system' proper, in so far as, by way of it, the subject has to learn to obliterate the false fullness of the non-notional (representational) content, all non-reflected presuppositions, in order to be able, finally, to begin from (being which is) nothing. It is against this background that one has to conceive the re-emergence of the term 'skull' on the last page of *Phenomenology*, where Hegel designates its itinerary as 'the Calvary of absolute Spirit' (*Hegel's Phenomenology of Spirit* (Oxford, Oxford University Press, 1977), p. 493). The literal meaning of the German term for Calvary, *Schädelstätte*, is 'the site of skulls'. The infinite judgement 'spirit is a bone (a skull)' acquires thereby a somewhat unexpected dimension: what are revealed to the Spirit in the backwards gaze of its *Er-Innerung*, inwardizing memory, are the scattered skulls of the past 'figures of consciousness'. The worn-out Hegelian formula according to which the Result, in its abstraction from the path leading to it, is a corpse, has to be invested once again: this 'path' itself is punctuated by scattered skulls.

20 See ch. 1 of Žižek, *Looking Awry*.

21 Is not the computer-generated virtual reality an exemplary case of reality conceived through the detour of its virtualization: i.e. of a reality wholly generated from its conditions of possibility?

22 Suffice it to recall here Kant's reflections on the meaning of the French Revolution: the very belief in the *possibility* of a free, rational social order, attested to by

the enthusiastic response of the enlightened public to the French Revolution, witnesses to the *actuality* of freedom, of a tendency toward freedom as an anthropological fact. See Immanuel Kant. *The Conflict of the Faculties* (Lincoln, University of Nebraska Press, 1992), p. 153.

23 This, of course, is a leftist reading of the Kennedy murder conspiracy theory; the reverse of it is that the trauma of Kennedy's death expresses a conservative longing for an authority which is not an imposture – or, to quote one of the commentaries on the anniversary of the Vietnam War: 'Somewhere within the generation now taking power, Vietnam may have installed the suspicion that leadership and authority are a fraud. That view may have subtle stunting effects upon moral growth. If sons don't learn to become fathers, a nation may breed politicians who behave less like full-grown leaders than like inadequate siblings, stepbrothers with problems of their own.' Against this background, it is easy to discern in the Kennedy myth the belief that he was the last 'full-grown leader', the last figure of authority which was not a fraud.

24 Another exemplary case of this paradoxical nature of the relationship between possible and actual is Senator Edward Kennedy's candidacy for presidential nomination in 1990. As long as his candidacy was still in the air, all polls showed him easily winning over any Democratic rival; yet the moment he publicly announced his decision to run for the nomination, his popularity plummeted.

25 What this notion of feminine castration ultimately amounts to is a variation on the notorious old Greek sophism 'What you don't have, you have lost; you don't have horns, so you have lost them'. To avoid the notion that this sophism can be dismissed as inconsequential false reasoning – i.e. to get a presentiment of the existential anxiety that may pertain to its logic – suffice it to recall the Wolf Man, Freud's Russian analysand, who was suffering from a hypochondriacal *idée fixe*: he complained that he was the victim of a nasal injury caused by electrolysis; however, when thorough dermatological examinations established that absolutely nothing was wrong with his nose, this triggered an unbearable anxiety in him: 'Having been told that nothing could be done for his nose because nothing was wrong with it, he felt unable to go on living in what he considered his irreparably mutilated state' (Muriel Gardiner, *The Wolf-Man and Sigmund Freud* (Harmondsworth, Penguin, 1973), p. 287). The logic is here exactly the same as if you do not have horns, you lost them; if nothing can be done, then the loss is irreparable. Within the Lacanian perspective, of course, this sophism points toward the fundamental feature of a structural/differential order: the unbearable absolute lack emerges at the very point when the lack itself is lacking.

26 As to this potentiality that pertains to the very actuality of power, see ch. 5 of Žižek, *For They Know Not What They Do*.

27 Another facet of this dialectical tension between possibility and actuality is the tension between a notion and its actualization: the content of a notion can be actualized only in the form of the notion's failure. Let us recall the recent Robert Harris alternative-history best-seller *Fatherland* (London, Hutchinson, 1992): its action takes place in 1964, with Hitler having won World War II and extending

his empire from the Rhine to the Ural Mountains. The trick the novel pulls is to stage what actually takes place today as the result of Hitler's victory: after his victory, Hitler organized Western Europe into the 'European Community', an economic union with twelve currencies under the domination of the German mark, whose flag consists of yellow stars on blue background (German documents from the early forties actually contain such plans!). The lesson of the novel is therefore that the 'notion' of Nazi Europe realized itself in the guise of the very 'empirical' defeat of Nazism.

28 The key question here is how this problematic of the Master *qua* metonymy of Death is affected by Lacan's later shift toward *jouissance*, which entails the splitting of the paternal figure into the Name-of-the-Father, the pure symbolic authority beyond enjoyment (the big Other is by definition beyond enjoyment – 'the big Other doesn't smell', as we may put it), and the Father-Enjoyment (*le Père-jouissance*): does the obscene Father *qua* Master of Enjoyment still function as 'metonymy of death', or does he rather epitomize 'life beyond death', the immortal, indestructible substance of enjoyment?

29 It is against this background that one is able to measure the subversive effect of a personal feature of Lacan noted by those who knew him. As is well known, he carefully cultivated the image of himself as being unbearable, demanding to the point of cruelty; yet at the same time he appeared witty and eccentric; those who knew him endeavoured to penetrate to the 'true person' behind this public mask, propelled by the desire for the reassuring guarantee that, beneath the mask, Lacan is 'human like the rest of us'. However, they were in for a bad surprise: what awaited them 'behind the mask' was no 'normal warm person', since even in private, Lacan stuck to his public image; he acted in precisely the same way, displaying the same mixture of courtesy and exacting cruelty. The effect of this uncanny coincidence between the public mask and the private person was the exact opposite of what one would expect (obliteration of all private, 'pathological' features; complete identification with the public symbolic role): the public symbolic role itself, as it were, collapsed into pathological idiosyncrasy, turned into a contingent personal tick.

11

Schelling-in-Itself: 'The Orgasm of Forces'

This extract is from *The Abyss of Freedom/Ages of the World* (1997, pp. 8–12, 14–18, 37–44, 94–5). Žižek here engages with the thought of the German Idealist philosopher F. W. J. Schelling, who produced a religio-metaphysical myth for the emergence of the rational order from an original chaos that anticipates Lacan's account of the relation of Real to Symbolic.

In Schelling's myth of creation, there is an originary divine 'vortex of drives', a dark undifferentiated freedom, out of which, by an act of differentiation (*Ent-Scheidung*, 'parting away from'), God produces himself as subject by means of '*logos*–light–desire': the Word, in conferring intentionality, transforms the 'rotary motion' into a 'linear progress' in time. Human history then repeats this transformation, passing from the cyclical rises and falls of the early pagan empires to the steady advance of the Christian epoch towards the Absolute ideal. What is here inadvertently indicated is the change within the Christian epoch from the feudal community with its self-enclosed tradition to the 'progressive' world of capitalism, the nostalgic resistance to which Fredric Jameson has located as the utopian ground of all narrative. Žižek's Lacanian reading of this myth is to see the shift from vortex to *logos* as the constitutive moment of the formation of the subject within language. The pulsations of drive, expanding and contracting, undergo a paradoxical restriction in which the emerging subject simultaneously finds itself inside and outside a boundary: the energy of the pulsations is trapped by the Word into acceptance of a limitation that creates an expansion, producing a subject able to see itself from outside at the moment it suffers a contraction of its force inside.

Žižek reads this as the Lacanian moment of symbolic castration, a 'primordial dissonance', in which the phallus is a 'something' standing for 'nothing', as the master-signifier that shows what is the case with all words, that in designating a presence they refer to an absence. With this crux the subject is faced with a 'forced choice': on the side of the drive, it cannot speak; on the side of the Word, it cannot be. In coming into being as subjects, we exchange the antagonism of the expansions and contractions of the drive for the contradictions of language; the vortex is exchanged for 'symbolic identity-and-difference'. Identity is first acquired piecemeal, crucially through an identification which is partial, picked up randomly as a 'unary trait' (Freud) to be turned into an ideal distinguishing mark. But the gain of symbolic identification is at the price of traumatic loss, or, in Schellingian terms, 'The God-Absolute becomes inexpressible at the very moment He expresses Himself in language'. The castration enforced by language bestows identity at the price of leaving an 'inexpressible' remainder: the drive is condemned to circle endlessly around the *objet a*, the fantasy of the restoration of the subject's loss.

This remainder cannot be accounted for in terms of a primordial experiential ground which no reflection can capture, but can only be grasped as the symbolic contradicting itself in its originary structure, revealed in the paradoxes (such as Zeno's) that result the moment the symbolic tries to reflect upon itself. We can neither arrive at a 'pre-reflective In-itself' nor reflect on our reflection, an aporia (articulated by Merleau-Ponty) that coincides with the Hegelian formulation that in the passage from a 'positing' to an 'external' standpoint (from subjective to objective), reflection is driven back to attempting, impossibly, to get outside itself. In the no-man's-land between positing and external reflection, Schelling lodges the images that God entertains in his mind before he creates the things of the world. Like temptations before their enactment, they play out their ghostly non-existence, having only a virtual reality while awaiting their actual use in the world in a structure of signification.

Whereas the virtual reality of ideas has a Platonic timeless necessity, the enigma of freedom emerges when they are taken up by subjects in the world. For Schelling it is freedom, rather than natural necessity, that is primordial, so that the human subject preserves from this *Urgrund* the possibility of throwing off its causal chains. Here Schelling confronts the aporia of free will versus determinism, and asks how the infinite God intervenes in the finite world; he thereby gets entangled in the problem of God's responsibility for evil. In an unusual move, Schelling rejects the notion of a Fall, rather seeing creation as a beginning in which God escapes from the 'divine madness' of the vortex of drives in order to find himself in symbolic difference. God's progress takes the form of an 'enchainment of polarities', in which the tension between opposite powers is continually resolved at higher and higher levels, but, in the struggle between ideal and real, matter is illumined into self-awareness rather than cast aside. This produces an irremediable tension in the human subject between the spiritual and the material, leaving it with a homelessness, finally cured only in death: here Schelling anticipates the modern split subject.

A System of Freedom

Schelling's basic insight that, prior to its assertion as the medium of rational Word, the subject is the pure 'night of the Self', the 'infinite lack of being', the violent gesture of contraction that negates every being outside itself, also forms the core of Hegel's notion of madness: when Hegel determines madness as withdrawal from the actual world, the closing of the soul into itself, its 'contraction', the cutting-off of its links with external reality, he all too quickly conceives this withdrawal as a 'regression' to the level of the 'animal soul' still embedded in its natural environs and determined by the rhythm of nature (night and day, etc.). Does this withdrawal, on the contrary, not designate the severing of the links with the *Umwelt*, the end of the subject's immersion in its immediate natural surroundings, and is it as such not the founding gesture of 'humanization'? Was this withdrawal into self not accomplished by Descartes in his universal doubt and reduction to *cogito*, which, as Derrida pointed out in his 'Cogito and the History of Madness',[1] also involves a passage through the moment of radical madness? Are we thus not back at the well-known passage from *Jenenser Realphilosophie*, where Hegel characterizes the experience of pure Self qua 'abstract negativity', the 'eclipse of (constituted) reality', the contraction into self of the subject, as the 'night of the world':

The human being is this night, this empty nothing, that contains everything in its simplicity – an unending wealth of many representations, images, of which none happens to him – or which are not present. This night, the inner of nature, that exists here – pure self – in phantasmagorical presentations, is night all around it, in which here shoots a bloody head – there another white shape, suddenly here before it, and just so disappears. One catches sight of this night when one looks human beings in the eye – into a night that becomes awful.[2]

And the symbolic order, the universe of the Word, *logos*, can emerge only from the experience of this abyss. As Hegel puts it, this inwardness of the pure self 'must enter also into existence, become an object, oppose itself to this innerness to be external; return to being. This is language as name-giving power.... Through the name the object as individual entity is born out of the I.'[3] What we must be careful not to miss here is how Hegel's break with the Enlightenment tradition can be discerned in the reversal of the very metaphor for the subject: the subject is no longer the Light of Reason opposed to the non-transparent, impenetrable Stuff (of Nature, Tradition...); his very kernel, the gesture that opens up the space for the Light of Logos, is absolute negativity qua 'night of the world', the point of utter madness in which fantasmatic apparitions of 'partial objects' wander around. Consequently, there is no subjectivity without this gesture of withdrawal, which is why Hegel is fully justified in inverting the standard question of how the fall regression into madness is possible: the true question is, rather, how the subject is able to climb out of madness and to reach 'normalcy'. That is to say, the withdrawal into self, the cutting-off of the links to the *Umwelt*, is followed by the construction of a symbolic universe that the subject projects on to reality as a kind of substitute-formation destined to recompense us for the loss of the immediate, pre-symbolic Real. However, as Freud himself asserted apropos of Schreber, is not the manufacturing of a substitute-formation that recompenses the subject for the loss of reality the most succinct definition of paranoiac construction as an attempt to cure the subject of the disintegration of his universe? In short, the ontological necessity of 'madness' resides in the fact that it is not possible to pass directly from the purely 'animal soul' immersed in its natural life-world to 'normal' subjectivity dwelling in its symbolic universe – the vanishing mediator between the two is the 'mad' gesture of radical withdrawal from reality that opens up the space for its symbolic (re)constitution. It was already Hegel who emphasized the radical ambiguity of the statement 'What I think, the product of my thought, is objectively true.' This statement is a speculative proposition that renders simultaneously the 'lowest truth', the erratic attitude of the madman caught in his self-enclosed universe, unable to relate to reality, *and* the 'highest truth', the truth of speculative idealism, the identity of thought and being. If, therefore, in this precise sense, as Lacan put it, normalcy itself is a mode, a subspecies of psychosis – that is, if the difference between 'normalcy' and madness is inherent in madness – in what does this difference between the 'mad' (paranoiac) construction and the 'normal' (social construction of) reality consist? Is 'normalcy' ultimately not merely a more 'mediated' form of madness? Or, as Schelling put it, is normal Reason not merely 'regulated madness'?

Hegel's notion of the 'night of the world' as the feminine kernel of subjectivity is thus profoundly 'Schellingian', in that it subverts the simple opposition between the Light of Reason and the impenetrable darkness of matter. Its ultimate consequence is that the emergence of reality, of the universe as such, is grounded in a fundamental and irreducible inversion/perversion of the 'proper' relationship between ontological forces – if their relationship were to be 'set straight', reality as such would disintegrate. Schelling sticks to this fundamental insight of *Weltalter* up to his late philosophy of mythology and revelation: the universe as such (the actual world) is the result of an original inversion/perversion of divine 'potencies': 'reality' emerges when the harmonious balance between the three primordial divine potencies (A^1, A^2, A^3) is disturbed: that is, when the first potency (A^1), which should serve as the passive ground for the other, higher potencies, usurps the leading place and thus changes from a benevolent enabling force, effective from the background, to an egoistic contractive force, destructive of every otherness. It is only through this perversion/inversion of potencies that the passage from mere potentiality to actuality can occur – the realm of harmony prior to the perversion of potencies is a realm of pure potentiality that lacks the firmness of actual being. Therein resides the great insight of German Idealism: the real, material world is not merely a (distorted) reflection of suprasensible Ideas in the mode of Plotinus's emanation, but involves a violent reversal of the proper hierarchical relation between Ideas. Schelling's name for this reversal is the force of egoism, of contractive Self-sameness (*Ichheit, Selbstheit*), that provides the firm ground of reality: this Self-sameness is neither passive matter nor universal notional content, but the active force of absolute contraction to a point of self-relating that can occur only in the sphere of the Spirit – matter cannot absolutely contract itself into itself, since it has its centre of gravity *outside* itself (as is proved by the phenomenon of gravity). In short, Schelling's crucial point is that the domain of Ideas becomes actual Spirit only through its 'egoist' perversion/inversion, in the guise of the absolute contraction into a real Person. One must be careful not to miss the point here: it is not only that what we experience as 'material reality' is the perversion/inversion of the true ideal order; reality emerges in so far as the true ideal order gets inverted in itself, runs amok – in Schelling's terms, *the inertia of external material reality is a proof of the divine madness, of the fact that God himself was 'out of his mind'*. (What Schelling is not ready to accept is the logical consequence of his reasoning: this perversion is unsurpassable, the Spirit in its actuality is irreducibly 'out of joint', the stain of perversion is the unavoidable price for the Spirit's actualization – the notion of a Reconciliation that would 'sublate' the contractive force of egoism in the ethereal medium of Spirit is purely fantasmatic, even when it puts on the technological dress of Virtual Reality and presents itself as the dream of cutting links with our material body and wandering freely in cyberspace.)

This perversion of the 'proper' hierarchical relationship between potencies is the key feature of the German Idealist notion of a philosophical 'system'. In so far as this perversion is a free act, the most elementary manifestation of freedom, one can see where the standard reproach (a topos from Kierkegaard to Heidegger), according to which the weak point of Schelling's essay on freedom is that it tries to think together what is incompatible (i.e. freedom and system), falls short. 'System', in the precise sense of German Idealism, is a totality that is all-encompassing, since it includes/contains its own inversion: in a 'system', the relationship between A and B, the 'higher' and the 'lower' principle, is only fully actualized when, within the domain of B, their proper relationship is inverted: that is, A itself is subordinated to B. We can also see in what sense the notion of system is strictly equivalent to the project of conceiving the Absolute 'not only as Substance, but also as Subject', as Hegel put it: the principle of subjectivity means that what is originally a subordinate moment of the Absolute can posit itself as its own Centre and subordinate to itself its own substantial presuppositions. Or, to put it in more popular terms, the gesture of the subject *par excellence* is that of wilfully putting at stake the entire substantial content for a capricious meaningless detail: 'I want *this*, even if the whole world goes down.' Therein resides what Hegel calls the 'infinite right of subjectivity': the subject's freedom has to actualize itself *against* Substance, and it can do so only by way of elevating a contingent, meaningless particular moment that the subject posits as its embodiment, over the entire substantial content.

This inclusion of the inversion of the 'proper' relationship is not only the key feature of Schelling's notion of freedom (as the freedom for good *and* evil, i.e. the freedom to invert the proper relationship), but also Fichte's and Hegel's, and even Kant's. Is not the aim of Fichte's 'doctrine of science' to explain how the subject at the transcendental level, the pure I, which 'posits' the entire objective content, experiences itself as passively determined by the universe of objectivity, how the proper relationship between Subject and Object is inverted? Is not the whole point of Hegel's theory of 'alienation' to explain how the product of social activity is reified into an autonomous substantial content that subordinates to itself its own generative force? And do we not encounter the same inversion in the fundamental Kantian deadlock that resides in the overlapping of the condition of impossibility (the inaccessibility of the noumenal realm to finite human conscience) with the condition of possibility (humanity can act morally, out of Duty, only in so far as the noumenal realm is inaccessible to human beings) – humanity's limitation to finitude, that is, the very condition that prevents it from ever being able to fulfil its ethical destination, is at the same time a positive condition of its ethical activity? *Subject, freedom* and *system* are thus three names for the same gesture of inversion.

Drives and their Rotary Motion

How, then, does Schelling succeed in accounting for this inherent inversion of the Absolute? Perhaps the most appropriate way is by focusing on the *problem of Beginning*, the crucial problem of German Idealism – suffice it to recall Hegel's detailed elaboration of this problem and all its implications in his *Science of Logic*. Schelling's fundamental thesis is that, to put it bluntly, *the true Beginning is not at the beginning*: there is something that precedes the Beginning itself – a rotary motion whose vicious cycle is broken, in a gesture analogous to the cutting of the Gordian knot, by the Beginning proper, that is, the primordial act of decision. The beginning of all beginnings is, of course, the 'In the beginning was the Word' from the Gospel according to St John: prior to it, there was nothing, that is, the void of divine eternity. According to Schelling, however, 'eternity' is not a nondescript bulk – a lot of things take place in it. Prior to the Word there is the chaotic-psychotic universe of blind drives, of their rotary motion, of their undifferentiated pulsating, and the Beginning occurs when the Word is pronounced that 'represses', rejects into the eternal Past, this self-enclosed circuit of drives. In short, *at the Beginning proper stands a resolution, an act of decision that, by way of differentiating between past and present, resolves the preceding unbearable tension of the rotary motion of drives*: the true Beginning is the passage from the 'closed' rotary motion to the 'open' progress, from drive to desire, or, in Lacanian terms, from the Real to the Symbolic. The beginning occurs when one 'finds the word' that breaks the deadlock, the vicious cycle, of empty and confused ruminations.

In this precise sense, the problem of the Beginning is the problem of 'phenomenalization': how does it happen that God pronounces the Word and thereby discloses himself, appears to himself? We must be careful not to miss this crucial point: as with Hegel, the problem is not how to attain the noumenal In-itself beyond phenomena; the true problem is how and why at all does this In-itself split itself from itself; how does it acquire a distance toward itself and thus clear the space in which it can appear (to itself).

How, then, can this phenomenalization of God, this pronunciation of the Word in him that magically, in an unfathomable way, dispels the impenetrable darkness of drives, occur? *It can only occur on condition that the rotary motion of drives that precedes the Beginning is itself not the primordial, unsurpassable fact.* That is to say, the notion of the vortex of drives as the ultimate foundation, the 'origin of all things', renders inconceivable the fact of freedom: how can a Word emerge out of this vortex and dominate it, confer on it its shape, 'discipline' it? Consequently, this ultimate Ground of reality, the primordial vortex of drives, this Wheel of Fate that sooner or later engulfs and destroys every determinate object, must be preceded by an unfathomable X that in a way yet to be explained 'contracts' drives. Is the primordial vortex of drives, however, not the ultimate ground that nothing can precede? Schelling would entirely agree with that, adding only that the point in question is precisely the exact status of this 'nothing': prior to *Grund*, there can only be an abyss (*Ungrund*); that is, far from being a mere *nihil privativum*, this 'nothing' that precedes Ground stands for the 'absolute indifference' *qua* the abyss of pure Freedom that is not yet the predicate-property of some Subject, but rather designates a pure impersonal Willing (*Wollen*) that wills nothing. At the outset of his 'prehistory', prior to the Beginning itself, God unavoidably, of the blind necessity that characterizes the workings of Fate (according to the first draft of *Weltalter*), 'contracts' Being – that is, a firm, impenetrable Ground. (Schelling, of course, plays upon the double meaning of the term 'contraction': to tighten-compress-condense *and* to catch, to be afflicted with, to go down with (an illness); the primordial Freedom 'contracts' Being as a painful burden that ties it down.) Prior to this primordial contraction, to this act of engendering ejecting one's Ground, God is, as Schelling puts it in an unsurpassed way in the second draft of *Weltalter*, a pure Nothingness that 'rejoices in its nonbeing'.[4]

God *qua* pure Freedom that hasn't yet contracted being thus *stricto sensu* doesn't exist. The spontaneous, self-generated 'breach of symmetry' (we are tempted to say: the primordial 'vacuum fluctuation', which sets in motion the development of the Absolute) is the primordial contraction by means of which God acquires being. This contraction of/into being is necessarily followed by a counter-stroke of expansion – why? Let us step back for a moment and reformulate the primordial contraction in terms of the passage from a self-contented Will that wants nothing to an actual Will that effectively wants something. The pure potentiality of the primordial Freedom, this blissful tranquillity, this pure enjoyment, of an unassertive, neutral *Will that wants nothing* actualizes itself in the guise of a *Will that actively, effectively, wants this 'nothing'* – that is, the annihilation of every positive, determinate content. By means of this purely formal conversion of potentiality into actuality, the blissful peace of primordial Freedom thus changes into pure contraction, into the vortex of 'divine madness' that threatens to swallow everything, into the highest affirmation of God's egoism, which tolerates nothing outside itself. In other words, the blissful peace of primordial Freedom and the all-destructive divine fury that sweeps away every determinate content are one and the same thing, only in a different modality: first in the mode of potentiality, then in the mode of actuality: 'the same principle carries and holds us in its ineffectiveness that would consume and destroy us in its effectiveness.'[5] Upon experiencing itself as negative and destructive, the Will opposes itself to itself in the guise of its own inherent counter-pole, the Will that *wants something* – that is, the positive Will to expansion. However, this positive Will's effort to break through the bars of its self-imposed contraction is doomed, since the antagonism of the two Wills, the contractive one and the expansive one, is here *under the dominance, in the power, of contraction*. God, as it were, repeatedly dashes against his own wall: unable to stay within, he follows his urge to break out; yet the more he strives to escape, the more he is caught in his own trap. Perhaps the best metaphor for this rotary motion is a trapped animal who desperately strives to disengage itself from a snare: although every spring only tightens the snare, a blind compulsion leads the animal to make dash after dash, so that it is condemned to an endless repetition of the same gesture. What we have here is Schelling's grandiose, 'Wagnerian' vision of God in the state of an endless 'pleasure in pain', agonizing and struggling with himself, affected by an unbearable anxiety, the vision of a 'psychotic', mad God who is absolutely alone, a One who is 'all' since he tolerates nothing outside himself – a 'wild madness, tearing itself apart'.[6] This rotary motion is horrible, because it is no longer impersonal: God already exists as One, as the Subject who suffers and endures the antagonism of drives. Schelling provides here a precise definition of anxiety: anxiety arises when a subject experiences simultaneously the impossibility of closing itself up, of withdrawing fully into itself, and the impossibility of opening itself up, of admitting an Otherness, so that it is caught in a vicious cycle of pulsation – every attempt at creation-expansion-externalization collapses back into itself. This God is not yet the Creator, since in creation the being (the contracted reality) of an Otherness is posited that possesses a minimal self-consistency and exists *outside* its Creator – this, however, is what God in the fury of his egoism is not prone to tolerate.

As Schelling emphasizes again and again, this all-destructive divine vortex remains even today the innermost base of all reality: 'if we were able to penetrate the exterior of things, we would see that the true stuff of all life and existence is the horrible.'[7] In this sense, all reality involves a fundamental antagonism, and is therefore destined to fall prey to Divine fury, to disappear in the 'orgasm of forces'.[8] 'Reality' is inherently fragile, the result of a balance between contraction and expansion that can, at any moment, explode into one of the extremes. Hogrebe resorts here to an analogy from cinema: if the projection of a film is to give rise to an 'impression of reality' in the spectator, the reel has to run at the proper speed – if it runs too quickly, the movement on the screen gets blurred, and we can no longer discern different objects; if it is too slow, we perceive individual pictures, and the continuity that accounts for the impression we are watching 'real life' gets lost.[9] Therein resides Schelling's fundamental motif: what we experience as 'reality' is constituted and maintains itself through a balance between the two antagonist forces, with the ever-present danger that one of the two sides will 'crack', run out of control, and thus destroy the 'impression of reality'. Is not this speculation confirmed by the premise of contemporary cosmology according to which the 'reality' of our universe hangs in the balance, that is, hinges on the fragile tension between expansion and gravitation? If the expansion were just a little bit stronger, the universe would 'explode', dissipate, and no firm, stable object would form; if, on the contrary, gravitation were a little bit stronger, it would long ago have 'collapsed', fallen in . . .

The Forced Choice of Symbolization

To recapitulate: the crux, the turning point, in the history of the Absolute is the unconscious act of *Ent-Scheidung*, the resolution that, by way of rejecting the vortex of drives, their 'mad dance', into the darkness of the 'eternal Past', establishes the universe of temporal 'progression' dominated by *logos*–light–desire.[10] Contrary to the commonplace according to which Schelling outlined the consequences of the thorough historicization of the Absolute, Schelling's greatest achievement was to *confine* the domain of history, to trace a line of separation between history (the domain of the Word, *logos*) and the non-historical (the rotary motion of drives). Therein resides Schelling's relevance for today's debate on historicism: his notion of the primordial act of decision/differentiation (*Ent-Scheidung*) aims at the gesture that opens up the gap between the inertia of the prehistoric Real and the domain of historicity, of multiple and shifting narrativizations; this act is thus a quasi-transcendental unhistorical condition of possibility and, simultaneously, a condition of the impossibility of historicization. Every 'historicization', every symbolization, has to 're-enact' this gap, this passage from the Real to history. Apropos of Oedipus, for example, it is easy to play the game of historicization and to demonstrate how the oedipal constellation is embedded in a specific patriarchal context, and so forth; it requires a far greater effort of thought to discern, in the very historical contingency of Oedipus, one of the re-enactments of the gap that opens up the horizon of historicity.

What exactly, then, is the relationship between historicization and the Real as its inherent limit? Freud's distinction between 'normal' repression (*Verdrängung*) and the primordial repression (*Ur-Verdrängung*) provides a key to it: the first presupposes the second. That is, for a certain content to be repressed, it is not sufficient for it to be pushed away from the domain of Consciousness/Preconscious – it must also be exposed to some attraction from the Unconscious, from the side of the already repressed. One should translate this opposition into topological terms: every part of the repressed content is 'historicizable'; that is, it should not be stigmatized into the untouchable taboo, since it can be retranslated back into the system Cs/Pcs – everything *except the very form of the Unconscious*, except the empty *place itself* that collects the repressed content. This empty place is created by the primordial repression that relates to 'normal' repression as a kind of transcendental, a priori frame to its empirical, a posteriori content. This gesture of 'primordial repression', of evacuating the place of the Thing, whose psychoanalytic name is *death drive*, cannot be historicized, since it is the non-historical condition of historicity itself. For that reason, *death drive* does not designate the positive content one should directly refer to in order to explain some event ('People kill each other in wars because of the death drive'), but the empty frame within which the game of historicization is taking place: it keeps open the minimal gap, the delay, between an event and the modes of its historicization, of its symbolic inscription; *death drive* stands for the fact that the passage from an event to its historicization is radically contingent, never grounded in the Real itself. (In a similar vein, Derrida speaks of the non-deconstructible conditions of deconstruction.[11])

How is the emergence of Word connected with the pulsating 'rotation' in God, that is, with the interchange of expansion and contraction, of externalization and internalization? How, precisely, does the Word discharge the tension of the rotary motion, how does it mediate the antagonism between the contractive and the expansive force? The Word is a *contraction in the guise of its very opposite, of an expansion*; that is, in pronouncing a word, the subject contracts his being *outside* himself, he 'coagulates' the core of his being in an external *sign*. In the (verbal) sign I *find myself outside myself*, as it were; I posit my unity outside myself, in a signifier that represents me:

It seems universal that every creature that cannot contain itself or draw itself together in its own fullness, draws itself together outside itself, whence, e.g., the elevated miracle of the formation of the word in the mouth belongs, which is a true creation of the full inside when it can no longer remain in itself.[12]

This notion of symbolization (of the pronunciation of Word) as the contraction of the subject outside itself – that is, in the form of its very opposite (of expansion) – announces the structural/differential notion of the signifier as an element whose identity stands for its very opposite (for pure difference): we enter the symbolic order the moment a feature functions as the index of its opposite (the moment the political Leader's hatred – of the 'enemies' – is perceived by his subjects as the very form of appearance of his unlimited love for the People; the moment the apathetic indifference of a *femme fatale* is perceived by her male admirers as the token of her intense passion; etc.). For the very same reason, phallus is for Lacan the 'pure' signifier: it stands for its own opposite. That is, it functions as the signifier of *castration*. The transition from the Real to the Symbolic, from the realm of pre-symbolic antagonism (of contraction and expansion) to the symbolic order in which the network of signifiers is correlated to the field of meaning, can take place only by means of a paradoxical 'pure' signifier, a signifier without signified: in order for the field of meaning to emerge, that is, in order for the series of signifiers to signify *something* (to have a determinate meaning), *there must be a signifier (a 'something') that stands for 'nothing'*, a signifying element whose very presence stands for the absence of meaning (or, rather, for absence *tout court*). This 'nothing', of course, is *the subject itself*, the subject *qua* $ (the Lacanian matheme, designating the subject with all content removed), the empty set, the void that emerges as the result of the contraction in the form of expansion: when I contract myself outside myself, I deprive myself of my substantial content. The formation of the Word is thus the exact opposite of the primordial contraction/abjection by means of which, according to Schelling's Stuttgart Seminars from the same time,[13] God expels – discharges, casts out, rejects out of himself – his real side, the vortex of drives, and thus constitutes himself in his Ideality, as a free subject: the primordial rejection is an act of supreme egoism, since in it, God as it were 'gets rid of the shit in himself' in order to purify and keep for himself the precious spiritual essence of his being; whereas in the formation of the Word, he articulates outside himself – that is, he discloses, (sur)renders – this very ideal-spiritual essence of his being. In this precise sense, the formation of the Word is the supreme act and the paradigmatic case of *creation*: 'creation' means that I reveal, hand over to the Other, the innermost essence of my being.

The problem, of course, is that this second contraction, this original act of creation, this 'drawing together outside itself', is ultimately always unfitting, contingent – it 'betrays' the subject, it represents him inadequately. Here, Schelling already announces the Lacanian problematic of a *vel*, a forced choice that is constitutive of the emergence of the subject: the subject either persists in himself, in his purity, and thereby loses himself in empty expansion, or he gets out of himself, externalizes himself, by way of 'contracting' or 'putting on' a signifying feature, and thereby alienates himself; that is, is no longer what he is, the void of pure, $:

...the subject can never grasp itself *as* what it is, for precisely in attracting itself [*sich-Anziehen*] it *becomes* an other; this is the basic contradiction, we can say the misfortune in all being – for either it *leaves* itself, then it is as nothing, or it attracts-contracts itself, then it is an other and not identical with itself. No longer uninhibited by being as before, but that which has inhibited itself with being, it itself feels this being as alien [*zugezogenes*] and thus contingent.[14]

Therein resides Schelling's reformulation of the classical question, 'Why is there something and not nothing?': in the primordial *vel*, the subject has to decide between 'nothing' (the unground/abyss of freedom that lacks all object-ive being, pure $\mathcal{B}$) and 'something', but always irreducibly in the sense of 'something extra, something additional, something foreign/put on, in a certain respect something contingent'.[15] The dilemma is therefore the following:

either it remains still (remains *as* it is, thus pure subject), then there is no life and it is itself as nothing, or it *wants* itself, then it becomes an other, something not the same as itself, *sui dissimile*. It admittedly wants itself *as* such, but precisely this is impossible in an *immediate* way; in the very wanting itself it already becomes an other and distorts itself.[16]

Everything thus turns around the primordial act by means of which 'nothing' becomes 'something', and Schelling's entire philosophical revolution is con-tained in the assertion that this act that precedes and grounds every necessity is in itself *radically contingent* – for that very reason, it cannot be deduced, inferred, but only retroactively presupposed. This act involves a primordial, radical and irreducible *alienation*, a distortion of the original balance, a constitutive 'out-of-jointedness': 'This whole construction therefore begins with the emergence of the first contingency – which is not identical with itself – it begins with a *dissonance*, and *must* begin this way.'[17] In order to emphasize the non-spontane-ous, 'artificial', 'corrupted' character of this act, Schelling plays on the multiple meanings of the German verb *Anziehen*: being attracted, drawn to something; contracting a disease; putting on some clothing; acting in a false, pretentious way. Apropos of this last feature, Schelling directly evokes what was later (by Jon Elster[18]) conceptualized as 'states which are essentially by-products':

There are certain moral and other qualities that one only has precisely to the extent that one does not have them, as the German language splendidly expresses it to the extent to which one does not put on [*sich anzieht*] those qualities. E.g., true charm is only possible precisely if it does not know about itself, whereas a person who knows of his charm, who puts it on, immediately stops being charming, and if he conducts himself *as* being charming will instead become the opposite.[19]

The implications of this are very radical and far-reaching: every positive feature, every 'something' that we are, is ultimately 'put on' – in short, *fake is original*. At this point, one is used to opposing Schelling to Hegel – that is, to the Hegelian logical necessity of the immanent self-deployment of the absolute Idea. Before yielding to this commonplace, however, it would be worth pausing to consider the fact that Hegel develops a homologous *vel* in his

Phenomenology of Spirit, apropos of the Beautiful Soul and the act. The choice that confronts the subject here is between inactivity and an act that is by definition contingent, branded with a merely subjective content. This contingency of the act disturbs the balance of the (social) Substance in which the subject is embedded; the reaction of the Substance thereby set in motion inexorably leads to the failure of the subject's enterprise. The true, critical, 'materialist' supplement to Schelling is to be sought elsewhere: in Marx, who, in his dialectics of the commodity form, also starts from the need of the abstract universal Value to embody itself in a contingent use-value, to 'put on' a use-value dress, to appear in the form of a use-value; however, as he is quick to add, *at least two* use-values (commodities) are needed if a Value is to express itself, so that the use-value of the first commodity gives body to the Value of the second commodity. And Lacan's definition of the signifier as that which 'represents the subject for another signifier' ultimately amounts to the same assertion of an irreducible duality: if a subject is to be represented by a signifier, there must be a minimal chain of two signifiers, one of which represents the subject for the other.

The crucial point not to be missed here is that, in so far as we are dealing with *Subject*, the 'contraction' in question is no longer the primordial contraction by means of which the original Freedom catches being and thereby gets caught in the rotary motion of contraction and expansion, but the contraction of the subject outside himself, in an external sign, which resolves the tension, the 'inner dispute', of contraction and expansion. The paradox of the Word is therefore that its emergence resolves the tension of the pre-symbolic antagonism, but at a price: the Word, the contraction of the Self outside the Self, involves an irretrievable externalization alienation. With the emergence of the Word, we pass from *antagonism* to the Hegelian *contradiction* between $ and S_1, between the subject and its inadequate symbolic representation. This 'contingency' of the contraction in the Word points toward what, in good old structuralist terms, is called 'the arbitrariness of the signifier': Schelling asserts the irreducible gap between the subject and a signifier the subject has to 'contract' if the subject is to acquire (symbolic) existence: the subject *qua* $ is never adequately represented in a signifier. This 'contradiction' between the subject and a (necessarily, constitutively inadequate) symbolic representation provides the context for Schelling's 'Lacanian' formulation according to which God-Absolute *becomes inexpressible at the very moment he expresses himself*, that is, *pronounces a Word*. Prior to his or her symbolic externalization, the subject cannot be said to be 'inexpressible', since the medium of expression itself is not yet given; or, to invoke Lacan's precise formulation, desire is *non-articulable* precisely as always-already *articulated* in a signifying chain. In this precise sense, 'subject is not substance': it has no substantial positive being 'in itself'; that is, it is caught between 'not yet' and 'no longer'. In other words, the subject never 'is', it 'will have been' – either the subject is *not yet* here, and we still have a pre-subjective bliss, or it is *no longer* here, since there is only a trace of its absence . . .

In short, by means of the Word, the subject finally *finds* itself, comes to itself: it is no longer a mere obscure longing for itself, since, in the Word, the subject directly attains itself, posits itself as such. The price for it, however, is the irretrievable *loss* of the subject's self-identity: the verbal sign that stands for the subject, that is, in which the subject posits itself as self-identical, bears the mark of an irreducible dissonance; it never 'fits' the subject. This paradoxical necessity on account of which the act of returning to oneself, of finding oneself, immediately, in its very actualization, assumes the form of its opposite, of the radical loss of one's self-identity, displays the structure of what Lacan calls 'symbolic castration'. This castration involved in the passage to the Word can also be formulated as the redoubling, the splitting, of an element into itself and its place in the structure. Apropos of the Word, Schelling refers to the medieval logic in which *reduplicatio* designated the operation by means of which a term is no longer conceived *simpliciter*, but is posited *as such*: *reduplicatio* points towards the minimal, constitutive gap that for ever separates an element from its re-marking in the symbolic network. Hogrebe invokes here the difference between an element and its place (*Platz*) in an anonymous structure.[20] Because of this structure of castration, Spirit is supernatural or extra-natural, although it grew out of nature: Nature has an ineradicable tendency to 'speak itself out', it is caught in the search for a Speaker (*die Suche nach dem Sprecher*) whose Word would posit it as such; this Speaker, however, can only be an entity that is itself not natural, not part of nature, but Nature's Other. Or, to put it in a slightly different way, Nature is searching for itself, it strives for itself; but it can only 'find itself', attain itself, *outside itself*, in a medium that is itself not natural. The moment Nature becomes *ein Aussprechliches* (something that can be spoken of in meaningful propositions), it ceases to be the *Aussprechendes* (that which is speaking):[21] the speaking agency is the Spirit *qua* $, the substanceless void of non-Nature, the distance of Nature toward itself. In short, the fundamental paradox of symbolization – the paradox the term 'symbolic castration' aims at recapturing – is that Nature can attain itself, its self-identity, only at the price of radical decentring: it can find itself only in a medium outside itself. A father becomes father 'as such', the bearer of symbolic authority, only in so far as he assumes his 'castration', the difference between himself in the immediate reality of his being and the place in the symbolic structure that guarantees his authority: the father's authority is radically 'decentred' with regard to father *qua* flesh-and-blood person; that is, it is the anonymous structure of the symbolic Law that speaks through him.

Notes

1 See Jacques Derrida, 'Cogito and the History of Madness', in *Writing and Difference* (Chicago, University of Chicago Press, 1978), pp. 31–63.

2 Quoted from Donald Phillip Verene, *Hegel's Recollection* (Albany, NY, SUNY Press, 1985), pp. 7–8.

3 Ibid., p. 8.

4 F. W. J. Schelling, *Die Weltalter*: *Fragmente In den unfassungen von 1811 and 1913*, ed. Manfred Schroeter (Munich, Biederstein, 1946), p. 134; see the translation in Žižek, *Abyss of freedom* p. 132. Significantly, Schelling resorts to the same formulation when, in his *Letters on Dogmatism and Criticism*, he describes the falsehood of a person entertaining the notion of his own death: when indulging in fantasies about one's own death, one always imagines oneself as miraculously surviving one's death and being present at the scene of one's own funeral in the guise of a pure gaze that observes the universe from which one is already absent, relishing the imagined pathetic reactions of the relatives, etc. We are thereby at the fundamental time-loop of fantasy: to be present as a pure gaze prior to one's own conception or decease. Is therefore the God prior to the primordial contraction, this pure gaze that finds enjoyment in contemplating its own non-being, also not a fantasy formation at its purest? Schelling emphasizes again and again that the passage of the pure *Seinkönnen* of the primordial Abyss into the contracted Ground cannot be accounted for or deduced: it can only be described (narrated) *post factum*, after it has already taken place, since we are dealing not with a necessary act but with a free act that could also not have happened – however, does this not amount to an implicit admission of the fact that its status is that of a retroactive fantasy?

5 Ibid., p. 13.

6 F. W. J. Schelling, *Sämtliche Werke*, ed. K. F. A. Schelling (Stuttgart, Cotta, 1856–61), vol. 8, p. 43.

7 Ibid., p. 715.

8 Ibid., p. 712.

9 See Wolfram, Hogrebe, *Prädikation und Genesis* (Frankfurt, Suhrkamp, 1989), p. 100.

10 One can see now why Schelling's philosophy is incompatible with the New Age attitude of Wisdom: wisdom is profound, i.e., it comes *from below*, from the depth of the eternal rotary motion (wisdom expresses itself in statements like 'Everything that is born must die,' 'The wheel of fortune is turning all the time,' etc.), whereas Schelling's endeavour is precisely to break this rotary motion and gain access to the domain of Word that intervenes *from above*.

11 This unhistorical gap that keeps open the space for historicization also allows us to account for the difference between the standard symbolic narrative and the fantasmatic narrative: the standard symbolic narrative remains within the space of historicization, whereas the fantasmatic narrative (of the primordial loss, castra-

tion) endeavours to tell the story of the emergence of the gap of historicization itself, of how the gap (the loss) itself took place.

12 Schelling, *Die Weltalter*, pp. 56–7.
13 See 'Stuttgart Seminars', in *Idealism and the Endgame of Theory: Three Essays by F. W. J. Schelling* (Albany, NY, SUNY Press, 1994), pp. 195–243.
14 F. W. J. Schelling, *On the History of Modern Philosophy* (Cambridge, Cambridge University Press, 1994), p. 115.
15 Ibid.
16 Ibid., p. 116.
17 Ibid.
18 See Jon Elster, *Sour Grapes* (Cambridge, Cambridge University Press, 1982).
19 Schelling, *History of Modern Philosophy*, p. 115.
20 See Hogrebe, *Prädikation und Genesis*, pp. 102–3.
21 Schelling, *Sämtliche Werke*, vol. 8, p. 629.

12

A Hair of the Dog that Bit You

This chapter is from *Lacan's Theory of Discourse: Subject, Structure and Society* (eds Mark Bracher et al. (Albany, NY: Suny Press, 1994), pp. 46–73). It articulates the problem of how to survive an accident: having been accidentally born into language, a birth which constitutes a defining cut, the subject can only endeavour to repair the damage by using language itself. This does not merely entail a struggle with words that continually fail to fit what they refer to, but also a commitment to language as a formal system. The difference shows up in the explication of Lacan's terms 'empty speech' and 'full speech': the opposition is not between inauthentic chatter and a 'full' subjective utterance, but between taking up a formal position and the utterance that it allows. There can be no substantial subjective utterance without a prior commitment to a wounding restriction – a 'symbolic wound'.

The wound testifies to the subject's failure to come up to the Symbolic injunction, bringing the sense that it has already done wrong. Kant's term for this condition is 'Radical Evil', an innate propensity for evil, arising from the very possession of free will. He has another term, 'Diabolical Evil', the performance of evil construed as a duty, a much more disturbing thought, because it makes Good and Evil indistinguishable: this makes the moral law reversible, leaving us at the founding moment, where the abstraction of the Law is completely blank, where Good and Evil impossibly intersect. Witness Don Giovanni, who, from his libertine perspective, ignores his 'pathological' interests (escaping damnation) in refusing to repent. However, there is no place in Kant's scheme for such an 'ethical' evil, for his two classes of Good and Evil are supposed to cover all the ground. 'Diabolical Evil' overlaps with Freud's notion of the 'death drive', in that both work against the tension between duty and pleasure (since the death drive invests the superego with an obscene *jouissance*). But whereas Kant sees freedom of choice as arising through the possibility of succumbing to one's pathological interests, Hegel takes this possibility as established by the 'original sin', a founding act of evil, which the subject cannot help but opt for in an act of suicidal egoism (eating the apple). Good then becomes the effort to restore an organic balance to society. In any case, the result is that 'the status of the subject as such is evil', in that, from the point of view of the Symbolic, the subject can never correspond to its idealized prescriptions. Thus, it is our very inadequacy, the wound, that is the basis of the moral law, and establishes us as ethical beings.

The chiasmic relationship of Good and Evil, whereby a 'free' choice is not a simple either/or, applies also to Kant's distinction between the Beautiful and the Sublime, which cannot just be taken as symbols of the Good and the Law respectively. It is rather that they both stand for aspects of the Law, Beauty as the Law in its function of Ego-Ideal (nature as harmonious), the Sublime in its Superego function (the terror of nature outfaced by the exigencies of the moral Law). The Sublime thus calls forth the possibility of evil as an ethical choice. This paradox is embodied in the figure of Hannibal Lecter in Jonathan Demme's *The Silence of the Lambs*, a 'sublime figure in the strict Kantian sense', for the threat of cannibalization he poses is not as monstrous as that of confronting a Lacanian analyst. Lecter's cruelty, his cannibalism – which includes eating his victims' entrails – stands as a *reductio ad absurdum* of the radical force of the analyst's act, because in insisting that the patient 'traverse' the fundamental fantasy (acknowledge the structural place of the fantasy in his subjecthood), the analyst deprives the patient of the core of his enjoyment: what has covered over the split in the subject is torn away. But, since Lecter offers his 'analysand', Agent Clarice Starling, something in return (the catching of a murderer) for her fundamental fantasy (the crying of the lambs), a *quid pro quo*, he is actually not as cruel as a Lacanian analyst. The notion that a painless cure is attainable (the wishful thinking of the film) is actually shown to be delusive, because there is a price to be paid for the symbolic resolution of trauma. Like Lecter, the analyst can be said to swallow 'the stuff' of a person, since the price for the cure is the analyst's disclosure of the *objet a*, whereby he displays as a mere semblance what maintains the consistency of the subject.

Monstrous apparitions such as Hannibal Lecter allegorize the terror springing from the tenuous hold of the subject upon the Symbolic: the split between the representation and what it endeavours to represent (the noumenon in Kant, the Thing in Lacan) becomes a scandal in post-Kantian philosophy. For Foucault a hallmark of the nineteenth century is that the structure of power and knowledge is distinguished by this failure to represent the unrepresentable Thing; sexuality breaks out through the very speech officially used to conceal it. Žižek illustrates with an example from *Madame Bovary*: when the novel was put on trial, an apparently 'innocent' description of the streets of Paris was seen as charged with obscene erotic connotations. The scandalous element, however, resided more in the epistemological shock at the treachery of language than in the offence to puritan sensibility. The issue of representation raises questions regarding the failure of binaries to constitute a perfect mode of reference. Although, logically, any universe of discourse is wholly divided by positive and negative judgements, Kant postulates an 'indefinite judgement' which upsets the binary division: in an indefinite judgement 'a non-predicate is affirmed', so a positive meaning is given to a predicate that is in a negative form. In postulating the indefinite judgement, Kant is unwittingly gesturing to what lies outside the binary.

By the same token, in popular culture, borderline phenomena such as vampires and zombies are referred to as the 'undead', a non-predicate that is affirmed, evidence of the 'unpresentable Thing'. For Lacan, in the wake of Heidegger's notion of 'being-towards-death', death is the impossible end point of the Symbolic as the lifeless stasis of its idealizations; as a result, the frustrated life-substance, the Freudo-Lacanian death drive, endlessly repeats itself in the Symbolic, in an attempt to regain what it has lost. When 'life' is withdrawn from the Symbolic, it emerges as an 'undead' substance, an 'ultimate object of horror', residing in an intermediate realm, 'between two deaths', dead to the Symbolic and awaiting its biological death. Žižek traces this 'undead' object to Lacan's mythical creature, the flat 'lamella', which designates the libido of the newly born, struggling amoeba-like against any form of division: the subject, tentatively emerging into the Symbolic, continues to be invested in its Real 'life', bound to the pursuit of the impossible fantasy that would make good its loss. Žižek illustrates this struggle between the alien, amoeba-like substance and the Symbolic subject, first with a scene of invasive assault from the horror film *Alien* and second from Syberberg's film version of *Parsifal*, in which the bleeding wound of Amfortas is displayed on a cushion as if it were an object in its own right. This 'undead' thing, which is the source of Amfortas's suffering and will not let him die, is finally healed with the instrument that caused it. In Syberberg's allegorical rendering, Žižek identifies this wound with the 'object' of psychoanalysis.

Jacques Lacan formulates the elementary dialectical structure of the symbolic order by stating that 'speech is able to recover the debt that it engenders',[1] a thesis in which one must recognize all its Hegelian connotation. The debt, the 'wound', opened up by the symbolic order is a philosophical commonplace, at least from Hegel onwards: with entry into the symbolic order, our immersion in the immediacy of the Real is for ever lost; we are forced to assume an irreducible loss; the word entails the (symbolic) murder of the thing, etc. In short, what we are dealing with here is the negative-abstractive power that pertains to what Hegel called *Verstand* (the analytical mortification dismembering of what organically belongs together). How, then, precisely, are we to conceive of the thesis that *logos* is able to recover its own constitutive debt, or, even more pointedly, that it is only speech itself, the very tool of disintegration, that can heal the wound it incises in the Real ('only the spear that smote you / can heal your wound,' as Wagner puts it in *Parsifal*)? It would be easy to provide examples here, first among them the ecological crisis: if there is one thing that is clear today, it is that a return to any kind of natural balance is for ever precluded; only technology and science themselves can get us out of the deadlock into which they have brought us. Let us, however, remain at the level of the notion. According to the postmodern *doxa*, the very idea that the symbolic order is able to square its debt in full epitomizes the illusion of the Hegelian *Aufhebung*: language compensates us for the loss of immediate reality (the replacement of 'things' with 'words') with sense, which renders present the essence of things – that is, in which reality is preserved in its notion. However – so the *doxa* goes on – the problem consists in the fact that the symbolic debt is constitutive and as such unredeemable: the emergence of the symbolic order opens up a *béance* that can never be wholly filled up by sense; for that reason, sense is never 'all'; it is always truncated, marked by a stain of non-sense.

Yet, contrary to common opinion, Lacan does not follow this path; the most appropriate way to track down his orientation is to take as our starting point the relationship between 'empty speech' (*parole vide*) and 'full speech' (*parole pleine*). Here, we immediately encounter one of the standard misapprehensions of Lacanian theory: as a rule, empty speech is conceived of as empty, non-authentic prattle in which the speaker's subjective position of enunciation is not disclosed, whereas in full speech, the subject is supposed to express his or her authentic existential position of enunciation; the relationship between empty and full speech is thus conceived of as homologous to the duality of 'subject of the enunciated' and 'subject of the enunciation'. Such a reading, however (even if it does not absolutely devalue empty speech but conceives of it also as 'free associations' in the psychoanalytical process, i.e. as a speech emptied of imaginary identifications), misses entirely Lacan's point, which becomes manifest the moment we take into account the crucial fact that for Lacan the exemplary case of empty speech is the password (*mot-de-passage*). How does a password function? As a pure gesture of recognition, of admission into a certain symbolic space, whose enunciated content is totally indifferent. If, say, I arrange with my gangster-colleague that the password that gives me access to his hide-out is 'Aunt has baked the apple pie', it can easily be changed into 'Long live Comrade Stalin!' or whatever else. Therein consists the 'emptiness' of empty speech: in this ultimate nullity of its enunciated content. And Lacan's point is that human speech in its most radical, fundamental dimension functions as a password: prior to its being a means of communication, of transmitting the signified content, speech is the medium of the mutual recognition of the speakers. In other words, it is precisely the password *qua* empty speech that reduces the subject to the punctuality of the 'subject of the enunciation': in it, he is present *qua* a pure symbolic point freed of all enunciated content. For that reason, full speech is never to be conceived of as a simple, immediate filling-out of the void that characterizes empty speech (as in the usual opposition of 'authentic' and 'non-authentic' speech). Quite the contrary, one must say that it is only empty speech that, by way of its very emptiness (of its distance from the enunciated content that is posited in it as totally indifferent), creates the space for 'full speech', for speech in which the subject can articulate his or her position of enunciation. Or, in Hegelese: it is only the subject's radical estrangement from immediate substantial wealth that opens up the space for the articulation of his or her subjective content. In order to posit the substantial content as 'my own', I must first establish myself as a pure, empty form of subjectivity devoid of all positive content.

And in so far as the symbolic wound is the ultimate paradigm of Evil, the same holds also for the relationship between Evil and Good: radical Evil opens up the space for Good in precisely the same way as empty speech opens up the space for full speech. What we come across here, of course, is the problem of 'radical Evil' first articulated by Kant in his *Religion within the Limits of Reason Alone*. By conceiving of the relationship Evil–Good as contrary, as 'real opposition', Kant is forced to accept a hypothesis about 'radical Evil,' on the presence, in man, of a positive counterforce to his tendency toward Good. The ultimate proof of the positive existence of this counterforce is the fact that the subject experiences moral Law in himself as an unbearable traumatic pressure that humiliates his self-esteem and self-love – so there must be something in the very nature of the Self that resists the moral Law: that is, that gives preference to the egoistical, 'pathological' leanings over following the moral Law. Kant emphasizes the a priori character of this propensity toward Evil (the moment that was later developed by Schelling): in so far as I am a free being, I cannot simply objectify that in me which resists the Good (by saying, for example, that it is part of my nature for which I am not responsible). The very fact that I feel morally responsible for my evil bears witness to the fact that, in a timeless transcendental act, I had to choose freely my eternal character by giving preference to Evil over Good. This is how Kant conceives of 'radical Evil': as an a priori, not just an empirical, contingent propensity of human nature toward Evil. However, by rejecting the hypothesis of 'diabolical Evil', Kant recoils from the ultimate paradox of radical Evil, from the uncanny domain of those acts that, although 'evil' as to their content, thoroughly fulfil the formal criteria of an ethical act: they are not motivated by any pathological considerations; that is, their sole motivating ground is Evil as a principle, which is why they can involve the radical abrogation of one's patho-logical interests, up to the sacrifice of one's life.

Let us recall Mozart's *Don Giovanni*: when, in the final confrontation with the statue of the Commendatore, Don Giovanni refuses to repent, to renounce his sinful past, he achieves something the only proper designation of which is a radical ethical stance. It is as if his tenacity mockingly reverses Kant's own example in the *Critique of Practical Reason*, wherein the libertine is quickly prepared to renounce the satisfaction of his passion as soon as he learns that the price to be paid for it is the gallows: Don Giovanni persists in his libertine attitude at the very moment when he knows very well that what awaits him is *only* the gallows and none of the satisfactions. That is to say, from the stand-point of pathological interests, the thing to do would be to perform the formal gesture of penitence: Don Giovanni knows that death is close, so that by atoning for his deeds he stands to lose nothing, only to gain (i.e. to save himself from posthumous torments); yet, 'on principle', he chooses to persist in his defiant stance of the libertine. How can one avoid experiencing Don Giovan-ni's unyielding 'No!' to the statue, to this living dead, as the model of an intransigent *ethical* attitude, notwithstanding its 'evil' content?

If we accept the possibility of such an 'evil' ethical act, then it is not sufficient to conceive of radical Evil as something that pertains to the very notion of subjectivity on a par with a disposition toward Good; one is compelled to advance a step further and to conceive of radical Evil as something that ontologically precedes Good by way of opening up the space for it. That is to say, in what, precisely, does Evil consist? Evil is another name for the 'death drive', for the fixation on some Thing that derails our customary life circuit. By way of Evil, man wrests himself from animal instinctual rhythm; that is, Evil introduces a radical reversal of the 'natural' relationship.[2] Here, therefore, is revealed the insufficiency of Kant's and Schelling's standard formula (the possibility of Evil is grounded in man's freedom of choice, on account of which he can invert the 'normal' relationship between universal principles of Reason and his pathological nature by way of subordinating his suprasensible nature to his egoistical inclinations). Hegel, who, in his *Lectures on the Philoso-*

phy of Religion, conceives of the very act of becoming human, of passage from animal to man, as the Fall into sin, is here more penetrating: the possible space for Good is opened up by the original choice of radical Evil, which disrupts the pattern of the organic substantial Whole. The choice between Good and Evil is thus in a sense not the true, original choice. The truly first choice is the choice between (what will later be perceived as) yielding to one's pathological leanings or embracing radical Evil, an act of suicidal egoism that 'makes place' for the Good – that is, that overcomes the domination of pathological natural impulses by way of a purely negative gesture of suspending the life circuit. Or, in Kierkegaard's terms, Evil is Good itself 'in the mode of becoming'. It 'becomes' as a radical disruption of the life circuit; the difference between them concerns a purely formal conversion from the mode of 'becoming' to the mode of 'being'.[3] This is how 'only the spear that smote you can heal the wound': the wound is healed when the place of Evil is filled out by a 'good' content. Good *qua* 'the mask of the Thing (i.e. of the radical Evil)' (Lacan) is thus an ontologically secondary, supplementary attempt to re-establish the lost balance. Its ultimate paradigm in the social sphere is the corporatist endeavour to (re)construct society as a harmonious, organic, non-antagonistic edifice.

The thesis according to which the possibility of choosing Evil pertains to the very notion of subjectivity has therefore to be radicalized by a kind of self-reflective inversion: *the status of the subject as such is evil.* That is, in so far as we are 'human', in a sense we *always-already* have chosen Evil. Far more than by his direct references to Hegel, the Hegelian stance of the early Lacan is attested to by the rhetorical figures that give body to this logic of the 'negation of negation'. Lacan's answer to the ego-psychological notion of the ego's 'maturity' as the capability to endure frustrations, for example, is that 'the ego as such is frustration in its essence':[4] in so far as the ego emerges in the process of imaginary identification with its mirror double who is at the same time its rival, its potential paranoid persecutor, the frustration on the part of the mirror double is constitutive of the ego. The logic of this reversal is strictly Hegelian: what first appears as an external hindrance frustrating the ego's striving for satisfaction is thereupon experienced as the ultimate support of its being.[5]

Why, then, does Kant hold back from bringing out all the consequences of the thesis about radical Evil? The answer is clear here, albeit paradoxical: what prevents him is the very logic that compelled him to articulate the thesis about radical Evil in the first place – namely, the logic of 'real opposition', which, as suggested by Monique David-Ménard,[6] constitutes a kind of ultimate fantasmatic frame of Kant's thought. If moral struggle is conceived of as the conflict between two opposing positive forces striving for mutual annihilation, it becomes unthinkable for one of the forces, Evil, not only to oppose the other, endeavouring to annihilate it, but also to undermine it from within, by way of assuming the very form of its opposite. Whenever Kant approaches this possibility (apropos of 'diabolical Evil' in practical philosophy, apropos of the trial against the monarch in the doctrine of law), he quickly dismisses it as unthinkable, as an object of ultimate abhorrence. It is only with Hegel's logic of negative self-relating that this step can be accomplished.

This dialectical coincidence of Good and radical Evil that is the 'unthought' of Kant can be further clarified by reference to the relationship between the Beautiful and the Sublime. That is to say, Kant, as is well known, conceives of beauty as the symbol of the Good. At the same time, in his *Critique of Judgement*, he points out that what is truly sublime is not the object that arouses the feeling of sublimity but the moral Law in us, our suprasensible nature. Are, then, beauty and sublimity simply to be conceived as two different symbols of the Good? Is it not, on the contrary, that this duality points toward a certain chasm that must pertain to the moral Law itself? Lacan draws a line of demarcation between the two facets of law. On the one hand, there is Law *qua* symbolic Ego-Ideal: that is, Law in its pacifying function, Law *qua* guarantee of the social pact, *qua* the intermediating Third that dissolves the impasse of imaginary aggressivity. On the other hand, there is law in its superego dimension: that is, law *qua* 'irrational' pressure, the force of culpability totally incommensurable with our actual responsibility, the agency in the eyes of which we are a priori guilty and that gives body to the impossible imperative of enjoyment. It is this distinction between Ego-Ideal and superego that enables us to specify the difference in the way Beauty and Sublimity are related to the domain of ethics. Beauty is the symbol of the Good: that is, of the moral Law as the pacifying agency that bridles our egoism and renders possible harmonious social co-existence. The dynamic sublime, on the contrary – volcanic eruptions, stormy seas, mountain precipices, etc. – by its very failure to symbolize (to represent symbolically) the suprasensible moral Law, evokes its superego dimension. The logic at work in the experience of the dynamic sublime is therefore as follows: true, I may be powerless in the face of the raging forces of nature, a tiny particle of dust thrown around by wind and sea; yet all this fury of nature pales in comparison with the absolute pressure exerted on me by the superego, which humiliates me and compels me to act contrary to my fundamental interests! (What we encounter here is the basic paradox of the Kantian autonomy: I am a free, autonomous subject, delivered from the constraints of my pathological nature precisely and only in so far as my feeling of self-esteem is crushed by the humiliating pressure of the moral Law.) Therein consists also the superego dimension of the Jewish God evoked by the high priest Abner in Racine's *Athalie*: 'Je crains Dieu et n'ai point d'autre crainte.' The fear of raging nature and of the pain other men can inflict on me converts into sublime peace not simply by my becoming aware of the suprasensible nature in me out of reach of the forces of nature, but by my taking cognizance of how the pressure of the moral Law is stronger than even the mightiest exercise of the forces of nature.

The unavoidable conclusion to be drawn from all this is that if Beauty is the symbol of the Good, the Sublime is the symbol of... Here, already, the homology gets stuck. The problem with the sublime object (more precisely: with the object that arouses in us the feeling of the sublime) is that it *fails* as a symbol – it evokes its Beyond by the very failure of its symbolic representation. So, if Beauty is the symbol of the Good, the Sublime evokes – what? There is only one answer possible: the non-pathological, ethical, suprasensible dimension, for sure, but *that dimension precisely in so far as it eludes the domain of the Good* – in short: diabolical Evil, Evil as an ethical attitude. In today's popular ideology, this paradox of the Kantian Sublime is what perhaps enables us to detect the roots of the public fascination with figures like Hannibal Lecter, the cannibal serial killer in Thomas Harris's novels: what this fascination ultimately bears witness to is a deep longing for a Lacanian psychoanalyst. That is to say, Hannibal Lecter is a sublime figure in the strict Kantian sense: a desperate, ultimately failed attempt of the popular imagination to represent to itself the idea of a Lacanian analyst. The relationship between Lecter and the Lacanian analyst corresponds perfectly to the relationship that, according to Kant, defines the experience of the 'dynamic sublime': the relationship between wild, chaotic, untamed, raging nature and the suprasensible Idea of Reason beyond any natural constraints. True, Lecter's evil – he not only kills his victims, but then goes on to eat parts of their entrails – strains to its limits our capacity to imagine the horrors we can inflict on our fellow creatures; yet even the utmost effort to represent Lecter's cruelty to ourselves fails to capture the true dimension of the act of the analyst: by bringing about *la traversée du fantasme* (the going-through of our fundamental fantasy), he literally 'steals the kernel of our being', the object *a*, the secret treasure, *agalma*, what we consider most precious in ourselves, denouncing it as a mere semblance. Lacan defines the object *a* as the fantasmatic 'stuff of the I', as that which confers on the $, on the fissure in the symbolic order, on the ontological void that we call 'subject', the ontological consistency of a 'person', the semblance of a fullness of being. And it is precisely this 'stuff' that the analyst 'swallows', pulverizes. This is the reason for the unexpected 'eucharistic' element at work in Lacan's definition of the analyst: namely, his repeated ironic allusion to Heidegger: 'Manage ton *Dasein!*' ('Eat your being there!') Therein lies the power of fascination that pertains to the figure of Hannibal Lecter: by its very failure to attain the absolute limit of what Lacan calls 'subjective destitution', it enables us to get a presentiment of the Idea of the analyst. So, in *The Silence of the Lambs*, Lecter is truly cannibalistic not only in relation to his victims, but also in relation to

Clarice Sterling: their relationship is a mocking imitation of the analytic situation, since in exchange for his helping her to capture 'Buffalo Bill', he wants her to confide in him – what? Precisely what the analysand confides to the analyst, the kernel of her being, her fundamental fantasy (the crying of the lambs). The *quid pro quo* proposed by Lecter to Clarice is therefore, 'I'll help you if you let me eat your *Dasein!*' The inversion of the proper analytic relationship consists in the fact that Lecter compensates her for it by helping her track down 'Buffalo Bill'. As such, he is not cruel enough to be a Lacanian analyst, since in psychoanalysis, we must pay the analyst so that he or she will allow us to offer him or her our *Dasein* on a plate.

What opens up the space for such sublime monstrous apparitions is the break-down of the logic of representation: that is, the radical incommensurability between the field of representation and the unrepresentable Thing, which emerges with Kant. In his philosophy, this crack, this space where such monstrous apparitions can emerge, is opened up by the distinction between negative and indefinite judgement. The very example used by Kant to illustrate this distinction is telling: the positive judgement by means of which a predicate is ascribed to the (logical) subject – 'The soul is mortal'; the negative judge-ment by means of which a predicate is denied to the subject – 'The soul is not mortal'; the indefinite judgement by means of which, instead of negating a predicate (i.e. the copula that ascribes it to the subject), we affirm a certain non-predicate – 'The soul is not-mortal'. (In German also, the difference is solely a matter of spacing: 'Die Seele ist nicht sterblich' versus 'Die Seele ist nichtsterblich'; Kant enigmatically does not use the standard 'unsterblich'.)

In this line of thought, Kant introduces in the second edition of the *Critique of Pure Reason* the distinction between positive and negative meaning of 'noumenon': in the positive meaning of the term, 'noumenon' is 'an object of a non-sensible intuition', whereas in the negative meaning, it is 'a thing in so far as it is not an object of our sensible intuition' (B307). The grammatical form should not deceive us here: the positive meaning is expressed by the negative judgement, and the negative meaning by the indefinite judgement. In other words, when one determines the Thing as 'an object of a non-sensible intui-tion', one immediately negates the positive judgement that determines the Thing as 'an object of a sensible intuition': one accepts intuition as the unquestioned base or genus; against this background, one opposes its two species, sensible and non-sensible intuition. Negative judgement is thus not only limiting; it also delineates a domain beyond phenomena where it locates the Thing – the domain of the non-sensible intuition – whereas in the case of the negative determination, the Thing is excluded from the domain of our sensible intuition, without being posited in an implicit way as the object of a non-sensible intuition; by leaving in suspense the positive status of the Thing, negative determination saps the very genus common to affirmation and negation of the predicate.

Therein consists also the difference between 'is not mortal' and 'is not-mortal': what we have in the first case is a simple negation, whereas in the second case, a *non-predicate is affirmed*. The only 'legitimate' definition of the noumenon is that it is 'not an object of our sensible intuition', that is, a wholly negative definition that excludes it from the phenomenal domain; this judgement is 'infinite', since it does not imply any conclusions as to where, in the infinite space of what remains outside the phenomenal domain, the noumenon is located. What Kant calls 'transcendental illusion' ultimately consists in the very (mis)reading of infinite judgement as negative judgement: when we conceive the noumenon as an 'object of a non-sensible intuition', the subject of the judgement remains the same (the 'object of an intuition'); what changes is only the character (non-sensible instead of sensible) of this intuition, so that a minimal 'commensurability' between the subject and the predicate (i.e. in this case, between the noumenon and its phenomenal determinations) is still maintained.

A Hegelian corollary to Kant here is that limitation is to be conceived of as prior to what lies 'beyond' it, so that it is ultimately Kant's notion of Thing-in-Itself that is revealed as too 'reified'. Hegel's position as to this point is subtle: what he claims by stating that the Suprasensible is 'appearance *qua* appearance' is precisely that the Thing-in-itself is *the limitation of the phenomena as such*. 'Suprasensible objects (objects of suprasensible intuition)' belong to the chimerical 'topsy-turvy world'. They are nothing but an inverted presentation, a projection, of the very content of sensible intuition in the form of another, non-sensible intuition. Or, to recall Marx's ironic critique of Proudhon in *The Poverty of Philosophy*: 'Instead of the ordinary individual with his ordinary way of speech and thought, we get this same ordinary way of speech and thought, without the individual.'[7] (The double irony of it, of course, is that Marx intended these lines as a mocking rejection of Proudhon's Hegelianism – that is, of his effort to supply economic theory with the form of speculative dialectics!) This is what the chimera of 'non-sensible intuition' is about: instead of ordinary objects of sensible intuition, we get the same ordinary objects of intuition, without their sensible character.

This subtle difference between negative and indefinite judgement is at work in a certain type of witticism wherein the second part does not immediately invert the first part by negating its predicate, but instead repeats it with the negation displaced on to the subject. The judgement 'He is an individual full of idiotic features', for example, can be negated in a standard mirror way – that is, be replaced by its contrary, 'He is an individual with no idiotic features'; yet its negation can also be given the form of 'He is full of idiotic features without being an individual'. This displacement of the negation from the predicate on to the subject provides the logical matrix of what is often the unforeseen result of our educational efforts to liberate the pupil from the constraint of prejudices and clichés: not a person capable of expressing himself or herself in a relaxed, unconstrained way, but an automatized bundle of (new) clichés behind which we no longer sense the presence of a 'real person'. Let us just recall the usual outcome of psychological training intended to deliver the individual from the constraints of his or her everyday frame of mind and to set free his or her 'true self', its authentic creative potentials (transcendental meditation, etc.): once he or she gets rid of the old clichés that were still able to sustain the dialectical tension between themselves and the 'personality' behind them, what take their place are new clichés that abrogate the very 'depth' of personality behind them. In short, he or she becomes a true monster, a kind of 'living dead'. Samuel Goldwyn, the old Hollywood mogul, was right: what we need are indeed some new, original clichés.

The mention of the 'living dead' is by no means accidental here: in our ordinary language, we resort to indefinite judgements precisely when we endeavour to comprehend those borderline phenomena that undermine established differences such as that between living and being dead. In the texts of popular culture, the uncanny creatures that are neither alive nor dead, the 'living dead' (vampires, etc.), are referred to as 'the undead': although they are not dead, they are clearly not alive like us ordinary mortals. The judgement 'He is undead' is therefore an indefinite, limiting judgement in the precise sense of a purely negative gesture of excluding vampires from the domain of the dead, without thereby locating them in the domain of the living (as in the case of the simple negation, 'He is not dead'). The fact that vampires and other 'living dead' are usually referred to as 'things' has to be rendered with its full Kantian meaning: a vampire is a Thing that looks and acts like us, yet is not one of us. In short, the difference between the vampire and the living person is that between indefinite and negative judgement: a dead person loses the predicates of a living being, yet he or she remains the same person. An undead, on the contrary, retains all the predicates of a living being without being one. As in the above-quoted Marxian joke, what we get with the vampire is 'the same ordinary way of speech and thought, without the individual'.

In lieu of a more detailed theoretical elaboration, it is appropriate at this point to approach the relationship of Lacan to Heidegger in a new way. In the fifties, Lacan endeavoured to read 'death drive' against the background of Heidegger's 'being-toward-death' (*Sein-zum-Tode*), conceiving of death as the inherent and ultimate limit of symbolization that provides for its irreducible

temporal character. With the shift of accent toward the Real from the
sixties onward, however, it is, rather, the 'undead' lamella, the indestructible,
immortal life that dwells in the domain 'between the two deaths', that emerges
as the ultimate object of horror. Lacan delineates the contours of this 'undead'
object toward the end of chapter 15 of his *Four Fundamental Concepts*,
where he proposes his own myth, constructed upon the model of Aristo-
phanes' fable from Plato's *Symposium*, the myth of *l'hommelette* (little female-
man omelette):

Whenever the membranes of the egg in which the foetus emerges on its way to
becoming a new-born, are broken, imagine for a moment that something flies off,
and that one can do it with an egg as easily as with a man, namely the *hommelette*, or the
lamella.

The lamella is something extra-flat, which moves like the amoeba. It is just a little
more complicated. But it goes everywhere. And as it is something . . . that is related to
what the sexed being loses in sexuality, it is, like the amoeba in relation to sexed beings,
immortal – because it survives any division, any scissiparous intervention. And it can
run around.

Well! This is not very reassuring. But suppose it comes and envelops your face while
you are quietly asleep. . . .

I can't see how we would not join battle with a being capable of these properties.
But it would not be a very convenient battle. This lamella, this organ, whose characteristic is not to exist, but which is nevertheless an organ . . . is the libido.

It is the libido, *qua* pure life instinct, that is to say, immortal life, or irrepressible life,
life that has need of no organ, simplified, indestructible life. It is precisely what is
subtracted from the living being by virtue of the fact that it is subject to the cycle of
sexed reproduction. And it is of this that all the forms of the *objet a* that can be
enumerated are the representatives, the equivalents. The *objets a* are merely its representatives, its figures. The breast – as equivocal, as an element characteristic of the
mammiferous organization, the placenta for example – certainly represents that part of
himself that the individual loses at birth, and which may serve to symbolize the most
profound lost object.[8]

What we have here, again, is an Otherness prior to intersubjectivity: the
subject's 'impossible' relationship to this amoeba-like creature is what Lacan
is ultimately aiming at by way of his formula $ \$ \diamond a $. The best way to clarify this
point is perhaps to allow ourselves the string of associations that Lacan's
description must evoke in so far as we like horror movies. Is not the alien
from Ridley Scott's film of that title the 'lamella' in its purest form? Are not all
the key elements of Lacan's myth contained already in the first truly horrifying
scene of the film, when, in the womblike cave of the unknown planet, the
'alien' leaps from the egglike globe when its lid splits off and sticks to John
Hurt's face? This amoeba-like, flattened creature that envelops the subject's

face stands for the irrepressible life beyond all the finite forms that are merely its representatives, its figures (later in the film, the 'alien' is able to assume a multitude of different shapes), immortal and indestructible. It suffices to recall the unpleasant thrill of the moment when a scientist cuts with a scalpel into a leg of the creature that envelops Hurt's face: the liquid that drips from it falls on to the metal floor and corrodes it immediately; nothing can resist it.[9]

The second association here, of course, is to a detail from Syberberg's film version of *Parsifal*, in which Syberberg depicts Amfortas's wound – externalized, carried by the servants on a pillow in front of him, in the form of a vagina-like partial object out of which blood is dripping in a continuous flow (like, *vulgari eloquentia*, a vagina in an unending period). This palpitating opening – an organ that is at the same time the entire organism (let us just recall a homologous motif in a series of science-fiction stories, like the gigantic eye living a life of its own) – epitomizes life in its indestructibility: Amfortas's pain consists in the very fact that he is unable to die, that he is condemned to an eternal life of suffering; when, at the end, Parsifal heals his wound with 'the spear that smote it', Amfortas is finally able to rest and die. This wound of Amfortas's, which persists outside himself as an *undead* thing, is the 'object of psychoanalysis'.

Notes

1   Jacques Lacan, *Écrits: A Selection* (New York, Norton, 1977), p. 144.
2   In this sense, the *femme fatale* who, in the *film noir* universe, derails man's daily routine, is one of the personifications of Evil: the sexual relationship becomes impossible the moment woman is elevated to the dignity of the Thing.
3   We must be careful here to avoid the trap of retroactive projection: Milton's Satan in his *Paradise Lost* is not yet the Kantian radical Evil – it appeared as such only to the Romantic gaze of Shelley and Blake. When Satan says, 'Evil, be thou my Good,' this is not yet radical Evil, but remains simply a case of wrongly putting some Evil at the place of Good. The logic of radical Evil consists rather in its exact opposite: that is, in saying 'Good, be thou my Evil' – in filling out the place of Evil, of the Thing, of the traumatic element that derails the closed circuit of organic life, by some (secondary) Good.
4   Lacan, *Écrits*, p. 42.
5   Lacan often makes use of the same rhetorical inversion to delineate the relationship of the ego to its symptoms: it is not sufficient to say that the ego forms its symptoms in order to maintain its precarious balance with the forces of the id. Ego itself is, as to its essence, a symptom, a compromise-formation, a tool enabling the subject to regulate his or her desire. In other words, the subject desires by means of his or her ego symptom.

6   Monique David-Menard, *La Folie dans la raison pure* (Paris, Vrin, 1990), p. 50.
7   Karl Marx, *Das Elend der Philosophie*, ed. Siegfried Landshut (Stuffgart, Redam, 1971), p. 494.
8   Jacques Lacan, *The Four Fundamental Concepts of Psycho-Analysis* (New York, Norton, 1979), pp. 197–8.
9   It is precisely this physical, tangible impact of 'lamella' that gets lost in *Aliens II*, which is why this sequel is infinitely inferior to *Aliens*.

13

Kant with (or against) Sade

In this new, previously unpublished essay Žižek examines the link made between Kant's formalist ethics, which disallows the consideration of personal motives, and Sade's insistence on enjoying unrestrained licentiousness. This connection was initially advanced by Adorno and Horkheimer, who justified it with an argument based on the historical change from an earlier morality resting on the notion of a Supreme Good to a bourgeois sentimentality that endeavoured to disguise the heartless mechanism of the market. They discerned in both Kant and Sade a rejection of such sentimentality: Kant insisted that ethical decision was not to be influenced by 'heteronomous content' (personal inclination); Sade that the pursuit of pleasure was to be rigidly performed. Moreover, the result of Sade's abandonment of the earlier metaphysical morality is not a release of raw passion, but a 'repressive desublimation' (Marcuse's term), a cold-blooded instrumentalization of the sexual, in which all feeling is excised. Hence, Sadean 'apathy' matches Kantian detachment, duty done solely for its own sake.

Lacan, independently of Adorno and Horkheimer, also puts 'Kant with Sade', but perceives in Sade the truth of Kantian ethics, in that both the Sadean and the Kantian subjects are autonomous legislators of their own morality. According to Lacan, the hidden ground of the Kantian innovation is a desire that is not articulated in a 'pathological' motive, a desire not to be compromised, aiming at a satisfaction 'beyond the pleasure principle'. The problem is that, while Kant tries to universalize the ethical choice that founds the moral order, he assumes a subject that deviates in its very uniqueness: there is an underlying fear that, instead of aspiring to noumenal transcendence, the subject will sink to its particular pathology. Kant prefers to presuppose an identity between the universality of the law and the particularity of the legislator. Lacan picks up on this by distinguishing between the 'subject of the enunciation' (the particular 'I' who speaks) and the 'subject of the enunciated' (the 'me' as universally defined). The failure to make such a distinction is implicit in the Cartesian notion of subjectivity, which postulates a subject whose particularity is a blot on the universal landscape, while at the same time being its ground.

The problem then emerges of whether to treat the subject with respect (*Achtung*) as a Kantian 'end-in-itself' (a contingent entity) or with disrespect as a mere means (universally defined). Since there is always a gap between the actuality of the subject and its symbolic status, respect relies on not approaching the other's castration too closely, in order that the semblance hiding the lack not be disturbed. This is precisely the opposite of what the Sadean sacrilege does, for it exposes the lack in the Other, following out the cold unconditional demand 'Enjoy!', and thus paralleling in its detachment Kant's categorical imperative, 'Do your duty!' By this means the Sadean pervert turns himself into the instrument of the Other's will, assigning his own internal division to his victim.

Here Žižek asks whether Sade is the whole truth of Kantian ethics, and whether in fact Kant's moral law is equivalent to Freud's superego. If it is equivalent, then Sade is the truth of Kant, in that an obscene superego is inherent in Kant's categorical imperative: if not, the moral law, far from being the arbiter of guilt, has its source in the subject's desire, not in the sense of a 'pathological' motive, but as representative of its own *jouissance*. For Lacan, it is the guilt that the superego induces that provides the proof that the subject is compromising on its desire. To get out of this trap, the subject has to find a way of framing a universal law that takes account of its particular *jouissance*. How is this consonant with the Kantian insistence that one must do one's duty?

No one before Kant had put the Law before the Good. A 'pseudo-Hegelian' criticism has it that Kant ignores the historical context around the ethical subject (see Žižek, *Plague of Fantasies*, p. 221), but Kant does not prescribe what its duty is. You have to do the work: God hasn't done it for you. It is the subject's responsibility to discover how the universal rule relates to the particular situation, a painful and violent experience. There is a gap between the act and the will: the act provides negative feedback, undermining the original intention (you are not what you thought you were). Part of the difficulty of keeping the balance between the universal rule and its particular application lies in the Sadean danger of allowing duty to become the excuse for a sadistic release of *jouissance*, where the subject believes itself to be the instrument of the Other's will. But this was never the implication of Kant's dictum 'You can because you must'. At the other extreme is the risk for the subject of effacing its subjecthood by too great a subordination. The Law is not something that we apply to a random empirical content, but the promise of an absent content that never comes. Since it is impossible to know the precise outcome of our acts, we never know if we have really obeyed, or if we have been driven by a hidden pathological motive. Because there is a lack of fit between the Law and obedient performances of it, we are guilty without knowing why. The very notion of a contentless Law has at its origin a founding repression. The symbolic form is never an expression of its content. It doesn't tell you what to do: it tells you that there is work to be done.

Therefore Kant's ethic is not the road to sadism; on the contrary, it prohibits the stance of the Sadean executioner, because duty has to be invested with a good will: but what Kant does not recognize is that *the faculty of desiring is not in itself "pathological"*', that desire can reside within a good will. As an example against Kant, Žižek cites Lacan's reading of Antigone, who obeyed an unconditional command without being at the mercy of an obscene superego. Far from her desire being attached to a mundane object with a subsequent yield of pleasure, it induced an act without either guilt or gain. For desire has a cause that lies outside 'pathological' motive, the Lacanian *objet a*, evidence of the Real within the subject.

'Kant *is* Sade' is the 'infinite judgement' of modern ethics, positing the sign of equation between the two radical opposites: that is, asserting that the sublime, disinterested, ethical attitude is somehow identical to, or overlaps with, the unrestrained indulgence in pleasurable violence. A lot – everything, perhaps – is at stake here: is there a line from Kantian formalist ethics to the cold-blooded Auschwitz killing-machine? Are concentration camps and killing as a neutral business the inherent outcome of the enlightened insistence on the autonomy of Reason? Is there at least a legitimate lineage from Sade to Fascist torturing, as is implied by Pasolini's film version of *120 Days*, which transposes it into the dark days of Mussolini's Salo republic? etc.

This link between Sade and Kant was first developed by Adorno and Horkheimer (A/H) in the (deservedly) famous Excursion II ('Juliette or Enlightenment and Morals') of the *Dialectic of Enlightenment*: A/H's fundamental thesis is that 'the work of Marquis de Sade displays the "Reason which is not led by another agency", that is to say, the bourgeois subject, liberated from a state of not yet being mature'.[1] Some fifteen years later, Jacques Lacan (without knowing about A/H's version) also developed the notion that Sade is the truth of Kant, first in his Seminar on *The Ethics of Psychoanalysis* (1958–9),[2] and then in the *écrit* 'Kant with Sade' of 1963.[3]

I

The first difference between A/H's and Lacan's 'Kant avec Sade' that strikes the eye is that, for A/H, Kant's practical philosophy is a sentimental / moralistic compromise that stands for a retreat from the radical consequences of Kant's criticism, while for Lacan, 'Kant avec Sade' is the truth of the Kantian ethical philosophy itself, of his 'critique of practical reason'. In short, A/H follow here the standard Young Hegelian opinion, stated in a most forcefully acerbic way by Heinrich Heine, that Kant's *Critique of Practical Reason* accomplishes a retreat from the unique anti-metaphysical, all-destroying thrust of the *Critique of Pure Reason*: in his moral philosophy, Kant makes a compromise with compassion for ordinary fellow humans (like his faithful servant Lampe, who obediently holds the umbrella for his master when it rains), providing them with necessary illusions (moral 'postulates') that enable them to lead a satisfying everyday life.[4] For A/H, this split is inherent in bourgeois society, where 'cold' objective market relations and the utilitarian logic of instrumental manipulation are supplemented by pathetic morality and sentimental philanthropism. Bourgeois ideology, in its everyday, 'normal' functioning, thus retracts from its own consequences – and, for A/H, the great merit of the bourgeois *poètes maudits* or thinkers like Sade or Nietzsche is that they leave off this moralistic sugar-coating and accept fully the consequences of the capitalist instrumental attitude. So, to put it succinctly, for A/H, the Sadean position is the true ethical implication of modern subjectivity (or, more radically, of the entire Enlightenment process from its early mythic origins), formulated in a consequent way, freed of all sentimental sugar-coating.

Kant thus goes only half-way: on behalf of the subject's autonomy, he abolishes the dependence on Reason, inclusive of ethical Reason, on any 'heteronomous' content (like the traditional, pre-modern ethics that relies on some substantial positive notion of Supreme Good), but he still wants to save the notion of ethical duty. He himself silently admits the fact that he cannot ground the priority of Good over Evil, of compassion over cruelty, etc., in the inherent formal structure of Reason itself, when he is compelled to claim that the Call of Conscience which requires us to do our Duty is a simple 'fact of Reason', something found in ourselves, a raw irrational fact. The sadist pervert's reduction of the sexual partner to a mere object, to a means to his own unlimited pleasure, is the hidden truth of the Kantian ethical injunction to treat other human beings with respect, to allow them a minimum of dignity.

A/H locate Sade in the long tradition of the orgiastic/carnivalesque reversal of the established order: the moment when the hierarchical rules are suspended and 'everything is permitted'. This primordial *jouissance* recaptured by the sacred orgies is, of course, the retroactive projection of the human alienated state: it never existed prior to its loss. The point, of course, is that Sade announces the moment when, with the emergence of bourgeois Enlightenment, pleasure itself loses its sacred/transgressive character and is reduced to a rationalized instrumental activity. That is to say, according to A/H, the greatness of Sade is that, on behalf of the full assertion of earthly pleasures, he not only rejects any metaphysical moralism, but also fully acknowledges the price one has to pay for it: the radical intellectualization/instrumentalization/regimentation of the (sexual) activity intended to bring pleasure. Here we encounter the content later baptized by Marcuse 'repressive desublimation': after all the barriers of sublimation, of cultural transformation of sexual activity, are abolished, what we get is not raw, brutal, passionate, satisfying animal sex, but, on the contrary, a fully regimented, intellectualized activity comparable to a well-planned sporting match. The Sadean hero is not a brute animal beast, but a pale, cold-blooded intellectual much more alienated from the true pleasure of the flesh than is the prudish, inhibited lover, a man of reason enslaved to the *amor intellectualis diaboli* – what gives pleasure to him (or her) is not sexuality as such, but the activity of outstripping rational civilization by its own means, by way of thinking (and practising) to the end the consequences of its logic. So, far from being an entity of full, earthy passion, the Sadean hero is fundamentally *apathetic*, reducing sexuality to a mechanical, planned procedure deprived of the last vestiges of spontaneous pleasure or sentimentality. What Sade heroically takes into account is that pure bodily sensual pleasure and spiritual love are not simply opposed, but dialectically intertwined: there is something deeply 'spiritual', spectral, sublime, about a really passionate sensual lust, and vice versa (as the mystical experience teaches us), so that the thorough 'desublimation' of sexuality also thoroughly intellectualizes it, changing an intense pathetic bodily experience into a cold, apathetic mechanical exercise.

Here again, as is clear to A/H, Sade paradoxically rejoins Kant: didn't Kant also despise the false morality supported by sentimental compassion or any other pathological feeling of satisfaction? Didn't he also preach as the only proper ethical attitude that of apathy, of doing one's duty only for the sake of duty? By drawing all ethical consequences from the formalized instrumental Reason – that is, by emphasizing its ethical neutrality and apathy, by pointing out how, if one sticks strictly to Reason alone, it is impossible to ground even the most elementary prohibition of murder – Sade's work is thus, according to A/H, not to be dismissed as an expression of the morbid sickness of our civilization: on the contrary, in the work of writers like Sade, 'sickness itself becomes the symptom of healing';[5] that is, its fearless exposure of the falsity of compassion and other philanthropic values opens up in a negative way the space for a society that would no longer need such ideological masks to conceal its own brutal actuality.

II

How, then, does Lacan stand in regard to the A/H version of 'Kant with Sade' (i.e. of Sade as the truth of Kantian ethics)? For Lacan also, Sade consequently deployed the inherent potential of the Kantian philosophical revolution, although Lacan gives to this a somewhat different twist – his point is that Sade honestly *externalizes* the Voice of Conscience (which, in Kant, attests the subject's full ethical autonomy, i.e. is self-posited/imposed by the subject) in the Executioner who terrorizes/tortures the victim...[6] The first thought that comes to mind here, of course, is: what's all the fuss about? Today, in our post-idealist Freudian era, doesn't everybody know what the point of the 'with' is: the truth of Kant's ethical rigorism is the sadism of the Law; that is, the Kantian Law is a superego agency that sadistically enjoys the subject's deadlock, his inability to meet its inexorable demands, like the proverbial teacher who tortures pupils with impossible tasks and secretly savours their failings? Lacan's point, however, is the exact opposite of this first association: it is not Kant who was a closet sadist; it is Sade who is a closet Kantian. That is to say, what one should bear in mind is that the focus of Lacan is always Kant, not Sade: what interest him are the ultimate consequences and disavowed premises of the Kantian ethical revolution. In other words, Lacan does not try to make the usual 'reductionist' point that every ethical act, as pure and disinterested as it may appear, is always grounded in some 'pathological' motivation (the agent's own long-term interest, the admiration of his peers, up to the 'negative' satisfaction provided by the suffering and extortion often demanded by ethical acts); the focus of Lacan's interest, rather, resides in the paradoxical reversal by means of which desire itself (i.e. acting upon one's desire, not compromising it) can no longer be grounded in any 'pathological' interests or motivations, and thus meets the criteria of the Kantian ethical act, so that 'following one's desire' overlaps with 'doing one's duty'. Suffice it to recall Kant's own famous example from his *Critique of Practical Reason*:

Suppose that someone says his lust is irresistible when the desired object and opportunity are present. Ask him whether he would not control his passions if, in front of the house where he has this opportunity, a gallows were erected on which he would be hanged immediately after gratifying his lust. We do not have to guess very long what his answer may be.[7]

Lacan's counter-argument here is that we certainly *do* have to guess what his answer may be: what if we encounter a subject (as we do regularly in psycho-analysis) who can only enjoy a night of passion fully if some form of 'gallows' *is* threatening him – that is, if, by doing it, he is violating some prohibition? Mario Monicelli's *Casanova '70* (1965), with Virna Lisi and Marcello Mas-troianni, hinges on this very point: the hero can only retain his sexual potency if doing 'it' involves some kind of danger. At the film's end, when he is on the verge of marrying his beloved, he wants at least to violate the prohibition of premarital sex by sleeping with her the night *before* the wedding. However, his bride unknowingly spoils even this minimal pleasure by arranging with the priest for special permission for the two of them to sleep together the night before, so that the act is deprived of its transgressive sting. What can he do now? In the last shot of the film, we see him crawling on the narrow porch on the outside of the high-rise building, giving himself the difficult task of entering the girl's bedroom in the most dangerous way, in a desperate attempt to link sexual gratification with mortal danger... So, Lacan's point is that if gratifying sexual passion involves the suspension of even the most elementary 'egoistic' interests, if this gratification is clearly located 'beyond the pleasure principle', then, in spite of all appearances to the contrary, *we are dealing with an ethical act*, then his 'passion' is *stricto sensu* ethical....[8]

Lacan's further point is that this covert Sadean dimension of an 'ethical (sexual) passion' is not read into Kant by our eccentric interpretation, but is inherent in the Kantian theoretical edifice.[9] If we put aside the body of 'circumstantial evidence' for it (isn't Kant's infamous definition of marriage – 'the contract between two adults of the opposite sex about the mutual use of each other's sexual organs' – thoroughly Sadean, since it reduces the Other, the subject's sexual partner, to a partial object, to his or her bodily organ which provides pleasure, ignoring him or her as the Whole of a human Person?), the crucial clue that allows us to discern the contours of 'Sade in Kant' is the way Kant conceptualizes the relationship between sentiments (feelings) and the moral Law. Although Kant insists on the absolute gap between pathological sentiments and the pure form of moral Law, there *is* one *a priori* sentiment that the subject necessarily experiences when confronted with the injunction of the moral Law, the *pain* of humiliation (because of man's hurt pride, due to the 'radical Evil' of human nature); for Lacan, this Kantian privileging of pain as the only a priori sentiment is strictly correlative to de Sade's notion of pain (torturing and humiliating the other, being tortured and humiliated by him) as the privileged way of access to sexual *jouissance* (Sade's argument, of course, is that pain is to be given priority over pleasure on account of its greater longevity – pleasures are passing, while pain can last almost indefinitely). This link can be further substantiated by what Lacan calls the Sadean fundamental fantasy: the

fantasy of another, ethereal body of the victim, which can be tortured indefinitely yet none the less magically retains its beauty (see the standard Sadean
figure of a young girl sustaining endless humiliations and mutilations from her
deprived torturer and somehow mysteriously surviving it all intact, in the same
way Tom and Jerry and other cartoon heroes survive all their ridiculous ordeals
intact). Doesn't this fantasy provide the libidinal foundation of the Kantian
postulate of the immortality of the soul endlessly striving to achieve ethical
perfection: that is, is not the fantasmatic 'truth' of the immortality of the soul its
exact opposite, the *immortality of the body*, its ability to sustain endless pain and
humiliation?[10] Judith Butler pointed out that the Foucauldian 'body' as the site
of resistance is none other than the Freudian 'psyche': paradoxically, 'body' is
Foucault's name for the *psychic* apparatus in so far as it resists the soul's
domination. That is to say, when, in his well-known definition of the soul as
the 'prison of the body', Foucault turns around the standard Platonic-Christian
definition of the body as the 'prison of the soul', what he calls 'body' is not
simply the biological body, but is effectively already caught up into some kind
of pre-subjective psychic apparatus.[11] Consequently, don't we encounter in
Kant a secret homologous inversion, only in the opposite direction, of the
relationship between body and soul: what Kant calls 'immortality of the soul' is
effectively the immortality of the other, ethereal, 'undead' *body*?

III

It is via this central role of pain in the subject's ethical experience that Lacan
introduces the difference between the 'subject of the enunciation' (the subject
who utters a statement) and the 'subject of the enunciated (statement)' (the
symbolic identity the subject assumes within and via his statement). Kant does
not address the question of who is the 'subject of the enunciation' of the moral
Law, the agent enunciating the unconditional ethical injunction. From within
his horizon, this question is itself meaningless, since the moral Law is an
impersonal command 'coming from nowhere'; that is, it is ultimately self-
posited, autonomously assumed by the subject himself). Via the reference to
Sade, Lacan reads absence in Kant as an act of rendering invisible, of 'repres-
sing', the moral Law's enunciator; and it is Sade who renders it visible in the
figure of the 'sadist' executioner-torturer. This executioner is the enunciator of
the moral Law, the agent who finds pleasure in our (the moral subject's) pain
and humiliation. A counter-argument offers itself here with apparent self-
evidence: isn't all this utter nonsense, since, in Sade, the element that occupies
the place of the unconditional injunction, the maxim the subject has to follow
categorically, is no longer the Kantian universal ethical command 'Do your

duty!', but its most radical opposite, the injunction to follow to their utmost limit the thoroughly pathological, contingent caprices that bring you pleasure, ruthlessly reducing all your fellow humans to instruments of your pleasure? However, it is crucial to perceive the solidarity between this feature and the emergence of the figure of the 'sadist' torturer-executioner as the effective 'subject of the enunciation' of the universal ethical statement-command. The Sadean move from Kantian Respect to Blasphemy – that is, from respecting the Other (fellow being), his freedom and autonomy, and always treating him also as an end-in-itself, to reducing all Others precisely to mere dispensable instruments to be ruthlessly exploited – is strictly correlative to the fact that the 'subject of the enunciation' of the Moral Injunction, invisible in Kant, assumes the concrete features of the Sadean executioner.

What Sade accomplishes is thus a very precise operation of *breaking up the link between two elements which, in Kant's eyes, are synonymous and overlapping:*[12] the assertion of an unconditional ethical injunction and the moral universality of this injunction. Sade keeps the structure of an unconditional injunction, positing as its content the utmost pathological singularity. But again, the crucial point is that this breaking up is not Sade's eccentricity – it lies dormant as a possibility in the very fundamental tension constitutive of the Cartesian subjectivity.[13] That is to say, the intervention of the subject undermines the standard, pre-modern opposition between the universal Order and the hubris of a particular force whose egoistic excess perturbs the balance of the universal Order: 'subject' is the name for the hubris, the excessive gesture, whose very excess grounds the universal Order; it is the name for the pathological abject, *clinamen*, deviation from the universal Order, which sustains this very universal Order. The transcendental subject is the 'ontological scandal', neither phenomenal nor noumenal, but an excess which sticks out from the 'great chain of being', a hole, a gap in the order of reality, and, simultaneously, the agent whose 'spontaneous' activity constitutes the order of (phenomenal) reality. If, for the traditional ontology, the problem was how to deduce chaotic phenomenal reality from the eternal Order of the true reality (how to account for the gradual 'degeneration' of the eternal Order), the problem of the subject is that of the imbalanced excess, hubris, deviation, which sustains the Order itself. The central paradox of the Kantian transcendental constitution is that the subject is not the Absolute, the eternal grounding Principle of reality, but a finite, temporal entity, and that precisely as such, it provides the ultimate horizon of reality. For that reason, one should reject the standard reading of the Kantian transcendental constitution according to which the subject is the agent of universality who imposes on the chaotic multitude of sensible impressions the universal form of Reason: in this case, the subject is directly identified with the force of universalization, and what is missed is the fact that subject is simultaneously *clinamen*, the out-of-joint excess, the paradoxical point at which an extreme excess itself, an element which sticks out, *Grounds* universality.

The exemplary case of the 'pathological', contingent element elevated to the status of an unconditional demand is, of course, an artist absolutely identified with his artistic mission, pursuing it freely without any guilt, as an inner constraint, unable to survive without it. The sad fate of Jacqueline du Pré confronts us with the feminine version of the split between the unconditional injunction and its obverse, the serial universality of indifferent empirical objects that must be sacrificed in the pursuit of one's Mission.[14] (It is extremely interesting and productive to read du Pré's life story not as a 'real story', but as a mythical narrative: what is so surprising about it is how closely it follows the pre-ordained contours of a family myth, just like the story of Kaspar Hauser, in which individual accidents uncannily reproduce familiar features from ancient myths.[15]) Du Pré's unconditional injunction, her drive, her absolute passion, was her art (when she was 4 years old, upon seeing someone playing a cello, she already immediately claimed that this is what she wanted to be . . .). This elevation of her art to the unconditional relegated her love life to a series of encounters with men who were ultimately all substitutable, one as good as the other – she was reported to be a serial 'man-eater'. She thus occupied the place usually reserved for the *Male* artist – no wonder her long tragic illness (multiple sclerosis, from which she was painfully dying from 1973 to 1987) was perceived by her mother as an 'answer of the Real', as divine punishment not only for her promiscuous sexual life, but also for her 'excessive' commitment to her art . . .

IV

On closer analysis, one would have to link the notion of respect to that of castration: *respect is ultimately always respect for (Other's) castration.* When we respect another subject, we do not do it on account of some outstanding property of this subject, but, on the contrary, on account of some fundamental lack that defines its very being – 'respect' means that we maintain a proper distance, that we do not approach the other too closely: that is, so closely that we dissolve the semblance that conceals/envelops the lack and thus render this lack fully visible. For example, one respects one's father in so far as one accepts his assertion of authority at its word, without provoking him too much into effectively demonstrating his authority, being well aware that in this way, one might render visible father's imposture, the fact that his authority conceals a fundamental impotence. (Which is why, for the respected person, the elementary gesture of undermining the respect others have is to expose their lack: for a cripple to show his deformed crippled leg, etc.) For this reason, cultures that insist on women wearing veils that cover them up, insist that they are doing this out of respect for women; for an Islamic 'fundamentalist', it is the Western liberal culture that treats women in a disrespectful way, shamelessly exposing them as objects of sexual pleasure . . . [16]

It is against this background that one should approach the Kantian notion of *Achtung*, of respect for the Other Person, who should never be treated only as a means. Things are here more unsettling than they may appear. Let us take a criminal who cruelly and intentionally killed another person; how do we show proper respect for him? By condemning him and shooting him, since this way we treat him as a free, reasonable person; whereas all the talk about the impact of social circumstances treats him 'disrespectfully' – that is, not as a free, responsible agent, but as a plaything of social mechanisms. Today's victimization and 'understanding' are thus much less respectful of human dignity than the Kantian – Hegelian notion of deserved punishment. (Hegel takes this to its logical conclusion by claiming that the murderer himself, in his capacity as a rational free being, *wants* his punishment: in punishing him, we merely realize his true rational Will that he is unaware of . . .) What the notion of respect thus involves is a split in the object of respect between the level of his symbolic ideal existence (a free being obeying universal laws) and the reality of his factual existence (a vile murderer): the only way to show respect for the other is to smash violently this reality of the factual existence on behalf of the symbolic ideal. On a somewhat different level, we encounter the same dilemma in the case of a person dying in debilitating, painful confusion, vomiting and regressing to childish and obscene rambling: when relatives opt for euthanasia to put an end to this painful spectacle, they do so not only to shorten the dying person's senseless pain, but also to retain his dignity: that is, to assure that he will be remembered by his relatives and friends as a dignified old person, not as a stinking, rambling idiot . . . Here we encounter the distinction between the Ego-Ideal and the Other *qua* real: do we really have the right to sacrifice the real Other for the sake of his Ego-Ideal, of the image of him retained for posterity? How can we be sure that the dying man did not find an intense *jouissance* in his 'undignified', drug-induced mortal delusions?

In Japanese culture, it is considered very crude and disrespectful to confront the other's gaze directly: averting the other's gaze, not looking him straight into the eyes, is considered not a sign of evasion, but a sign of respect.[17] (Instead of veiling the object we are looking at, as in Islam, the veil is here, as it were, 'internalized', transposed to the eye itself . . .) Perhaps this feature gives a clue to what respect is: as we have already seen, to respect the Other means that one does not approach him or her too closely. So how does this work with Kant? What is worthy of respect in a person is, for Kant, his or her sublime dimension: that is, his or her noumenal freedom, the fact that he or she is an ethical being. In what, then, does respect consist here? In a first attempt, one is tempted to say that, in so far as the Kantian Sublime stands for the failure of imagination to successfully 'schematize' the noumenal dimension of Freedom, what makes a man worthy of respect is the very gap of castration that for ever separates him as a 'real person' from his freedom as symbolic feature (a real person can never fully live up to his noumenal Duty). But is this the only possible reading? Isn't it also that, when we approach the Other Person too closely, we discover not that the acts that appeared ethical were effectively done for pathological reasons, but that his or her transcendental Freedom itself is that which is properly Monstrous. What respect veils is not the gap between Freedom and the pathological reality of a person, but the uncanny, monstrous obverse of transcendental Freedom itself.

V

Although, in contrast to Kant, the Sadean blasphemy openly displays the castration – not the executioner's, but the Other's, rendering the Other visible in his or her utter, shameful impotence – they both meet in the fundamental coldness of the subject who follows the unconditional injunction. Edward Said draws attention to Mozart's letters to his wife Constanze from 30 September of 1790 – that is, from the time when he was composing *Cosi fan tutte*. After expressing his pleasure at the prospect of meeting her again soon, he goes on: 'If the people were to be able to see into my heart, I would have to be almost ashamed of myself...' At this point, as Said perspicuously perceives, one would expect the confession of some dirty private secret (sexual fantasies of what he will do to his wife when they will finally meet, etc.); however, the letter goes on: 'everything is cold to me – cold like ice'.[18] It is here that Mozart enters the uncanny domain of 'Kant avec Sade', the domain in which sexuality loses its passionate, intense character, and turns into its opposite, a 'mechanical' exercise in pleasure executed by cold distance, like the Kantian ethical subject doing his duty without any pathological commitment... Isn't this the underlying vision of *Cosi*: a universe in which subjects are determined not by their passionate engagements, but by a blind mechanism that regulates their passions? What compels us to bring *Cosi* close to the domain of 'Kant avec Sade' is its very insistence on the *universal* dimension already indicated by its title: 'they are all doing this', determined by the same blind mechanism ...In short, Alfonso, the philosopher who organizes and manipulates the game of changed identities in *Cosi*, is a version of the figure of the Sadean pedagogue educating his young disciples in the art of debauchery. It is thus oversimplified and inadequate to conceive this coldness as that of the 'instrumental reason'.

Kant and Sade have in common not only this coldness of the unconditional injunction (*Do your duty!* or *Enjoy!*) that compels the subject to sacrifice his attachment to all contingent, 'pathological' objects; it is interesting to note that they also share the same symptomatic gesture by means of which they shrink from the ultimate consequences of their theoretical edifice. In both cases, the term that allows this operation is that of *nature*: 'Nature is, in Sade as well as in Kant, the symptom of that which remains unthought in these two thinkers of the universal.'[19] That is to say, in both cases we are dealing with a certain structurally necessary ambiguity of this term. Kant first defines nature as the Whole of phenomena, of phenomenal reality, in so far as it is held together by (and subject to) universal laws; later, however, he also speaks of another, noumenal Nature as the kingdom of ethical goals, as the community of all rational ethical beings. Thus, the very excess of Freedom over nature (the natural enchainment of causes and effects) is again naturalized... Sade, on the other hand, first conceives of nature as the indifferent system of matter subject to eternal change, inexorably following its course, submitted to no external Divine Master; however, in his claim that, when we find pleasure in torturing our fellow beings and destroying them, up to the interruption of the very natural cycle of reproduction, we effectively fulfil Nature's innermost request, he secretly introduces another form of nature, no longer the usual indifferent run of things 'beyond Good and Evil', but Nature which is already somehow subjectivized, turned into a transgressive/diabolic entity commanding us to pursue evil and to find pleasure in the destruction and sacrifice of every form of morality and compassion. Isn't this second nature – what Lacan referred to as the 'Supreme Being of Evilness' – the Sadean counterpoint to (or reversal of) the Kantian Nature *qua* the community of suprasensible rational beings, the kingdom of ethical Goals? This ambiguity can also be stated in the following terms: what effectively brings pleasure to the Sadean hero? Is it the mere 'return to the innocence of nature', the unconstrained following of the laws of nature that also demand destruction, or is pleasure none the less inherently linked to the moral Law it violates, so that what brings us pleasure is the very awareness that we are committing a blasphemy? This ambivalence between innocence and blasphemous corruption is irreducible. (Another aspect of this same ambivalence is Sade's oscillation between the *solipsism* of pleasure and the *intersubjective* logic of blasphemy: is the point merely that I must ignore the Other's dignity, reducing him to an instrument to satisfy my whims, so that the Other is not subjectivized but reduced to an impersonal tool, a kind of masturbatory resource for my solitary pleasure; or is it that I get pleasure out of the very awareness that I am humiliating the Other and causing him

unbearable pain?[20]) So, in both cases, in Kant as well as in Sade, the 'elementary' neutral notion of Nature as the indifferent mechanism that follows its
course is supplemented by another, 'ethical' notion of Nature (the suprasensible kingdom of ethical goals, the diabolical commandment to pursue the evil
path of destruction . . .), and, in both cases, this second notion of nature masks
a certain gesture of shrinking back, of avoiding the confrontation with the
ultimate paradox of one's position: the uncanny abyss of freedom without any
ontological guarantee in the Order of Being.

VI

The fundamental difference between A/H and Lacan resides in the fact that,
for A/H, Sade is the truth of Kant in the sense that the Kantian ethical *formalism*
implies the radical instrumentalization of all contingent ('pathological') *content*
– each and every other human being, each 'neighbour', is reduced to a
potential object of manipulation in the service of the subject's survival –
while for Lacan, *it is the sadist pervert himself who occupies the place of the object* –
that is, who assumes the position of the pure object-instrument of the Other's
jouissance, displacing the division constitutive of subjectivity on to the other, on
to his victim. In this respect, the sadist perversion is very close to obsessional
neurosis, with the only (yet crucial) difference that the sadist pervert is active in
order to generate the Other's *jouissance*, while the obsessional neurotic is active
for precisely the opposite reason: in order to *prevent* the Other's enjoyment
(*pour que ça ne bouge pas dans l'autre*, as they put it in French).

This, however, is not the whole story. The decisive question is: is the
Kantian moral Law translatable into the Freudian notion of the superego or
not? If the answer is yes, then 'Kant with Sade' effectively means that Sade is
the truth of Kantian ethics. If, however, the Kantian moral Law cannot be
identified with the superego (since, as Lacan himself puts it in the last pages of
Seminar XI, moral Law is equivalent to desire itself, while the superego precisely feeds on the subject's compromising of his or her desire; that is, the guilt
sustained by the superego bears witness to the fact that the subject has somewhere betrayed or compromised his or her desire[21]), then Sade is not the entire
truth of Kantian ethics, but a form of its perverted realization. In short, far from
being 'more radical than Kant', Sade articulates what happens when the subject
betrays the true stringency of Kantian ethics. Sade is thus the truth of Kant in so
far as we interpret the Kantian ethical imperative as an objectivized apparatus
establishing what our duty is (so that we can use it as an excuse: 'What can I do,
the categorical imperative tells me this is my duty!'); however, in so far as duty
itself cannot serve as an excuse to do one's duty, Sade (the sadist perversion) is

no longer the truth of Kantian ethics. This difference is crucial in its political consequences: in so far as the libidinal structure of 'totalitarian' regimes is perverse (the totalitarian subject assumes the position of the object-instrument of the Other's *jouissance*), 'Sade as the truth of Kant' would mean that Kantian ethics effectively harbours totalitarian potentials;[22] however, in so far as we conceive of Kantian ethics as precisely *prohibiting* the subject from assuming the position of the object-instrument of the Other's *jouissance* – that is, as calling on him to assume full responsibility for what he proclaims his Duty – then Kant is the anti-totalitarian *par excellence* ...

And the same goes also for Freud himself: the dream about Irma's injection that Freud used as the exemplary case to illustrate his procedure of analyzing dreams is a dream about *responsibility* (Freud's own responsibility for the failure of his treatment of Irma) – this fact alone indicates that responsibility is a crucial Freudian notion. But how are we to conceive it? How are we to avoid the usual trap of the *mauvaise foi* of the Sartrean subject responsible for his existential project: that is, of the existentialist motif of ontological guilt that pertains to the finite human existence as such, as well as the opposite trap of 'putting the blame on the Other' ('since the Unconscious is the discourse of the Other, I am not responsible for its formations, it is the big Other who speaks through me, I am merely its instrument ...')? Lacan himself pointed the way out of this deadlock by referring to Kant's philosophy as the crucial antecedent of the psychoanalythic ethics of the duty 'beyond the Good'. According to the standard pseudo-Hegelian critique, the Kantian universalist ethic of the categorical imperative fails to take into account the concrete historical situation in which the subject is embedded, and which provides the determinate content of the Good: what eludes Kantian formalism is the historically specified particular Substance of ethical life. However, this reproach can be countered by claiming that the unique strength of Kant's ethics resides in this very formal indeterminacy: moral Law does not tell me *what* my duty is, it merely tells me *that* I should accomplish my duty; that is, it is not possible to derive the concrete norms I have to follow in my specific situation from the moral Law itself – *which means that the subject him or herself has to assume responsibility for 'translating' the abstract injunction of the moral Law into a series of concrete obligations*. In this precise sense, one is tempted to risk a parallel with Kant's *Critique of Judgement*: the concrete formulation of a determinate ethical obligation has the structure of an aesthetic judgement – that is, of a judgement whereby, instead of simply applying a universal category to a particular object or of subsuming this object under an already given universal determination, I as it were *invent* its universal-necessary-obligatory dimension and thus elevate this particular contingent object (act) to the dignity of the ethical Thing. So there is always something sublime about pronouncing a judgement that defines our duty: in it, I 'elevate an object to the dignity of the Thing' (Lacan's definition of sublimation).

Full acceptance of this paradox also compels us to reject any reference to 'duty' as an excuse: 'I know this is heavy and can be painful, but what can I do, this is my duty? . . .' The standard motto of ethical rigour is: 'There is no excuse for not accomplishing one's duty!'; although Kant's 'Du kannst, denn du sollst!' ('You can, because you must!') seems to offer a new version of this motto, he implicitly complements it with its much more uncanny inversion: 'There is no excuse for *accomplishing* one's duty!'[23] The reference to duty as the excuse to do our duty should be rejected as hypocritical; suffice it to recall again the example of the severe sadistic teacher. Of course, his excuse to himself (and to others) is: 'I myself find it hard to exert such pressure on the poor kids, but what can I do – it's my duty!' The more pertinent example is that of a Stalinist politician who loves mankind, but none the less carries out horrible purges and executions; his heart is breaking while he is doing it, but he cannot help it, it's his Duty towards the Progress of Humanity . . . What we encounter here is the properly *perverse* attitude of adopting the position of the pure instrument of the big Other's Will: it's not my responsibility, it's not me who is effectively doing it, I am merely an instrument of the higher Historical Necessity . . . The obscene *jouissance* of this situation is generated by the fact that I conceive of myself as exculpated for what I am doing: isn't it nice to be able to inflict pain on others with the full awareness that I'm not responsible for it, that I merely fulfil the Other's Will? . . . This is what Kantian ethics prohibits. This position of the sadist pervert provides the answer to the question: How can the subject be guilty when he merely realizes an 'objective', externally imposed necessity? By subjectively assuming this 'objective necessity' – that is, by finding *enjoyment* in what is imposed on him.[24] So, at its most radical, Kantian ethics is *not* 'sadist', but precisely what prohibits assuming the position of a Sadean executioner. What, then, does this tell us about the respective status of coldness in Kant and in Sade? The conclusion to be drawn is not that Sade sticks to cruel coldness, while Kant somehow has to allow for human compassion, but quite the opposite: it is only the Kantian subject that is effectively thoroughly cold (apathetic), while the sadist is *not 'cold' enough*; his 'apathy' is a fake, a lure concealing the all too passionate engagement on behalf of the Other's *jouissance*.

In a final twist, Lacan thus none the less undermines the thesis of 'Sade as the truth of Kant': it is no accident that the seminar in which Lacan first deployed the inherent link between Kant and Sade also contains the detailed reading of *Antigone* in which Lacan delineates the contours of an ethical act that *does* successfully avoid the trap of the Sadean perversion as its hidden truth – in insisting on her unconditional demand for her brother's proper burial, Antigone does *not* obey a command that humiliates her, a command effectively uttered by a sadistic executioner . . . So the main effect of Lacan's seminar on the *Ethics of Psychoanalysis* is precisely to break up the vicious cycle of 'Kant avec Sade'. How is this possible? Only if – in contrast to Kant – one asserts that *the faculty of desiring is not in itself 'pathological'*. In short, Lacan asserts the necessity of a 'critique of *pure* desire': in contrast to Kant, for whom our capacity to desire is thoroughly 'pathological' (since, as he repeatedly stresses, there is no a priori link between an empirical object and the pleasure this object generates in the subject), Lacan claims that there is a 'pure faculty of desire', since desire *does* have a non-pathological, a priori object-cause. This object, of course, is what Lacan calls *objet petit a*.

Notes

1 Max Horkheimer und Theodor W. Adorno, *Dialektik der Aufklaerung* (Frankfurt, Fischer Verlag, 1971), p. 79.

2 See especially chapter 6 of Jacques Lacan, *Le Séminaire, livre VII: l'éthique de la psychanalyse* (Paris, Éditions du Seuil, 1986).

3 See Jacques Lacan, 'Kant avec Sade', in *Écrits* (Paris, Éditions du Seuil, 1966), pp. 765–90.

4 Doesn't the same hold even for Derrida, who, in his *Spectres of Marx* (Paris, Galilée, 1993), in what is arguably the lowest philosophical point of his *oeuvre*, in order to prove that, in spite of the ruthless radicality of deconstruction, he is also a good, caring human being, enumerates in ten points what is wrong with today's world (from the sad plight of the homeless in our cities to narco-cartels . . . – see pp. 134– 9). In a strict parallel to the Young Hegelian criticism of Kant, Laclau's critical analysis of Derrida (see Ernesto Laclau, 'The Time is Out of Joint', in *Emancipation(s)* (London, Verso, 1996), pp. 66–93) emphasized how the Lévinasian ethical attitude of 'openness to the spectral Other', to the unique Event of its emergence, cannot be strictly deduced from the basic premiss of deconstruction (the constitutive displacement, i.e. the coincidence of conditions of possibility with the conditions of impossibility) – from the same premisses, one can also draw the exactly opposite conclusion: i.e. the need for a strong force of domination which, temporarily at least, contains the threat of dissemination.

5 Horkheimer and Adorno, *Dialektik*, p. 102.

6 In clinical terms, one can say that Sade radicalizes the Kantian obsessional economy into a full-blown perverse position.

7 Immanuel Kant, *Critique of Practical Reason* (New York, Macmillan, 1993), p. 30.

8 '. . . if, as Kant claims, no other thing but the moral law can induce us to put aside all our pathological interests and accept our death, then the case of someone who spends a night with a lady even though he knows that he will pay for it with his life, *is the case of the moral law*' (Alenka Zupančič, 'The Subject of the Law', in *Cogito and*

the Unconscious, ed. by Slavoj Žižek (Durham, NC, Duke University Press, 1998), p. 89).

9   The most obvious proof of the inherent character of this link of Kant with Sade, of course, is the (disavowed) Kantian notion of 'diabolical Evil', i.e. of Evil accomplished for no 'pathological' reasons, but out of principle, 'Just for the sake of it'. Kant evokes this notion of Evil elevated into a universal maxim (and thus turned into an ethical principle) only in order to disclaim it immediately, insisting that human beings are incapable of such utter corruption; however, shouldn't we counter this Kantian disclaimer by pointing out that de Sade's entire edifice relies precisely on such an elevation of Evil into an unconditional ('categorical') imperative? For a closer elaboration of this point, see chapter 2 of Žižek, *Indivisible Remainder*.

10 Regarding this point, see Zupančič, 'Subject of the Law'.

11 See Judith Butler, *The Psychic Life of Power* (Stanford, Calif., Stanford University Press, 1997), pp. 28–9.

12 See Monique David-Menard, *Les Constructions de l'universel* (Paris, PUE, 1997).

13 Hegel was already aware of this reversal of the Kantian universal into the utmost idiosyncratic contingency: isn't the main point of his critique of the Kantian ethical imperative that, since the imperative is empty, Kant has to fill it with some empirical content, thus conferring on contingent particular content the form of universal necessity?

14 See Hilary and Piers du Pré, *A Genius in the Family: An Intimate Memoir of Jacqueline du Pré* (London, Chatto and Windus, 1997).

15 Conversely, it is sometimes also productive to read myths as 'real stories'. In this way, if one reads a myth with total 'realist' *naïvéte*, the point of the narrative emerges clearly.

16 Of course, the catch here is that woman's self-respect is defined in terms of her role within the patriarchal normative system of exchanges.

17 Therein resides the subversive effect of Ozu's films, which as a rule passes unobserved in the West: his films depict couples who, shown in standard American shots, directly return each other's gaze and look into each other's eyes. The emotional impact of this is much stronger in Japan than in Europe or the USA.

18 See Edward W. Said, 'Cosi fan tutte', *Lettre international 39* (Winter 1997), pp. 69–70.

19 David-Menard, *Les Constructions*, p. 64.

20 As Claude Lefort pointed out (see his *Écrire a l'épreuve du politique* (Paris, Calman Lévy, 1992), pp. 108–10), the same tension is discernible in the inconsistency of Sadean pedagogy: although Sade's goal is the asocial individual who exploits others merely as means for his pleasure, the only way to bring about such an individual in today's society 'degenerated' by religion is through a new pedagogy that expresses the will to corrupt innocent young girls by introducing them into the art of unconstrained pleasures. Sadean heroes thus none the less tend to form a new, 'authentic' community, an élitist closed circle of those initiated in the art of pleasures . . .

21 See Zupančič, 'Subject of the Law', as well as Bernard Baas, *Le Désir pur* (Louvain, Peeters, 1992).

22 A feature which, perhaps, points in this direction is Kant's well-known thesis that Reason without intuition is empty, while Intuition without reason is blind: is not its political counterpart Robespierre's dictum according to which Virtue without Terror is impotent, while Terror without Virtue is lethal, striking blindly?

23 For a more detailed account of this key feature of Kant's ethics, see chapter 2 of Žižek, *The Individisible Remainder*.

24 See Alenka Zupančič, *Die Ethik des Realen. Kant mit Lacan* (Vienna, Turia und Kant, 1995).

14

Of Cells and Selves

This new, previously unpublished essay is a critique of 'Deep Ecology', the ethico-political position in which *Homo sapiens* is considered to be on the same level as other species, with obligations towards them. Both in its neo-Spinozistic pantheist form (in which even rocks and stones figure as objects of concern) and in its 'New Age' spiritualized mode (in which man is hierarchically supreme yet involved in a caretaking capacity), the human being is subordinate to the cosmic whole: this split is traceable to a contradiction within Cartesian subjectivism, for which, on the one hand, one is no more than a mote in the universe, while, on the other, one is a self-seeking operator.

An even more extreme version of Deep Ecology sees the end result of human development as proceeding towards a higher form of consciousness, a 'properly *psychotic* fantasy', since it leaves behind the contingent nature of all subjectivity and thereby runs the risk of that loss of freedom, which, for Kant, attends the dreadful face-to-face confrontation with the noumenal God (see also Žižek, *Plague of Fantasies*, p. 229). The psychotic structure of this fantasy, its absence of freedom is equivalent to the erasure of sexual difference, as if the monstrous asexual Thing could immortalize itself – perhaps by cloning? There is an analogy here between this totalizing fantasy which cancels out all freedom in the pursuit of freedom and the contradictions that Kant reveals in his antinomies of pure reason and Lacan in his sexuation formulas.

The question of what ethical judgement is proper to cloning produces similar contradictions, there being an underlying fear that the human being can be reduced to genetic specification together with the belief that the soul is *sui generis*; the arguments produced by the Roman Catholic Church, the social theorist Jürgen Habermas and the Deep Ecologists all go down this road. In their argument it is as if Kant's moral dictum 'You can, because you must' has been turned into 'You cannot, because you should not'. This is tantamount to saying that the materialist reduction is impossible because you ought not to perform it, as it is actually possible. To escape this double bind requires a surrender of both the materialist order and the divine. If, then, there is no ontological completeness, the self has to remain unspecified. Freedom can be guaranteed only by a 'reality' that is neither ordered nor unified, but has an ontological flaw within it. This counters the logical picture of the world implied in both the noumenal universe of Deep Ecology and the 'postmodern' attempt to produce a digital version of 'reality'.

How, then, can one get distinct entities out of an initial disorder, or, biologically speaking, how does a cell emerge from the confusion of the environment? In one biological account (Varela) the very act of origin involves the creation of a boundary which sets off 'inside' from 'outside': a limit occurs in the environment that becomes a self-limitation, an 'autopoiesis'. There is a parallel here to the formation of the self, in that it comes into existence the moment it 'posits itself self-referentially' ('the self-referential loop'), defining itself in a retrospective mediation of its own activities; or, as Hegel has it, it 'posits its presuppositions'. The self has only a virtual existence, maintained in its performance, not knowing 'what kind of a Thing it is in the Real', wholly determined neither by its genome nor by environmental causes. The anxiety about meeting a clone, that imaginary substantializing of the self's particular identity, is therefore directed at something impossible, a 'doubling of the soul', which finds representation in the Romantic *Doppelgänger*, the uncanny horror of which resides in its possession of that which I lack, the *objet a*, that particularly which I believed was uniquely mine.

Because of the incessant mediation between the self and the social, there is a 'gap of causality', since there is no way in which causal links can be traced in either direction. The determinist causal chain is thus broken, which spares psychoanalysis from the accusation that it is unscientific: the unconscious 'intervenes when something "goes wrong" in the order of causality that encompasses our daily reality'. This unconscious intervention is the driving force of the self-reflexive pursuit, which for the German Idealists is the continuous act of negation, the separation of the 'I' from the 'Not-I', and for psychoanalysis is the death drive's endless symbolic repetitions tested out in the world, 'a void insisting indefinitely on its fulfilment'.

Žižek notes that a 'gap of causality' has also appeared in biology regarding the evolution of organs, in that some that have lost their original purpose become co-opted for tasks for which they were not developed, thus breaking the direct causal link claimed by vulgar Darwinism. Similarly, Lacan sees subjects as gratuitously burdened with an excess of drive which stubbornly strives for satisfaction. Language, it is suggested (Stephen Jay Gould), rather than being an adaptive system, now serves its own ends regardless of evolutionary development, displaying a 'purposiveness without purpose' (Kant), indicating human purpose unrelated to cause.

Who's Afraid of the Big Bad Clone?

Let us begin with the inherent antagonism of today's 'Deep Ecology', discernible in its split into two main orientations: on the one hand, anti-anthropocentric Spinozian Deep Ecology, for which all forms of life are strictly equivalent, so that the rights of all elements of a biosphere, rivers and rocks included, have ultimately the same weight as the rights of man; on the other hand, New Age animist spiritualism, which conceives of the entire universe as a living organism whose development to date has culminated in man, its Omega-point, its steward-guardian (which is why references to *anima mundi* and the 'anthropic principle' abound here). According to this view, we are today on the brink of a new cosmo-spiritual alteration which will deliver man from his narrow egoism and bring about a new solidarity of Life... This inherent split of Deep Ecology is grounded in the ambivalent relationship of modern Cartesian science to so-called anthropocentrism: the non-anthropocentric point of view that asserted itself with it (man as a tiny particle of dust in the endless universe...) is strictly correlative with its 'anthropocentric' stance of the ruthless exploitation of nature. More precisely, we encounter here an exemplary case of the split between man and subject: Cartesian 'subjectivism' is radically non-anthropocentric and 'anti-humanist'; that is, the moment Cartesian subjectivity is asserted, the pre-Cartesian humanist notions of man as the 'mirror of the universe', fitting into the hierarchy of beings as the highest product of divine creativity, is done with... [1]

In other words, the 'pragmatic contradiction' of Spinozian Deep Ecology resides in the fact that it itself commits the sin with which it reproaches animist New Age spiritualism (i.e. of being even more anthropocentric than Cartesianism, since man is for it the Omega-point of the entire universe): the paradox of Deep Ecology is that, in its very rejection of anthropocentrism, it charges man with the duty of subordinating the narrow interests of the human species to the interests of all other forms of life and of the entire biosphere. Does it not thereby elevate man into a kind of 'functionary of Life'? One can only ask of man to sacrifice his narrow interests and take into account the interests of the Whole of Life if one conceives of him as a 'universal being', the being in which life in its entirety became aware of itself – birds, trees, rivers and rocks are clearly not able to plead their own cause, let alone the cause of all other living beings... Deep Ecology thus in no way escapes the charge of anthropocentrism: the very demand it addresses to man to sacrifice himself for the interests of the entire biosphere confers on him the exceptional status of universal being; that is, the very apparent humiliation of man to a being whose duty is to sacrifice himself for the higher aim of preserving the biosphere is the form-of-appearance of its opposite. That is to say, is not the ability to disengage oneself from one's own limited situation and to self-objectivize oneself – to look at oneself as an insignificant part of a larger totality – the highest, exclusive spiritual capacity?

For this reason, when the very authors who condemn the anthropocentrist 'Cartesian paradigm' refer to the anthropic principle, they are not simply inconsistent: the man whose centrality is asserted in the anthropic principle is not the modern subject, but the pre-modern 'crown of creation', the highest link in the positive 'chain of Being', the point at which the universe itself, this gigantic living organism, arrives at consciousness of itself. More precisely, what one usually gets is the notion that we – humanity – are on the threshold of evolving into a higher entity, a universal cosmic consciousness, a kind of Mega-Brain – that is, of accomplishing the leap to a new stage of cosmic evolution with regard to which humanity as we know it is just a lower preparatory stage. This properly *psychotic* fantasy of leaving behind the level of subjectivity, with its contingent finitude, is one of the popular motifs of New Age techno-ideology: we are on the threshold of the transformation of human intelligence into something 'more than human', a higher-order Entity towards which we stand like animals (or even cells) stand to us:

We're heading toward something which is going to happen very soon – in our lifetimes – and which is fundamentally different from anything that's happened in human history before.... If I try to extrapolate the trends, to look at where technology's going sometime early in the next century, there comes a point where something incomprehensible will happen. Maybe it's the creation of intelligent machines. Maybe it's telecommunications merging us into a global organism. If you try to talk about it, it sounds mystical, but I'm making a very practical statement here. I think something's happening now – and will continue to happen over the next few decades – which is incomprehensible to us, and I find that both frightening and exciting.[2]

One cannot but recall again Kant's reflections on the necessary limitation of human cognitive faculties in his *Critique of Practical Reason*. The 'frightening and exciting' prospect of the 'global organism' into which we will be merged is, as to its consequences for the status of subjectivity, exactly what Kant aimed at when he evoked the prospect of direct insight into the noumenal Thing which would deprive us of the very freedom which makes us ethical agents: instead of providing ecstatic immersion in the ultimate Reality, this insight would turn us into lifeless puppets deprived of human dignity (which, of course, is just the obverse facet of ecstatic immersion). In Lacanian terms: through such an insight, the Symbolic directly overlaps the Real, which, by definition, brings about a psychotic effect. Or, to put it in yet another way, such a direct insight into the Thing would amount to the *end of sexual difference*; sexuality as we know it would be eclipsed by the monstrous asexual Alien Thing which reproduces itself by direct cloning (such an object is a common motif in science fiction, its best-known example being the gigantic planet which materializes Thought in Stanislav Lem's *Solaris*. What is crucial to bear in mind here is that, from the Lacanian perspective, the inaccessibility of the noumenal Thing to our cognition in Kant's philosophy is directly linked to the fact that we, finite humans, are sexed beings (an indirect proof of how sexuation is correlative to cognitive limitation – that is, to the inaccessibility of the noumenal Thing – is provided by the fact that the structure of the Kantian antinomies of pure reason – dynamic versus mathematical antinomies – which bear witness to the ultimate constraint of our cognitive capacity perfectly replicates Lacan's 'formulas of sexuation' that render the difference between masculine and feminine modes of subjectivity[3]).

Is, then, the hidden truth of Kant's *You can, because you must!* its reversal *You cannot, because you should not!*? The philosophico-ethical problems of (bioge-netic) cloning seem to point in this direction: the argument of those who oppose cloning is that we *should not* pursue it, at least not on human beings, because it is *not possible* to reduce a human being to a positive entity whose innermost psychic properties can be manipulated. Is this not another variation on Wittgenstein's 'You *should not* talk about what you *cannot* talk about!'? The underlying fear that gains expression in this prohibition, of course, is that the order of reason is actually obverse: that is, that the ontological impossibility is grounded in ethics. We should claim that we cannot do it, because otherwise *we may well do it*, with catastrophic ethical consequences. This paradox of prohibiting the impossible emerges at its purest in the conservative reaction of the Catholic Church to cloning: if the church effectively believes in the immortality of the human soul, in the uniqueness of human personality, in how I am not just the result of the interaction between my genetic code and my environs, then why oppose cloning and genetic manipulations? Are those Christians who oppose cloning not yet again involved in the game of prohibit-ing the impossible – biogenetic manipulation *cannot* touch the core of human personality, so we should *prohibit* it? In other words, is it not that *these Christian opponents of cloning themselves secretly believe in the power of scientific manipulation, in its capacity to stir up the very core of our personality?* Of course, their answer would be that, by treating himself as just the result of the interaction between his genetic code and his environs, man freely renounces his dignity. The problem is not genetic manipulation as such, but the fact that its acceptance signals how man conceives of himself as just another biological machine and thus robs himself of his unique dignity. However, the answer to this is, again: but why should we not endorse genetic manipulation and simultaneously insist that human persons are free responsible agents, since we accept the proviso that these manipulations do not really affect the core of our Soul? Why do the Christian opponents still talk about the 'unfathomable mystery of the conception' man should not meddle with, as if, none the less, by pursuing our biogenetic explorations, we may touch some secret better left in shadow – in short, as if, by cloning my body, *I at the same time also clone my immortal Soul...?*[4]

Cloning thus confronts us with the most fundamental ethico-ontological alternative. One can pretend that all the furor caused by its prospect is just a repetition of the standard reaction to every great technological invention, from machinery to cyberspace: the moral furor and fear, which express the subject's perplexity, is then followed by 'normalization'; that is, the new invention slowly becomes part of our lives, we get used to it, invent new norms of conduct with it . . . However, things are none the less more radical here, since what is at stake is the very core of 'human freedom'. In an essay for *Süddeutsche Zeitung*, Jürgen Habermas defended the prohibition of cloning with a line of argumentation which implies an interesting paradox. His main point is that cloning involves a situation which somehow resembles that of slavery: an inherent part of myself, a part which at least partially co-determines my psychic and bodily identity, becomes the result of a purposeful intervention/manipulation of another human being. In short, Habermas's argument is that what makes cloning ethically problematic is the very fact that my genetic base – which hitherto depended on the blind chance of biological inheritance – is at least partially determined by the conscious and purposeful (i.e. *free*) decision and intervention of another person: what makes me unfree, what deprives me of a part of my freedom, is, paradoxically, the very fact that what was hitherto left to chance (i.e. to blind natural *necessity*) becomes dependent on the *free* decision of another person. Here we encounter the crucial difference from slavery: when a slave is subordinated to another's Will, he is thereby deprived of his own personal freedom; however, when a clone is produced and its genome (ca. 6 billion genetic marks comprising the entirety of inherited 'knowledge') is changed by genetic manipulation, he is not in any homologous sense deprived of his freedom, it is only the part of him that previously depended on natural chance that is subordinated to another person's freedom. For this reason, the case analogous to the liberation of a slave is here neither the liberation of the subject from determination by a genetic code, nor a situation in which the concerned subject himself, after growing up and mastering biotechnology, would be able to manipulate himself, to intervene in his body in order to change it according to his free decision, but just the negative gesture of abolishing the determination of my genetic code by another person's decision and manipulative intervention. In short, I regain my freedom in so far as the structure of my genome is again left to the blind chance of natural necessity... Does Habermas thereby not confront the aforementioned Kantian dilemma? Does his solution also not imply that a certain minimum of ignorance is the condition of our freedom, so that through knowledge and a manipulative intervention into the genome deprive us of a part of our freedom? Here, the alternative is inevitable: either our genome does determine us, and then we are just 'biological machines', and all the talk about prohibiting cloning and genetic manipulations is just a desperate strategy for avoiding the inevitable, for sustaining the false appearance of our freedom by constraining our scientific knowledge and technological capacities based on it; or our genome does not determine us thoroughly, in which case, again, there is no real cause for alarm, since the manipulation of our genetic code does not really affect the core of our personal identity...

Are we thus back at the well-known conservative wisdom which claims that the only way to save human freedom and ethical dignity is to restrain our cognitive capacities and renounce probing too deeply into the nature of things? If we think to the end the consequences of the notion of subject *qua* the 'crack in the chain of being', we can none the less avoid this debilitating deadlock. The mistake of the identification of (self-) consciousness and/or freedom with misrecognition, with an epistemological obstacle, is that it stealthily (re)introduces the standard, pre-modern, 'cosmological' notion of reality as a Whole of Being, the positive order of things: in such a fully constituted positive 'chain of being', there is, of course, no place for the subject, so the dimension of subjectivity can only be conceived of as something which is strictly co-dependent with the epistemological misrecognition of the true positivity of being. Consequently, the only way effectively to account for the status of (self-) consciousness is to assert *the ontological incompleteness of 'reality' itself:* there is 'reality' only in so far as there is an ontological gap, a crack, in its very heart – that is, a traumatic excess, a foreign body which cannot be integrated into it. This brings us back to the notion of the 'night of the world': in this momentary suspension of the positive order of reality, we confront the ontological gap on account of which 'reality' is never a complete, self-enclosed, positive order of being. It is only this experience of the psychotic withdrawal from reality, of the absolute self-contraction, which accounts for the mysterious 'fact' of transcendental freedom – that is, for a (self-) consciousness which is effectively 'spontaneous', whose spontaneity is not an effect of misrecognition of some 'objective' process. At a different level, apropos of the artificial life created on the computer screen, Chris Langton encounters the same deadlock, and proposes the same false idealist way out:

After working for a long time creating these artificial universes, and wondering if such life would ever wonder about its own existence and origins, I find myself looking over my shoulder and wondering if there isn't another level on top of ours, with something wondering about me in the same way. . . . the universe as we know it is an artifact in a computer in a more 'real' universe.[5]

This more 'real' universe, of course, would be none other than the Kantian noumenal reality. The trap to be avoided is thus to conclude, from the fact that our universe is inconsistent, lacking, the existence of *another*, 'deeper' reality which provides the proper ontological foundation of our universe: that is, to accept that our reality stands towards some other, inaccessible noumenal reality in the same relationship as the simulated digital reality to our everyday 'real' reality. This ideological trap is strictly symmetrical to the opposite trap: to the 'postmodern' notion according to which our 'real' reality and the simulated reality on the screen are ultimately equal ontologically; that is, according to which 'real life' itself is just another cyberspace window, so that, when we shift from 'real life' to cyberspace and back, we are ultimately just shifting to and from different virtual universes – see Langton's answer to the reproach that the artificial models of evolutionary process in a computer only simulate evolution:

But what's the difference between the process of evolution in a computer and the process of evolution outside the computer? The entities that are being evolved are made of different stuff, but the process is identical.[6]

Here we encounter the problem of *un discours qui ne serait pas du semblant*:[7] how to locate the difference between a perfect simulation and the original itself? how to distinguish between a purely logical living system, existing only in an abstract mathematical world, and 'real' biological life? Implicit in the assertion of their ultimate identity is the Platonic precedence of purely logical digital life: this life renders the ideal pattern which can only be imitated/copied in an imperfect way by the 'real' biological life. All possible versions of the relationship between 'real' and digital life can thus be arranged into four basic options: (1) the 'naïve-realist' notion of our everyday reality as fully existing, as the 'original' imitated by its virtual simulations; (2) the notion that our everyday reality itself is an imperfect simulation of some higher, inaccessible reality; (3) the notion that real life and its digital simulation share the same logical structure or generative matrix, which is the only Real, that which remains the same in all possible universes; (4) the relativist notion that there simply is no Real, that there are only simulations referring to each other, as in an endless hall of mirrors. What all four versions exclude, of course, is the Lacanian impossible Real as opposed to reality.

The Self-referential Loop

The basic problem of the new evolutionary thought – that of the emergence of the ideal life-pattern – is none other than the old metaphysical enigma of the relationship between chaos and order, between the Many and the One, between parts and their whole: how can we get 'order for free'; that is, how can order emerge out of initial disorder? how account for a whole which is larger than the mere sum of its parts? How can a One with a distinct self-identity emerge out of the interaction of its multiple constituents? A series of contemporary researchers, from Lynn Margulis to Francisco Varela, assert that the true problem is not how organism and its environs interact or connect, but rather the opposite one: *how does a distinct self-identical organism emerge out of its environs*? How does a cell form the membrane which separates its inside from its outside? The true problem is thus not how an organism *adapts* to its environs, but how it is that *there is something, a distinct entity, which has to adapt itself* in the first place. And it is here, at this crucial point, that the biologist's language starts to resemble uncannily the language of Hegel. When Varela, for example, explains his notion of autopoiesis, he repeats almost verbatim the Hegelian notion of life as a teleological self-organizing entity. His central notion, that of a loop or bootstrap, points towards Hegel's 'positing the presuppositions':

Autopoiesis attempts to define the uniqueness of the emergence that produces life in its fundamental cellular form. It's specific to the cellular level. There's a circular or network process that engenders a paradox: a self-organizing network of biochemical reactions produces molecules, which do something specific and unique: they create a boundary, a membrane, which constrains the network that has produced the constituents of the membrane. This is a logical bootstrap, a loop: a network produces entities that create a boundary, which constrains the network that produces the boundary. This bootstrap is precisely what's unique about cells. A self-distinguishing entity exists when the bootstrap is completed. This entity has produced its own boundary. It doesn't require an external agent to notice it, or to say, 'I'm here'. It is, by itself, a self-distinction. It bootstraps itself out of a soup of chemistry and physics.[8]

The conclusion to be drawn is thus that the only way to account for the emergence of the distinction between 'inside' and 'outside' constitutive of a living organism is to posit a kind of self-reflexive reversal by means of which – to put it in Hegelese – the One of an organism as a Whole retroactively 'posits' as its result, as that which it dominates and regulates, the set of its own causes: that is, the very multiple process out of which it emerged. In this way, and only in this way, an organism is no longer limited by external conditionis, but is fundamentally *self-limited*. Again, as Hegel would have put it, life emerges when the external limitation (of an entity by its environs) turns into self-limitation. This brings us back to the problem of *infinity*: for Hegel, true infinity does not stand for limitless expansion, but for active *self-limitation* (self-determination), in contrast to being-determined-by-the-other. In this precise sense, life (even at its most elementary, as a living cell) is the basic form of true infinity, since it already involves the minimal loop by means of which a process is no longer simply determined by the Outside of its environs, but is itself able to (over)determine the mode of this determination and thus 'posits its presuppositions' – infinity acquires its first actual existence the moment a cell's membrane starts to functions as a *self*-boundary... Do these notions not reactualize Hegel's conceptual determinations of the elementary structure of life? When Hegel includes minerals in the category of 'life', as the lowest form of organism, does he not anticipate Margulis, who also insists on forms of life which *precede* vegetable and animal life? The further key fact is that we thus obtain a minimum of *ideality*: a property emerges which is purely virtual and relational, with no substantial identity:

My sense of self exists because it gives me an interface with the world. I'm 'me' for interactions, but my 'I' doesn't substantially exist, in the sense that it can't be localized anywhere.... An emergent property, which is produced by an underlying network, is a coherent condition that allows the system in which it exists to interface at that level – that is, with other selves or identities of the same kind. You can never say, 'This property is here; it's in this component.' In the case of autopoiesis, you can't say that life – the condition of being self-produced – is in this molecule, or in the DNA, or in the cellular membrane, or in the protein. Life is in the configuration and in the dynamical pattern, which is what embodies it as an emergent property.[9]

Here we encounter the minimum of 'idealism' which defines the notion of Self: a Self is precisely an entity without any substantial density, without any hard kernel tht would guarantee its consistency. If we penetrate the surface of an organism and look deeper and deeper into it, we never encounter some central controlling element which would be its Self, secretly pulling the strings of its organs. The consistency of the Self is thus purely and entirely virtual; it is as if it were an Inside which appears only when viewed from the Outside, on the interface screen: the moment we penetrate the interface and endeavour to grasp the Self 'substantially', as it is 'in itself', it disappears like sand between our fingers... The materialist reductionists who claim that 'there really is no self' are thus right, but they none the less miss the point: at the level of material reality (inclusive of the psychological reality of 'inner experience'), there effectively is no Self. The Self (Subject) is not the 'inner kernel' of an organism, but a surface effect: that is, a *'true' human Self in a sense functions like a computer screen*. What is 'behind' it is nothing but a network of 'selfless' neuronal machinery... We all know of *tamagochi*, the toy which reduces the other with whom we communicate (usually a pet animal) to the purely virtual presence on a screen. We play the game with him *as if* there were a real living creature behind the screen; we get excited, cry for it, etc., although we know very well that there is nothing behind, just a meaningless digital network. If we take seriously what I just said, we cannot avoid the conclusion that the Other Person with whom we communicate is ultimately also a kind of *tamagochi*: when we communicate with another subject, we get signals from him or her, we observe his or her face as a screen, but not only do we, partners in communication, never get to know what is 'behind the screen', *the same goes for the concerned subject himself*; the subject himself does not know what lies behind the screen of his (self-) consciousness, what kind of a Thing he is in the Real. (Self-) consciousness is a surface screen which produces the effect of 'depth', of a dimension beneath it; yet this dimension is accessible only from the standpoint of the surface, it is a kind of surface-effect. If we effectively reach behind the screen, the very effect of the 'depth of a person' dissolves; what we are left with is just a set of meaningless neuronal, biochemical, etc. processes. For that reason, the usual polemics of the respective role of 'genes versus environment' (of biology versus cultural influence, of nature versus nurture) in the formation of the subject misses the key dimension, that of the *interface* which connects and distinguishes the two. The 'subject' emerges when the 'membrane', the surface which delimits the Inside from the Outside, instead of being just a passive medium of their interaction, starts to function as their active mediator.

Geneticists predict that in about 10 to 15 years they will be able to identify and manipulate each individual's exact genome. Potentially, at least, each individual will thus have at his disposal the complete formula of what he or she 'objectively is'. How will this 'knowledge in the real', the fact that I will be able to locate and identify myself completely as an object in reality, affect the status of subjectivity? Will it lead to the end of human subjectivity? Lacan's answer is negative: what will continue to elude the geneticist is not my phenomenal self-experience (say, the experience of a love passion that no knowledge of the genetic and other material mechanisms determining it can take from me), but the fundamental fantasy, the fantasmatic core inaccessible to my conscious experience. Even if science is able to articulate the genetic formula of what I objectively am, it will still be unable to articulate my 'objectively subjective' fantasmatic identity, this objectal counterpoint to my subjectivity, which is neither subjective (experienced) nor objective. A further point to be noted is that this prospect of self-objectivization is strictly correlative to its opposite, to the rising unpredictability of our lives in today's 'risk society': nobody can be sure about the long-term effects of genetic manipulations of plants and animal species, not to speak of the standard ecological concerns about the greenhouse effect, etc. Are we not dealing here with the self-referential paradox of how to include in observed behaviour the knowledge about expected behaviour? That is to say, as any introduction to systems – theory will tell us, the problem with predictability is not only that it is difficult to predict the behaviour of complex systems – these systems are 'complex' in the more specific sense of their elements agents being 'adaptive' that is, of performing their acts on the basis of their expectations of how other agents will act, and changing their strategy upon getting new feed back. What further complicates the picture is the fact that the rationality of the agents is limited: no one among them possesses a global overview of the situation *This* is what makes the global situation unpredictable: what one cannot predict is how many features of the global situation will be *ignored* by particular agents. How are we to take into account the way the process under observation will be affected by the subject's very intervention? This contemporary experience of unpredictability should not be confused with the uncertainty about daily lives which was always part of the human experience. What we are dealing with today is, rather, the 'inexistence of the big Other': the substantial 'big Other', not only society but even nature itself, at least the natural life-cycle on Earth, is experienced as an unstable system which one cannot rely on to continue unperturbed and to ignore our human follies. The dreadful prospect always lurks of some of our acts (genetic manipulation, etc.) giving rise to the 'butterfly effect', and unexpectedly setting in motion a process which will end in a global catastrophe for the whole of humanity.

So, again, even if science defines and starts to manipulate the human genome, this will not enable it to dominate and manipulate man's subjectivity: what makes me 'unique' is neither my genetic formula (genome) nor the way my dispositions developed owing to the influence of the environment, but the unique self-relationship which emerges out of the interaction between the two. More precisely, even the word 'interaction' is not quite adequate here, in so far as it still implies the mutual influence of two given sets of positive conditions (genes and environment), and thus does not cover the crucial feature of *self-relating*, the self-referential loop due to which, in the way I relate to my environment, I never reach the 'zero-level' of being passively influenced by it, but always-already relate to myself in relating to it; that is, I always-already, with a minimum of 'freedom', determine in advance the way I will be determined by the environment, up to the most elementary level of sensible perceptions. The way I 'see myself', the imaginary and symbolic features which constitute my 'self-image', or, even more fundamentally, the fantasy which provides the ultimate co-ordinates of my being is neither in the genes nor imposed by the environment, but the unique way each subject *relates to him or herself*, 'chooses him or herself', in relationship to his or her environs, as well as to (what he or she perceives as) his 'nature'. We are thus dealing with a kind of 'bootstrap' mechanism which cannot be reduced to the interaction of myself as a biological entity with my environment: a third mediating agency emerges (the subject, precisely), which has no positive substantial Being, since, in a way, its status is purely 'performative', That is, it is a kind of self-inflamed flame, nothing but the outcome of its activity – what Fichte called a *Tathandlung*, the pure act of self-referential self-positing. Yes, I emerge through the interaction between my biological bodily base and my environs – but what both my environs and my bodily base are is always 'mediated' by my activity... It is interesting to note how today's most advanced cognitive scientists take over (or, rather, develop out of their own research) this motif of minimal self-reference which the great German Idealists were trying to formulate in terms of 'transcendental spontaneity'.[10] So, in the case of clones (or, already today, of identical twins), what accounts for their difference, for the uniqueness of each of the two, is not simply that they were exposed to different environments, but the way each of the two formed a unique structure of self-reference out of the interaction between their genetic substance and their environment.

Significantly, anxiety about encountering one's genetic clone is often confounded with the anxiety that arises when I am in danger of being deprived of my symbolic identity, since I am compelled to identify fully with imposed imaginary and/or symbolic features – to be like my mother or father or some other ideal-ego figure. (This situation is best exemplified by Billy Wilder's *Fedora*, a film in which a daughter is forced to take over the identity of her mother, an old actress: she undergoes plastic surgery to look like her mother when she was still young, she is taught to talk and to behave like her, etc., so that her mother's career is prolonged – everyone thinks that the mother has somehow succeeded in staying and looking young... This situation ultimately drives the daughter to suicide, of course she is unable to sustain this radical deprivation of her identity.) The crucial difference between this situation and that of cloning is that here we are dealing with *symbolic* violence, with the violent imposition of an alien symbolic identity, of a 'self-image' which is not the direct Real of someone's genes, but freely created by another subject through his or her self-relating. The proof of it is the very anxiety people experience apropos of being cloned: this fear of encountering an exact double already presupposes that I experience myself as the absolute singularity of a subject, so that the imposed sameness with another subject will consist of an imposed imaginary and/or symbolic identity, of an imposed 'self-image', not of the direct genetic sameness-in-the-real. In clear contrast to it, a true clone would feel no anxiety at being the same as his genetic double, since he would lack the very sense of absolute singularity which constitutes the self-referential identity of a subject.

Here it is crucial to reassert the old Lacanian lesson of the mirror-phase: I constitute myself as Ego only by recognizing myself in the mirror-image – that is, by encountering my virtual double, with whom I then engage in an ambiguous love–hate relationship (loving him because he is like me, hating him for the very same reason, because he threatens to occupy my place). So, in a way, there is no Ego without its clone double. The uncanniness of the double, however, hinges on the fact that the subject (as opposed to the Ego or the Self) is in itself 'barred', empty; that it is a unique point of self-relationship which has no double, no objective counterpoint: the horror of encountering a double is horror at the prospect that I will encounter the objective counterpoint of my unique subjectivity. For that reason, the horror that the motif of encountering a double evokes in us is something distinctly modern – that is, linked to the emergence of modern (Kantian) subjectivity, as demonstrated by the sudden change in the perception of the theme of the *double* at the end of eighteenth century. Till that time, the theme of the double mostly gave rise to comic plots (two brothers who look alike are seducing the same girl; Zeus seducing Amphitrion's faithful wife disguised as Amphitrion, so that, when Amphitrion unexpectedly returns home, he encounters *himself* leaving his bedroom; etc.). All of a sudden, however, in the historic moment that exactly fits the Kantian revolution, the topic of the double became associated with horror and anxiety – encountering one's double or being followed and persecuted by him is the ultimate experience of terror, something which shatters the very core of the subject's identity.

The horrifying aspect of the theme of the double has thus something to do with the emergence of the Kantian subject as pure transcendental apperception, as the substanceless void of self-consciousness that is *not* an object in reality. What the subject encounters in the guise of his double is himself *as object*: that is, his own 'impossible' objectal counterpoint. In pre-Kantian space, this encounter was not traumatic, since the individual conceived of himself as a positive entity, an object within the world. Another way to make the same point is to locate in my double, in the encountered object that 'is' myself, the Lacanian *objet petit a*: what makes the double so uncanny, what distinguishes it from other inner-worldly objects is not simply its resemblance to me, but the fact that it gives body to 'that which is in myself more than myself', to the inaccessible/unfathomable object that 'I am', to that which I for ever *lack* in the reality of my self-experience . . . The true point of anxiety is thus not that of doubling the body, but that of doubling my unique Soul. What makes me creep at the very thought of encountering my double is not that he looks exactly like me, but that, in his personality, he 'is' another me, that he clones the very uniqueness of my personality.

The Gap of Causality

Regarding this uniqueness, it is interesting to note how authors who write about neurobiology always feel compelled to emphasize the margin of undecidability which escapes complete determination by neurological processes. Oliver Sacks's work is exemplary here: he isolates the physiological foundation of severe mental disorders (brain lesions, etc.), but none the less focuses on how the individual 'subjectivizes' the disorder, what attitude he adopts towards it, how he constructs his universe to supplement his malfunction – therein resides the seductive charm of his clinical accounts. Sacks's point is that there is (almost) always a space to supplement the physiological disorder with a symbolic activity. For example, when confronted with a patient who is condemned to the irretrievable loss of his memory on account of his damaged brain, Sacks quotes Luria, his great Soviet teacher, who wrote to him that 'a man does not consist of memory alone. He has feeling, will, sensibilities, moral being – matters of which neuropsychology cannot speak. And it is here, beyond the realm of an impersonal psychology, that you may find ways to touch him, and change him. . . . Neuropsychologically, there is little or nothing you can do; but in the realm of the Individual, there may be much you can do.'[11] One is almost tempted to add that this description is all too 'idealist': what psychoanalysis offers is precisely a *materialist* theory of how the domain of 'interface' introduces a gap between the two orders, that of genes (biological heritage) and that of cultural influence of the environs, and thus disturbs any univocal relationship of causality between the two. It is in this sense that Lacan strictly opposes cause to the law (of causality):

Cause is to be distinguished from that which is determinate in a chain, in other words from the *law*. By way of example, think of what is pictured in the law of action and reaction. There is here, one might say, a single principle. One does not go without the other.... There is no gap here ... Whenever we speak of cause, on the other hand, there is always something anti-conceptual, something indefinite.... In short, there is a cause only in something that doesn't work.... It is at this point that I am trying to make you see by approximation that the Freudian unconscious is situated at that point, where, between cause and that which it affects, there is always something wrong. The important thing is not that the unconscious determines neurosis – of that one, Freud can quite happily, like Pontius Pilate, wash his hands. Sooner or later, something would have been found, humoral determinates, for example – for Freud, it would be quite immaterial. For what the unconscious does is to show the gap through which neurosis recreates a harmony with a real – a real that may well not be determined.[12]

The Unconscious intervenes when something 'goes wrong' in the order of causality that encompasses our daily activity: a slip of tongue introduces a gap in the connection between intention-to-signify and words, a failed gesture frustrates my act... However, Lacan's point is, precisely, that psychoanalytic interpretation does not simply fill in this gap by way of providing the hidden complete network of causality that 'explains' the slip: the Cause whose 'insistence' interrupts the normal functioning of the order of causality is not another positive entity; as Lacan emphasizes, it rather belongs to the order of the *non-realized*, thwarted – that is, *it is in itself structured as a gap*, a void insisting indefinitely on its fulfilment. (The psychoanalytic name for this gap, of course, is death drive, while its philosophical name in German Idealism is 'abstract negativity', the point of absolute self-contraction which constitutes the subject as the Void of pure self-relating.) This same gap is discernible also in the work of Richard Dawkins, who finishes the chapter on 'Memes: The New Replicators' in his *The Selfish Gene* with:

We have the power to defy the selfish genes of our birth and, if necessary, the selfish memes of our indoctrination. We can even discuss ways of deliberately cultivating and nurturing pure, disinterested altruism – something that has no place in nature, something that has never existed before in the whole history of the world. We are built as gene machines and cultured as meme machines, but we have the power to turn against our creators. We, alone on earth, can rebel against the tyranny of the selfish replicators.[13]

Dawkins wisely abstains from speculating about the evolutionary origins of this unique capacity, which is precisely the capacity of the subject to turn against the (biological – genes – as well as cultural – memes –) Substance of its own being.[14]

The author whose work is of special interest with regard to this gap of causality is Stephen Jay Gould. In his insistence on the excess of organs and on tinkering (*brioolage*) in nature, Gould, in a properly 'dialectical materialist' way, endeavours to mediate between the 'vulgar materialism' of the orthodox Darwinians and the 'idealist' insistence on the precedence of the identity of the Form of an organism over its adaptive changes, advocated by the proponents of 'autopoiesis'. For Gould, the paradigm of evolution is that of 'over-determination': an organ that was naturally selected for some function takes over another function which has nothing in common with the previous one (see his deservedly famous example of the spandrels of San Marco) – Gould calls this 'exaptation', as opposed to direct adaptation:

Under the spandrel principle, you can have a structure that is fit, that works well, that is apt, but was not built by natural selection for its current utility. It may not have been built by natural selection at all.... Exaptations are useful structures by virtue of having been coopted – that's the 'ex-apt' – they're apt because of what they are for other reasons. They were not built by natural selection for their current role.... Just because something arises as a side consequence doesn't condemn it to secondary status.[15]

The importance of Gould resides in this insistence that nature cannot be opposed to culture as the domain of strict adaptation to the domain in which adaptation is no longer operative: there is a gap in nature itself between an organ and its adaptive function, a gap which leaves the space open for this organ's exaptation.[16] Is Gould here not close to Lacan who, in *Seminar XX*, also emphasizes that what characterizes the animal universe is an excess of organs which are, as it were, in search of their possible use? The problem with the animal body is not that it is never perfectly adapted, that it never has enough organs to fit perfectly into its environs, but that it has *too many* organs, remainders from past situations, which lie dormant for possible future unforeseen uses... According to Gould, this holds especially for language, which is not an adaptive system with a function, but emerged as a by-product of some other adaptive process. Symbolic order is in excess with regard to adaptive economy; it involves what Freud already referred to as the 'economic problem of masochism'; it cannot be accounted for as a tool or means within some adaptive activity (the necessity of co-operation, etc.). One is tempted to mention here *chindogu*, the Japanese art of uselessly overfunctional objects, i.e. of objects/inventions which become meaningless and provoke laughter by means of their very excessive functionality, like glasses (binoculars) with electrically operated windscreen wipers to enable us to see clearly when it rains. It is as if *chindogu* inverts Kant's well-known definition of art in his *Critique of Judgement* ('purposiveness without purpose'): what we are dealing with here is rather the paradox of a purpose without purposiveness; that is, in a *chindogu*, the instrumental purpose is not only clearly discernible, but is stretched to the absurd, and thus rendered absurd, purposeless, through this very exaggeration. And is language not the ultimate *chindogu*: an entity that serves a precisely defined goal, which, however, can only be defined from within the horizon of language itself, and not through the adaptation to some external goals or conditions?

Notes

1   A further antagonism exists between Deep Ecology and ecofeminism, which aims at replacing Deep Ecology's anti-anthropocentrism with anti-androcentrism and, consequently, reproaches Deep Ecology with retaining basic patriarchal premisses.

2   W. Daniel Hillis, 'Close to the Singularity', in *The Third Culture*, ed. John Brockman, New York, Touchstone, 1996), pp. 385–6.

3   Jacques Lacan, 'A Love Letter', in *The Seminar of Jacques Lacan: On Feminine Sexuality, The Limits of Love and Knowledge, Book XX, Encore 1972–1973*, trans. Bruce Fink (New York and London, W. W. Norton & Co., 1998; orig. Paris, Éditions du Seuil, 1975), pp. 78–89.

4   I rely here on conversations with Mladen Dolar.

5   Christopher G. Langton, 'A Dynamical Pattern', in *Third Culture*, ed. Brockman, p. 354.

6   Ibid., p. 353.

7   Jacques Lacan, unpublished seminar, XVIII, 1970–1.

8   Francisco Varela, 'The Emergent Self', in *Third Culture*, ed. Brockman, p. 212.

9   Ibid., pp. 215–16.

10   See e.g., Erich Harth, *The Creative Loop* (Harmondsworth, Penguin, 1995).

11   Quoted from Oliver Sacks, *The Man who Mistook his Wife for a Hat* (London, Picador, 1986), p. 32.

12   Jacques Lacan, *The Four Fundamental Concepts of Psycho-Analysis* (New York, Norton, 1978), p. 22.

13   Richard Dawkins, *The Selfish Gene* (Oxford, Oxford University Press, 1989), pp. 200–1.

14   The Freudian hypothesis of the Unconscious as the gap of causality also enables us to throw new light on some phenomena usually associated with parapsychology: since thought is ultimately a kind of electromagnetic vibration, the prospect is looming of a machine capable of directly 'reading' our mind (according to some reports, there are already scanners able to discern elementary emotional attitudes, like fear or joy . . .). However, an interesting problem emerges here for a Freudian: what if we accept the psychoanalytic premiss of the split subject? What if we are dealing with a subject who *does not really desire what he wants*? What if, in an even more intricate way, when I pretend to like something, I deceive myself in thinking that I merely pretend to like it, being unaware that I really like it, so that the true goal of my pretending is to convince myself that I am just pretending? What if

I want something, what if I daydream constantly about it, but only in the mode of empty fantasizing, so that the actualization in real life of the object of my daydreaming – say, of some extremely perverse sexual practice – would fill me with disgust and bring about a total disintegration of my personality? In such cases, what will the scanner that 'reads my mind' identify as the content of my will? Not to mention the problem of language: is not the presupposition of a scanner directly reading my thoughts that language is merely a secondary medium for the expression of my thoughts? What, however, if it is only the language articulation which confers the definitive form on the diffuse content of my thoughts?

15 Stephen Jay Gould, 'The Pattern of Life's History', in *Third Culture*, ed. Brockman, p. 59.

16 Is not a fine musical example of 'exaptation' provided by the sublime aria of Florestan which opens Act II of *Fidelio*? Beethoven had to make use of the obligatory double structure of the great tenor's aria (the slow introductory part followed by the fast enthusiastic part which contains the declaration of love, of a decision to take revenge, etc.). How was he to do it with the starved character lying half-dead in the dark dungeon without his enthusiastic outburst appearing simply ridiculous in these circumstances? His ingenious solution was to have the hero explode in enthusiasm when, in a dying vision, an image of his beloved Leonora appears to him: the formula of the fast-paced enthusiastic conclusion of the aria is thus ingeniously trans-functionalized, 'exapted', and used to render the delirious raving of a dying man.

Slavoj Žižek: Bibliography of Works in English

The Sublime Object of Ideology. London and New York, Verso, 1989.

For They Know Not What They Do: Enjoyment as a Political Factor. London and New York, Verso, 1991.

Looking Awry: An Introduction to Jacques Lacan through Popular Culture. Cambridge, Mass., and London, MIT Press, 1991.

Everything You Always Wanted to Know about Lacan (but were Afraid to Ask Hitchcock), ed. Slavoj Žižek. London and New York, Verso, 1992.

Enjoy Your Symptom! Jacques Lacan in Hollywood and Out. New York and London, Routledge, 1992.

Tarrying with the Negative: Kant, Hegel, and the Critique of Ideology. Durham, NC, Duke University Press, 1993.

Mapping Ideology, ed. Slavoj Žižek. London and New York, Verso, 1994.

The Metastases of Enjoyment: Six Essays on Women and Causality. London and New York, Verso, 1994.

The Indivisible Remainder: An Essay on Schelling and Related Matters. London and New York, Verso, 1996.

Gaze and Voice as Love Objects, ed. Renata Salecl and Slavoj Žižek. Durham, NC, Duke University Press, 1996.

The Plague of Fantasies. London and New York, Verso, 1997.

The Abyss of Freedom/Ages of the World. Slavoj Žižek/F.W.J. von Schelling. Schelling's *Die Weltalter,* trans. Judith Norman. Ann Arbor, Mich., Michigan University Press, 1997.

Cogito and the Unconscious, ed. Slavoj Žižek. Durham, NC, Duke University Press, 1998.

The Ticklish Subject: A Treatise in Political Ontology. London and New York, Verso, 1998.

Many of Slavoj Žižek's works, in different versions and combinations, have been translated into other languages (Dutch, French, German, Japanese, Korean, Portuguese, Serb, Spanish, Swedish).

Index